Structural Criminology

A volume in the
CRIME, LAW, AND DEVIANCE
Series

Structural Criminology

JOHN HAGAN

In collaboration with
Celesta Albonetti
Duane Alwin
A. R. Gillis
John Hewitt
Alberto Palloni
Patricia Parker
Ruth Peterson
John Simpson

Rutgers University Press
New Brunswick, New Jersey

First published in the United States
by Rutgers University Press, 1989

First published in the United Kingdom
by Polity Press, 1988

ISBN 0-8135-1375-8

Contents

Preface and Acknowledgements

Crime data do not speak for themselves. Indeed they often have a one dimensional quality that deflects attention from the structural relations between individuals, groups, organizations and state based agencies that produce them. Such lessons are among the first learned by students in undergraduate and graduate sociology courses about crime and delinquency. However, what too often follows is an embarrassing silence about how theories of crime can be meaningfully connected either to new primary data about crime or to secondary data received from official agencies. How can these data be made to reflect the structural processes that are so often at the heart of the sociological understanding of crime?

Research carried out over the past decade with the collaborators in this volume represents an effort to come to terms with this question. The empirical essays that make up this book are explicit in their efforts to illustrate how social structure can be built back into our research, so that our analyses can better inform us about the structural foundations of crime. I believe that these foundations are a key to making sociological sense of crime and its control, and that we therefore must make explicit the ways in which we operationalize and explore the social structure of crime in our research.

This book has an important social structure of its own, in that each collaborator is my coauthor on one or more chapters. Alberto Palloni is coauthor of parts of the Prologue and Epilogue, portions of which appeared respectively in the *Annual Review of Sociology* and *Criminology*. Patricia Parker is coauthor of the chapter on 'White-Collar Crime and Punishment', which appeared originally in the *American Sociological Review*. Ruth Peterson is the first author of the chapter on 'The Addictive Sanction', a different version of which appeared in the *American Sociological Review*. John Hewitt and Duane Alwin are coauthors for the chapter on 'Ceremonial Justice', which appeared in a somewhat different form in *Social Forces*. Celesta Albonetti is coauthor of the chapter on 'Race, Class and the Perception of Criminal Injustice', which appeared in the *American Journal of Sociology*. John Simpson and A. R. Gillis are coauthors for the chapters on 'The Class Dynamics of the Family' and 'Feminist Scholarship and Power-Control Theory', different versions of which appeared in the *American Journal of Sociology* and the *British Journal of Sociology*. I take responsibility for the final form these chapters assume here, as for the others that I have developed on my own, including the chapter on 'The Corporate Advantage', which appeared initially in *Social Forces*.

I am grateful to Lisa Lapointe for secretarial assistance on this project, and to the Faculty of Law and the Department of Sociology of the University of Toronto for more general support. This book is dedicated to Linda, Jeremy and Joshua.

Prologue

Toward a Structural Criminology

INTRODUCTION

This book is a collection of empirical essays concerned with the development of criminological theory and the analysis of criminological data. Each chapter is particularly concerned with the strategy used to link theory development to data analysis, which makes this a book about methodology as well as a book about theory. More specifically, this is a book about the use of a structural methodology to develop theoretical perspectives on crime and delinquency.

'Methodology' is a term with many meanings. The meaning we adopt in this volume is suggested by Hirschi and Selvin (1967: 4) when they note that the core of methodology 'lies in the relation between data and theory, the ways in which sociologists use empirical observations to formulate, test, and refine statements about the social world'. The thesis of this book is that sociologists who study crime frequently have failed in their methodology because they have ignored a sociological premise that underwrites much criminological thinking. This premise, sometimes implicit and sometimes explicit, is that the meaning and explanation of crime is found in its social structure. It distinguishes an approach to the study of criminality that we call structural criminology. However, before we argue the value of this premise, we must first clarify what is meant by it.

Social structure is formed out of relations between actors. These actors may be individual or corporate in form, and their relations may be ones of solidarity as well as subordination. These structural relations are organized along both horizontal and vertical lines. However, structural relations organized along vertical, hierarchical lines of power are of greatest interest to criminologists. Perhaps this is because crime itself implies a power relationship. To perpetrate a crime is often to impose one's power on others, while to be punished for a crime is to be subjected to the power of others. Of course, these power relations are subject to change. Therefore the study of social structure often is concerned with changes in power relations, that is, with structural change over time. Structural criminology is distinguished by its attention to power relations and by the priority it assigns them in undertaking research on crime.

In the chapters that follow we will see that in many instances the power relationships to be explored are instrumental, as in the use of rights of ownership to manipulate corporate resources in the commission of white-collar crimes. However, in other instances the power relationships include a symbolic dimension, as in the relational assignment of victim and villain statuses to users and dealers of drugs. The instrumental and symbolic dimensions of these power relationships will most often be complimentary. That is, power usually brings preferential symbolism, as when corporate criminals are seen as more reputable and credible than street criminals. In any case, what distinguishes a structural criminology is its attention to instrumental and symbolic uses of power, both in relation to criminal behaviour and in the study of reactions to this behaviour.

So what makes structural criminology unique is its insistence that crime be understood and therefore studied in terms of power relations. Dominant criminological paradigms both imply and deny what structural criminology requires. That is, our theories often imply that crime is a product of power relations, but our methodologies conventionally ignore this premise. We first make this point briefly in relation to three traditions in criminological theory, and then by a more systematic review of three research literatures.

Labelling theory (e.g., Becker, 1963; Lemert, 1967) focuses our attention on the roles of crime control agents in defining crime, making clear that there can be no crime without reactions to it by empowered others. Yet research guided by labelling theory seldom measures in power related terms the interaction of actors with reactors in this crime defining process. Put another way, power often is inferred from status attributes in this tradition, but there is seldom measurement of the actual power relationships involved. Similarly, conflict theory (e.g., Turk, 1969b; Quinney, 1970; Chambliss, 1973; Taylor, Walton and Young, 1973) focuses our attention on the roles of class and status group members in guiding the reactions of crime control agents to the group-linked behaviours of others. However, research in the conflict tradition seldom has measured class or status group memberships in the kinds of relational terms that determine the location of individuals in positions of power. Finally, control theory (e.g., Hirschi, 1969) focuses attention on links between individual actors and institutions like the family. However, research by control theorists is more concerned with measuring the attitudinal and behavioural consequences of these links than with attending to the linkages themselves and the group-linked power relationships they reflect. We elaborate this last point through the development of a power-control theory of gender and delinquency in the latter part of this volume.

Meanwhile, the larger point we are making in no way diminishes the importance of the above theoretical traditions. Each is important for its unique explanatory insights. Each has helped spawn new research literatures. And most importantly, for our purposes, *each calls attention to the role of social structure in defining and explaining crime*. The problem is in the translation of these theoretical insights into the structural study of crime. Methodologically, the structural implications of these theoretical traditions are ignored. So far we have made this point largely by assertion. We make this point next by introducing three research literatures that form the background of the essays that constitute the remainder of this book. These research literatures respectively address issues of class and criminality, criminal sentencing, and the family and delinquency. Each of these research literatures is highly influenced by one or more of the above theories; each would be better guided by a methodology that is more consistent with the structural premises of these theories.

CLASS AND CRIMINALITY

The literature on class and criminality is important, complicated, and perhaps therefore predictably controversial. The importance of this literature derives from the fact that so many of our theories are based on assumptions about what the relationship between class and criminality is. The complications derive from the many meanings and measures that attach to the concepts of class and criminality. The father figure of modern criminology, Edwin Sutherland (1945; 1949), raised but did not resolve many of these issues, while inventing one of modern sociology's most popularly applied concepts: 'white-collar crime'.

Sutherland's approach to the study of white-collar crime was explicitly structural in his consideration of differential social organization, in his insistence that white-collar crime was organized crime, and in his use of corporations as units in his most famous research (1949). Nonetheless, Sutherland's definition of white-collar crime in the same work, 'as crime committed by a person of respectability and high social status in the course of his occupation'(9), has troubled researchers ever since (see Geis and Meier, 1977). This definition not only shifts attention away from corporations as the units of study, it grounds the measurement of class position in gradational notions of 'respect' and 'status'.

Structural measures of class position, grounded in relations of ownership and authority, speak more directly to the kinds of theoretical issues (i.e., issues of power and its corporate corruption) that interested Sutherland.

Structurally conceived variables directly speak to these issues by measuring the location of individuals in positions of ownership and authority, rather than by making inferences indirectly from titles of occupations or scales of occupational prestige (see, for example, Wright, 1985; Robinson and Kelly, 1979). As a result, structural measures of class do not simply locate individuals above or below one another, they locate individuals in terms of their *relation* to one another in the social organization of work. When issues of class are addressed in this book we incorporate relational, or in other words structural, measures of class into our analyses. This is a key point in the structural methodology we propose.

The substitution of relational measures of class for gradational measures of status clarifies one aspect of the relationship between class position and white-collar criminality that previously remained moot. It does so by making explicit that owners of businesses and persons with occupational authority are located in positions of power that allow use of organizational (usually corporate) resources to commit larger crimes than persons located in employee positions without authority. As we note in several chapters of this volume, and particularly in chapter 1, it is this element of power in the social organization of work, rather than the simple relationship between status and the size of white-collar crimes, that is of theoretical interest and importance. Wheeler and Rothman (1982: 1406) make the crucial point that the corporation and access to its resources 'is for white-collar criminals what the gun or knife is for the common criminal – a tool to obtain money from victims'. Status measures obscure this structural insight.

However, theoretically meaningful measures of class are only a part of the issue of class and criminality. Sutherland anticipates another part of our difficulties in his assertion that some civil offences are also crimes. Insofar as there exists a 'legal description of acts as socially injurious and legal provision of a penalty for the act', Sutherland (1945: 44) insists that such acts are, for the purposes of our research, crimes. This position is not much debated today, but it is nonetheless typically ignored in terms of the class and criminality debate. Doing so may void much of the gain that can result from implementing relational measures of class. Alternatively, if Sutherland's approach to the definition of white-collar crime is taken seriously, and combined with relational measures of class, it can have important implications.

For example, statistics on the many and sometimes deadly white-collar crimes have the potential to change the way we think about the class-crime connection. This point is effectively made through the consideration of one kind of white-collar crime, or a form of what Schrager and Short (1978: 333) call 'organizational crime': those crimes of corporate actors (individuals and collectivities) that cause physical harm to employees.

'Occupational deaths' far outnumber deaths resulting from murder. It is estimated (e.g., Page and O'Brian, 1973; US Department of Labor, 1972; Glasbeek and Rowland, 1979) that 'every year 14,000 Americans are killed in on the job accidents; and that more than 2 million are injured. Fatalities from job-related illnesses are estimated (accurate data is scarce) to run as high as 200,000 a year.' In Canada (see Reasons et al., 1981), 'occupational deaths' rank third after heart disease and cancer as a source of mortality, accounting for more than ten times as many deaths as murder. While it cannot be assumed that all or most such deaths result from the intentions of employers to see employees die, nonetheless there is reason to think that the majority of such deaths are not the result of employee carelessness either. One recent estimate (see Reasons et al. 1981: 7) is that 'approximately 39% of the job injuries in the U.S. are due to illegal working conditions while another 24% are due to legal but unsafe conditions. At the most, a third of accidents are due to unsafe acts.' Meanwhile, there are numerous and well-documented examples of employers intentionally, knowingly or negligently creating hazards; failing to follow administrative orders to alter dangerous situations; and covering up the creation and existence of such hazards. The case of asbestos poisoning involving administrative decisions within the Johns-Mansville corporation is one of the best known of these examples. Ermann and Lundman (1980) argue that such deaths occur in large numbers and can be called 'corporate homicides'.

This is not the place to debate the fine points in defining corporate homicide, or to attempt to establish with any precision how many such homicides occur. It is enough to note that such deaths occur in substantial numbers; that while we have only briefly considered their consequences for employees, corporate homicides also involve many consumers and the general public; and that corporate homicides seem likely to rival in number or exceed those deaths resulting from homicide conceived in more traditional terms. Our immediate interest is in the meaning of behaviours like corporate homicide for the class-crime controversy, structural criminology, and the methodology of criminological research. To pursue these interests we first make several comparative points about more traditional street crimes of violence.

The point is well-made by Wolfgang and his colleagues (1972) that while the prevalence of violent street crimes is low in the general population, the incidence among some of the offenders involved is quite high. Wilson (1975) uses this finding as an important argument for selective incapacitation. However, this work also makes a broader methodological point: that while a behaviour may not be highly prevalent in the general population, its high incidence among selected members of that population may nonetheless be important in developing an understanding of the behaviour and its distribution across the general population. Random samples and correlational techniques often obscure this point through their reliance on central tendencies. This is particularly likely when correlational techniques are used to analyse self-report surveys of the randomly sampled general population. The problem is that behaviours of greatest interest and importance to the understanding of the class-crime connection may be highly concentrated among relatively few persons who are easily missed among the central tendencies that are the conventional focus of these analyses. This problem is compounded by difficulties of sampling small class segments (e.g., the employer or capitalist class makes up a minute part of the general population) and the inappropriate operationalization of categorizing concepts such as class. The low prevalence of the behavioural events and the inadequate or inappropriate measurement of class categories appear to be interrelated problems.

So if crimes such as corporate homicide occur with high incidence, but low prevalence, and among highly selected sub-populations (for example, particular employers in particular industries), they are unlikely to be identified in meaningful ways with correlational analyses based on self-report data from the general population and the measurement of status rather than class. Instead, we may need relational measures of class, purposive samples, and modes of analysis that are unaffected by highly skewed distributions. These concerns are prominent in the chapter on 'White-Collar Crime and Punishment', which focuses on the 'quasi-criminal' as well as 'criminal' infractions of securities violators.

Finally, implicit in the preceding references to street crimes of violence and corporate crime is the likelihood that crime is not a unidimensional concept. Rather, it is likely that class measured in relational terms is connected to different crimes in different ways. For example, among adults, while class may be related negatively to the direct physical attacks involved in street crimes of violence, class is more likely to be related positively to the harms caused less directly by criminal acts involving commercial enterprise. Similarly, among juveniles it may be that some common acts of delinquency are related positively to class (see Hagan et al., 1985), while more 'serious' acts of delinquency are related negatively to class (cf., Colvin and Pauly, 1983). It frequently appears that gradational measures of status are not related to crime and delinquency at all (Tittle et al., 1978); however, as we argue in greater detail in the chapters on 'White-Collar Crime and Punishment' and 'The Class Dynamics of the Family and Delinquency', there is increasing reason to believe that relational measures of class are connected to crime and delinquency in interesting, albeit more complicated ways. A structural criminology urges that we incorporate relational class measures, reconsider what is meant by criminality, and move beyond the easy assumption that the relationship between class and criminality is linear or additive in form.

If power relations influence criminal behaviour, it is likely that they also influence reactions to these behaviours, although perhaps again in more complicated ways than is commonly assumed in the methodology of this research. Research on criminal sentencing is probably the most highly developed literature on reactions to crime. Perhaps this is because the issue of equality in sentencing is so highly visible and symbolically important to the criminal justice system (Arnold, 1967). It may be that symbolic issues characteristically are addressed in simplified ways; that is, it may be that for an issue to become important symbolically, it must be simply framed. In any case, this seems frequently to be true in discussions of equality in sentencing, to the detriment of research in this area.

The measurement of class is again a significant factor in this research literature. While the largest volume of research on equality in sentencing has focused on the issue of race (Kleck, 1981), it may be that class is the more salient factor (Hagan and Bumiller, 1983). Once more, however, this point may be obscured by the substitution of status for class measures (e.g., Chiricos and Waldo, 1975). Structural, that is relational, measures of class make more explicit than status measures the ways in which class might influence sentencing. For example, relational measures of class highlight positions of persons who are unemployed members of the surplus population. It may be the fact of unemployment, more directly than low social status, that leads to punitive sentencing decisions. As we note in the chapters on 'The Corporate Advantage' and 'Ceremonial Justice', it may be a position of powerlessness, rather than a relative deprivation of status, that better accounts for punitive sentencing decisions. Indeed, what is potentially most interesting is that the law scarcely bothers to deny this.

Many sentencing guidelines and criminal codes designate unemployment as a legitimate criterion in determining pre-trial release status and the post-conviction use of probation. Perhaps this is why the research literature on sentencing has not devoted much attention to the direct and indirect influence of unemployment on sentencing decisions (although see, for example, Lizotte, 1978). The search has been for extra-legal influences that would discredit sentencing decisions in terms the system itself defines as illegitimate. Race is clearly illegitimate, and therefore has received the greater attention. The structural significance of unemployment and its embeddedness in the decision-making rules is overlooked in this kind of analysis.

Meanwhile, race also is often considered in an astructural fashion. Typically, the significance of the race of the offender being sentenced is assumed, apart from whom or what he or she has offended against, and without consideration of the period or place where the sentencing has occurred. Once more, this may be because the influence of race is so clearly understood as illegitimate. However, the structural context in which race operates may be determinative of the nature of its influence. The significance of race derives from specific kinds of power relationships.

The best understood examples of this involve the role of race in the sentencing of crimes where the race of the victim is also salient. For example, homicide and assault are characteristically *intra*racial offences. When black offenders assault or kill black victims, the less powerful positions of the black victims often combine with the paternalistic attitudes of white authorities to justify lenient treatment (Kleck, 1981; see also Myrdal, 1944; Garfinkel, 1949). Rape, on the other hand, is more frequently *inter*racial. When blacks violate white victims, the high sexual property value attached to the white victims (which derives from the power positions of their significant others) and the racial fears of authorities can justify severe treatment (LaFree, 1980; see also Wolfgang and Riedel, 1973). Robbery is also increasingly interracial. The higher value attached to white property by its more powerful owners and the fears of white authorities may here also lead to more severe sentences for black offenders (Thomson and Zingraff, 1981).

Note, however, that the above studies only consider crimes involving victims of interpersonal violence (homicide, assault, rape), or the threat of it (robbery). These offences are important, but nonetheless only a small part of 'the crime problem' in industrial societies. However, this kind of structural analysis can also be extended to a broader range of offences, including the so-called 'victimless' crimes. For example, in our chapter on 'The Addictive Sanction' we show that during a Nixon Administration anti-drug crusade an important set of symbolic distinctions was developed involving the relational identification of 'victims' and 'villains' within the drug trade. This crusade involved a compromise between conservative and liberal impulses in which 'big dealers' were identified as villains, while middle-class youth and blacks (but the latter only insofar as they were rarely big dealers in a racially stratified drug trade) were reconceived as victims. The preferred victim status derived from the relative power of middle-class parents and was generalized to ordinary black drug offenders (Peterson, 1985). The most dramatic effects of this new conceptualization were the increasingly punitive treatment of big dealers in the place and period studied (1969 to 1973 in the

Southern Federal District Court of New York City), combined with the lenient treatment of ordinary black drug offenders and the very severe treatment of black big dealers. More generally, these findings suggest that while there may be a trend toward equality in American criminal sentencing, there are also patterns of differential leniency and severity that only become apparent through consideration of the structural and symbolic contexts in which sentencing decisions are made. Studies that focus on a single period and place, without some consideration of how variation in these contextual variables affect relational conceptions of victims and villains, miss a key element in the structural understanding of reactions to crime.

A structural understanding of criminal sentencing also includes consideration of the different kinds of actors, corporate as well as individual, that are involved in criminal cases. We have already noted that the organizational form of the corporation is important in understanding the class-crime connection (see also Reiss, 1981; Ermann and Lundman, 1978; Wheeler, 1976), and more generally it seems apparent that 'those interests that have been successfully collected to create corporate actors are the interests that dominate the society' (Coleman, 1974: 49). Corporate actors can be powerful participants in the legal process. Of course, the corporation itself is a 'legal fiction', with, as H. L. Mencken aptly observed, 'no pants to kick or soul to damn'. Thus corporations are 'juristic persons' that the law chooses to teat, for many practical purposes, like 'natural persons'. The limits noted by Mencken of this legal analogy become apparent when we turn to the study of criminal sentencing and encounter the impossibility of imprisoning or executing corporations. A result is that little research has been done on the relative experiences of individual and corporately organized actors in the criminal courts. Nonetheless, important possibilities exist to meaningfully study the power of corporate actors in criminal cases.

One possibility in studying the sanctioning of white-collar criminals is to make the use of corporate resources a central variable in examining the treatment that individual offenders receive. Wheeler and Rothman (1982) illustrate how such measures may be applied, and our analysis of the sanctioning of securities violators in the chapter on 'White-Collar Crime and Punishment' demonstrates that such measures can be important in understanding how alternative kinds of statutes are used to prosecute white-collar offenders. This work gives good reason to believe that employers are becoming quite adept in using the power that derives from their structural location in the social organization of work to distance and disengage themselves from the crimes that they nonetheless encourage subordinates to commit (see also Farberman, 1975; Baumhart, 1961; Brenner and Molander, 1977). The effect is to leave the latter more open to the application of criminal sentences.

A second possibility involves studying the role of corporate actors in initiating and influencing prosecutions of individual actors. Grocery stores, department stores, drug stores and many other kinds of commercial establishments are heavily involved in bringing criminal charges against individuals. This makes possible the analysis of the relative influence of corporate and individual actors in using the criminal courts. Although little of this kind of research has yet been done, we present some evidence in the chapter on 'The Corporate Advantage' that corporate actors are more likely than individuals to obtain convictions in the criminal cases they initiate against individuals, and that the likelihood of conviction increases with the size of the organization. On the other hand, this same research suggests that when corporate actors are in the role of complainants, disparities by characteristics of individuals in sentencing decrease. The argument is that corporate actors as compared to individuals encourage formal rationality to prevail, simultaneously making convictions more likely and disparities in sentencing less frequent. More research is needed, but the point is made that the power of corporate and individual actors to influence case outcomes can be compared in significant ways.

Important differences also exist in the power of actors within the court system to influence judicial outcomes, although this too remains largely unstudied. Actors in the judicial system do not simply exist alongside one another, but in relation to one another, with some actors in the judicial system exercising more power than others in the determination of outcomes.

For example, while common sense may suggest that judges alone control criminal sentencing, Eisenstein and Jacob (1977: 37) note that 'the judge does not rule or govern, at most, he manages, and often he is managed by others.' More specifically, both probation officers and prosecutors are often involved in sentencing decisions, giving recommendations for the sentences to be imposed. Probation officers are involved through the preparation of pre-sentence reports that usually offer either evaluations or recommendations for sentencing. Carter and Wilkins (1967; see also Myers, 1979; Hagan, 1975b) cite the close relationship between recommendations of probation officers and final dispositions and suggest that probation officers are a cause of disparities in judicial sentencing. However, prosecutors can also have a strong interest in sentencing, particularly, as we note in the chapters on 'White-Collar Crime and Punishment' and 'The Addictive Sanction', as a means of ratifying plea bargains. Judges are sensitive to this. Simmel (1950) noted that triads are inherently unstable, which adds interest to the power relationships between probation officers, prosecutors and judges in sentencing. The evidence presented in the chapter on 'Ceremonial Justice' suggests that prosecutors are actually much more powerful than probation officers in determining final outcomes. Sentencing may indeed be a lonely task, as judges (e.g., Frankel, 1972) lead us to believe. Nonetheless, sentencing does not occur within a social vacuum: judges too are social actors, influenced by the power relationships that surround and organize their work.

There remains the issue of how all of this is perceived by the general public, which returns us to the symbolic aspect of criminal sentencing and criminal justice more generally. Criminal justice is a variable and symbolic phenomenon, open to systematic variation in perception. One reflection of this is that persons located in varying positions of power differ in the quality of the criminal justice they perceive. Again, a key to understanding the social structure of these perceptions involves locating individuals in class positions. The chapter on 'Race, Class and the Perception of Criminal Injustice', reports that members of the surplus population and blacks are more likely than others to perceive criminal injustice. Beyond this, black members of the professional managerial class are particularly likely to perceive criminal injustice. Speculation as to why this is the case brings us back to criminal justice decision-making. Albonetti et al. (1988) demonstrate in a recent paper that black offenders relative to whites experience a poorer return on class resources (i.e., income and education) in bail decisions. It may be that more generally black professionals experience various kinds of harassment from authorities that they had expected their class resources to end. Again, the meaning of race is not inherent; it varies with the power relationships in which it operates and is experienced.

THE FAMILY AND DELINQUENCY

Power relations may also be important in conditioning and/or mediating links between the family and delinquency, and perhaps ultimately adult criminality as well. The latter half of this book employs the structural methodology we have advocated to explore this possibility. This part of the book begins with an introductory chapter that outlines a 'Power-Control Theory of Gender and Delinquency.' Power-control theory is built around the premise that the family is a neglected link between gender relations and class relations in the causation of delinquency. Of course, the family has not always been neglected in delinquency research. Quite the contrary: to focus on the family as a causal factor in delinquency is to run the risk of seeming old-fashioned (see Hirschi, 1973).

Wilkinson (1974) notes that the family was first emphasized as a causal factor in delinquency research at the turn of the century, and was accepted as an important variable until about 1930. For the next twenty years, the family, and especially family breakdown, was rejected as a causal factor, and although some signs of renewed interest emerged in the 1950s, research on the family has been limited. In explanation, Wilkinson suggests that in the early 1900s the family was seen as important because of its near exclusive control over the development of children, and because of a very negative attitude toward divorce. However, in the 1930s the family's protective, religious, recreational, and educational functions began to shift to other institutions. At the same time, attitudes toward divorce were softening. Of course, none of this meant that the family was now of no importance, but Wilkinson suggests that we began to think and act more as if this was the case. Wilkinson summarizes our situation this way: '. . . the decline in concern for the . . . home . . . came about not because scientific evidence provided conclusive grounds for rejecting it, but because cultural and ideological factors favouring its acceptance early in this century became less important . . .' (735).

Of course, the forms and meanings of family life have indeed changed over time, with, as we will see, interesting implications for our understanding of class relations and delinquency. Variations in family life and the settings in which they occur are both a challenge and an opportunity for understanding the place of the family in the causation of crime and delinquency. For example, this variation can be used to set scope conditions across which theories of the family and its effects can be explored. A premise of power-control theory is that dominance relations between spouses determine gender divisions in the domestic social control of sons and daughters. These patterns of social control are in turn linked to gender variations in delinquency and the intergenerational reproduction of gender relations. The predominant mediating relationship in this framework is that mothers more than fathers are assigned responsibility for controlling their daughters more than their sons. This sexual stratification in the parental control of children accounts for substantial gender variation in delinquency. In turn, the challenge for power-control theory is to identify variations in family structure that constitute scope conditions within which this sexual stratification of social control labour can explain gender differences in delinquency.

Dominance relations at work and in the family are core components of power-control theory. A typology of family class structures is provisionally identified and explored in chapter 7, in terms of the translation of gender-linked power relations at work (outside the family) into gender-linked power relations in the home. It is important in doing this to acknowledge that relationships between gender in the workplace and gender in the home are likely to be socially and historically contingent. This is because different kinds of family relations are likely to have different kinds of meanings and effects in different times and places. Nonetheless, we must begin our exploration of these family relations somewhere, and power-control theory does so by suggesting a prototypical framework in which relations of dominance in the workplace are assumed to produce and reproduce relations of dominance in the home.

What makes the study of family relations and delinquency of interest for the understanding of class relations and delinquency is the premise that work relations are a source of family relations: that is, that relations of dominance in the household derive from relations of dominance in the workplace. These are the class dynamics of the family. Relations of dominance refer here to the use of power and authority for the control of organized aggregates. Following Dahrendorf (1959: 198), these 'organized aggregates' include all 'imperatively coordinated associations'. That is, they include the family as well as the workplace. The particular form of structural criminology we propose here, power-control theory, argues that to understand the effects of class position in the workplace on crime and delinquency it is important to trace the way that work relations structure family relations, particularly relations between fathers and mothers and, in turn, relations between parents and their children, especially mothers and their daughters.

The family class structures that we identify provisionally in later chapters can be thought of as ranging between patriarchal and egalitarian forms. These family structures often reproduce themselves. For example, daughters in most families, but especially in patriarchal families, are controlled more than sons and in ways that make it less likely, at least until relatively recently, that these daughters will develop the kinds of attitudes that in adulthood lead to work outside the home. This leads to the intergenerational reproduction of patriarchal families in which husbands engage in paid labour outside the family, while wives engage in unpaid labour inside the home. Again, patriarchal families are characterized by the control that they impose on daughters, particularly through intense mother-daughter relationships, and by the relative infrequency of risk-taking and delinquent behaviour among daughters compared to sons in these families. Egalitarian families are more likely to reproduce themselves by treating daughters similarly to sons, with results that make daughters more like sons in attitudes toward risk-taking, work prospects, as well as delinquency.

The theoretical significance of patriarchal family structures may in the past have been obscured by the tendency to conceive measures of parent-child relationships primarily as indicators of affection or attachment rather than of power and authority, and by the tendency of prior research to overlook the gender stratification of these relationships. These latter points are developed in considerable detail in the chapter on 'Feminist Scholarship and Power-Control Theory'.

The approach we propose for studying the family and delinquency encourages the class analysis of delinquency, and perhaps ultimately of adult criminality as well, to take a more relational form. It suggests, for example, that we focus on workplace relations between actors and on how these relations position spouses relative to one another in the family. In doing so we inevitably will find, as we do in the chapter on 'The Class Dynamics of the Family and Delinquency', that the ideal typical Western industrial family – for example, a patriarchal family with the father employed in a position of authority outside the home and the mother not so employed – is only one (and perhaps a declining) possibility in a changing world of work and family relations. The theory predicts that gender-specific authority relations between parents and children follow from gender specific work relations outside the home, and that therefore gender differences in delinquency will be most acute in patriarchal family structures, and less so in more egalitarian family structures. This combination of interlocking relationships between work and family suggests a link between class and delinquency that has eluded past criminological research.

In short, power-control theory proposes an end to a gender bias that may have obscured our vision of a base on which the relationship between class and criminality is built. Said differently, our historical preoccupation with male criminality may have obscured a fuller view of the class dynamics of the family. This broader, structural vision may help us to understand a combined role of gender and class in the causation of crime and delinquency, and deviance more generally. The latter prospect of a more general structural theory of deviance is explored in the final chapter, 'Gender and The Search for Deviant Role Exits'. This chapter applies power-control theory in an attempt to explain gender differences in thoughts about suicide and running away from home.

A CAUTIONARY CONCLUSION

The chapters that follow offer empirically developed examples of a structural criminology. However, as we turn to these empirical essays we should be careful to dispel any unintended suggestion that a structural criminology can or should answer all questions about crime and delinquency. Rather the purpose of a structural criminology is to suggest how meaningful questions about crime and delinquency can be asked, and begin to be answered. This beginning leaves important questions unanswered. For example, this beginning includes an explicit assumption that vertical, hierarchical relations of power and subordination are more important in the study of criminality than horizontal, non-hierarchical relations of attachment and solidarity. There is an interesting base of support for this assumption in the research literature on parental and peer influences, which generally shows that the effects of the former on delinquency are stronger than the effects of the latter. Nonetheless both hierarchical and non-hierarchical relations are important, and a key to explanatory success may ultimately involve conceptually linking the two kinds of relations among actors and groups. We also began with an implicit assumption that power relations derived from ownership and authority in the social organization of work are crucial to the meaningful study of crime and deliquency. Yet exactly when and how these separable sources of power and subordination exercise their influence remains unsettled in the study of social stratification as well as in the study of criminality. In this and other ways, the fates of sociology and criminology are closely entwined. A *structural* criminology is a *sociological* criminology. With these points in mind, the chapters that follow illustrate how the work of a structural criminology can proceed.

PART I

Social Structure, Crime and Punishment

I

White-Collar Crime and Punishment

Gibbons (1979: 65) accurately observes that, 'in many other areas of sociology, it is possible to list a considerable number of important contributors . . . , but in criminology, Sutherland stands virtually alone.' Sutherland's contributions occurred at the micro- and macrostructural levels reflected in his concepts of differential association and differential social organization (see, for example, Schuessler, 1973: Part 1). The coordinating premise was that differential social organization structures the differential association of people and the definitions learned from them. Sutherland (1983) applied his concepts most provocatively to the explanation of white-collar crime, arguing that 'businessmen are not only in contact with definitions which are favourable to white-collar crime but also . . . are isolated from and protected against definitions which are unfavourable to such crime' (Sutherland, 1983: 250).

However, the full structural implications of Sutherland's work remain undeveloped. This may in part result from his much debated definition of white-collar crime as 'crime committed by a person of *respectability* and high social *status* in the course of his occupation' (Sutherland, 1983: 7, emphasis added). While Sutherland often implied much more, status today is understood as a social-psychological concept which refers to the perceived relative position of an individual in a hierarchy of respect. This gradational conception has caused confusion in the study of white-collar crime and its sanctioning (see Geis and Meier, 1977), and recently has led to the unexpected finding by Wheeler et al. (1982) that high status white-collar offenders receive more severe sentences than low status white-collar offenders.

But do studies so conceived (see also Hagan et al., 1980) actually get to the core of what concerned Sutherland? Geis (1984: 146) suggests they do not, reasoning that, 'Sutherland, for all his definitional uncertainty, was particularly concerned with the use of positions of power and influence in the corporate, professional, and political world to abuse and even exploit others. Neither education nor income nor even status, which Sutherland stressed – actually cut to the scientific-ideological essence of the concept.' The problem is that a contemporary understanding of the concept of status glosses over what is potentially most salient in Sutherland's attention to differential social organization: the differential power that derives from structural location in the social organization of work.

Sutherland (1949: 224) probably would have agreed, for he noted that 'although the concept of "status" is not entirely clear, it seems to be based principally upon power' (see also Schuessler, 1973: 49, 57). He was also explicit about the power that derives from forms of business organization (Sutherland, 1973), and insisted further that 'white-collar crime is organized crime' (1949: chapter 14). This emphasis has resulted in important efforts (Wheeler and Rothman, 1982) to distinguish between crimes committed by individuals acting alone and those committed through occupational and organizational roles.

However, the above efforts have not yet formed the basis of a structural theory of white-collar crime and punishment. The class structure of these organizational crimes has not been articulated, and a structural theory of white-collar crime and punishment that incorporates the role of power has neither been explicitly formulated nor subjected to empirical test.

In this chapter we outline and test a structural theory that begins with a *relational* conception of class (see Wright, 1980: 325; see also Hagan et al., 1985). The need for such a conception is linked directly to Sutherland's observation that the most flagrant white-collar crime is also organized crime, in the sense that these crimes make use of organizational positions and resources. It is not gradational status, but rather structural position in the social organization of work that makes such forms of organized crime possible. Relational conceptions of class penetrate to the heart of this matter by locating individuals in structural terms. The relational indicators we use in this chapter, ownership and authority, locate individuals in class positions that are directly relevant to the perpetration of white-collar crime as organized crime. We develop this point further, after introducing the substantive focus of our study.

SECURITIES VIOLATIONS AS WHITE-COLLAR CRIMES

We focus in this chapter on the class structure and legal sanctioning of securities violations in the Province of Ontario, Canada. Securities markets are among the pre-eminent institutions of modern capitalist societies (Baker, 1984), and their manipulation is therefore a pre-eminent white-collar crime with national and international implications. The latter point has particular relevance to the data we analyse. The Province of Ontario plays a primary role in regulating the Toronto Stock Exchange, Canada's busiest securities market. In North America, this market is second only in its volume to the New York Stock Exchange. The United States is the largest trading partner of Canada, and the Toronto Exchange is a focal point in the interpenetration of the two economies. It is difficult to miss the element of power in this relationship and its implications for securities regulation.

'Throughout its history,' writes Wallace Clement (1977: 7), 'Canada has conformed to the pressures of external demands and internal opportunism.' Prior to World War I, the source of these demands was British: after World War I, they were increasingly American. In both cases, Canada encouraged and facilitated resource extraction as a source of foreign capital and as a base of industrialization. The result was an unequal alliance in which the United States became the 'extractive power', dominating much of Canada's industry and its resource markets. Through most of this century, therefore, Canada has been much more concerned with stimulating than restricting capital investment, much of which was foreign, but some of which was domestic. Predictably, the regulation of securities was of low priority during this period, and the manipulation of securities was common (see, for example, Kryzanowski, 1978: 124). By the mid-1960s Canada had earned an unfavourable international reputation for securities manipulation that itself posed a threat to investment (LaPrairie, 1979). Re-establishing 'investor confidence' and the 'credibility of the marketplace' became prominent concerns. This led to a strengthening of enforcement efforts, including passage of the Ontario Securities Act of 1966 (see Johnston, 1977).[1] These efforts have more recently included an investigation by the Ontario Securities Commission of Conrad Black, Chairman of the giant Argus Corporation and reputedly the most powerful corporate entrepreneur in Canada (Newman, 1982), as well as an investigation of the multinational participants in a set of real-estate transactions involving the block sale of over 10,000 Toronto apartments eventually valued at over half a billion dollars. These cases attracted the attention of the national (*Globe and Mail*, 1983a, 1983b) and the international press (*Wall Street Journal*, 1983a, 1983b, 1983c) and helped stimulate the current research.

The structure and enforcement of Canadian securities legislation offers a unique opportunity to explore definitional issues raised by Sutherland, but never since explored empirically. Sutherland (1945) noted that many white-collar law violations are prosecuted under non-criminal statutes, but that these statutes and the violations specified nonetheless are criminal in the sense of including two necessary elements: 'legal description of acts as socially injurious and legal provision of a penalty for these acts' (Sutherland, 1945: 132). These criteria, rather than a strict reliance on criminal-code constructions (see Tappan, 1947), were what Sutherland used in selecting cases for his classic study. Although Sutherland's position on this definitional issue today prevails in theoretical discussions of white-collar crime (Wheeler, 1976), empirical studies (Hagan et al., 1980; Wheeler et al., 1982) since Sutherland have been restricted to samples convicted under criminal statutes.

In Canada, securities violations are prosecuted under both kinds of statutes; the Ontario Securities Act and the Criminal Code. Both statutes describe socially injurious offences and specify fines and imprisonment as penalties.[2] It is commonly asserted that, 'criminal code prosecution will be undertaken where the conduct of the accused has been flagrant or persistent, or is clearly indicative of malice' (Johnston, 1977: 373). Sutherland, and a structural theory of white-collar crime and punishment, cast doubt on such assumptions, asserting that power as well is at least part of the equation (e.g. Chambliss, 1984). We already have made the point that power was not meaningfully operationalized in past studies. To this is added the further problem that since Sutherland, only persons convicted under criminal statutes have been sampled for study. The empirical implications of this problem are made explicit in table 1.1, where we have cross-classified the statute of prosecution and the disposition of cases prosecuted in the Province of Ontario from 1966 to 1983. Since Sutherland, only cases of the type found in cell four (which comprise little more than a third of the cases)

TABLE 1.1 *The selection problem: Cross-classification of charge by disposition*[a]

Type of charge		Unconvicted		Convicted		Row
				Disposition		
Securities	(1)	Unconvicted Securities Defendants (31)	35.6 41.3 15.3	(2) Convicted Securities Offenders (56)	64.4 43.8 27.6	42.9 (87)
Criminal	(3)	Unconvicted Criminal Defendants (44)	37.9 58.7 21.7	(4) Convicted Criminal Offenders (72)	62.1 56.3 35.5	57.1 (116)
Column		(75)	36.9	(128)	63.1	(203)

[a] Percentaged by row, column, and cell, respectively, with cell frequencies in parentheses.

of this table have been studied. This may constitute a severe form of sample selection bias. However, before addressing this issue further, we describe our data in greater detail, and elaborate the theory, concepts and indicators to be used in this study.

THE DATA AND THE THEORY

The sampling frame for this study consists of all cases referred for prosecution under the Securities Act or the Criminal Code in Ontario from 1966 to 1983. Rather than rely exclusively (as have past studies) on case file data, we interviewed investigators from provincial agencies about the cases they developed during this period. All investigators (whether currently employed by the agencies or not) who could be located were interviewed about their cases, resulting in a sample of 203 cases which are considered in this analysis.[3] The interview method allowed us to collect information on the class position, organizational involvement, and other aspects of the suspects' cases not included in official case files and therefore not considered in previous research.

Information collected from the above interviews and case files forms the basis of our test of a structural theory. The fundamental premise of such a theory is that class position influences involvement in white-collar criminal *behaviour* as well as the *punishment* of this behaviour. Indeed, it is our argument that the latter cannot be understood fully without consideration of the former. This is because the punishment of white-collar crime is not simply a function of class position, but also of the kinds of organized white-collar criminal behaviour that certain class positions make possible. To make these points, we must identify the classes we will consider. First, however, we must justify using the kind of data we have collected for the study of white-collar criminal behaviour and its punishment.

Our data consist of cases referred for prosecution, and thus may not be a random sample of behaviours. Our justifications for using these cases to study white-collar criminal behaviour as well as punishment are three-fold. First, the most commonly assumed source of non-randomness is that the 'bigger fish', for various reasons, get away. However, Wheeler and Rothman (1982: 1423) make a compelling case against this assumption:

The simple fact is that we really don't know, in the case of common crime, simple white-collar crime, or complex white-collar crime what the relationship is between the magnitude of the take and the likelihood of getting caught. We see no reason in principle for that relationship to differ greatly across types of crime, and we rather imagine that in both simpler and more complex offenses law enforcement officials must trade off their estimated likelihood of conviction against the magnitude of the take. The same felt need to maintain a winning record, to favour cases that will conclude expeditiously with negotiated pleas of guilt, will obtain regardless of the form the illegality takes.

Of course Wheeler and Rothman are correct in saying that we really don't know what the forms of these biases might actually be. However, beyond their own cogent reasoning we offer, as the second justification for our use of the data chosen, that these data start at an earlier stage, referral for prosecution, than any other empirical study of these issues we have found. Third, lacking some involvement of authorities, such as referral for prosecution, there is a problem of establishing a basis for the assumption that crimes actually have taken place for study. Referral for prosecution is the first decisive commitment to the proposition that a crime has occurred. While the above justifications individually may not be determinative, in combination we believe they weigh heavily in favour of the kind of sample we have selected.

Our analysis considers occupants of four class positions; employers, managers, the petty bourgeoisie, and workers. Note that our interest is in the structural location of individuals in these class positions rather than in the individuals themselves. The positions are defined in the relational (i.e. structural) terms summarized in table 1.2. This operationalization derives from the Marxist work of Wright (1980; Wright and Perrone, 1977; Wright et al., 1982), but is adapted to the criminal population involved. Thus the first indicator derives from a question which asks whether the accused is involved in a legitimate or illegitimate occupation. This indicator locates the individual in the legitimate or illegitimate economic sector. The second indicator taps ownership of the means of production by asking whether the individual owns a business. The third indicator measures authority in the workplace by asking whether the individual has one or more levels of subordinates beneath him/her.

Employers work in the legitimate sector, own a business, and have subordinates; they comprise 27.09 per cent of our sample. *Managers* also work in the legitimate sector and have subordinates, but they do not own a business; they make up 19.70 per cent of our sample. The *petty bourgeoisie* work in the legitimate sector and own a business, but have no subordinates; they constitute 9.36 per cent of our sample. (The petty bourgeoisie are usually identified as a dying class, and therefore excluded from Marxist analyses (see Wright and Perrone, 1977: 43). However, such entrepreneurs, operating 'paper' or 'shell companies' are a more lively group in the securities area, and we therefore include them in our analysis.) The above three classes are treated as dummy variables, with *workers* designated as the comparison or omitted category. Workers are located in the illegitimate or legitimate sector, they are not owners of legitimate businesses and they have no subordinates;

TABLE 1.2 Criteria for class categories

Class	Economic sector	Ownership of means of production	Authority in workplace	Distribution
Employers	Legitimate	Owner	Has subordinates	27.09% (55)
Managers	Legitimate	Nonowner	Has subordinates	19.70% (40)
Petty bourgeoisie	Legitimate	Owner	No subordinates	9.36% (19)
Workers	Legitimate or illegitimate	Nonowner	No subordinates	43.85% (89)

they make up 43.85 per cent of our sample. A measure of prior record (none/one or more prior convictions) is considered simultaneously with the preceding class variables in our analysis. This is the most frequently included control variable in studies of sanctioning. Additional control variables were included at several stages of our analysis, but eliminated for lack of effect, as discussed further below. The structural theory we are proposing assumes that employers, managers and the petty bourgeoisie are more likely than workers to engage in organized forms of white-collar crimes that are more extensive in their scope. Offences may be organized informally by affiliated individuals, or they may occur through the use of formal organizations including, most notably, businesses. As Sutherland (see Schuessler, 1973: 21) notes, 'criminals perfect an organization and with organization their crimes increase in frequency and seriousness'. Our theory is premised on the assumptions that organizations, especially formal business organizations, make resources available for the perpetration of grander crimes than is otherwise the case, and that organizations also frequently provide effective covers for the commission of these crimes. Measures of the form and scope of white-collar crimes are therefore required. A key requirement of the measure of the form of the offence is that it effectively indicates whether the crime was organized in an informal and/ or formal way. Our measure of the organization of the offence is derived from Wheeler and Rothman (1982) and is based on information obtained from investigators as to whether the offence was committed (a) by a single individual; (b) by an individual acting with one or more affiliated persons; or (c) by an individual acting through an organized association, business organization, partnership or family business. (In thirteen cases during the period of our study an organization rather than an individual was charged;

these cases were not included in this analysis.) The joint variation of this measure of the organization of the offence with the preceding measures of class position will allow us to explore the class structure of white-collar crime as organized crime.

Both class position and organization of the offence are expected to influence the scope of the white-collar crimes. However, difficulties in measuring the scope of securities crimes became apparent as we began to ask for dollar estimates of losses. An example of this problem is provided in the following response of an investigator when asked about the dollar loss in a specific case:

Well, I don't know. It would be a guesstimate, and a bad one at that. People want to know how much money is involved in a scheme like this. Well, the only thing you can allege is how much money was lost by a total number of victims . . . You know bloody well that —— took in, over four or five years of operating on Bay Street, something in those days approaching if not exceeding several million dollars, or something like that, and that it was done by multiplying the number of shares sold by the top market price of the unit that was reached on a given day by the number of shareholders, or something like this, and we ended up with some grand glorious figure . . . I don't think it was done fairly . . . but in order to respond to it they had to make a few admissions and it was done for that very purpose.

To deal with this kind of problem of accuracy, we asked investigators to estimate in each case broad categories of dollar loss (none, hundreds, thousands, millions), number of victims (none, less than a hundred, thousands, many thousands, millions), and the geographical spread of the crime (none, local, national, international). When assigned ordinal ranks and summed, these items form a scale, called 'scale of offence' with an alpha reliability coefficient of 0.63. Further analysis revealed that the measure of dollar loss correlated least with the other items, and when it was excluded from the scale the alpha coefficient increased to 0.72. Use of either scale produces similar substantive results in the analysis that follows; the latter two-item scale is the basis of results presented below.

Our attention shifts next to the prosecution of these white-collar crimes. Here we consider the strength of the evidence in the case, whether plea negotiation was involved, and the type of charge placed against the offender. Investigators ranked the evidence in their cases as strong, uncertain or weak; indicated whether or not plea negotiation occurred; and case files were used to indicate whether the offence was prosecuted under the Securities Act or the Criminal Code. Although conviction under the Securities Act can result in imprisonment, the maximum penalities allowed are lower than under the Criminal Code (see note 2), and the stigma of a *criminal* conviction is avoided. A structural theory of white-collar crime and punishment therefore predicts that persons located in positions of power will be less likely to be prosecuted under the criminal code. Yet we noted above that seriousness of the offence and malice of motive conventionally are assumed to increase the likelihood of criminal prosecution. The issue, then, is not simply whether powerful persons are more likely than others to benefit from securities convictions, but rather whether this benefit applies with scope of the offence (our measure of seriousness) and strength of evidence (which must include a consideration of intent, and therefore malice) taken into account.

The dependent variable for our analysis is the severity of sentence imposed. The relationship between type of charge and actual sentence imposed is of particular concern. We have already indicated that 'sentence exposure' is greater under the Criminal Code than under the Securities Act. Nonetheless, type charge and actual sentence severity are independent events in that exposure under the Criminal Code and the Securities Act overlap, with neither specifying statutory minimum sentences and both allowing commitments to prison, albeit for differing maximum lengths of time. Empirically, more than half (57 per cent) of the persons convicted under the Criminal Code receive sentences of less than one year in prison, the maximum term allowed under the Securities Act. However, as we report further below, the relationship between type of charge and sentence severity is strong. The implication is that the two statutes encourage differential sentence severity, without requiring this outcome by statutory definition.

We present results based on several measures of sentence severity below. The most familiar of these measures is an adapted eleven-point scale widely used in the sentencing literature (see Tiffany et al., 1975; Diamond and Zeisel, 1975) to reflect variation in the punitiveness of sentences in an approximate interval form.[4] This scale recently has received criticism in the sentencing literature (see Blumstein et al., 1983: 82), the argument being that sentence severity is a discrete rather than a continuous variable. We demonstrate below that the level of measurement assumed makes little substantive difference for the purposes of this study. The substantive interest of a structural theory of white-collar crime and punishment is in how positions of power influence sentencing, with the assumption being that the bias is in the direction of leniency.

A final exogenous variable included in our analysis is the year in which the case was processed. We noted that beginning in 1965 there was an increasing emphasis on securities enforcement in Ontario. Ontario is probably not unique in this regard. Katz (1980) speaks of a 'social movement against white-collar crime' that began in the United States in the late 1960s, and public-opinion data documents an increasing concern with the occurrence of such crimes (e.g. Cullen et al., 1982; Schrager and Short, 1980). Wheeler et al. (1982: 657) suggest that the status effects found in their data may result from the aftermath of Watergate, but they are unable to test this hypothesis because their data come only from the post-Watergate period. Canada experienced a major political scandal, dubbed 'Harbourgate' (see *Toronto Star*, 1975), that resulted in similar calls for stricter treatment of white-collar criminals. The interesting issue for a structural theory of white-collar crime and punishment is whether such 'movements' have the kinds of effects conventionally assumed. The structural theorist is skeptical. By including year in our analysis, we will be able to explore this issue.

A final set of control variables were incorporated at several points in the data analyses presented in this chapter. These variables included the age of the defendant, whether the defendant was represented by private counsel, the co-operativeness of the defendant with investigators and prosecutors, and the defendant's prior reputation in the community.[5] These variables had no causal significance for the sanctioning decisions that interest us. The results of including these variables are therefore not presented. There were only five women in our data, so the effects of gender could not be analysed.

METHODS

Below we explore a causal model of white-collar crime and punishment that incorporates the variables, save the last group, described above. These variables were presented in an assumed logical-temporal sequence that is consistent with the structural theory we wish to explore. Clearly, this theory is not sufficiently developed to allow a deductive model-testing approach. Instead, a series of equations is used inductively to determine causal linkages between variables. However, before doing so, it is necessary that we address the issue of selection bias noted above.

Recall that our dependent variable is sentence and that past studies of the sanctioning of white-collar offenders have dealt only with offenders *convicted* of white-collar *crimes*: cell four of table 1.1. Yet decisions to charge with non-criminal rather than criminal statutes, and to acquit, dismiss or withdraw charges rather than convict, may result in a highly selected pool of offenders to be sentenced. Parameter estimates based on such samples may be biased and inconsistent.

We address this problem of selection bias in two ways. First, as indicated above, we adopt Sutherland's strategy and include persons charged with Securities Act as well as Criminal Code violations. Second we conceptualize sentencing as a two-stage process, involving first a decision as to whether to convict, and subsequently, if conviction occurs, a decision as to sentence severity. Heckman (1974, 1975, 1979; see also Berk, 1983) outlines a procedure that allows us to combine information from these two decisions in a meaningful way. This procedure involves two equations: the first is a probit equation that estimates whether an accused person is convicted, and the second is an OLS equation for sentence severity that is corrected for selection bias.

The first equation is:

$$\text{Probit } (P_i) = \mathbf{X}_i\mathbf{B} \qquad (1.1)$$

where P_i is the probability of the ith accused person being convicted; $\mathbf{X}_i$ is a row vector of co-variates; and $\mathbf{B}$ the corresponding volume vector of parameters. The second equation is:

$$Z_i = A_i\mathbf{v} + \theta_o\lambda_i + E_i \qquad (1.2)$$

where Z_i is sentence severity; $A_i\mathbf{v}$ is a set of explanatory variables and parameters; λ_i is a regressor derived from equation (1.1) and defined as the 'hazard' or risk that the offender will be convicted, with θ_o as its regression coefficient (i.e. the estimator of the co-variance between the errors in the equation predicting conviction and the errors in the equation predicting sentence severity); and E_i is an error term.

The above strategy allows us to include information from cases in all four cells of table 1.1. Including securities as well as criminal cases, and treating type of charge as an endogenous variable, will allow us to explore the effects of selection through charging practices. Comparison of OLS sentence equations that do and do not include the correction factor derived from the Heckman procedure will allow us to explore the effects of selection through conviction.[6]

THE ANALYSIS

We begin with the probit model of determinants of conviction used to create the correction factor described above. Probit estimates for this model are presented in table 1.3 along with the correlations of the predictor variables with the correction factor (λ). As one might hope, strength of evidence is the strongest predictor of conviction, and therefore the strongest correlate of the correction factor.[7] Prior record and year are also significantly related to conviction and are the next strongest correlates of the correction factor. (The signs of the significant correlates of conviction are reversed as correlates of the correction factor; since the correction factor is a control variable with no substantive significance in itself, the direction of these correlations is irrelevant).

The consequences of including the correction factor in our analysis are indicated in table 1.4, which presents the results of estimating sentence

TABLE 1.3 Probit estimates of determinants of conviction and correlations with (correction factor)

	Estimate	Standard error	Correlation with
Year	− 0.092[b]	0.026	0.320
Petty bourgeoisie	0.028	0.384	− 0.105
Managers	− 0.225	0.303	0.107
Employers	− 0.037	0.279	− 0.008
Prior record	0.805[a]	0.358	− 0.342
Organization of offence	0.062	0.139	− 0.116
Scope of offence	0.019	0.077	− 0.062
Strength of evidence	1.068[b]	0.181	− 0.631
Plea negotiation	0.472	0.272	− 0.174
Type charge	− 0.232	0.215	0.131
Constant = 5.341			

[a] Significant at the 0.05 level.
[b] Significant at the 0.001 level.

equations containing our independent variables, first without and then with the correction factor included. This table makes clear the importance of type of charge to sentence severity. In both the uncorrected (b = 3.307) and corrected (b = 3.542) equations, charge is the only significant ($p < 0.001$) predictor: persons charged under the Criminal Code receive much more severe sentences. The important implication of our analysis thus far is that type of charge is crucial to sentence severity. This suggests the necessity of a causal model approach that treats type of charge as an intervening variable in the sentencing of white-collar offenders. On the other hand, there is little evidence that looking only at convicted offenders will bias our analysis. Re-estimating the corrected sentence equation makes little difference substantively. We proceed, then, by estimating a causal model of sentencing decisions that considers only convicted offenders. Later in the analysis we return to the full sample of convicted and unconvicted offenders to provide a further check on our results. Before turning to our causal model, we will make a few further points about the coding of sentence severity in these analyses.

When the sentence-severity scale described above and in note 4 is used as the dependent variable in the uncorrected OLS sentence equation estimated in table 1.4, the standardized effect of type of charge on sentence is 0.629. Above we noted a criticism of this scale: that it obscures discrete differences in types of sentences imposed. To explore this issue we estimated separate probit equations that modelled the likelihood of offenders receiving fine,

TABLE 1.4 Uncorrected and corrected sentence equations

Variables	Uncorrected equation			Corrected equation		
	b	B	SE	b	B	SE
Year	− 0.084	− 0.167	0.051	0.020	0.040	0.092
Petty bourgeoisie	− 0.348	− 0.041	0.674	− 0.354	0.041	0.672
Managers	− 0.198	− 0.030	0.588	0.170	0.025	0.656
Employers	0.164	0.028	0.546	0.150	0.026	0.545
Prior record	0.439	0.064	0.510	− 0.358	− 0.052	0.812
Organization of offence	0.072	0.024	0.272	0.019	0.006	0.277
Scope of offence	0.050	0.029	0.149	0.037	0.021	0.149
Strength of evidence	− 0.132	− 0.024	0.440	− 1.607	− 0.285	1.250
Plea negotiation	− 0.456	− 0.080	0.442	− 0.983	− 0.171	0.608
Type charge	3.307[a]	0.629	0.402	3.542[a]	0.674	0.443
				− 2.905		2.306
R^2	0.429			0.437		
Constant	8.625			5.136		

[a] Significant at the 0.001 level.

probation and jail sentences. These equations contained the identical independent variables as the uncorrected sentence equation estimated in table 1.4. Again in each of these equations only type of charge was significant in its effect. These equations revealed that persons charged under the Criminal Code were much less likely than those charged under the Securities Act to receive fines (B = 2.304, p < 0.05). We also assigned sentences ordinal ranks of three for imprisonment, two for probation, and one for fines, and regressed this scale on the independent variables in an OLS equation. We use this coding in the causal model presented below, and the result again is that only type of charge is significant in its effect, with a standardized coefficient of 0.701. So regardless of the measure used, it is clear that type of charge is crucial to sentence severity.

We proceed now to our causal model.[8] Paths less than 0.10 in significance or weaker than 0.10 in strength were deleted from the model, and the equations were then re-estimated. Metric coefficients are indicated in figure 1.1 (in parentheses) next to the standard-form path coefficients. This model further clarifies the importance of type of charge in the sentencing of white-collar offenders. Thus while as noted above only charge exerts a direct effect (B = 0.656) on sentence severity, a number of other variables influence sentence indirectly through type of charge. As conventionally assumed, the

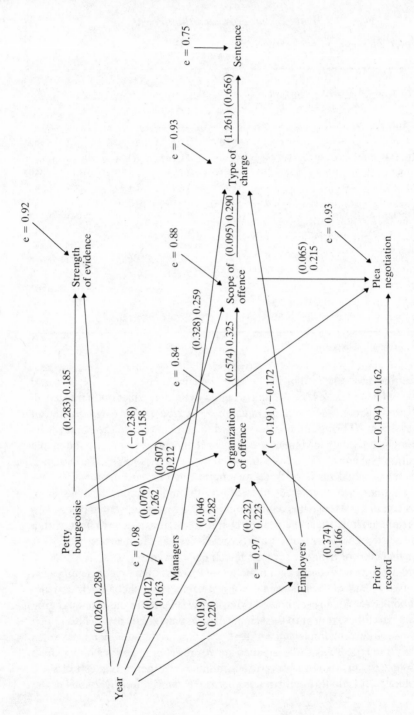

Figure 1.1 Causal model of white-collar crime and punishment

greater the scope of the offence (B = 0.290), the more likely the person is to be charged with a criminal offence. However, with scope of offence and other variables held constant, there are also two important class effects: compared to workers, managers (B = 0.259) are *more* likely, and employers (B = − 0.172) *less* likely, to be charged under the Criminal Code.

To understand further the role of class position in our model, we consider next the influence of organization of the offence. Recall that our organizational measure has three values that represent individuals acting alone (31.8 per cent), with affiliated others (18.2 per cent), and through formal organizations (50 per cent), most notably business organizations. So informally organized offences are the least frequent in our sample, with formally organized offences most frequent. In our preliminary analyses, we created dummy variables to measure separately the impact of the informal and formal organization of offences on their scope. Offences committed with formal (B = 0.528, $p < 0.001$) and informal (B = 0.517, $p < 0.001$) organization were about equal in scope, with both kinds of offences much broader in scope than unorganized offences. Recall, however, that formally organized offences were much more frequent than informally organized offences. Furthermore, employers were more likely to be involved in formally than informally organized offences. (A separate probit analysis of the effects of class position on organization of offence revealed that employers are much less likely than workers to act alone (B = 0.904, $p < 0.05$), and equally likely to commit their offences with informally affiliated others (B = 0.221, $p > 0.05$), and much more likely to commit their offences through formal organizations (B = 0.849, $p < 0.05$)). In other words, it appears that employers make good use of the formally organized business resources available to them. That is, of course, consistent with the structural theory we propose.

The three-valued version of the organizational variable is used in the causal model presented. Again in this model, scope of offence is in large part determined by its organization: organized offences are bigger (B = 0.325). Beyond this, it is employers who are particularly likely to perpetrate organized offences (B = 0.223). Again, our structural theory assumes that this is because employers are best positioned to use organizational resources in committing white-collar crimes. A structural theory of white-collar crime and punishment is therefore unsurprised to find that the correlation between being an employer and scope of offence is significant and positive (r = 0.164); that the effect of employer position on scope of offence is largely indirect through organization of offence (0.223 × 0.325 = 0.73); and that the correlation between being an employer and sentence severity is negligible and non-significant (r = 0.002). Given the scope of employer offences, the weakness of the latter correlation is suggestive of an inequality of outcomes, made possible in part by a reduced likelihood of employers being charged with criminal offences.

Thus far, our account of the model estimated in figure 1.1 suggests that managers are treated with disproportionate severity, and employers with disproportionate leniency. However, the model becomes even more interesting when we take into account the year in which the case was processed. This part of the model indicates a shift over time toward the prosecution of what would commonly be regarded as more important cases. Year of the case exerts a positive direct effect on scope of the offence through organization of the offence ($0.282 \times 0.325 = 0.092$). Over time, managers ($B = 0.163$) and employers ($B = 0.220$) were more likely to be prosecuted than workers.

The prominence of the above year effects made us wonder if there might be evidence of a 'Watergate' or 'Harbourgate' effect. More specifically, we wondered if it could have been the increased charging of employers over time that led to a reduced prosecution of employers under the Criminal Code. To answer this question we first re-estimated the type-of-charge equation, including an interaction term formed by multiplying year, coded first as an interval and then as a binary variable, times the employer variable. With year coded as an interval variable, the interaction effect is significant ($t = 1.716$, $p < 0.05$, one-tailed). With year coded as a binary variable, the interaction effect remains marginally significant ($t = 1.526$, $p < 0.10$, one-tailed).

Table 1.5 further clarifies the above findings by presenting the results of estimating the type-of-charge equations in the before- and after-Watergate periods. Before Watergate, the effect of an employer on being charged under the Criminal Code was positive and non-significant ($b = 0.214$, $p > 0.10$). After Watergate, this effect is significantly negative ($b = -0.316$, $p < 0.05$). In other words, it is only after Watergate, and the increased prosecution of employers, that the apparent leniency in the use of Securities Act charges with employers occurs. Recall that managers were also more likely to be prosecuted after Watergate. However, before ($b = 0.406$, $p < 0.10$) and after Watergate ($b = 0.356$, $p < 0.05$), managers are *more* likely than workers to be charged under the Criminal Code (between periods, $t = 0.232$, $p < 0.10$).

Two final concerns remain. The above equations were estimated using the sample of convicted offenders and OLS regression. The concerns are whether using only the convicted sample and using OLS regression with a binary dependent variable bias our results. Since we are not directly concerned with sentencing in this part of the analysis, we can again use the full sample, and we can use probit in place of OLS regression.

TABLE 1.5 OLS estimates of determinants of type of charge by time period

Variables	1966–1973 (N = 54) b	B	SE	1974–1983 (N = 72) b	B	SE
Year	0.045	0.154	0.042	0.027	0.158	0.020
Petty bourgeoisie	−0.120	−0.086	0.227	0.277	0.145	0.234
Managers	0.406	0.236	0.286	0.356[a]	0.324	0.148
Employers	0.214	0.160	0.282	−0.316[a]	−0.313	0.140
Prior record	0.045	0.032	0.222	0.210	0.172	0.150
Organization of offence	−0.105	−0.184	0.117	0.025	−0.038	0.079
Scope of offence	0.100[a]	0.316	0.052	0.135[b]	0.360	0.044
Strength of evidence	−0.053	0.126	−0.063	0.073	0.041	0.208
Plea negotiation	−0.291	−0.227	0.185	0.014	0.132	0.014
R^2	0.218			0.243		
Constant	−2.557			2.154		

[a] Significant at the 0.05 level.
[b] Significant at the 0.01 level.

The results are presented in Table 1.6.[9] These results confirm that it was only after Watergate that employers were significantly less likely than workers ($B = -0.797$, $p < 0.05$) to be charged under the Criminal Code ($t = 3.25$, $p < 0.01$). On the other hand, we also find that after ($B = 0.517$, $p < 0.10$) as well as before Watergate ($B = 1.340$, $p < 0.10$), managers were significantly more likely than workers to be charged with Criminal Code offences. This effect declines, but not significantly, after Watergate ($t = 1.145$, $p > 0.10$). More generally, the effect of year within the second time period ($B = -0.083$, $p < 0.10$) and the above class effects suggest that the increased prosecution of managers and employers after Watergate was offset by a reduced use of criminal charges. For our purposes, the most important conclusion is that in this period, employers were particularly unlikely to be charged under the Criminal Code. Indeed, occupants of this class position were in this period the least likely in the sample to be charged as criminal offenders. Meanwhile, members of the managerial class continued to be the persons most vulnerable to these charges.

DISCUSSION AND CONCLUSIONS

We have proposed a structural theory of white-collar crime and punishment.

TABLE *1.6 Probit estimate of determinants of type of charge by time period*

Variables	1966–1983 (N = 203) Estimate (B)	SE	1966–1973 (N = 81) Estimate (B)	SE	1974–1983 (N = 123) Estimate (B)	SE
Year	− 0.005	0.021	0.215[b]	0.103	− 0.083[a]	0.049
Petty Bourgeoisie	− 0.743[b]	0.344	− 0.686	0.569	− 0.408	0.483
Managers	0.524[a]	0.278	1.340[a]	0.814	0.517[a]	0.328
Employers	− 0.464[a]	0.256	0.324	0.501	− 0.797[b]	0.326
Prior record	− 0.250	0.275	0.282	0.579	− 0.013	0.356
Organization of offence	− 0.031	0.127	− 0.136	0.217	0.051	0.180
Scope of offence	0.187[c]	0.072	0.037	0.109	0.400[d]	0.111
Strength of evidence	0.283[a]	0.148	0.150	0.233	0.416[a]	0.214
Plea negotiation	− 0.293	0.240	− 0.978[a]	0.546	− 0.010	0.317
Constant	− 0.079		− 14.740		4.856	

[a] Significant at the 0.10 level, one-tailed.
[b] Significant at the 0.05 level.
[c] Significant at the 0.01 level.
[d] Significant at the 0.001 level.

This theory urges that a relational conception of class replace earlier considerations of socio-economic status. Sutherland might well have seconded this change, for it allows a more direct consideration of the role of power that he also emphasized. Empirical results of our work suggest that the substitution of class for status measures is crucial.

For example, recall Sutherland's concern that white-collar crime is a form of organized crime. Our class-based analysis of securities violations indicates why and how this is the case. Employers are located in positions of power that allow them to use organizational resources to commit white-collar crimes. As might be expected, these organizational crimes are also the largest in scope (measured in terms of numbers of victims and geopolitical spread) in our data. However, persons located in the employer class do not receive sanctions commensurate with these crimes. Our data indicate that in large part this is because employers are less likely than others to be charged under the Criminal Code. Employers are instead more likely to be charged with Securities Act violations that carry less stigma and lower sentence exposure. Subsequent analyses revealed that these patterns were most noticeable following Watergate. This was an era in which the enforcement of securities laws increased, with a new emphasis on large, organized offences committed by managers as well as employers. Employers apparently were spared some of the consequences through the use of Securities Act rather than Criminal Code charges.

On the other hand, the post-Watergate attention to securities violations was felt most acutely in the managerial class. The prosecution of members of this class increased over time, and before as well as after Watergate managers were more likely than others to be subjected to Criminal Code charges. The implication is that persons located in this class were scapegoats for the 'social movement against white-collar crime' that Katz (1980) and others describe. The question is why?

Our answer begins with the uniquely powerful positions that employers occupy in modern capitalist economies (see also Hagan et al., 1985). Employers are in positions of power that allow them to be distanced from criminal events and that can obscure their involvement in them. Sutherland (1949: 226) made this point in noting the 'obfuscation as to responsibility' that accompanies corporate positions of power. Two intriguing studies (Baumhart, 1961; Brenner and Molander, 1977) published in the *Harvard Business Review* suggest that this problem of distance and disengagement is not only large but growing. The latter of these studies reports that the percentage of managing executives who indicate an inability to be honest in providing information to their employers has nearly doubled since the earlier research. About half of those surveyed in the latter study thought that their employers frequently did not wish to know how results were obtained, so long as the desired outcomes were accomplished. Such tendencies, and the indication that they are increasing, may explain the greater liability of managers than employers to criminal sanctioning, particularly in the post-Watergate era when the 'failure to know and/or recall' defence became common.

Two further factors complement the above argument and should be noted with regard to employer-class leniency. The first is the role that the complexity of employers' offences may play in insulating them from criminal prosecution. Investigators frequently noted in our interviews the difficulty judges had in understanding securities offences, and the hesitancy judges therefore felt in reaching judgments of guilt in criminal cases:

The biggest problem is convincing the courts of what their offense was, because the courts don't understand securities frauds . . . There are only a smattering of provincial court judges that have a knowledge of securities law, and a lot of them will take the easy way out and give accused the benefit of the doubt.

Consider such a judge hearing the following investigator's description of a typical employer class case:

All right, what happened was this . . . ah geez, it's so complicated . . . He got control of an old public mining company. And he also at the same time had a private company called ——. He then changed the name of the public mining company to ——. So now he had two entities. He got control of the mining company by issuing debentures of his private company for the shares of the public company . . . Then he had the name changed. So now he's got these debentures which were one time private and are now in the public and he can convert them for shares of the debentures. So then he got into a scheme with —— and his own wife where he took the debentures now, that are now owned by that public company, he took them and put them into ——, a stockbroker, as legitimate bonds. And he arranged with —— and —— to buy and sell the bonds because he figured out that as long as you keep a bid on the bonds that gave them a price, even though they were worthless, they were convertible debentures due in 1994 or something, you know, they were just, nothing behind them at all, but as long as somebody was willing to put a bid in on them and there was a buy at least once a month, then the deal would go through and the IBM print-out would show a price on the bond and he could get margin on it from the broker. And by using this margin, they were able to buy and sell these Dune shares . . .

In such complicated cases, it undoubtedly is easier to convince a judge of a more specific securities charge than of a criminal conviction that requires a demonstration of malice.

A related factor is the international scale of many employers' cases. In many such cases, the additional cost involved in securing a criminal conviction may explain reliance on the Securities Act. An investigator observes:

The principals in —— were involved in a tremendous seam that was taking place in Holland, and in the Netherlands, the Antilles and in the Bahamian Islands, and places like that, and they (OSC investigators) put a tremendous amount of work in it, spent all sorts of money trying to prove what had gone on and they (the OSC) went to the Attorney General's department and . . . no criminal charges were laid. You know, it was a matter of economics. Because it would have meant bringing witnesses from practically all over the country, all over the world, to give evidence.

The above factors help further explain the reluctance to pursue employer-class cases under the Criminal Code.

We turn finally to the broader implications of our findings. Our findings contrast most noticeably with those of Wheeler et al. (1982), who report a linear, additive relationship between socio-economic status and sentence severity in white-collar cases. Wheeler et al. (1982: 680) note that this relationship is surprising and controversial, and they encourage further research to evaluate three alternative explanations of their results. The first explanation focuses on the kinds of sample selection problems we have examined; the second on a kind of Watergate effect we have explored; the third on 'historical patterns that link greater social obligations with higher social status' (Wheeler et al., 1982: 658). Our categorical measure of class suggests a more complicated link between class and court outcomes than is found in the study by Wheeler et al., and our findings are more supportive of the first two explanations of their results than the third. This is important because, as Wheeler et al. (1982: 658) note, acceptance of the third explanation would require 'modification of most currently held views', including the widely respected views of Sutherland.

Beyond this, Marxists and non-Marxists alike should find our results of interest, for they are relevant to both functionalist and structural Marxist theories of capital formation and law. We noted at the outset Canada's chronic dependence on foreign as well as domestic infusions of capital to extract its resources and develop its industrial base. It is through securities markets that such capitalization must occur. For much of Canada's history these markets were given as free a rein as possible, so as to develop as quickly as possible. When in the 1960s these markets fell into disrepute, a new mandate for enforcement emerged. We have noted that this mandate did not develop in Canada alone, but it was felt particularly acutely in the enforcement of Canadian securities laws. As in the United States (i.e. Canada is culturally as well as economically dominated), this 'social movement' reached its peak in the post-Watergate era. There was a felt need to rebuild 'investor confidence' and the 'credibility of the marketplace'. It is in this kind of context that the classic conflict between the desire for free enterprise and the need for government regulation comes most openly into view. Both functionalist and structural Marxist theories have something to say about this.

The laissez-faire functionalist assumption is that freedom from regulation facilitates economic enterprise, at least insofar as the exchanges involved are consensually based. The role of the state is therefore to prohibit and punish unwilling exchanges, while giving due consideration to the potential costs and gains of alternative sanctions (see Humphries and Greenberg, 1984: 188). This concern for balance is captured nicely in the observation of the outgoing Chairman of the Ontario Securities Commission that 'our role is not solely investor protection, but it is to create an environment which leads to an efficient market place' (*Globe and Mail*, 1985: B1). The goal, of course, is the efficient formation of capital.

Structural Marxist theories of law seek to explain how such goals influence legal behaviour. These theories, in contrast with older instrumental Marxisms, acknowledge a 'relative autonomy of law', and seek to determine when this autonomy will be observed as well as violated (e.g., Balbus, 1973). The tendency after Watergate of employers more than others to be charged under the Securities Act rather than the Criminal Code suggests a violation of autonomy. We have speculated that an increasing distancing and disengagement of employers from unlawful behaviour that employers nonetheless implicitly or explicitly encourage among others, namely managers, may account for the above result, and further explain the finding that managers were especially liable to criminal prosecution in the post-Watergate era. These are structural conditions that may protect employers and leave managers more vulnerable to criminal prosecution. Both functionalist and structural Marxist theories of capital formation and law are relevant to the understanding of these conditions. Meanwhile, conceptualization and measurement of such practices as distancing and disengagement will provide the kind of elaboration and specification that a structural theory of law requires to be more fully developed and tested in terms of traditional criteria of causality. Our results indicate that the substitution of class for status measures is a crucial precondition to such developments.

NOTES

1 Three court cases attracted particular attention during this period: R. v. Jay (1965), 2 Ontario Reports 471; R. v. Lampard (1968), 2 Ontario Reports 470; R. v. MacMillan (1968), 1 Ontario Reports 475. These cases were highly publicized and earned the designation of 'scandals', especially the last, which was popularly known as the 'Windfall Oil and Miles Affair'.

2 The Securities Act specifies offences which for an individual can result in fines of up to $2000 and imprisonment for one year. The act deals specifically with takeover bids, proxies, insider reporting and financial disclosure, and also includes a general offence provision. The Criminal Code specifies offences which for an individual can result in imprisonment for ten years. These offences include conspiracy, spreading false news, false pretences or statements, fraud, false prospectus, fraudulent manipulation of stock exchange transactions, gaming in stocks and merchandise, broker reducing stock by selling for his own account (short sales), and breach of trust by public officials.

3 The file system of provincial agencies provided our initial enumeration of 226 cases referred for prosecution from 1966–1983. When investigators primarily responsible for cases could not be located (this occurred in 43 cases), alternative sources of information were used (news accounts, related case files, and other investigators). In 23 cases this information was eventually judged inadequate, and these cases were omitted from the analysis presented here. Removal of these cases does not change the structure of the causal model presented, but it does improve the performance of the scope-of-offence scale described in this chapter.

4 This scale takes the following values: suspended sentence without supervision (1); fine (2); probation with supervision to 12 months, with or without fine (3); probation with supervision to 36 months, with or without fine (4); prison to 6 months with or without fine or probation (5); prison to 12 months, with or without fine or probation (6); prison to 24 months, with or without fine or probation (7);

prison to 36 months, with or without fine or probation (8); prison to 48 months, with or without fine or probation (9); prison to 60 months, with or without fine or probation (10); prison to 72 months, with or without fine or probation (11).

5 Age was coded in actual years, private counsel as a dummy variable, and cooperativeness and reputation as Likert scales.

6 For discussions of possible limitations of the Heckman procedure in correcting for selection bias, see Berk (1983) and Goldberger (1981). We simply note here that the selection equation itself gives little indication that the kinds of class bias that are of concern in the research literature on white-collar crime influence our results through the process of conviction.

7 Although there was no indication of this in our interviews with investigators, it is possible that the influence of strength of evidence was exaggerated by the investigators' retrospective knowledge of case outcomes. For this reason among others we return below to the full sample of convicted and unconvicted offenders to conduct a final check on our results.

8 We believe that the analysis is free of common technical or specification problems. None of the independent variables are correlated as high as 0.6, the Durbin-Watson d-statistics for equations estimated below are concentrated between 1.5 and 1.8, scattergrams reveal no outlier problems, and our attempts to incorporate additional explanatory variables do not alter the structure or substance of our results.

9 Smith (1984: 36) points out that the following statistic has a *t*-distribution and can be used to test for significant differences between pairs of probit coefficients across equations:

$$t = \frac{b_1 - b^2}{\sqrt{\dfrac{(V_1)\,(SEB_1)^2 + (V_2)\,(SEB_2)^2}{V_1 + V_2}}}$$

Where

b = Probit coefficient for population i
V = $N - K - 1$ for population i
SEB = Standard error for probit coefficient for population i.

2

The Corporate Advantage

To the extent that criminologists have talked in recent years about corporate entities and criminal law (e.g., Schrager and Short, 1978), they have been most concerned with the illegal and unethical activities of commercial organizations, and with the failure of the criminal law to deal with them (e.g., Ermann and Lundman, 1980). The point of this important and growing body of work is to demonstrate that commercial organizations are ineffectively pursued as criminals. Yet there is another, and potentially even more important, aspect of this situation. That is that corporate entities are nonetheless very active participants in the criminal justice process, pursuing through the police and courts many individuals who commit crimes against them. In other words, corporate entities not only have successfully avoided large scale criminal prosecutions, they also have proven themselves effective in using criminal prosecutions to penalize those individuals who offend against them. It is the latter part of this imbalanced situation that we will examine in this chapter.

CORPORATE ENTITIES AS JURISTIC PERSONS

We will follow Coleman (1974: 14) in interchangeably using the terms 'corporate entity' and 'corporate actor' to refer not only to what are commonly called corporations, but also to other collective entities such as churches, associations, unions and schools, all of whom may enlist the criminal law to prosecute and convict individuals who commit crimes against them. These corporate entities constitute 'juristic persons' who for legal purposes are treated much like 'natural persons'. Indeed, it may be this apparent legal equivalence drawn between juristic and natural persons that has distracted social scientists from considering the distinctive roles these respective parties play in the criminal justice system. Thus, the formal legal assumpion is that juristic and natural persons have equal rights and interests in law as a protection against those who offend against them. However, the preceding assumption is a formal legal abstraction that is inconsistent with social and economic inequalities that differentiate corporate and individual entities. In other words, the 'juristic person' is a legal form (Balbus, 1973) that obscures more than it reveals. Coleman (1974) states the problem clearly when he notes that '. . . a symmetric allocation of rights between corporations and persons can lead in practice to an asymmetric realization of interests' (76); and when he concludes that '. . . among the variety of interest that men have, those interests that have been successfully collected to create corporate actors are the interests that dominate the society' (49). Our concern in this chapter is with how, and with what consequences, corporate advantages in the criminal justice process may have been achieved. The work of Max Weber (1969) is relevant to these issues.

THE DOMINATION OF LAW

Weber regarded the law, criminal and civil, as bearing a close correspondence to the economy, and to the corporate entities that comprise it. The connecting link in this system of thought was the notion of logical formalism, or formal rationality. In fact, much of Weber's work on law addressed a fundamental question that ultimately was left unresolved: did formal rationality in legal thought contribute to the rise of capitalism, or alternatively, did capitalism contribute to the rise of logical rationality in legal thought? Regardless of the answer given to this question, Weber made the following point quite clear, 'The tempo of modern business communication requires a promptly and predictably functioning legal system,' or, said differently, 'The universal predominance of the market consociation requires . . . a legal system the functioning of which is *calculable* in accordance with rational rules' (40). Thus corporate entities have a generalized interest in formal rational legal processes, and a mainstay of formal rationality is the domination of law.

By domination, Weber means the probability that commands will be followed. *A key form of domination for our purposes involves the probability that corporate victims will be better able than individual victims to get individual offenders convicted.* Weber notes that such forms of domination are sustained in large part by efforts to raise or cultivate their legitimacy. Thus '. . . the continued existence of every domination . . . always has the strongest need of self-justification through appealing to the principles of legitimation' (336).

Weber concludes that '*Rationally* consociated conduct of a dominational structure finds its typical expression in *bureaucracy*, and therefore the purest type of legal domination is that which is carried on by and through a bureaucratic administrative staff.' The effectiveness of bureaucracy in the service of this goal is readily explained:

> Bureaucracy tends toward *formalistic impersonality*. The ideal official administers his office *sine ira et studio*, without hatred or passion, hence also without 'love' or 'enthusiasm'; under the pressure of a plain sense of duty, 'without regard of person' he treats equally all persons who find themselves in factually equal situations. (xliii, emphasis in original)

Thus one key feature of a bureaucratically organized criminal justice system is the presumed capacity to rise above consideration of the extra-legal characteristics of the persons it processes. Such a system is expected instead to deal only with legally relevant aspects of offenders' cases. Note that this expectation directly contradicts the instrumental Marxist assumption that discrimination against economic and ethnic minorities is an inevitable product of criminal justice decision-making in a capitalist society. In contrast to this expectation, we have argued that corporate entities should have an objective interest in the very feature of formal impersonality that a bureaucratically organized criminal justice system is expected to provide: it is this feature that adds the legitimacy, and in turn the predictability and calculability, that are essential to successful commercial enterprise.

If the above reasoning is correct, in historical as well as cross-sectional data, *we should expect the participation of corporate actors as victims in the criminal justice process to be characterized by an increased formal equality in the treatment of offenders*. However, it is essential to emphasize the word *formal* here, because as Balbus (1973: 652) suggests, '. . . the systemic application of an equal scale to systemically unequal individuals necessarily tends to reinforce systemic inequalities . . .' That is, it is important to emphasize that although individual offenders might be treated more equally when corporate victims are involved, they collectively would still fare worse (i.e., because as a *group* they would experience a higher probability of conviction).

A final implication of the above discussion is that corporate actors will not only be anxious to make use of the criminal justice system, but also that they will more easily co-ordinate their goals with the organizational priorities of this system. Both organizational forms have an interest in the bureaucratic pursuit of the formal rational application of law. Furthermore, as bureaucracies themselves, many corporate actors may be better suited than individuals to work effectively with the criminal justice system. For example, the element of formal impersonality may better equip corporate actors to decide which crimes against them are more promising cases for criminal prosecution.

Also, because corporate actors may be more impersonal as well as less involved emotionally in their cases, they may be less likely to intrude on the criminal justice process once a case is under way; or, in the course of a case to indicate a change of preference with regard to the prosecution of it. Thus corporate victims may work more effectively than individual victims with criminal justice organizations, and *corporate actors may therefore be more satisfied than individuals with the results they achieve*. This type of prediction is anticipated by Coleman's observation that corporate actors (including not only corporations but also government agencies like those that constitute the criminal justice system) prefer to work with other corporate actors as compared to individuals. Coleman captures the irony and significance of this situation when he notes that 'These preferences are often rationally based: the corporate actor ordinarily stands to gain more from a transaction with another corporate actor than from one with a person. But the rational basis makes the preference no less real in its consequences for persons.'

Three testable hypotheses are contained in the above discussion: (i) that corporate actors will be more successful than individuals in obtaining convictions against offenders, (ii) that equal treatment of offenders will be more likely to accompany corporate than individual victim involvement in the criminal justice system, and (iii) that corporate actors will be more satisfied than individuals with the work of this system. This chapter presents a cross-sectional empirical test of these hypotheses. First, however, it will be useful to provide a brief discussion of the changing historical role of victims in the criminal justice system. The thesis of this discussion is that the historical emergence of corporate entities has been associated with significant changes in the role of the victim.

THE ROLE OF THE VICTIM VIEWED HISTORICALLY

If the Weberian picture of corporate participation in the criminal justice process we have provided is correct, it should be possible to identify historical changes in the role of crime victims that correspond to changes in the surrounding economy and society (cf. Tigar and Levy, 1977). Such changes can be identified. In their broadest outline: a resort to blood feuds directly involved victims in achieving early notions of criminal justice in tribal societies; a form of private prosecution and compensation continued to involve victims, but with some notable modifications, in feudal societies; and the emergence of modern capitalism found victims of crime replaced by public prosecutors in pursuit of a more impersonal, formal rational form of justice.

Thus, early societies, based on kinship ties and tribal organization functioned without centralized systems of criminal justice and they assigned a prominent role to presumed victims in resolving 'criminal' disputes through blood feuds. In these societies, victims and their kin were expected to put things right by avenging what they perceived as crimes against them: 'All crime was against the family; it was the family that had to atone, or carry out the blood-feud' (Traill, 1899: 5).

Feudalism and Christianity were accompanied by a gradual elimination of blood feuding and an emerging system of compensations. What is significant in this is that as feudalism developed, between 700 and 1066, lords and bishops gradually replaced kinship groups as recipients of the compensatory payments (Hibbert, 1963; Jeffrey, 1957). This was a very significant beginning of the decoupling of victims from an emerging criminal justice system. Gradually, the state began to receive a part of the compensation payments. Schafer (1976: 914) notes that 'Before long the injured person's right to restitution began to shrink, and after the Treaty of Verdun divided the Frankish Empire, the fine that went to the state gradually replaced it entirely.' Thus, it was now the state that was replacing the victim as a central actor in the criminal justice process. Finally, although the proceedings of this period (including oaths and ordeals) could be quite formal, at least from a modern viewpoint, they also were quite irrational (see Whitelock, 1952: 139–42; also Thayer, 1898; Maine, 1960).

The transition in England to a more modern form of criminal justice occurred during the reign of Henry II (1154–1189). During this period the feudal system of law disappeared and a system of common law emerged (Jeffrey, 1957: 660). Nonetheless, a system of private prosecutions based on the initiative taken by victims of crime remained in effect in England well into the nineteenth century. In fact, the final decline of the victim's role in the criminal justice system did not begin until the Enlightenment, with the work of Cesare Beccaria. Writing in the eighteenth century, Beccaria (1963) applied the 'principle of utility' in arguing that criminal law should serve the interests of society rather than the individual victim. What is significant throughout this work is the effort to model a criminal justice system on the same principles of calculation and reason that formed the foundations of modern capitalism (for elaboration of this point, see Halevy, 1960). Thus Balbus (1977) is able to note direct parallels between the emergence of modern legal forms and the commodity forms that characterize modern capitalism.

With Beccaria and Bentham (1970), then, the formal rationality that Weber associates with modern capitalism found a very fundamental expression. The most important implication of this was that victims should play no direct role in criminal justice decisions about prosecution and punishment. From the utilitarian viewpoint, the crime is against *society*, and the state must therefore use calculation and reason in pursuing its prosecution and in deterring its repetition. However, as indicated earlier, in England the right and power to accuse, collect evidence and manage prosecutions for the state resided with individual citizens well into the nineteenth century (McDonald, 1976: 659–65). Indeed this access to the law was regarded as an important right of private citizens, and it was not until the middle of the nineteenth century that the principal inadequacy of this arrangement was acknowledged: namely, that offenders were escaping prosecution because victims could not afford to exercise their legal rights. After several unsuccessful attempts to solve this problem in other ways, the office of the Director of Public Prosecutions was established in England in 1879. The ultimate effect of this change, and those discussed above, was a final loosening of the coupling of the victim to the criminal justice system, and a new autonomy for the state in overseeing victim-offender disputes.

It is clear then that a new kind of criminal justice emerged alongside the rise of the corporate form and the emergence of modern capitalism. It is our argument that this new form of criminal justice is particularly effective in facilitating and legitimating use of the criminal law for the protection of corporate property against individuals. Put simply, our argument is that the new 'autonomy' of the state in matters of criminal justice better serves corporate than individual interests. The remainder of this chapter is an empirical exploration of this argument.

PRIOR RESEARCH

In spite of the importance we have attached in this discussion to corporate victims of crime, very little empirical attention has been given to them. Several victimization surveys involving corporate actors have been conducted as part of the National Crime Survey Program in the United States (US Department of Justice, 1975). However, only two types of commercial crime, robbery and burglary, are considered in this work, and the sampling is restricted almost entirely to commercial establishments. Beyond this, a small collection of articles on crimes against businesses has been brought together in a single volume (Smigel and Ross, 1970); there are several studies of shoplifting and its control (e.g., Cameron, 1964; Hindelang and Gottfredson, 1976; Robin, 1967); and the United States government has made some attempt to collect information on the costs of several types of commercial victimization (US Department of Commerce, 1974). Among these sources, it is the victimization research that is most instructive.

Victimization data collected on burglary and robbery in thirteen American cities (US Department of Justice) are brought together, and weighted to produce population estimates, in Appendix tables 2.1 and 2.2 of this chapter. These data provide preliminary support for our focus on the corporate influence on criminal law. For example, as might be expected given the opportunities and benefits of crimes against corporate actors, both for burglary and robbery, the per capita rates of victimization of commercial establishments are higher than for individuals and households. Across the thirteen cities, on a per capita basis, commercial establishments experience more than three times the burglaries and five times the robberies as households and individuals. Furthermore, in every city, for both burglary and robbery, commercial establishments are more likely than individuals and households to report the victimizations they experience to the police. Across thirteen cities, approximately three-quarters (76.1 per cent) of the commercial burglary victims report their experiences to the police, while about half (51.6 per cent) of the household burglary victims report their experiences to the police. Similarly, 82 per cent of the commercial robberies and 57 per cent of the individual robberies are reported to the police. Undoubtedly, this difference is influenced by the types and amounts of corporate insurance coverage. Nonetheless, it remains significant that on a per capita basis, commercial victims are much more likely than individual victims to require and make use of the criminal justice system. Of course, individuals and households outnumber commercial organizations, so that when the above findings are weighted back to the population, commercial establishments are reduced in their apparent significance. Even then, however, we find that commercial establishments are very important clients of the criminal justice system. Thus across the thirteen American cities, commercial establishments are responsible for more than a third, and in some cities (e.g., Cincinnati in the case of burglary and Miami in the case of robbery) more than half, of both the burglaries and robberies reported to the police. In other words, the representation of commercial victims in the criminal justice process is large and disproportionate.

Some comments should be added to these findings. First, these data deal with burglary and robbery only, while thefts (by employees and customers) are clearly the most frequent crimes experienced by commercial victims. Second, these data consider only commercial establishments, ignoring other kinds of corporate victims. Finally, these data stop at the point where victims indicate that they reported incidents to the police. In other words, the picture provided by victimization data is suggestive, but partial. Research reported in the remainder of this chapter considers in greater detail the involvement of corporate victims in the criminal justice process, in one Canadian jurisdiction.

THE CURRENT RESEARCH

The data analysed in the remainder of this chapter consist of cases involving victims of crime for whom an offender is charged in a collection of suburban communities adjacent to Toronto, Canada. Our focus on only those cases where an offender is charged is deliberate. We have already shown with victimization data that commercial organizations are more likely than individual victims to report crimes against them to the police. We now want to consider the role of these victims in the criminal justice system. Focusing on cases where charges are laid increases the likelihood that the victims we consider have something more than a passing contact with the system.

Several kinds of data are considered. First, a population of 1,000 cases drawn from police department files from September 1976 to January 1977 is used to establish parameters for the jurisdiction under study. Then a stratified sample of 40 post-disposition interviews with 200 individual and 200 corporate victims is analysed. The interviews with the individual victims represent the latter half of a panel design involving before and after court contacts which took place between June 1976 and December 1978; the corporate interviews began in September 1977 and continued until September 1978. Individual victims for whom an offender was charged were eliminated from the sampling frame in three circumstances: if the victim was a juvenile, if the crime was against a person's property and resulted in less than five dollars damage, or if the crime was against a person who could not, or would not, recall it. The panel design involving individual victims began with 305 victims and stopped after 200 of these victims could be recontacted for the follow-up, post-disposition interview.[1]

In establishing the sampling frame for the corporate interviews, two research decisions had to be made. First, which member of the corporate entity should be interviewed? Our decision was to have the interviewer determine who in the organization was most responsible for making charging and other decisions in the relevant case. In practice, this arrangement seemed to work effectively; however, it also raised the second issue to be faced. That issue was: which cases involving corporate victims should be considered? Many corporate actors – especially the retail department stores – were victimized repeatedly. It would have made little sense to interview representatives of these organizations repeatedly. Instead we formulated as a sampling criterion that each organization was to be interviewed only once about a crime (involving a charged suspect) which was representative of those experienced. This was done in one of two ways. Working with a listing of all cases involving corporate victims for whom an accused was charged, we first sorted the cases by organization. Again as in the case of individual victims, property crimes involving less than five dollars in losses were not considered. If a modal type of case for a corporate victim was present (e.g., shoplifting for many retail stores), a case for interview was selected among these at random. Alternatively, if no modal type of case existed, a case was selected at random from the larger grouping. The resulting sampling frame was made up of cases involving 334 corporate actors.

The variables and their values included in our analysis are listed in Appendix table 2.1. Our analysis focuses first on a set of court outcomes: whether the defendant was held for a bail hearing, convicted, and the type of sentence received; and second on victims' reactions to these outcomes: the perceived appropriateness of the disposition and the overall satisfaction with the outcome of the case.

There may be initial discomfort with the idea of considering cases involving corporate and individual victims in a single analysis; a discomfort that probably follows from the observation that some types of cases, for example shoplifting, only involve corporate actors. However, it is not at all clear that this fact makes shoplifting cases *qualitatively* different from other offences commited against corporate actors and individuals. Certainly the law provides no separate offence category for shoplifting (i.e., the charge is typically theft), and we have noted that it treats both corporate and individual victims as 'persons'. Furthermore, Sellin and Wolfgang (1964) have demonstrated that shoplifting and other types of property crimes can be located, along with a variety of other crimes that cause bodily injury, on a common scale of seriousness. Their point, empirically confirmed, is that in everyday life, and particularly in everyday law enforcement, certain equivalences can and must be formed (348). Beyond this, our argument is that differences between cases involving corporate actors and individuals are a matter of degree, not kind, involving such things as the impersonality versus intimacy involved in the victim-accused relationship. Consideration of such variables is a part of our analysis; an analysis that successfully 'accounts' for an important difference in the outcomes of cases involving corporate and individual victims.

A wide range of independent variables are considered in the analysis, some deriving from our theoretical interests, others from the conventions of this kind of criminal justice research (see, for example, Hagan and Bumiller, 1983). For example, in the first part of the analysis, dealing with court outcomes, we consider a number of characteristics of the victim: whether the victim is an individual or a corporate entity, and if the former, the victim's sex and socio-economic status; the seriousness of the victimization as measured by the Sellin-Wolfgang scale; whether property was returned to the victim, the willingness of the victim to accept any responsibility for the crime, whether the victim gave testimony, the intimacy of the victim-accused relationship,[2] and whether the victim is a 'repeat player' in the sense of having experienced the same type of crime previously. If the victim is a corporate actor, we consider whether it is involved in retailing, public or private in its base, local to multinational in scale, the number of employees in the representative's division, the number of organizational units, the number of employees in the organization, the centralization of the organization and the perceived relationship between the organization and its clients. A number of characteristics of the accused were also taken from police files for this part of the analysis, including the marital status, sex, condition at arrest and employment status of the accused. Information from the files was also used to determine whether a statement was taken from the accused, the police perception of the demeanour of the accused, and the number of prior convictions, the most serious prior disposition and the number of charges against the accused. Finally, for this part of the analysis we included from these files information on whether the victim mobilized the police, filed the complaint, whether a warrant was issued, and the initial decision whether to hold the person for a bail hearing. The last variable was included only for the adjudication and sentencing outcomes, to determine if early processing decisions are coupled to those made later.

There is some overlap in the independent variables included in the first and second parts of the analysis. The type of victim and crime, seriousness of victimization, return of property to the victim, victim responsibility, the relationship between victim and accused, and whether the victim mobilized the police, filed the complaint and gave testimony, are all considered as before. Similarly, four aspects of the accused – employment status, prior convictions, most serious prior disposition and number of other charges – are included in the same way as before. In addition to these variables, we consider a number of others that come from our interviews and that plausibly influence the response to court outcomes.

The remorse of the accused, as perceived by the victim, is included as measured in a Likert-type scale. We also consider characteristics attributed to the accused by the victim, measured in the form of a summed semantic differential scale that includes evaluations of the accused as honest-dishonest, responsible-irresponsible, kind-cruel, gentle-brutal, safe-dangerous, good-bad, predictable-unpredictable, stable-unstable, mature-immature, friendly-unfriendly. Victim ratings of the importance of five goals of sentencing – reformation, general deterrence, individual deterrence, punishment and incapacitation – are considered. A summed five item law and order scale (see Hagan, 1975a) is included. A 'citizen responsibility' scale was constructed in the same way from responses to two items: (i) there isn't much individual citizens can do to prevent crime, and (ii) preventing crime is the job of the police, not the job of the average citizen. Separate consideration is given to the victim's belief in free will ('To what extent to you believe that human beings act on their own free will?') and conceptions of individual responsibility ('Do you feel that human beings should be responsible for their actions?'), both coded as Likert scales. Consideration is also given to whether the victim attended trial and to the victim's knowledge of the disposition. Victims who did not know the disposition were told it before being asked to respond to the case outcomes. The last of the independent variables we include is the disposition of the case. We are interested not only in the direct effect of this variable on the victim's response to the criminal justice process, but also in the effects of statistically holding this variable constant.

Tabular and regression techniques are used to analyse our data. Two of our five dependent variables are binary and violate technical assumptions of homoskedasticity. Under these conditions, ordinary least squares regression may produce inefficient, though unbiased, parameter estimates. We therefore ran weighted least squares solutions as well as ordinary least squares regressions when the binary dependent variables were involved. This procedure produced changes in some coefficients, but no alterations in substantive conclusions. To conserve space and maintain consistency, we present only the results of the ordinary least squares regressions in this chapter. Unless otherwise indicated, in the regression phase of the analysis we consider only those effects that are statistically significant at the 0.10 level,[3] with betas of 0.10 and larger. Throughout the analysis we focus on those factors that distinguish the involvement of corporate and individual victims in the criminal justice process.

THE ANALYSIS

The preliminary part of the analysis focused on a comparison of the population and interview data to determine if any systematic sources of error or bias were present in the latter. Although no important discrepancies were discovered, several findings did stand out. First, we found that nearly two-thirds of the victims in the population were corporate entities (N = 643), while just over a third were individuals (357). Also both in the population and in the interviews significantly more corporate (79.5 per cent and 75.0 per cent) than individual victims (65.5 per cent and 62.2 per cent) saw accused persons in their cases convicted. We analyse this relationship between type of victim and likelihood of conviction further below. Meanwhile, we can note that these preliminary findings are certainly consistent with our first hypothesis about corporate influence in the criminal justice process; that is, that corporate actors are more successful than individuals in obtaining convictions against offenders.

Before pursuing our multivariate analysis, several additional bivariate relationships are presented in table 2.1. The first two findings in this table reveal that corporate victims are more likely than individual victims to believe they could have prevented the incident and less likely to believe that crime prevention is the job of the police. The implication is that corporate victims are well aware of the fact that they present more opportunities for crime than individuals, and that they could, and perhaps should, assume a greater responsibility for the crimes committed against them. As we have indicated, however, the paradox of this situation is that corporate victims are more likely to see accused persons convicted.

Table 2.1 also establishes several other things: individual victims are significantly more likely to know the accused, attend court and know the case outcome. These indicators suggest that corporate victims are more detached from the accused, and decoupled from the criminal justice system, than are individual victims. We note these findings here because, as we suggest later, they may facilitate a more formal rational influence of corporate victims on the criminal justice process.

Finally, there is evidence in table 2.1, consistent with our third hypothesis above, that corporate victims respond more positively to the criminal justice experience than do individual victims. Corporate victims are less likely than individual victims to be dissatisfied with the sentences the courts generally impose, and more likely to be satisfied with the competence of the police, the overall outcome of the case, and with the specific sentence imposed in the immediate case. All but the last of these differences is statistically significant. In other words, and perhaps with good reason, corporate victims express a greater satisfaction with the criminal justice system than do individual victims. Since some of this satisfaction may derive from the greater success of corporate victims in obtaining convictions, we go on next to a multivariate analysis of this success.

In table 2.2 we use a step-wise multiple regression procedure to assess the impact of several variables on the greater success of corporate victims in obtaining convictions. These variables were selected in terms of our expectations about corporate participation in the criminal justice process. Thus the first of the variables is the victim-accused relationship, measured in terms of the intimacy, or conversely, the impersonality, of this relationship. Our expectation is that an impersonal relationship is more likely to allow a sustained prosecution, while intimacy between the victim and accused more often does not. Second, we consider the presence of a statement from the accused. Offenders who make incriminating statements are more easily convicted, and corporate entities may be able to use their

TABLE 2.1 Type of victim by response to victimization and court experience

	Perceived ability to prevent incident	Prevention of crime job of police	Knowledge of offender	Attended court	Knowledge of case outcome	Sentences generally too easy	Satisfaction with police competence	Satisfied with sentence	Satisfied with overall outcome
Individual	10.5% (21)	18.0% (36)	40.0% (80)	57.0% (114)	50.5% (101)	64.0% (128)	79.5% (159)	43.5% (87)	53.0% (106)
Organization	26.5% (53)	9.0% (18)	18.0% (36)	21.0% (42)	26.0% (52)	53.0% (106)	88.5% (177)	46.0% (92)	66.0% (132)
	$x^2 = 11.02$ $p = 0.001$	$x^2 = 8.21$ $p = 0.004$	$x^2 = 23.51$ $p = 0.001$	$x^2 = 55.20$ $p = 0.001$	$x^2 = 29.02$ $p = 0.001$	$x^2 = 5.25$ $p = 0.072$	$x^2 = 5.25$ $p = 0.014$	$x^2 = 3.27$ $p = 0.351$	$x^2 = 16.35$ $p = 0.006$

TABLE 2.2 *Decomposition of the effect of type of victim on adjudication (N = 400)*

	(1)		(2)		(3)		(4)		(5)	
	B	F	B	F	B	F	B	F	B	F
Type of victim	0.16	10.18	0.14	7.17	0.12	5.63	0.09	2.99	0.09	3.12
Statement taken			0.22	21.15	0.18	11.94	0.18	11.91	0.17	11.63
Accused demeanour					−0.14	6.83	−0.14	6.93	−0.13	6.68
Victim-accused relationship							−0.12	5.39	−0.12	5.62
Repeat player									−0.07	2.21
Mediated effect			0.02		0.02		0.03		0.00	

resources more selectively in picking cases for prosecution where such statements can be generated. We include also the demeanour of the accused. One aspect of 'good' demeanour, as perceived by the police, is an acknowledgement of guilt; again, corporate victims may be better able to generate cases with accused persons who have been reduced to this demeanour. Finally, we consider whether the victim is a 'repeat player', in the sense of having been a victim previously of a similar crime (Galanter, 1974). Corporate entities are more likely to be repeat players ($r = 0.53$), and this experience may be expected to improve their prospects for successful prosecutions. The above variables were introduced into the regression equations in table 2.2 in the order that they increased the explained variance in convictions.

Examination of table 2.2 reveals that three of the above four variables are indeed involved in the success of corporations in obtaining convictions. Thus the statistical significance of the type of victim was reduced below the 0.05 level after the introduction of three of these variables.[4] The largest of the mediated effects (0.03) in table 2.2 is produced by the introduction of the victim-accused relationship. In other words, the impersonality of corporate actors is a key factor in their higher rate of convictions. Only slightly less important is the apparent ability of corporate victims to select and/or generate accused persons who give statements to the police and who demonstrate co-operative demeanour (both mediated effects = 0.02). The only variable that does not operate as expected is whether the victim is a repeat player. Apparently this experience does not *directly* account for the success of organizations. Indeed, the correlation between this experience and convictions is only 0.07. On the other hand, we have found evidence that corporate entities seem to more generally choose cases for prosecution with an eye toward what the courts are most likely to convict. Said differently, corporate entities choose their cases impersonally and strategically, a pattern that would seem to facilitate the formal rational enforcement of criminal law.

TABLE 2.3 Correlation and regression coefficients for individual victims

Independent variables	Bail (N = 188)				Adjudication (N = 188)				Sentence (N = 130)			
	r	b	B	F	r	b	B	F	r	b	B	F
Seriousness of victimization	0.17	0.02	0.15	4.20[b]					0.31	0.08	0.29	11.07[b]
Return of property					0.23	0.18	0.15	3.70[b]				
Victim-accused relationship									− 0.13	− 0.03	− 0.15	3.02[a]
Accused condition at arrest	0.20	0.14	0.17	5.11[b]								
Accused employment status	− 0.08	− 0.11	− 0.14	3.85[b]	− 0.30	− 0.22	− 0.23	9.47[b]	− 0.16	− 0.26	− 0.16	3.87[a]
Statement taken	0.16	0.18	0.22	8.59[b]								
Accused demeanour	0.17	0.17	0.19	7.05[b]								
Accused most serious disposition	0.36	0.11	0.35	14.38[b]					0.38	0.18	0.30	6.21
Number of charges against accused					− 0.12	− 0.06	− 0.23	7.98[b]				
Complaint	− 0.15	− 0.10	− 0.13	3.28[a]								
Warrant					− 0.18	− 0.27	− 0.19	6.52[b]				
Victim's sex	0.07	− 0.12	− 0.15	3.67[a]					− 0.06	− 0.40	− 0.26	8.49[b]
	R² = 0.29				R² = 0.25				R² = 0.38			
	Intercept = 0.15				Intercept = 0.64				Intercept = 3.41			

TABLE 2.4 Results of dummy variable regressions involving sex of victim and involvement with the accused

Dummy variables	Bail				Adjudication				Sentence			
	r	b	B	F	r	b	B	F	r	b	B	F
Female victim–involved with accused	− 0.06	0.08	0.09	1.24	− 0.14	− 0.02	− 0.02	0.04	− 0.12	0.12	0.06	0.49
Female victim–not involved with accused	− 0.02	0.12	0.13	2.91[a]	0.02	0.02	0.03	0.08	0.18	0.42	0.22	6.15[b]

Note: In this and tables 2.4–2.6 [a] indicates statistical significance at the 0.10 level, [b] indicates the 0.05 level and [c] indicates the 0.01 level.

There was no evidence in our data that corporate victims were any more likely than individual victims to see accused persons held for a bail hearing or severely sentenced. However, a comparison in tables 2.3 and 2.5 of factors producing these outcomes in cases of individual and corporate victims reveals some striking differences that are consistent with our earlier discussion. For example, in cases with individual victims (see table 2.3), the independent variable that most consistently predicts bail, adjudication and sentencing decisions is the employment status of the accused. In these cases, unemployed accused, whom we elsewhere in this volume identify as members of the surplus population, are more likely to be held for bail ($B = -0.14$), convicted ($B = -0.23$), and sentenced severely ($B = -0.16$). It may be possible to legally justify detention of an unemployed accused for a bail hearing in terms of formal standards for the making of these decisions (see Nagel, 1980; Morden, 1980). However, similar justifications do not exist at conviction and sentencing, and measured against normative expectations about equality before the law, these effects are extra-legal. In contrast, in table 2.5, where cases involving corporate victims are considered, the employment status of the accused does *not* play a significant role at conviction and sentencing. These findings support our second hypothesis that formally equal treatment of offenders increases with corporate involvement in the criminal justice system.

Of related interest is the finding that persons accused of crimes against women are more likely than are persons accused of crimes against men to be held for a bail hearing ($B = -0.15$) and to be sentenced severely ($B = -0.26$). Interpretation of these effects is complicated by the fact that they only become apparent when other variables are held constant ($r = -0.07$ and -0.06). Our concern in offering an interpretation of these effects was with the complicating role that the victim's relationship with the accused might play. To explore this we created two dummy variables representing female victims who *were* and *were not* intimately involved with the accused.[5] The 'omitted category' for these dummy variables was male victims uninvolved with the accused. The results of substituting these dummy variables for their component parts in the regression equations of table 2.3 are presented in table 2.4. These results reveal two things: (i) offender involvement with female victims lessens the probability of conviction ($r = -0.14$), and when conviction occurs, tends to result in more lenient sentencing ($r = -0.12$); (ii) other variables held constant, offenders accused of crimes against female victims with whom they are uninvolved are more likely to be held for bail hearings ($B = 0.13$) and receive severe sentences ($B = 0.22$). In other words, female victims who are uninvolved with the offender receive greater protective treatment from the courts than do female victims who are involved with the accused. These

TABLE 2.5 *Correlation and regression coefficients for organizational victims*

Independent variables	Bail (N = 200)				Adjudication (N = 200)				Sentence (N = 157)			
	r	b	B	F	r	b	B	F	r	b	B	F
Seriousness of victimization									0.32	0.08	0.19	7.29[b]
Victim responsibility					− 0.16	− 0.12	− 0.12	3.17[a]				
Victim testimony									− 0.06	− 0.33	− 0.13	3.41[a]
Accused marital status					0.13	0.07	0.12	2.78[a]	− 0.23	− 0.23	− 0.17	4.96[a]
Accused condition at arrest					0.06	0.16	0.13	3.43[a]				
Accused employment status	− 0.16	− 0.14	− 0.16	4.93[b]								
Statement taken					0.26	0.26	0.32	16.85[b]	0.26	0.47	0.28	11.66[b]
Accused demeanour					− 0.21	− 0.12	− 0.14	3.59[a]				
Accused prior convictions	0.42	0.03	0.29	7.44[b]								
Accused most serious disposition	0.39	0.06	0.18	2.77[a]								
Number of charges against accused					− 0.04	− 0.04	− 0.13	2.87[a]				
Mobilization					0.15	0.14	0.17	6.34[b]				
Bail decision					0.15	0.15	0.15	3.94[b]	0.39	0.53	0.27	12.39[b]
Number of employees					0.10	0.01	0.14	3.32[a]				
	R^2 = 0.27				R^2 = 0.28				R^2 = 0.47			
	Intercept = 0.09				Intercept = 1.11				Intercept = 2.87			

results are suggestive of another type of inequality before the law that accompanies disputes between individuals.

Rather different findings emerge in table 2.5, where cases involving corporate victims are considered. For example, in addition to the finding pertaining to the employment status of the accused noted above, the two most important determinants of being held for a bail hearing are the number of prior convictions and the most serious prior disposition against the accused. Beyond this, the most consistent influence on adjudication and sentencing is whether the accused was held for a bail hearing ($B = 0.15$ and 0.27). Overall, then, there is a tendency in cases involving corporate victims to give greater attention to legal variables (or in other words to formal rational considerations), and to prior organizational decisions. The former finding is again supportive of our second hypothesis above; the latter reliance on bail decisions at the later stages of adjudication and sentencing suggests a pattern in which decision-making is routinized and reaffirmed as the defendant moves through the criminal justice process. One possible further indication of this routinization is that the largest explained variance in tables 2.3 and 2.4 occurs at the sentencing stage in cases involving corporate victims ($R^2 = 0.47$). It may be here that the court is most certain of what it is doing. Finally, it is of significance to note that at the conviction stage, larger corporate entities are apparently more successful than smaller corporate entities in obtaining convictions (i.e., the beta for number of employees is 0.14). Insofar as size is a reflection of power and resources, this finding is consistent with our focus on the corporate advantage in the criminal justice process. More generally, the findings from this part of the analysis are also supportive of the link we have drawn between formal rationality and the involvement of corporate victims in the criminal justice process.

The final part of our analysis deals with the specific reactions of individual and corporate victims to the sentences imposed in their cases, and with their overall satisfaction with the outcomes in these cases. As earlier, there are clear differences in the responses of individual and corporate victims (see table 2.6). Among these, the most significant again involves the employment status of the accused. If the accused is a member of the unemployed surplus population, individual victims are more likely to think the sentence was too lenient ($B = -0.16$) and to be dissatisfied ($B = -0.15$) with the overall outcome of the case. The reader will recall the earlier finding that in cases with individual victims, unemployed accused were more likely to be held for a bail hearing, convicted and sentenced severely. In this analysis we have held disposition constant. *Thus, individual victims apparently want more severe sanctioning for accused members of the surplus population than they already receive.* No similar pattern exists when corporate victims are considered. Again,

TABLE 2.6 Correlation and regression coefficients for perceived sentence severity and satisfaction with outcome in cases with individual and organizational victims

	Perceived sentence severity, individual victims (N = 188)				Satisfaction with case outcome, individual victims (N = 188)				Perceived sentence severity, organizational victims (N = 200)				Satisfaction with case outcome, organizational victims (N = 200)			
	r	b	B	F	r	b	B	F	r	b	B	F	r	b	B	F
Seriousness of victimization	0.17	0.03	0.16	3.68[a]	0.17	0.14	0.24	9.19[c]								
Victim responsibility	−0.11	−0.15	−0.13	2.67[a]												
Characteristics attributed to accused	0.27	0.01	0.25	10.50[c]												
Complainant					−0.14	−0.72	−0.22	8.06[c]					−0.17	−0.79	−0.20	6.65[c]
General deterrence-victim ranking									−0.19	−0.09	−0.16	3.09[a]	−0.15	−0.19	−0.14	2.73[a]
Individual deterrence-victim ranking					−0.18	−0.12	−0.21	6.92[c]								
Law and order attitudes	−0.17	−0.03	−0.18	5.68[b]	0.02	0.05	0.15	3.70[a]								
Individual responsibility					−0.07	−0.50	−0.15	3.01[a]								
Victim testimony					−0.08	−0.48	−0.15	3.62[a]								
Accused employment status	−0.12	−0.16	−0.16	3.89[b]	−0.15	−0.26	−0.25	9.25[c]								
Disposition					0.00	0.61	0.19	3.68[a]	0.19	−0.07	−0.19	5.50[b]	−0.26	−0.25	−0.26	11.31[c]
Trial attendance																
Relationship between organization and clients													0.16	0.24	0.16	4.23[b]
	R^2 = 0.25				R^2 = 0.25				R^2 = 0.19				R^2 = 0.23			
	Intercept = 2.06				Intercept = 3.04				Intercept = 5.15				Intercept = 3.08			

then, the implication is that corporate victims encourage, or at least facilitate, formal equality in the treatment of accused. However, we again emphasize that this gain is offset by the greater collective likelihood of conviction in these cases.

There is further evidence that individual victims who support a 'law and order' orientation think sentences in their cases are too lenient and are dissatisfied with their case outcomes ($B = -0.18$ and -0.21). Also, those individual victims who attribute negative characteristics to the accused also find the sentences in their cases too lenient ($B = 0.25$).

The reactions of corporate victims to their case outcomes are more narrow or circumscribed in character. While individual victims do not vary in their reactions to court outcomes according to their concerns about deterrence, or for that matter in relation to any other goal of sentencing, corporate victims do. Among corporate victims, a concern with individual deterrence is associated with a perception that the sentence is too lenient ($B = -0.16$), and a concern with general deterrence is associated with a dissatisfaction with the overall case outcome ($B = -0.14$). The other consistent response of corporate victims is to the actual severity of the disposition in the case. As one might expect, the more lenient the disposition, the more likely the corporate victim is to regard the sentence as too lenient ($B = -0.19$) and to be dissatisfied with the overall outcome of the case ($B = -0.26$). These findings seem quite consistent with Coleman's observation that insofar as corporate actors come to replace individuals in influencing the allocation of organizational resources, these decisions '. . . are more and more removed from the multiplicity of dampening and modifying interests of which a real person is composed – more and more the result of a balance of narrow intense interests of which corporate actors are composed' (49). Corporate actors here seem narrowly focused on the deterrence of future crimes against them.

DISCUSSION AND CONCLUSIONS

To date, criminal justice research has not given much attention to the structural contexts in which criminal justice decisions are made. One source of this *a*structural attitude is undoubtedly the importance Anglo-American law attaches to individuals. Notions of individual rights permeate our system of criminal law and are reflected in the modern ideal of 'individualized justice'. However, one purpose of this chapter is to argue that there is a 'myth of individualism' that is stretched beyond plausibility, for example, by the legal conceptualization of corporate entities as 'juristic persons' who are accorded the same formal status as 'natural persons.' Criminal justice research has accepted uncritically the myth of individualism insofar as it has neglected to explore the consequences of the involvement of these 'juristic persons' as victims in criminal justice decision-making. Making the role of corporate entities explicit in this system is one way of adding a structural dimension to this area of work.

We hypothesized that the involvement of these new juristic persons in the criminal justice system has resulted in a corporate influence in the criminal justice process that is characterized by (i) the greater success of corporate than individual actors in getting individual offenders convicted, (ii) a greater likelihood of formal equality in the treatment of individuals prosecuted for crimes against corporate than individual victims, and (iii) a greater satisfaction of corporate than individual victims with their experiences in the criminal justice system. We noted that an increase in formal equality in the treatment of individuals prosecuted for crimes against corporate actors (hypothesis ii) is offset by the possibility that as a group, these individuals may still be more likely to be convicted for crimes against these corporate entities (hypothesis i). This combination of possibilities may also serve to increase the legitimacy as well as the efficiency with which criminal justice agencies serve corporate actors, and therefore anticipates the greater satisfaction corporate actors are hypothesized to take from the criminal justice experience (hypothesis iii). To put all this in Weberian terms, we are suggesting that there is an 'elective affinity' between corporate actors and agencies of criminal justice.

There is much in our data that supports the perspective just outlined. Our historical review of victim involvement in criminal justice decision-making revealed that it was not until the Enlightenment and the rise of modern capitalism that the role of the state-supported public prosecutor fully emerged, and consequently reduced the involvement of private victims in criminal justice operations. We noted that this 'new autonomy' of the state might better serve the interests of corporate than individual victims. Thus our review of contemporary victimization data from thirteen American cities revealed that as compared to individuals, commercial organizations experience and report crimes to the police in large and disproportionate numbers. While we have no data to indicate precisely when the increased involvement of corporate actors began, it is reasonable to assume that it has paralleled the tremendous growth of commercial retailing in this century. The purpose of the current study has been to examine how the involvement of corporate victims may influence contemporary criminal justice operations. We have explored this issue within a Canadian jurisdiction.

Overall, our data provide support for the perspective outlined above. For example, corporate actors actually outnumber individuals as victims in the jurisdiction studied.[6] Corporate actors are more likely than individuals to obtain convictions, and, the larger the organization, the greater is the likelihood of conviction. The greater success of corporate actors as compared to individuals in obtaining convictions is explained by their more impersonal relationships with accused, and by their selection of accused who give statements to the police and who convey a demeanour that acknowledges their guilt. The picture that emerges is of corporate entities that use their resources in an impersonal, formal rational, efficient fashion. One of these resources, the use of private security personnel, deserves further study. It is likely that size of organization acts as a proxy in our data for quantity and quality of private security arrangements. Access to private security may well be a crucial part of what we have called 'the corporate advantage'.

We also considered separately factors that lead to bail, conviction and sentencing decisions in cases involving corporate, as contrasted with individual, victims. Measured against legal standards of equality before the law, we found that the involvement of individual victims is associated with the operation of extra-legal factors in the decision-making process. For example, in cases with individual victims, accused members of the unemployed surplus population are more likely to be held for a bail hearing, convicted and sentenced severely. Furthermore, even when the severity of dispositions in these cases is held constant, individual victims of accused members of the surplus population still express a greater desire for severe sanctions and a dissatisfaction with overall case outcomes. The implication is that individual victims are a part (although not as large a part as they might wish) of the differential imposition of the sanctions noted above. A different pattern emerges when corporate victims are involved. More influential here are factors that derive from contact of the accused with criminal justice organizations (e.g., bail decisions, prior convictions and dispositions, and statements given to the police) and corporate concerns about individual and general deterrence. Measured against legal expectations, corporate victims again seem to be part of a more formal rational application of law.

We have argued that the form and content of criminal justice found in modern capitalist societies facilitates and legitimates the use of criminal law for the protection of corporate property against individuals. That is, we have argued that the modern criminal justice system better serves corporate than individual interests. One consequence of this situation is that criminal justice agencies originally thought to have emerged for the purposes of protecting individuals against individuals today are devoting a substantial share of their resources to the protection of large affluent corporate actors. It is important to note that this may not be the unique fate of modern institutions of criminal justice. For example, the Post Office has long complained of a related set of pressures generated by the growth of commercial enterprise; and it is interesting to note that in the same way commercial retailers have encouraged the development of private security services to do what the criminal courts will not, similar commercial interests have generated a private mail industry to do what the Post Office will not. Thus the patterns we have observed probably have parallels and consequences beyond those explored in this chapter. This is another way of saying that the corporate domination of our everyday lives is probably a more pervasive phenomenon than the subject matter of this chapter may have unintentionally implied.

APPENDIX

APPENDIX TABLE 2.1 Variables, values and descriptive statistics for analyses

Independent variables (individual and organizations)	Values	$\bar{x}$	s
Type of victim	Individual = 0	0.50	0.50
	Organization = 1		
Type of crime	Person = 0		
	Property = 1		
Seriousness of victimization	Sellin-Wolfgang Scale	3.36	2.47
Return of property to victim	Property not returned = 0	0.37	0.48
	Property returned = 1		
Victim responsibility	Denies responsibility = 0	1.26	0.44
	Accepts responsibility = 1		
Victim testimony	Victim did not testify = 0	0.23	0.43
	Victim testified		
Victim-accused relationship	Intimacy scale	6.45	4.25
Repeat player	No = 0		
	Yes = 1		
Accused marital status	Divorced, separated, common law = 0	1.05	0.65
	Single = 1		
	Married, widowed = 2		
Accused sex	Female = 0	0.88	0.33
	Male = 1		
Accused condition at arrest	Sober = 0	0.23	0.42
	Intoxicated = 1		
Accused employment status	Unemployed = 0	0.44	0.50
	Employed = 1		
Accused demeanour	Good = 0	0.67	0.47
	Bad or indifferent = 1		
Accused prior convictions	Actual number	2.98	4.80

APPENDIX TABLE 2.1 cont.

Accused most serious prior disposition	None = 0 Fine = 1 Probation = 2 Prison = 3	1.18	1.26
Number of charges	Actual number	0.56	1.61
Statement taken	No statement = 0 Statement taken = 1	0.39	0.49
Warrant	No warrant = 0 Warrant executed = 1	0.14	0.35
Mobilization	Other than by victim = 0 By victim = 1	0.56	0.50
Complaint	Other than victim = 0 Victim = 1	0.27	0.44
Perceived remorse of accused	Likert Scale (high to low)	2.90	0.75
Characteristics attributed to accused	Summated semantic differential (positive to negative)	42.53	7.93
Reformation-victim ranking	Likert Scale (high to low)	1.56	0.91
General deterrence-victim ranking	Likert Scale (high to low)	1.92	1.03
Individual deterrence-victim ranking	Likert Scale (high to low)	1.64	0.92
Punishment-victim ranking	Likert Scale (high to low)	2.58	1.24
Incapacitation-victim ranking	Likert Scale (high to low)	2.46	1.17
Law and order attitudes	Summated Likert Scale (high to low)	11.70	2.96
Citizen responsibility	Summated Likert Scale (high to low)	7.78	1.58
Belief in free will	Likert Scale (high to low)	7.28	2.63
Individual responsibility	Likert Scale (high to low)	5.58	3.83
Knowledge of disposition	No = 0 Yes = 1	0.39	0.49
Disposition	Withdrawn, dismissed or acquitted = 0 Absolute discharge = 1 Peace bond or fine = 2 Probation = 3 Prison = 4	2.39	1.46
Trial	Victim did not attend = 0 Victim attended = 1	0.39	0.49
Independent variables (Organizations only)			
Type of organization	Retail = 0 Other = 1	0.42	0.49

APPENDIX TABLE 2.1 cont.

Independent variables (individual and organizations)	Values	$\bar{x}$	s
Organizational base	Private = 1 Public = 0	1.38	0.49
Scale of organization	Local = 1 Regional = 2 Provincial = 3 Interprovincial = 4 National = 5 Multinational = 6	3.20	2.04
Number of employees in division	Actual number	99.76	342.85
Number of organizational units	Actual number	44.18	126.41
Number of employees in organization	Actual number	352,359.91	449,393.03
Centralization of organization	Likert Scale (decentralized to centralized)	3.52	1.09
Relationship between organization and clients	Likert Scale (depersonalized to personalized)	3.90	0.87
Dependent variables (Individuals and organizations)			
Bail hearing	Not held for hearing = 0 Held for hearing = 1	0.21	0.40
Adjudication	Not guilty = 0 Guilty = 1	0.72	0.45
Sentence	Absolute discharge = 1 Peace bond or fine = 2 Probation = 3 Prison = 4	2.96	0.83
Perceived severity of disposition	Too severe = 1 About right = 2 Not severe enough = 3	2.45	0.52
Satisfaction with outcome	Very satisfied = 1 Satisfied = 2 Neutral = 3 Dissatisfied = 4 Very dissatisfied = 5	2.69	1.52

APPENDIX TABLE 2.2 Victimization data on burglary in thirteen American cities

	Boston	Buffalo	Cincinnati	Houston	Miami	Milwaukee	Minneapolis	New Orleans	Oakland	Pittsburgh	San Diego	San Francisco	Washington	13 cities
Burglary incidents per 1000 population	149	97	143	164	85	152	177	112	174	93	138	115	75	128.7
% reported to police	56%	50%	55%	46%	58%	54%	52%	47%	57%	50%	50%	51%	57%	51.6%
Incidents reported to police weighted to population	17,360 (56.7%)	7,200 (60.4%)	12,375 (48.9%)	32,016 (70.4%)	6,090 (50.4%)	19,926 (76.9%)	14,768 (74.3%)	10,199 (62.8%)	13,224 (56.2%)	8,100 (66.5%)	17,650 (74.4%)	16,932 (64.6%)	11,229 (62.3%)	187,069 (64.2%)
Burglary incidents per 1000 establishments	576	3.9	566	518	292	321	436	448	637	293	358	253	330	411.3
% reported to police	78%	75%	84%	71%	79%	82%	71%	68%	77%	73%	80%	72%	79%	76.1%
Incidents reported to police weighted to population	13,260 (43.3%)	4,725 (39.6%)	13,490 (29.6%)	6,004 (49.6%)	5,986 (23.1%)	5,986 (25.7%)	5,112 (25.7%)	6,052 (37.2%)	10,318 (43.8%)	4,088 (33.5%)	6,080 (25.6%)	9,288 (35.4%)	6,794 (37.7%)	104,133 (35.8%)
Per capita ratio of commercial to household burglaries	3.9	3.3	4.0	3.2	3.4	2.1	2.5	4.0	3.7	3.2	2.6	2.2	4.4	3.2
Total no. of incidents reported to police weighted to population	30,620	11,925	25,311	45,506	12,094	25,912	19,880	16,251	23,542	12,188	23,730	26,220	18,023	291,202

APPENDIX TABLE 2.2 cont.

	Boston	Buffalo	Cincinnati	Houston	Miami	Milwaukee	Minneapolis	New Orleans	Oakland	Pittsburgh	San Diego	San Francisco	Washington	13 cities
Robbery incidents per 1000 population	31	16	15	17	10	18	21	18	22	15	11	29	17	18.5
% reported to police	53%	51%	51%	47%	65%	51%	49%	53%	53%	56%	46%	44%	63%	57%
Incidents reported to police weighted to population	5,089 (64.9%)	2,295 (73.0%)	2,091 (54.6%)	6,157 (60.8%)	1,430 (43.4%)	4,182 (80.0%)	2,793 (67.9%)	3,392 (54.6%)	2,650 (52.4%)	2,744 (65.3%)	2,438 (74.0%)	6,160 (66.1%)	4,914 (70.4%)	47,235 (63.8%)
Robbery incidents per 1000 establishments	132	56	72	140	104	49	91	173	137	77	49	80	88	96.0
% reported to police	83%	77%	87%	78%	69%	95%	88%	83%	83%	97%	85%	77%	90%	82%
Incidents reported to police weighted to population	3,237 (35.1%)	847 (27.0%)	1,740 (45.4%)	3,978 (39.2%)	1,863 (56.6%)	1,045 (20.0%)	1,320 (32.1%)	2,822 (45.4%)	2,407 (47.6%)	1,455 (34.7%)	855 (26.0%)	3,157 (33.9%)	2,070 (29.6%)	26,796 (36.2%)
Per capita ratio of commercial to personal robberies	4.3	3.5	4.8	8.2	10.4	2.7	4.3	9.6	6.2	5.1	4.5	2.8	5.2	5.2
Total no. of incidents reported to police weighted to population	9,226	3,142	3,831	10,135	3,293	5,227	4,113	6,214	5,057	4,199	3,293	9,317	6,984	74,031

NOTES

1 An examination of the population and sample data revealed no systematic evidence of error or bias in the latter. The panel design forms the basis for an analysis reported in Hagan (1983, chaps. 3–4). Only the follow-up interviews are used here.

2 Our measure of the intimacy of the victim-accused relationship is based on ordinally ranked responses to five interview questions: How well did you know the offender? How frequently did you talk to the offender? Did you know the offender's name? Would you say that you generally liked the offender before this incident? Did you feel that the offender generally liked you before this incident? Responses to these items were combined into an additive measure of intimacy.

3 Our decision to use the 0.10 level is based on the exploratory character of the research.

4 Introduction of additional variables reduced the statistical significance of this relationship below the 0.10 level used elsewhere in this chapter, however, the mediating influences of subsequent variables were not sufficiently large to justify substantive discussion.

5 Our measure of the intimacy of the victim's involvement with the accused is the scale discussed in note 2, dichotomized at the mean.

6 How this suburban Canadian jurisdiction compares to other jurisdictions is, of course, an issue that calls for further research.

3

The Addictive Sanction

INTRODUCTION

This chapter attempts to make theoretical sense of an anomaly in the research literature on criminal sentencing. The anomaly is that while a popular theory of criminal sentencing, conflict theory, traditionally has predicted that non-white offenders would receive more severe sentences than white offenders (Quinney, 1970; Chambliss and Seidman, 1971), there are a surprising number of studies that show the reverse to be the case (Kleck, 1981). This anomaly is made more noteworthy by a national survey (see IUCPSR, 1979) which shows that white as well as black Americans, but blacks even more than whites (see chapter 5), share the traditional conflict viewpoint. Can so popular a theory be wrong? Below we argue that the anomaly we have identified is based on a simplistic conception of the role of race in criminal sanctioning. When conflict theory is informed by a conception of race and other variables that is more sensitive to their structural, that is relational and contextual meanings, the anomaly disappears. Data from a fourteen-year period on the sentencing of drug offenders in the Southern Federal District of New York is analysed in assessing this argument.

THE ANOMALY OF PRIOR RESEARCH

In this chapter we draw a distinction between an individual-processual and a structural-contextual approach to sentencing research. The first of these approaches emphasizes the premise that sentencing is the end result of a decision-making process involving many stages. Farrell and Swigert (1978b: 442) make the premise of this approach explicit when they note that 'The discrete ordering of events – the social characteristics of the defendants prior to their entry into the system, their accumulated criminal histories, the type of legal representation, pretrial release, the mode of adjudication, and final disposition – constitutes a series of stages that allows the researcher to assert the causal sequence of relationships.' This process is often likened to the operation of a leaky sieve, in that additional offenders are deselected fom further consideration at succeeding stages of the system. Using increasingly sophisticated structural equation models and log linear techniques, much of the best work of the 1970s involved the clarification and elaboration of individual-processual models of this selection process that leads to sentencing (e.g., Burke and Turk, 1975; Bernstein et al., 1977a). We contribute further to this tradition by statistically addressing a problem of parameter estimation that this kind of selection process can produce.

However, sentencing is not only a matter of individuals being processed through a criminal justice system. Both the individuals and the system occupy variable positions or locations within a social structure. Thus individual processing decisions can vary by social context. Recent studies incorporate this premise of a structural-contextual approach. For example, using data sets from several jurisdictions, Balbus (1973), Eisenstein and Jacob (1977), Levin (1977), Hagan et al. (1980) and Myers and Talarico (1987) have linked variations in political environments to sentencing behaviour. Within single jurisdictions, Lizotte (1978) has linked individuals' class as well as racial positions in the social structure to sentencing outcomes, and in the previous chapter we examined the consequences of corporate entities as compared to individuals acting as victim-complainants in the criminal justice process. Each of these studies adds some feature of structural and contextual variation to the consideration of the individual processing that leads to sentencing decisions.

Our point is not that individual-processual and structural-contextual approaches are mutually exclusive. Indeed, each of these approaches is increasingly persuasive as it includes consideration of the other. A preliminary way of making this point is to demonstrate how the findings, anomalous and otherwise, of prior individual-processual studies can be combined and better understood through an analysis of their varied structural and contextual characteristics. To do this, we consider studies[1] that include information on the zero-order relationship between race and sentencing.[2] Twenty-six of these studies[3] present data in a categorical form that allows us to re-calculate gammas for the race-sentence relationship.[4] Our interest is in determining whether variation in these relationships can be explained in terms of the structural contexts in which the original studies were done.

For example, we begin by regressing the above race-sentence gammas on the years covered by the studies.[5] Our expectation is that the legal structure of race relations has improved over the last half-century, however slowly and imperfectly, so that the changing temporal context of these studies should reveal a gradual decline in race-sentence relationships. Consistent with this expectation, the result of our regression analysis is an equation $y = -0.0065 \times + 12.9$, where the annual decline in the estimated effect of race on sentence is 0.0065. While the latter change may initially seem small, over the forty-one year period of the studies considered, the cumulative decline in the effect of race is estimated to be 0.262, with a predicted gamma for the first year in our data set (1932) of -0.342, and for the last year (1973) of -0.075. The standardized coefficient for year in this equation is -0.383 ($p < 0.05$, $t = 1.91$). Adding region and type of crime considered to the equation reduces the standardized coefficient for year only slightly, to -0.377. Thus the influence of time on the race-sentence relationship is prominently and persistently negative.

The above analysis may be indicative of a simple trend toward equality in criminal sentencing. However, while we think this is partly true, we also think that the situation is more complicated than this conclusion suggests. One sign of this complication is the anomaly described by Kleck (1981: 799):

For a variety of specific crimes, jurisdictions, and judges, various researchers have produced data indicating more lenient treatment of black defendants than whites, although the admittedly scattered findings were usually deemphasized or discounted as merely anomalous results . . . For example, Bullock (1961) found significantly shorter prison sentences were assigned to blacks convicted of murder; Levin's (1972) Pittsburg data indicate that blacks received more lenient dispositions than whites for eight of nine offense categories; and Bernstein and her colleagues (1977) found that blacks received significantly less severe sentences than whites. Gibson (1978: 469) studied sentences given by individual judges and found that seven of eleven judges gave a higher percentage of severe sentences to whites than to blacks.

Another sign that the pattern is more complicated (than a simple trend toward equality) emerges from consideration of several 'outlying' gammas in the above regression analysis.[6] The largest of these outliers is a gamma of 0.86 from a study of rape cases by Wolfgang and Reidel (1973). This coefficient reflects in part the fact that gammas can be inflated in tables that have one cell with a low frequency; but it also reflects the fact that there is a very strong relationship between race and sentence in this study. The second outlier noted above is a gamma of -0.22 from a study of homicide cases by Garfinkel (1949). Inspection of the data from both of these studies indicates that during an earlier part of this century in the south, black offenders with white victims were likely to receive particularly severe sanctions. We should not be surprised: inter-racial crimes represent conflict across assumed structural positions in a racially stratified society (LaFree, 1980). However, closer inspection of these data also illustrates another important point: that homicide is less likely than rape to be an *inter*-racial crime. Because *intra*-racial offences between blacks often result in *lenient* sanctioning, studies focusing on homicide are much less likely than those focusing on rape to pick up racial disparities when only a zero-order relationship between the race of the *offender* and sentence is considered. Thus the Garfinkel study manifests two countervailing trends that form the basis of a suppression effect: the lenient sanctioning of black intra-racial offences, and the severe sanctioning of crimes committed by blacks against whites (see also Bowers and Pearce, 1980). In number of cases, the former outweigh the latter in the Garfinkel study, resulting in the negative coefficient.

To what extent could the above kind of suppression effect confuse current and past findings on race and sentencing? We will argue that these kinds of patterns can complicate our understanding of sentencing even in the case of crimes involving no identifiable victim (the majority of offences). For example, while black drug offenders traditionally have been seen as 'villains' in America's problems with drugs, today there may also be contexts in which black offenders are seen as the 'victims' of America's drug problems. Our point is that race can have a symbolic meaning that can alter the relational position of minority offenders in some structural contexts. A modern tendency to see some black offenders as victims may partially explain the diminishing relationship between race and sentencing observed above, and the anomaly of black offenders sometimes receiving more lenient sentences than whites. We turn now to a more detailed consideration of this possibility in the context of drug law enforcement.

VICTIMS AND VILLAINS IN THE POLITICS OF DRUGS

Through most of this century the issue of race has been manifest in the American moral crusade against drugs (Musto, 1973; Reasons, 1974; Gusfield, 1975). Musto (1973: 5) observes that as early as '. . . the nineteenth century addicts were identified with foreign groups and internal minorities who were already actively feared and the objects of elaborate and massive social and legal constraints'. For example, the Chinese were associated with opium (Cook, 1969; 1970; Musto, 1973; Reasons, 1974), southern blacks with cocaine (Musto, 1973), and Mexicans with marihuana (Musto, 1973; Bonnie and Whitebread, 1974). It made little difference that contrary to emerging stereotypes, '. . . evidence clearly indicates that the upper and middle classes predominated among narcotic addicts in the period up to 1914' (Duster, 1970: 9). Only after passage of the Harrison Narcotic Act in 1914 did this situation change, so that 'by 1920 medical journals could speak of the "overwhelming majority (of drug addicts)" from the "unrespectable parts" of society' (11). By persuading the public to associate narcotics use with disenfranchised minorities, and by establishing minority users as the symbolic villains in this unfolding crime drama, lobbyists were able to lay a foundation for the first American legislative prohibition of narcotics.

However, the symbolic implications of deviant behaviour are not static. As Gusfield (1967: 187) notes, '. . . deviance designations have histories . . . What is attacked as criminal today may be seen as sick next year and fought over as possibly legitimate by the next generation.' Our interest is in demonstrating how such changes may have influenced the sanctioning of drug offenders. To do this, it is necessary to focus on a time and setting that allows detailed analysis. We have chosen the period of the 1960s and 1970s because it includes the most recent and concerted national effort to mobilize criminal justice resources against drug crimes; a period whose culmination was the Nixon administration's 1970 reform of the federal drug laws. We have selected the Southern Federal District of New York because it is widely recognized as the 'premier' prosecution office in the USA (e.g., Katz, 1980), among other reasons for its pursuit of major drug cases (Moore, 1977). Located in the southern tip of Manhattan, this district is in the heart of what frequently is called the 'Drug Capital of the World'. By any measure, New York City is a major port of entry and centre of distribution for illicit drugs, with a large and diverse offender population.

An analysis of public opinion, media materials, and legislative activities summarized below suggests a sub-division of the time period we will consider into three parts (1963 to 1968, 1969 to 1973, 1974 to 1976), the most significant of which is the middle interval. During this middle period public concern about drugs seemed to peak. This point can be made first through a consideration of Gallup Poll data providing national opinion rankings of 'the most important problem the country faces today'. Drugs were not among ranked social problems in these data prior to 1970, and were not consistently ranked after 1973. However, from February 1971 to August 1973, through six Gallup pollings, drugs were never less than fifth in the national rankings, and usually second or third in ranked importance behind the Vietnam War and economic issues (see Gallup, 1972; 1978a; 1978b; 1979).

Change in the treatment of an issue in the mass media is another index of shifts in public concern (Davis, 1952; Berk et al., 1980; Stinchcombe et al., 1980; Humphries, 1981). Quantitative changes in media attention to the drug problem were noted by counting (see Peterson, 1983) from 1960 through 1978: (1) articles about drug use and abuse in American periodicals referenced in the *Reader's Guide to Periodical Literature*; (2) references to drug-related news items in the *New York Times Index*; and (3) drug-related editorials and lines therein appearing in the *New York Times*.[7] We gave particular attention to the *New York Times* because it is the only daily paper with wide circulation both in New York City and around the country, the latter giving it the status of a national daily newspaper (Lidz and Walker, 1980).

Although there is some variation by source, overall there was a rather dramatic increase in the coverage of drug problems that began in the late 1960s and declined dramatically by the mid-1970s. Thus the data from the above sources all lead to the same general conclusion: for the period under examination, drug use, abuse and trafficking were issues of much greater concern in the late 1960s and early 1970s than during either the early and mid-1960s or the mid- to late 1970s.

The qualitative changes that accompanied these quantitative shifts are of even greater interest and importance. We will examine these qualitative changes by first reviewing the content of drug-related editorials appearing in the *New York Times* between 1960 and 1978. We focus on editorials, first, because unlike routine news stories and feature articles which basically describe facts and features of events or trends, editorials (along with letters to the editor and columns) take specific positions and express opinions of approval or disapproval. Second, editorials may be directed at criminal justice officials, including judges, therefore influencing sanctioning decisions directly. Third, we are impressed by the findings of Berk et al. (1977) in their study of changes in the California Penal Code that: (1) there is a direct causal link between editorials and changes in legislation; (2) editorials are far more important in influencing legislation that crime-related news articles or letters to the editor; and (3) editorials determine the types of letters to the editor and articles to appear in newspapers.

The most important qualitative change in the eighteen years from 1960 to 1978 was the distinction increasingly made between dealers and users of drugs. This distinction became particularly salient during the Nixon administration, as the former group became the symbolic villains, and the latter group the symbolic victims, in the changing imagery of America's drug problems. The significance of this distinction lies in its origins and consequences. As we have seen, in the earlier part of this century it was sufficient to condemn drug offenders, who were presumed to be mostly of minority status, in an undifferentiated fashion. However, in the 1960s the composition of the drug abusing population changed. Whether this change was linked to the growing popularity of the anti-war movement, or to a more general 'morals revolution' (Gusfield, 1975), its consequence was clear: '. . . for the first time in the twentieth century, the objects of the drug control laws were persons from the dominant middle class whose value system served as the basis for the development and enforcement of the criminal code' (Susman, 1975: 23–4).

The symbolic politics of such a situation were problematic. The legitimacy of the criminal justice system was threatened almost as much by the general public's view that it was inappropriate to subject their children to criminal punishment as it had been by youthful drug and protest behaviour itself (Glaser, 1974; Susman, 1975; Rosenthal, 1977; Galliher and Basilick, 1979). The answer seemed to lie in what Gusfield refers to as 'altered deviance designations' (i.e., in a redefinition of what constituted the 'real' drug problem). Pushers, especially high level dealers, became the designated villains in this new portrayal of the problem. Conceived as part of organized drug networks with ties to the underworld, professional traffickers were designated as the real source of the drug problem. They were assigned responsibility for the street crimes of addicts forced to steal to pay the high price of drugs, and for the acts of violence committed by addicts under the influence of drugs so acquired. Their sins also included preying upon innocent victims, especially middle-class youth. 'For material gain, he corrupted the young and introduced them to the joys and horrors of addiction. Thus the concept of the innocence of youth could be preserved and the source of corruption focused on the pusher.' (Lidz and Walker, 1980: 80).

These new deviance designations were reflected during 1969–73 in editorial coverage of drug-related events in the *New York Times*, as well as in the penalty provisions and intent of the Nixon administration's Comprehensive Drug Abuse Prevention and Control Act of 1970. Beginning with the former, *Times* editors repeatedly called for a scaling down of penalties for 'soft' drugs, users and youthful offenders. Indeed, judges who imposed overly harsh penalties on these types of offenders were criticized openly (*New York Times*, 15 July 1969: 38; 22 October 1969: 46; 8 December 1969: 46; 24 January 1970: 30; 30 August 1970: IV, 12; 26 September 1970: 28; 25 January 1971: 42; 22 January 1972: 28; 20 February 1972: IV, 12; 2 August 1972: 36; 15 January 1973: 28; 9 February 1973: 34; 17 April 1973: 40). In sharp contrast to these liberal views, *Times* editors supported 'throwing the book' at veteran pushers and dealers in hard drugs. As one editorial saw it, 'The penalties for those who prey on the innocent by peddling drugs can hardly be too severe' (*New York Times*, 15 July 1969: 38; see also *New York Times*, 9 January 1973: 38; 10 January 1973: 40; 7 March 1973: 42; 30 April 1973: 30).

We turn finally to the relevant legislation. On 27 October 1970 President Nixon signed into the law the Comprehensive Drug Abuse Prevention and Control Act. The most outstanding feature of this Act was that it reversed the trend of more than half a century: it lowered penalties for violations of traditional drug laws and removed mandatory penalties for most offences, all at a time when public and political concern about drug use and its consequences (e.g., street crime, violence, drug-related deaths) was increasing dramatically. However, this apparent paradox can be explained in terms that reinforce the above discussion of altered deviance designations.

In enacting the 1970 penalty provisions, Congress also focused on two target populations: young middle- and upper-class drug users, the symbolic victims; and hardcore traffickers and professional drug criminals, the symbolic villains. The penalties that emerged from Congressional debate reflected compromises reached to deal with these two target populations. Reduction of first offence possession and of distribution of small amounts of marihuana for no remuneration to misdemeanours, removal of mandatory minimum penalties, and a provision for special first offender treatment, all served to minimize the possibility of subjecting middle- and upper-class youth to criminal penalties, and their presumed negative consequences. On the other hand, the retention of a possession offence for the purpose of bargaining with informants, relatively minor reductions in maximum penalties for trafficking offences, provisions of mandatory special parole terms, and the provision of extreme sanctions for two new offence categories (Continuing Criminal Enterprise and Dangerous Special Drug Offender) of questionable constitutionality, and supplementary criminal enforcement provisions, provided the coercive policies required for handling (and warning) the second targeted population: major drug traffickers.

In sum, the penalty provisions of the 1970 Act were a set of compromises which permitted Congress to: (1) maintain a coercive approach to the drug problem, for the purpose of dealing with the 'evil' activities of those deviants designated as responsible for the drug problem, namely the symbolic villains, the big drug dealers; (2) protect 'misguided' but otherwise innocent middle- and upper-class youth, the symbolic victims, from stigmatization as criminal felons; (3) provide a symbolic gesture (an offer of appeasement) to disaffected youth believed to be alienated from the criminal justice system, and society in general; and (4) express Congressional and societal condemnation of indiscriminate and non-medical use of controlled substances. The question remains whether this explanation of the paradox of declining penalties in a time of increasing public concern can also account for the lenient treatment of minority offenders. We believe it can.

We suggest that the same symbolic distinction drawn between users as victims, and dealers as villains, can be used to explain the more lenient treatment of minorities. A factual premise that underwrites this suggestion is that the opportunity structure of the drug trade, like more conventional opportunity structures in America, is racially stratified. That is, more minority drug offenders are users than dealers, and very few minority offenders are *big* dealers (Ianni, 1974). Of course, there is no logical necessity that the benefit of leniency would extend to minority as well as majority users. However, coming as it did on the heels of the civil rights era, our expectation is that this otherwise anomalous form of equity held sway in the formation of the new drug strategy. Indeed, we believe that it was this coalition of conservative purpose (i.e., a moral crusade against the symbolic villains of the drug trade) and liberal impulse (i.e., the recognition and treatment of youthful, better educated, and minority offenders as symbolic victims of the world of drugs) that best accounts for the emergence of a new drug strategy. As indicated above, our expectation is that this strategy became most pronounced in the structural context represented by the years 1969 to 1973: it is during these years that we expect well-educated youth, minority offenders and users of drugs to have received the most lenient treatment. During these same years, big drug dealers are expected to have experienced particularly severe treatment.

One final point should be made. The lenience we expect for minority drug offenders is premised on their designation as victims. However, in those infrequent instances where minority offenders are identified as big dealers, the symbolic protection we have postulated obviously is absent. If the perspective we have offered is correct, then we should not expect in these instances to encounter the anomaly of lenient treatment for minority offenders.

A NOTE ON THE SOCIAL STRUCTURE OF DRUG LAW
ENFORCEMENT

The social organization of drug law enforcement is complicated by the fact that drug crimes typically occur in private, among consenting and collaborating persons who have no interest in notifying authorities about their activities or providing incriminating information and evidence (Skolnick, 1966; Zinberg and Robertson, 1972; Blumberg, 1973; Glaser, 1974). The resulting problem is that there usually are no complainants or victims to generate cases reactively. Such cases must therefore be pursued *pro*-actively (Reiss, 1971). We have described above a period between 1969 and 1973 when public pressure for prosecution of the villains of the drug trade, big dealers, was particularly acute. The Nixon administration was eager to respond to this pressure by using the prosecutorial resources of the federal courts. However, for reasons we have noted and others that are obvious, 'Going after higher levels of the narcotic business pyramid, to say nothing of the apexes, is a long, hazardous, and at best uncertain affair' (Chein et al., 1964: 331).

Prior research in a variety of settings (Cloyd, 1979; Hagan et al., 1980) indicates that the development of co-operative witnesses through plea bargaining is the major means of successfully building such cases proactively. In exchange for lenient penalties, key informants and witnesses are encouraged to provide the evidence necessary for the successful prosecution of others. As Hagan et al. (1980: 805) note with regard to the proactive prosecution of white-collar cases, the problem comes down to '. . . how to get the leverage required to "turn witnesses" and the key to obtaining this leverage is to forge a connection between plea negotiations and concessions and coercion in sentencing.' As we will discuss further in chapter 4, this connection involves a tightened coupling of the prosecutorial and judicial subsystems of court operations.

If the above description of drug law prosecution is correct, we should expect two results. First, that the relationship between plea and sentence severity is strongest from 1969 to 1973, the period of the most proactive prosecutorial policy. Second, that the effect of plea on sentence severity is stronger among big dealers than users, where the most important information and prosecutions are to be obtained.

One final point should be made here. In addition to the instrumental sources of concessions in plea bargaining we have noted, there may be symbolic considerations at work as well. The drug offender who pleads guilty communicates a far different symbolic message than the offender who protests his/her innocence. It is the difference, for example, between remorse and defiance. Gusfield (1981: 185) goes even further in according a symbolic significance to this kind of confession, suggesting that, 'It is in the honor that Vice pays to Virtue by masking itself that Virtue mounts its pedestal.' It is for these reasons, as well as for those noted above, that we expect varied and pronounced plea effects in the data analysed below.

THE MEASUREMENT OF STRUCTURAL CHANGE AND A CORRECTION OF SELECTION BIAS

Imprisonment has been an addictive response to federal drug crimes. It remains a persistent, if not the preferred, punishment. However, this does not mean that the allocation of this sanction among individuals has remained constant. Indeed, our argument is that this allocation has changed in response to the changing symbolic politics of American drug law enforcement. To demonstrate this kind of social change, it is necessary to have information on joint variations in dependent and independent variables within varied structural contexts. Duncan (1975) notes that analyses of the latter kind allow identification of social change of a 'structural' form, that is, social change, '. . . in a deeper sense of the term'. Laslett (1980: 217–18) goes on to observe that, 'According to this perspective, social change "in a deeper sense of the term" involves change in social relationships – in social organization as a whole – and not simply changes in the distribution of the individual components within the whole.' The data considered in this study allow the above kind of analysis: they include crucial information on all 4,371 drug offenders sentenced from 1963 to 1976 in the Southern Federal District of New York City.[8] The analysis proceeds within three structural contexts derived from the above discussion: 1963 to 1968, 1969 to 1973, and 1974 to 1976.

Sentencing can be thought of as a two stage process (Wheeler et al., 1982), involving first a decision as to whether to imprison, and second, if imprisonment is selected, a decision about the length of sentence. However, as we noted in the context of conviction and sentencing in chapter 1, there are problems associated with simply treating such decisions as separate occurrences. In this context, there are at least three problems: (1) the two phases of the sentencing process are left disconnected, while in practice they are not; (2) the separate results make it difficult to reach summary judgements about the overall influence of explanatory variables; and (3) the parameter estimates for the separate analysis of length of imprisonment will be biased. The last point requires elaboration (see also Heckman, 1974; 1975; Fligstein and Wolf, 1978; Berk, 1983).

As we have noted, the decision about length of imprisonment follows from the decision to imprison at all. This initial decision results in a selected pool of offenders who have exceeded a threshold on the criteria that determine use of this sanction. When such selection occurs, length of imprisonment will be a function not only of the linear combination of regressors ordinarily considered, but also of what Heckman (1975) terms the 'hazard rate', or risk of not being selected into the imprisoned population, i.e., the risk of exceeding or not exceeding the threshold. Estimation procedures, such as ordinary regression, which fail to take into account the 'hazard rate' will yield biased and inconsistent estimates of the structural coefficients (see Berk, 1983).

As we noted in chapter 1, what is required is a procedure that provides information about the two decisions, in this case type and length of sentence, but that also allows us to combine this information in a meaningful way. Heckman (1974; 1975) outlines such a procedure that for our purposes involves two equations like those considered in chapter 1: the first is a probit equation that estimates whether a drug offender receives an institutional sentence, and the second an OLS equation for sentence length that is corrected for selection bias.

THE ANALYSIS

We now apply Heckman's estimation procedures in analysing the impact of twenty-two explanatory variables on sentences received by federal drug offenders for the three periods previously identified: 1963–8, 1969–73 and 1974–6. Again, our aim is to draw general conclusions about the relationship between changes in the social environment surrounding the sanctioning process and the sentences received by convicted federal drug offenders. The twenty-two explanatory variables included in our analysis are identified in table 3.1, and descriptive statistics are provided for each. Although the coding of most of these variables is straightforward, several require comment.

The last of the offender characteristics, status, is a composite measure coded (1) if the defendant is 22 years old or less, high school educated and white, and (0) otherwise. Since age, education and race are all included separately in the analysis as well, significant status effects represent interactions that persist beyond the main effects of the component measures. The legally relevant offender characteristics include distinctions between prosecution under pre- and post-1970 statutes, as well as indicators of whether the offender is a user and/or big dealer. Users were identified as such in the court records. We identified big dealers when they were designated as 'prime movers' in marginal notes in court records, or when their drug-related criminal activities involved 100 pounds or more of a narcotic substance.[9] Characteristics of judges include whether they were appointed to the bench during the Nixon administration and a measure of the average severity of the sentences given by individual judges in non-drug cases over the period of the study. Our expectation is that Nixon appointees will be more punitive than non-Nixon appointees, especially between 1969 and 1973. The legal process variables include measures of whether the offender pleaded guilty or went on trial, and of whether a pre-sentence report was prepared.

For comparative purposes, before presenting our corrected regression analysis, we consider uncorrected results of the length of imprisonment equation within the three separate time periods. These data are presented in table 3.2. Although these results are not corrected for selection, and therefore we have not calculated significance tests for differences between periods, they nonetheless provide some preliminary support for the theoretical perspective we have proposed. For example, beginning with our most direct measure of villain status, big dealers receive substantially more severe treatment than other drug offenders in all time periods, with their most severe treatment coming between 1969 and 1973. Alternatively, non-

TABLE 3.1 Variables, means and standard deviations for the total population of drug offenders and for the population of imprisoned offenders

Variables	Value	Total population (N = 437)		Imprisoned population (N = 3056)	
		Mean	Standard deviation	Mean	Standard deviation
A Offender's status characteristics					
1 Male sex: Yes 1		0.908	0.289	0.940	0.238
No 0					
2 Age	In years	33.370	9.371	35.148	8.829
3 Race: Non-white 1		0.350	0.477	0.365	0.482
White 0					
4 Education: < High school graduate 1		0.637	0.481	0.701	0.458
≥ high school graduate 0					
5 Marital status: Unattached 1		0.511	0.500	0.464	0.499
Attached 0					
6 Status: Middle status youth 1		0.038	0.191	0.009	0.092
Non-middle status youth 0					
B Legally relevant offender and case characteristics					
7 Prior convictions	Total number	3.781	5.101	4.346	5.230
8 Pre-1970 trafficking: Yes 1		0.298	0.457	0.379	0.485
No 0					
9 Post-1970 trafficking: Yes 1		0.321	0.467	0.321	0.467
No 0					

10	Pre-1970 importing:	Yes	1	0.017	0.127	0.020	0.140
		No	0	0.005	0.069	0.004	0.063
11	Post-1970 importing:	Yes	1				
		No	0				
12	Conspiracy:	Yes	1	0.198	0.399	0.192	0.394
		No	0				
13	Illegal communication:	Yes	1	0.012	0.108	0.011	0.103
		No	0				
14	Charge seriousness		Months maximum possible prison	177.079	53.730	189.456	47.006
15	Gun used:	Yes	1	0.063	0.242	0.074	0.262
		No	0				
16	Narcotic drug:	Yes	1	0.432	0.495	0.436	0.496
		No	0				
17	Drug user:	Yes	1	0.300	0.458	0.292	0.455
		No	0				
18	Big dealer:	Yes	1	0.014	0.116	0.018	0.135
		No	0				

C *Characteristics of the judge*

19	Nixon judge:	Yes	1	0.215	0.411	0.209	0.407
		No	0				
20	Judge severity		Average sentence in non-drug cases	45.543	8.109	45.996	8.126

D Legal process variables

21	Plea:	Not guilty	1	0.355	0.478	0.447	0.497
		Guilty	0				
22	Pre-sentence report:	Yes	1	0.800	0.400	0.761	0.427
		No	0				

TABLE 3.2 *Uncorrected regression of length of imprisonment (in months) on independent variables for different social contexts*

Variable	Period I 1963–1968			Period II 1969–1973			Period III 1974–1976		
	b	β	Standard error	b	β	Standard error	b	β	Standard error
Male sex	6.210	0.033	5.580	11.045	0.042	7.334	9.662	0.028	9.554
Age	1.267[c]	0.235	0.171	0.798[b]	0.103	0.231	0.972[b]	0.123	0.245
Race (non-white)	− 5.769[a]	− 0.064	2.915	− 16.528[b]	− 0.119	4.175	− 10.405[a]	− 0.063	4.722
Marital status (unattached)	0.411	0.005	2.905	− 16.446[c]	− 0.122	3.905	− 10.441[a]	− 0.069	4.285
Education	− 6.216	− 0.048	3.994	4.842	0.035	4.026	7.875	0.051	4.584
Status	− 12.634	− 0.020	19.204	− 11.418	− 0.018	17.477	5.893	0.007	22.327
Prior record	0.045	− 0.005	0.300	1.762[c]	0.133	0.390	2.033[c]	0.148	0.432
Pre-1970 trafficking	10,808[a]	0.097	5.389	45.152[c]	0.308	11.426	49.255	0.169	31.996
Post-1970 trafficking	—	—	—	16.874	0.125	10.275	21.014	0.139	25.239
Pre-1970 importing	− 0.592	− 0.003	8.128	35.713	0.037	28.815	—	—	—
Post-1970 importing	—	—	—	18.439	0.017	30.823	67.178[a]	0.079	34.015

	Model 1			Model 2			Model 3		
Conspiracy	—	—	—	17.068	0.100	10.722	23.457	0.151	25.276
Illegal communication	—	—	—	16.803	0.036	15.317	-29.656	-0.041	25.446
Charge seriousness	0.107[b]	0.136	0.033	-0.051	-0.036	0.060	-0.239	-0.088	0.157
Gun use	—	—	—	-0.870	-0.003	8.197	5.116	0.025	6.048
Narcotic drug	—	—	—	7.038	0.052	5.051	18.955[a]	0.085	7.089
Drug user	-3.321	-0.035	3.162	-9.631[a]	-0.059	4.682	-18.839[c]	-0.118	4.666
Big dealer	45.707[a]	0.065	21.192	88.567[c]	0.135	17.903	54.779[c]	0.145	10.970
Nixon judge	—	—	—	17.973[b]	0.100	5.436	2.832	0.019	4.282
Judge severity	0.077	0.014	0.166	0.027	0.003	0.234	-0.128	-0.013	0.284
Plea (not guilty)	11.115[b]	0.124	2.905	31.541[c]	0.235	3.885	35.828[c]	0.235	4.432
Pre-sentence report	2.774	0.029	3.077	25.438[a]	0.074	9.965	-17.835	-0.041	13.748
	$R^2 = 0.159$			$R^2 = 0.254$			$R^2 = 0.276$		
	Intercept $= -12.006$			Intercept $= 24.634$			Intercept $= 29.167$		
	Mean sentence $= 69.525$			Mean sentence $= 69.138$			Mean sentence $= 66.380$		

[a] $p \leq 0.05$.
[b] $p \leq 0.01$.
[c] $p \leq 0.001$.

white offenders receive more lenient treatment than white offenders in all time periods, with this disparity again being most acute during the middle years. Also consistent with our perspective, Nixon judges are more punitive than other judges, specifically during the Nixon years, 1969–73. There are additional effects that are partially consistent with our perspective. The plea variable, which we argued would have particular instrumental and symbolic importance during the anti-drug crusade, does jump in its influence during the middle interval, while it is even more important (albeit slightly) in the final period. Similarly, our most direct measure of victim status, being a drug user, results in increasingly more lenient treatment across the three time periods. Finally, although the age, education and status variables do not act entirely as expected, their effects do not particularly conflict with our viewpoint either. Overall, our perspective receives considerable support: there are various indications of the symbolic politics we described. Much of the variation from our expectations seems to involve a continuing influence of these politics into the third period. However, before more definitive conclusions are reached, we use previously described procedures to correct for selection bias.

The first step in this correction involves the estimation of the probit equation in each of the three periods. The dependent variable here is the decision between a prison and non-prison sentence. Since the probit results are built into the corrected regression analysis that follows, we will discuss these findings, presented in table 3.3, only briefly.

Our most direct measures of villain and victim statuses influence imprisonment in ways that are consistent with the perspective we have suggested. Thus users are *more* likely than others to go to jail from 1963 to 1968, but *less* likely to do so from 1969 to 1973. It is difficult to interpret these effects in any way other than the altered deviance designations we have described. Meanwhile, although the effect of being a big dealer is not significant during any of the three periods, the effect coefficient for this variable is largest during the middle interval. As expected, the effect of plea is significant in all periods, and also largest from 1969 to 1973. And, while we were unable to find any significant status effects above, we now find that middle class membership decreases significantly the likelihood of imprisonment in all time periods and, again as expected, this effect is strongest from 1969 to 1973. Education and age also have their own effects on imprisonment, with education having the bigger impact, and with the likelihood of high school educated offenders being jailed lowest from 1969 to 1973. Nixon judges show a greater reluctance to imprison offenders than other judges during the last two periods, while judges with high severity scores for non-drug cases also are more willing in drug cases to use prison as a sanction. The latter findings are discussed further below. Finally, although non-white offenders are less likely than white offenders to get jail sentences in all three periods, counter to our expectations, this effect is smallest and statistically non-significant from 1969 to 1973. This last finding, as well as those more consistent with our perspective, is taken into account through the incorporation of risk factors in the corrected regression equation whose results are presented in table 3.4.

A comparison of the results reported in tables 3.2 and 3.4 indicates that inclusion of risk factors as regressors in the corrected equations alters many of the coefficients and standard errors. This is because the correction factor is highly correlated with many of the exogenous variables in the prison sentence length equations. Although there are exceptions, the tendency is for the coefficients to become larger in table 3.4, where selection bias is taken into account. For example, the major consequence of correcting for selection bias on the effect parameters for race is to increase by two months in the first and second periods, and three months in the third period, the advantage that accrues to non-whites in drug sentencing. Thus while non-whites received sentences (net of twenty-one other variables and the correction factor) nearly eight months ($b = -7.745$) shorter than whites from 1963 to 1968, this difference jumped to more than eighteen months ($b = -18.320$) from 1969 to 1973, and remained close to this level ($b = -16.920$) from 1974 to 1976. The t-tests reported in table 3.5 indicate that the differences between periods I and II, and I and III, are statistically significant. Again, our explanation is that data cover a period in which the historical association of the drug problem with minority and low income populations was declining. Big drug dealers were now seen as the symbolic villains.

Consistent with this theme, including the correction factor in the prison sentence length equation augments, but does not alter, the pattern of influence of the big dealer variable. In each period, the corrected equation reveals an increment of seven additional months of imprisonment for big dealers. The respective coefficients for the uncorrected and corrected equations are: 45.7 and 52.8 (1963–8), 88.6 and 96.0 (1969–73), and 54.8 and 62.4 (1974–6). Both the rise and decline in the severity of the sentences big dealers receive across the three periods are statistically significant (see tables). We view the unique and severe sentences for big dealers during the period of heightened concern about drugs as substantiating our argument that big dealers were, from 1969 to 1973, the symbolic villains of the anti-drug crusade.

We have noted the instrumental and symbolic significance of the plea variable in this crusade. Again, estimates from the corrected model indicate that the penalty for pleading not guilty is greater in each period and substantially greater in the 1969–73 and 1974–6 periods: $b = 14.4$ for

TABLE 3.3 *Probit regression of type of sentence (prison/non-prison) on independent variables for different social contexts*

Variable	Period I 1963–1968			Period II 1969–1973			Period III 1974–1976		
	Coefficient	Standard error	Correlation with risk factor	Coefficient	Standard error	Correlation with risk factor	Coefficient	Standard error	Correlation with risk factor
Male sex	0.449[b]	0.167	0.283	0.727[c]	0.124	0.748	0.818[c]	0.131	0.698
Age	0.018[b]	0.006	0.345	0.025[c]	0.005	0.652	0.036[c]	0.005	0.749
Race (non–white)	−0.233[a]	0.112	−0.218	−0.084	0.091	−0.123	−0.210[a]	0.089	−0.330
Marital status (unattached)	0.010	0.111	0.019	−0.071	0.083	−0.232	−0.075	0.081	−0.199
Education	0.138	0.138	0.211	0.261[b]	0.084	0.565	0.175[a]	0.083	0.305
Status	−0.858[a]	0.396	−0.345	−1.006[c]	0.215	−0.771	−0.734[b]	0.208	−0.566
Prior record	0.039[b]	0.012	0.431	0.019	0.010	0.354	0.026[a]	0.010	0.355
Pre-1970 trafficking	1.407[c]	0.157	0.883	0.528[b]	0.160	0.545	0.966	0.634	0.240
Post-1970 trafficking	—	—	—	0.609[b]	0.160	0.678	0.405	0.484	0.257

Pre-1970 importing	1.661[c]	0.375	0.799	−0.082	0.458	0.53	—	—	—
Post-1970 importing	—	—	—	0.122	0.563	0.132	−0.088	0.605	0.057
Conspiracy	—	—	—	0.550[b]	0.174	0.640	0.395	0.485	0.256
Illegal communication	—	—	—	1.368[c]	0.321	0.762	0.668	0.360	0.295
Charge seriousness	0.003[b]	0.001	0.319	0.004[c]	0.001	0.687	0.004	0.003	0.195
Gun use	—	—	—	−0.042	0.201	−0.037	0.196	0.133	0.193
Narcotic drug	—	—	—	0.109	0.106	0.184	0.394[b]	0.109	0.527
Drug user	0.426[b]	0.129	0.383	−0.278[a]	0.094	−0.517	0.027	0.082	0.013
Big dealer	1.484	2.692	0.114	2.015	1.603	0.245	0.950	0.503	0.161
Nixon judge	—	—	—	−0.259[a]	0.119	−0.391	−0.300[b]	0.080	−0.512
Judge severity	0.008	0.008	0.053	0.027[c]	0.006	0.689	0.026[c]	0.005	0.620
Plea (not guilty)	0.440[b]	0.142	0.364	0.666[c]	0.093	0.840	0.520[c]	0.089	0.708
Pre-sentence report	−0.457[c]	0.111	−0.526	0.211	0.206	0.132	−0.072	0.217	−0.100

[a] $p \leq 0.05$.
[b] $p \leq 0.01$.
[c] $p \leq 0.001$.

TABLE 3.4 *Corrected regression of length of imprisonment (in months) on independent variables for different social contexts*

	Period I 1963–1968			Period II 1969–1973			Period III 1974–1976		
Variables	b	β	SE	b	β	SE	b	β	SE
Male sex	10.970	0.059	5.821	24.710[a]	0.095	10.990	49.870[b]	0.145	12.950
Age	1.449[c]	0.268	0.183	1.115[b]	0.150	0.307	2.277[c]	0.288	0.359
Race (non-white)	− 7.745[a]	− 0.086	3.007	− 18.320[c]	− 0.137	4.209	− 16.920[b]	− 0.102	4.863
Marital status (unattached)	0.438	0.005	2.923	− 17.740[c]	− 0.138	4.007	− 15.000[b]	− 0.099	4.250
Education	− 3.704	− 0.029	4.126	9.780[a]	0.073	4.880	13.130[a]	0.085	4.679
Status	− 38.290	− 0.055	22.800	− 45.590	− 0.076	27.330	− 59.400[a]	− 0.074	26.270
Prior record	0.370	0.042	0.333	1.800[c]	0.141	0.423	2.584[c]	0.188	0.449
Pre-1970 trafficking	40.020[b]	0.682	11.480	56.750[c]	1.458	13.590	85.800[a]	2.212	31.980
Post-1970 trafficking	—	—	—	32.280[a]	0.830	13.980	58.680[a]	1.513	25.380
Pre-1970 importing	31.770[a]	0.541	14.050	39.320	1.010	28.730	—	—	—
Post-1970 importing	—	—	—	25.350	0.651	30.970	84.590[a]	2.181	34.140

Conspiracy	—	—	—	31.490[a]	0.809	13.950	61.190[a]	1.578	25.410
Illegal communication	—	—	—	49.170[a]	1.263	23.900	32.240	0.831	26.190
Charge seriousness	0.139[c]	0.177	0.034	0.049	0.036	0.083	0.030	0.011	0.157
Gun use	—	—	—	0.842	0.003	8.241	9.374	0.046	5.983
Narcotic drug	—	—	—	10.040	−0.078	5.152	41.030[a]	0.184	8.115
Drug user	0.528	0.006	3.425	−13.900[a]	−0.090	5.470	−16.990[c]	−0.106	4.540
Big dealer	52.750[a]	0.075	21.360	95.990[c]	0.153	18.380	62.410[c]	0.165	10.780
Nixon judge	—	—		12.370[a]	0.073	5.921	9.550	−0.063	4.843
Judge severity	0.112	0.018	0.194	0.687	0.083	0.347	0.961[a]	0.092	0.367
Plea (not guilty)	14.450[c]	0.161	3.140	41.320[c]	0.322	7.128	55.360[c]	0.364	6.095
Pre-sentence report	2.726	−0.028	3.635	27.850[a]	0.085	10.010	−26.570	−0.062	13.420
Risk of imprisonment (λ_i)	41.310[a]		14.290	41.280		25.090	97.080[c]		21.700
	$R^2 = 0.159$			$R^2 = 0.250$			$R^2 = 0.285$		
	Intercept $= -69.33$			Intercept $= -134.8$			Intercept $= -248.9$		

[a] $p \leq 0.05$.
[b] $p \leq 0.01$.
[c] $p \leq 0.001$.

1963–8, 41.3 for 1969–73, and 55.3 for the 1974–6 period. Table 3.5 indicates that these differences across time periods are all significant. We view the substantial increase in the impact of the plea effect over time as support for our argument that the proactive character of an anti-drug crusade requires the use of plea bargaining, and that a plea of guilty symbolizes contrition and possibly remorse.

Correcting for selection bias has important consequences for the measured effects of being a drug user, the symbolic victims in our perspective. When the uncorrected equations were estimated, users did not appear to receive substantially different sentences relative to other offenders in periods I and II. In contrast, the corrected equations reveal that when selection bias is controlled, there is a substantial 13.4 month difference in the coefficients for periods I and II which is statistically significant, as is the difference (16.5 months) between the effect parameters in periods I and III (see table 3.5). Furthermore, the corrected equation suggests that, in the

TABLE 3.5 t-statistics for differences in the value of beta coefficients comparing the effects of independent variables on the corrected model of prison sentence length across social contexts

Variable	Period I compared with Period II		Period I compared with Period III		Period II compared with Period III	
	Difference	t	Difference	t	Difference	t
Male sex	− 13.740	− 4.710[b]	− 38.890	− 12.630[b]	− 25.150	− 7270[b]
Age	0.334	0.672	− 0.828	− 1.586	− 1.162	2.010[a]
Race (non-white)	10.580	5.540[b]	9.175	4.610[b]	− 1.400	− 0.657
Marital status (unattached)	− 17.300	− 9.250[b]	− 14.560	− 7.660[b]	− 2.740	1.350
Education	− 13.480	− 6.330[b]	− 16.830	− 8.020[b]	− 3.350	− 1.530
Status	7.300	1.450	21.110	4.260[b]	13.810	2.670[b]
Prior record	− 1.430	− 3.760[b]	− 2.210	− 3.540[b]	− 0.784	− 1.190
Pre-1970 trafficking	− 16.730	− 4.710[b]	− 45.780	− 9.780[b]	− 29.050	− 6.100[b]
Post-1970 trafficking	—	—	—	—	− 26.400	− 5.970[b]
Pre-1970 importing	− 7.550	−. 1.620	—	—	—	—
Post-1970 importing	—	—	—	—	− 59.240	− 10.390[b]
Conspiracy	—	—	—	—	− 29.670	− 6.710[b]
Illegal communication	—	—	—	—	16.930	3.390[b]
Charge seriousness	0.090	0.370	0.109	0.350	0.019	0.055
Gun use	—	—	—	—	− 10.216	− 3.830[b]
Narcotic drug	—	—	—	—	− 30.990	− 12.060[b]
Drug user	− 13.370	− 6.310[b]	− 16.460	− 8.210[b]	3.090	1.380
Big dealer	− 43.240	− 9.720[b]	− 9.660	− 2.420[a]	33.580	8.770[b]
Nixon judge	—	—	—	—	2.820	1.220
Judge severity	− 0.575	− 1.100	− 0.849	− 1.600	− 0.274	− 0.459
Plea (not guilty)	− 26.870	− 11.790[b]	− 40.910	− 18.940[b]	− 14.040	− 5.460[b]
Pre-sentence report	− 30.580	− 11.580[b]	23.840	8.110[b]	54.420	15.910[b]
Risk of imprisonment (λ_i)	0.030	0.007	− 55.770	− 13.120[b]	− 55.800	− 11.530[b]

[a] $p \leq 0.05$.
[b] $p \leq 0.01$.

earliest years, drug users received *more* rather than less severe sentences than non-users, although this pattern is neither substantial ($b = 0.528$) nor statistically significant. In contrast, drug users in the later periods received sentences that were substantially and significantly *less* severe than those received by non-users (in the corrected equations, $b = -13.9$ for 1969–73, and $b = -16.99$ for 1974–6). We interpret this new found lenience as reflecting the altered status of users as symbolic victims.

Of the several variables that are important to the perspective we have proposed, controlling for selection bias has the greatest impact on the findings for status. The uncorrected equation indicated a decline over time in the impact of this variable on prison sentence length. This is a somewhat puzzling finding since it suggests that middle class youth received the smallest break in sentencing (compared to traditional offenders) during the period when sources of public and elite opinion were converging in advocating more lenient handling of such offenders; and, when legislative provisions (e.g., discretionary sentencing and special first offender provisions) should have facilitated the awarding of lenient penalities to middle class youthful drug offenders. Importantly, however, correcting for selection bias eliminates this puzzling finding. Consistent with our perspective, the corrected equations reveal that the tendency is for the impact of status to increase rather than decrease over time. Middle class youth received substantially larger breaks in sentencing during the final two periods when concern about the fate of these symbolic victims in the hands of the criminal justice system was more pronounced. The 7.3 months difference in the coefficients comparing the impact of status during the 1963–8 period with the 1969–73 period does not quite reach statistical significance. However, the remaining differences in coefficients across time periods are substantial and statistically significant. Finally, we should note that a significant change in the main effect of education precedes the status effect: between 1969 and 1973, better educated drug offenders received more than nine months shorter sentences ($b = 9.780$) than those less educated; between 1974 and 1976 this difference widened to more than thirteen months ($b = 13.130$).

A FURTHER TEST

There is an additional way to examine, with the present data, the implications of the perspective we proposed. Above we argued that the leniency expected for non-white drug offenders derived from their tendency to be restricted to the lower levels of the drug trade. A consequence of this situation, we argued, was the generalized designation of non-white offenders as symbolic victims rather than villains of America's drug problems.

However, on those rare occasions when non-whites do rise to the position of big dealers, the protection of symbolic victim status is no longer a concern, and the predicted leniency should disappear. We now explore this implication of our perspective by considering big dealers separately from more ordinary drug offenders. This phase of our analysis also allows consideration of a second unexamined expectation of our perspective, that the plea variable has a bigger effect among big dealers. We argued that this would be the case because of the instrumental use of plea bargaining in proactively prosecuting big dealers, and because of the symbolic significance of guilty pleas, as contrasted with protestations of innocence, by big dealers.

To conduct this part of the analysis we have combined data from the last two time periods and regressed sentence length, separately for big dealers and for ordinary drug offenders, on those independent variables (race, marital status, pre-1970 trafficking, drug user, plea and pre-sentence report) which were substantively and statistically related to this criterion variable. The decision to combine the data for the last two periods followed from the fact that the number of big dealers was too small to permit a reliable regression analysis within each period. Since our prior analysis revealed considerable carry-over of the politics of the second period into the third, this approach seems justified. No correction for selection bias is attempted in this part of our analysis because for big dealers there is none: they are all imprisoned.

Table 3.6 presents the results of the above analysis. First the findings for race: the unstandardized coefficient for ordinary offenders indicates that non-whites receive sentences that average six months less than those received by whites ($b = -6.685$); in contrast, non-white big dealers receive prison sentences that average more than 19 months *longer* than those received by white big dealers. While the latter finding in itself is not statistically significant (an unsurprising outcome given the small number of non-white big dealers), the *difference* in the impact of race for ordinary drug offenders and big dealers is significant beyond the 0.001 level. In a period when big dealers were viewed as the source and symbol of the drug problem, *non-white big dealers* may have been seen as even more suspect and villainous, since they in particular may be perceived as inflicting their evil on an already victimized population: non-white users. In any case, this finding provides further evidence for our perspective.

Meanwhile, the unstandardized regression coefficients for the plea variable indicate that this is the single most important predicator of sentence length for both ordinary offenders and big dealers, but that plea has a significantly greater impact for big dealers than for ordinary offenders. Ordinary drug offenders who plead not guilty are subject to average prison sentences that are more than thirty-six months longer than their counterparts

TABLE 3.6 *Regression of length of prison sentence (in months) on significant independent variables or ordinary drug offenders and big dealers, 1969–1976*

Independent variables	Ordinary offenders (N = 2025) b	Big dealers (N = 53) b	Difference	t
Race (non-white)	− 6.686[a]	19.385	− 26.071	− 13.254[c]
Marital status (unattached)	− 18.290[c]	− 13.789	− 4.501	2.425[a]
Pre-1970 trafficking	20.502[c]	50.380	− 29.878	− 14.344[c]
Drug user	− 15.700[c]	− 18.489	2.759	1.340
Plea (not guilty)	36.271[c]	126.796[c]	− 90.525	− 48.203[c]
Pre-sentence report	13.119	57.767	− 44.648	− 14.045[c]

R^2 = 0.155 R^2 = 0.342
Intercept = 48.317   Intercept = 11.074
Mean sentence = 65.265   Mean sentence = 164.15

[a] $p \leq 0.05$.
[b] $p \leq 0.01$.
[c] $p \leq 0.001$.

who plead guilty. By comparison, big dealers who plead not guilty are subject to average prison sentences that are more than 126 months longer than those received by big dealers who plead guilty. These findings are consistent with our thesis regarding the proactive prosecution of big dealers and the symbolic significance of their protestations of innocence. Among big dealers, the plea variable operates to tighten the coupling of the prosecutorial and judicial subsystems, in this case in the service of a political crusade against drugs.

SOME CONCLUSIONS

From his review of the literature on race and sentencing, Gary Kleck (1981: 799) concludes that, 'Students of the criminal justice system . . . have sought to explain patterns of more severe treatment of blacks, while overlooking or downplaying the pattern of lenient treatment of black defendants.' In doing so, prior theorizing and research implicitly have treated the meaning of race as a constant. Explicit in our analysis is the premise that the meaning of race varies. There are hints of such an understanding in prior studies of inter- and intra-racial crimes with victims. However, we have argued that racial categories have broader symbolic connotations that can influence societal reactions to the more frequent victimless crimes as well. Furthermore, we have suggested that these symbolic meanings have histories that can include important alterations in designations of deviance.

For example, the politics of the American drug prohibition began with the portrayal of minorities as the symbolic villains behind a growing drug menace. With the increasing non-medical use of drugs by middle-class youth in the 1960s, older conceptions of the drug problem became problematic. A new strategy was required. However, this was not to be a strategy that gave up a reliance on imprisonment as the ultimate sanction; instead, this sanction was redistributed. Big dealers became the new symbolic villains, while middle-class youth *and* non-whites (the latter insofar as they rarely were big dealers in a racially stratified drug trade) were reconceived as symbolic victims. We have argued that inclusion of blacks in the latter category was the product of a compromise between conservative and liberal impulses that facilitated a more specialized allocation of penal sanctions. This modern anti-drug crusade reached its peak between 1969 and 1973, a structural context that included the Nixon administration's passage of a new drug law.

We were able to identify in our data a series of effects consistent with the above perspective. The most dramatic of these effects included a peak in the punitive treatment of big dealers between 1969 and 1973. Lenient treatment of non-white offenders peaked during these same years. The latter ultimately was revealed to be a lenience restricted to *ordinary* non-white drug offenders. Indeed, there were signs that non-white *big dealers* received the most severe sentences of all.

The above findings were reinforced by a series of follow-up interviews we conducted with three former heads of the drug enforcement division of the US Attorney's Office of the Southern District of New York. When asked to explain the general pattern of leniency we found for non-white drug offenders, one former prosecutor answered with the immediate response that, 'Sure, three blacks equal one Italian, and three Italians equal one Corsican.' Asked to elaborate, this former Assistant US Attorney noted that the world of drugs is not only racially, but also ethnically stratified. The remainder of the interview, and the others we conducted, are best characterized as reflecting a casual, jaded, and sometimes paternal indifference to black drug crime that is well captured in contemporary American films like *Prince of the City*, which not coincidentally is set in the same time and place as the current study.

There is, however, a more ominous side to the new drug strategy that is reflected in the race-period-big dealer interaction noted above. Indeed there are dramatic examples of the extremely severe treatment of black big dealers. The case of Leroy 'Nicky' Barnes offers a vivid illustration. On 19 January

1978, Barnes was sentenced to life imprisonment *without* parole on drug conspiracy charges *and* under the seldom used Continuing Criminal Enterprise provision of the 1970 Federal Drug Act.[10] Regarded as possibly Harlem's biggest drug dealer, Barnes was listed in the New York Police Department's Blue Book of 'Black Major Violators'. In imposing such a severe sentence, the judge in the case explained that Barnes 'is "a great danger" to the community . . . His narcotics trafficking affected "the lives of thousands of people". And the saddest part of all . . . is that the great majority of people he is affecting are people in his own neighborhood [Harlem]' (*New York Times*, 20 January 1978). If our argument about the symbolic politics of drugs described above has merit, then this latter comment may be interpreted as consistent with our view that non-white big dealers are regarded as more villainous, and therefore deserving of more severe penalties, because they 'sin' against an already victimized population. The following comment from a *Time* magazine article (written prior to Barnes' 1978 conviction) is also noteworthy in light of our perspective.

Whatever the reasons, the failure to make an arrest stick has earned Barnes the street name 'Mr Untouchable'. He is not a retiring man. Of medium height, he projects a presence larger than his size. He is muscular and recently shaved the beard he sported for years. He prefers luxurious motor cars and elaborate custom clothing. To the street people, he is a presence. To the police, this symbolic quality is as significant as the crimes they allege he has committed.

To them he embodies the new trend in drug trafficking, in which blacks and Hispanics, the new ethnic successors in organized crime, have taken over from their predecessors, the Italian street gangsters. (*Time* magazine, 5 June 1977: 16)

It is noteworthy that Nicky Barnes and other big dealers in our sample received particularly long sentences when they pleaded not guilty. We suggested that the severe sanctioning of these refusals to plead guilty reflected a coupling of the prosecutorial and judicial sub-systems for a shared goal: the anti-drug crusade initiated by the Nixon administration. In the next chapter we suggest that this kind of tight coupling can occur through the recommendations that prosecutors make to judges for sentencing. However, we are not suggesting that this kind of coupling is characteristic of criminal justice decision-making. For example, probation officers also recommend sentences, but they may not be as influential as prosecutors in their recommendations. In the next chapter we suggest that criminal justice outcomes more characteristically are the products of rather loosely coupled sub-systems.

More generally, we offer this study as an argument for a structural-contextual approach to sentencing research that takes into account the changing symbolic politics of American crime and punishment. Our re-analysis of the results of prior studies, and the analysis of new data presented here, suggest that there may not only be a trend toward equality in American criminal sentencing, but also patterns of differential lenience and severity that only contextualized analyses can reveal. The symbolic politics of race and sentencing in America are more variable and more complicated than previously acknowledged.

NOTES

1 These studies were identified through a review of existing bibliographies (e.g., Kleck, 1981) and a search of Sociological Abstracts, Crime and Delinquency Abstracts, and Legal Abstracts. For reasons explained in the footnote that follows, only studies reporting zero-order relationships between race and sentencing are included. They are: Atkinson and Newman (1970), Baab and Ferguson (1968), Bedau (1964; 1965), Bensing and Schroeder (1960), Farrell and Swigert (1978a; 1978b), Garfinkel (1949), Gerard and Terry (1970), Gibson (1978), Green (1961; 1964), Hagan et al. (1979), Hagan et al. (1980), Johnson (1957), Judson et al. (1969), Lemert and Rosberg (1948), Lizotte (1978), Martin (1934), Partington (1965), Pope (1975a; 1975b), Uhlman and Walker (1979), Wolf (1964), Wolfgang et al. (1962), Wolfgang and Reidel (1973), Zimring et al. (1976). Where the same data set is used in more than one published study, only one is included.

2 The traditional approach to the issue of racial disparities in sentencing is to examine whether a zero-order relationship between race and sentencing persists when legitimized influences on sentencing (e.g., type of offence, prior record) are taken into account. This is the essence of what we have called the individual-processual approach. However, there is also an important benefit to examining zero-order relationships found between race and sentencing across available studies, with the purpose of seeing what characteristics of the range of contexts considered produce variation in these relationships. In other words, we can use these zero-order relationships as a dependent variable for an aggregated, structural-contextual analysis. We contemplated using measures of net effects of race on sentencing as dependent variables in parallel fashion. However, because the variables introduced into these kinds of multivariate analyses are so different in type and measurement, and because the legitimacy of variables like prior record is so open to debate (Farrell and Swigert, 1978b), the results of such an exercise could not be given a clear interpretation. Meanwhile, the traditional conflict perspective and the surveyed public presume that there is a zero-order relationship between race and sentence to be explained. It is true that the possibility of suppression effects complicates this presumption, and we consider important implications of this point in this chapter.

3 Five of the studies (Baab and Ferguson, 1968; Bernstein et al., 1977; Farrell and Swigert, 1978a; Hagan et al., 1980; Lizotte, 1978) do not present data in categorical form. However, consistent with the pattern observed below, all of

these studies are relatively recent, and all report small (from 0.03 to − 0.08) zero-order relationships between race and sentencing.

4 In the analysis that follows, race is measured as black or white and sentence as two or more ordered categories. The use of gamma as our measure of association follows the precedent of an analogous review of studies of the relationship of social class and criminality by Tittle et al. (1978; see also Smith and Vischer, 1980). For a discussion of some of the prospects and problems of cumulating studies as we have done here, see Rosenthal (1980). For a discussion of gamma, see Mueller et al. (1977: 215–17).

5 For those studies that cover more than one year, the middle year is used. The first order autocorrelation coefficient for these data is − 0.113, which indicates that successive observations are not highly correlated, and that therefore autoregression is not a serious problem.

6 Exclusion of these outliers from the above analysis produces little change in the results.

7 The major reason for including the *Reader's Guide* measure is to confirm that the levels of concern in the *New York Times* and the *New York Times Index* represent general tendencies across the nation.

8 These case data originally were collected by the probation department of the Southern Federal District of New York (Manhattan) in order to make information available to sentencing judges. The case data were put into machine readable form by the authors.

9 While the use of 100 pounds as a cut-off is somewhat arbitrary, selection of this amount was based on the minimum volume of drugs typically involved in major drug cases as indicated in the *Annual Reports* of the US Attorney for the Southern District.

10 Under the 1970 Act, a person is considered to be engaging in a continuing criminal enterprise if she or he: (1) commits a felony which is part of a continuing series of drug offences; (2) acts in concert with at least five other persons to commit these offences; (3) commands some organizational or supervisory position with respect to the group; and (4) obtains substantial income from the enterprise. None of the big dealers in our population of drug offenders were sentenced for this offence during the period of our investigation. While the Barnes case was not processed until 1977, it is not irrelevant to the present analysis. Indeed, the 1978 conviction represented the culmination of efforts, begun in 1973, to criminally sanction Leroy 'Nicky' Barnes for drug trafficking. On several attempts during 1973 and 1974, state law enforcement agents were unsuccessful in prosecuting Barnes, earning him the title 'Mr Untouchable'.

4

Ceremonial Justice

Conceptions of justice change, and with them the structures for carrying out justice. The most significant conceptual change of this century in the realm of criminal justice is a shift from the classical to the positivist view of crime and punishment. Put simply, the positivist position is that punishments must fit the individual criminal rather than the crime. Thus, where the classical theorists – such as Beccaria, Bentham, and Romilly – urged a close fit between infraction and reaction, the positivists – Lombroso, Ferri, and Garofalo – were more anxious to match the sanction to its recipient (Mannheim, 1960; Vold, 1958). This shift found encouragement in the American political environment at the turn of the century.

It was during the Progressive era that the themes of positivism were reflected in North American crime and delinquency legislation (Hagan and Leon, 1977; Platt, 1969). First in juvenile court laws, and then in adult probation statutes, the Progressives created legal structures to match their new conceptions of the delinquent and the criminal. The Progressive assumption, quite simply, was that 'if the laws are the right laws, and if they can be enforced by the right men ... everything would be better' (Hofstadter, 1968: 202). The 'right laws' in this case were those allowing attention to the needs of individual offenders (see Matza, 1964).

The most conspicuous structural manifestations of the new individualized or socialized justice (Pound, 1930) were the grafting of juvenile and adult probation departments onto existing criminal justice systems, and the resulting involvement of probation officers in the pre-sentencing process. Following Meyer and Rowan (1977), it is our thesis that the attachment of probation subsystems to the American courts had more to do with the making of legal myths than with the restructuring of the way decisions actually are made. In this sense, the rise of probation was more ideological than instrumental in significance, resulting in ritualized court practices characterized more by ceremony than substance. Meanwhile, prosecutors continued to be the more powerful actors in court decision-making. We contend that an understanding of the relationship between myth and ceremony in the criminal courts is essential to the development of an accurate and comprehensive understanding of court operations.

OLD AND NEW THEORIES OF CRIME PUNISHMENT

Dominant theories of crime and punishment often assume a tight fit between structure and function in the criminal courts. For example, the Marxian class conflict model often posits modern capitalism as an economic infrastructure that requires a coercive system of criminal justice to preserve the domination of one class by another. An instrumental form of this perspective assumes that the courts are structured such that class-linked, extra-legal offender characteristics exercise a strong influence on decision-making. Alternatively, a Durkheimian consensus perspective posits a close correspondence between the widely shared values of a society and the criminal justice system that both expresses and preserves this system of values through the even-handed enforcement of laws. The assumption of this perspective is that legally defined offence characteristics exercise a strong influence on decision-making. In other words, the instrumental Marxist and Durkheimian consensus models disagree on the factors assumed to influence legal decision-making, but they agree that this decision-making is structured in a way that one or the other set of factors exercises a substantial influence.

Yet, the evidence commonly cited to affirm or deny the instrumental Marxist and Durkheimian consensus positions is inconsistent (see Hagan and Bumiller, 1983). There are important circumstances such as those examined in earlier chapters, where class and racial variables have substantial effects. However, those studies which reveal the influence of race and class position in sentencing decisions often find that their influence is relatively weak. Meanwhile, those studies which question the influence of race and class in sentencing decisions rarely find evidence that legal or court-related variables exercise a profound impact on sentence dispositions. The single finding that is consistent throughout this empirical literature is that, whether legal or extra-legal factors are the focus of the analysis, the unexplained variance in sentencing looms large. This observation holds even in the case where the two types of variables are combined (e.g., Hogarth, 1971).

It is our contention that these findings may be symptomatic of what some theorists have called a 'loosely coupled system'. Leaving aside temporarily the precise meaning attached to this concept, we note that there is some precedent for a conception of looseness in the American criminal justice system. Perhaps most significantly, Reiss (1971) speaks of American criminal justice as a 'loosely articulated hierarchy of subsystems' (114–20). Similarly, Eisenstein and Jacob (1977) note that even 'the judge does not rule or govern, at most, he manages, and often he is managed by others' (37). Reiss goes on to suggest that 'the major means of control among the subsystems is internal to each' with the significant consequence that 'each subsystem creates its own system of justice'. If true, these observations have important theoretical and methodological implications for the direction of criminal justice research.

CRIME AND PUNISHMENT AS A LOOSELY COUPLED SYSTEM

We begin with a connotative definition. Loose coupling is meant to evoke the image of entities (e.g., court subsystems) which are responsive to one another, while still maintaining independent identities and some evidence of physical or logical separateness (Weick, 1976). Meyer and Rowan (1977) add to this conception an enumeration of characteristics associated with loosely coupled formal organizations – structural elements are only loosely linked to one another and to activities, rules are often violated, decisions often go unimplemented, or if implemented have uncertain consequences, techniques are often subverted or rendered so vague as to provide little co-ordination. We argue here that many of these characteristics are manifest in the criminal justice system, and furthermore that the consequences of this loose coupling can be recognized at the level of individual sentencing decisions. At this level of analysis, Glassman (1973) suggests that entities may be considered loosely coupled to the extent that: (a) they share few variables in common; (b) the variables shared in common differ substantially in their degree of influence; or (c) the variables shared in common are weak in comparison to other variables considered. The concept of loose coupling, therefore, has implications for analysis of processes at both micro- and macro-levels.

A salient advantage of loosely coupled systems is that they can easily take on new appendages demanded by changes in the external environment, while at the same time selectively ignoring the activities of these new appendages. The importance of this capability, in Weberian terms, is that the organization is able to maintain and often increase its institutional legitimacy without dramatically changing its day-to-day practices. The more such organizations change, the more, for many practical purposes, they remain the same. For purposes of our discussion, the result may be interpreted as a propagation of myth and ceremony in the administration of criminal justice.

MYTH, CEREMONY AND INDIVIDUALIZED JUSTICE

As we noted at the outset, the notion of individualized justice emerged in an era of social reform, as part of broader efforts to humanize the bureaucratic structures of post-industrial society. The standards of individualized justice, including most notably attempts to attend to the social needs of individuals, represent what Meyer and Rowan (1977) call 'institutionalized rules'. They suggest that as legitimated institutional rules arise in given domains of work activity (e.g., the criminal courts), formal organizations form and expand by incorporating these rules as structural elements. Correspondingly, we have indicated that as the conception of individualized justice grew in popularity in this century, there emerged an organized probation movement (see Chute, 1956; Timascheff, 1941) whose principal goal was legislation recognizing a new profession of probation workers, functioning in probation departments within the juvenile and criminal courts. This new profession was to operationalize the institutional rules of individualized justice through the preparation of pre-sentence reports describing the offender's social and legal history and containing the probation officer's individualized recommendation for sentence (see Hagan, 1975b).

The willingness of the courts to take on the profession of probation work as a subsystem may, of course, be explained in terms of the legitimation needs of the court. However, Meyer and Rowan (1977) note that legitimacy and efficiency can be inversely related. Thus, 'specific contexts highlight the inadequacies of the prescriptions of generalized myths, and inconsistent structural elements conflict over jurisdictional rights' (356). It is in these contexts that systemic decoupling is most likely to occur, with the consequence that conflicts may be avoided and legitimacy maintained. In other words, decoupling can preserve myths and prevent demystification.

The institutional rule of individualized justice requires a skilful mixture of coupling and decoupling for its preservation. On the one hand, Matza (1964) notes, and our review of the sentencing literature confirms, that 'the principle of individualized justice results in a frame of reference that is so large, so all-inclusive, that any relation between the criteria of judgement and the disposition remains obscure' (115). The institutional dilemma, then, centres on the basis for reaching judgement. Individual justice presumably demands attention to individual needs – but, which needs? How known? And, by whom discerned? Matza argues that there is only one possible answer to these questions, based on the 'professional training, experience, and judgment' of court agents, whereby 'any system with an extremely wide frame of reference in which the items included . . . are neither specifically enumerated nor weighted must come to rely heavily on professional judgment' (16). Hence, the significance of the pre-sentence report and recommendation of the probation officer for arriving at sentencing decisions. Yet reliance on the professional judgements of probation officers is a workable solution to the dispositional dilemmas of individualized justice only insofar as these recommendations do not seriously impede the efficiency needs of the court. It is only under these conditions that the court can function as a tightly coupled system. Alternatively, a problem arises when efficiency needs require outcomes different from those recommended by probation officers. It is under these circumstances that decoupling becomes a means of ceremonially preserving the myth of individualization.

The criminal courts have responded to the potential disjunction between individualization and efficiency by expanding the decision-making network. Recommendations are requested not only from the agent of individualization – the probation officer – but from the agent of the state – the prosecutor – as well. The prosecutor, of course, represents a set of interests antithetical to individualization, being concerned instead with the efficient processing of large numbers of cases. The significance of including the prosecutor in the making of sentencing decisions is that when efficiency needs (e.g., rewarding guilty pleas and punishing resource-taxing claims of innocence) become salient, the prosecutor's recommendation can be followed and the probation officer's ignored. In the end, the prosecutor is the more powerful actor. In terms of its ceremonial effects, this strategy requires procedures followed in almost all court systems: that the prosecutor's recommendation for sentence is presented orally in court, while the probation officer's recommendation is submitted in writing as part of the pre-sentence report undisclosed to the offender or to members of the public (see Zastrow, 1971). The practice of not disclosing the probation officer's recommendation can conceal the fact that an elaborate pre-sentencing process aimed at individualization has effectively been ignored. This process is mystified still further in some jurisdictions by concluding the pre-sentence report with an 'evaluation' in place of the more explicit recommendation; in other jurisdictions no report is requested at all. In other words, there are various means of loosening the coupling between the judiciary and the probation subsystem, while still maintaining the general myth and ceremony of individualization which is fundamental to probation work.

The rest of this chapter pursues these themes through a quantitative analysis of sentencing in one criminal court jurisdiction, King County (Seattle), Washington, in 1973. We first develop a model which incorporates theoretically relevant sources of variation in the sentencing process. Then, after describing our data and methods, we present an analysis and interpretation of this model using structural equation models.

MODEL, METHOD AND DATA

The model we will examine here provides a structural perspective on what is often referred to as a labelling process. The label involved, of course, is the disposition imposed on the person convicted. Our population consists of the 1,832 adult felony convictions in the King County Superior Court in 1973 (Bayley, 1973), and our analyses are based on a systematic random sample of 504 cases obtained from the case files of the court. Our model, represented in figure 4.1, incorporates six classes of variables – offender-, offence-, and court-related characteristics, recommendations made to the judge, judge differences in the propensity for using particular sentences, and finally, the disposition ultimately imposed.

The model developed here conceptualizes sentencing as a *process*. This allows us not only to specify the influences of factors associated with differing perspectives as they occur temporally, but also to articulate complex linkages of variables reflecting different theoretical orientations as they impinge on one another. For example, although the sentencing literature (reviewed briefly above and in chapter 3) indicates that the effects of offender characteristics, e.g., race, net of offence-related factors (the so-called legal factors) are not overwhelmingly large in magnitude, it is still possible that these variables indirectly influence sentencing decisions through offence- and court-related factors. In viewing the effects of these variables in processual terms we are able to highlight the structurally relevant ways in which they are connected.

Reading figure 4.1 from left to right, causal consideration is given first to *offender* characteristics emphasized in the instrumental Marxist conflict perspective. Our data provide measures of a number of offender characteristics – age, education, occupation, marital status, race, sex, work history, and family integration. The first four of these variables were shown to be of little consequence for sentencing in a preliminary analysis using these data (Hewitt, 1975). The remaining four offender characteristics are included in the analysis presented here. Each of these variables is coded in binary form with the presumed disadvantaged level of the variable assigned the higher value (for example, for race, white = 0 and non-white = 1). The work history variable reflects stable vs. unstable employment, where an individual's work history is considered unstable if there were two or more periods of unemployment or one period of six or more months duration during the two years prior to conviction. In the class terms used elsewhere in this volume,

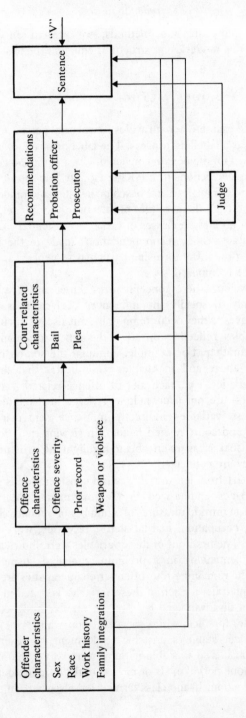

Figure 4.1 Determinants of sentencing

this identifies a surplus population. Family integration indicates whether the defendant had children for whom he or she was responsible, had ties with a family of origin, or was married and living with a spouse.

Second in the causal ordering depicted in figure 4.1 is the set of *offence* characteristics emphasized in the Durkheimian consensus perspective. The consensus model indicates that 'the application of sanctions reflects threats to the most basic values of the society' (McDonald, 1976). One such value strongly condemns the use of violence, and so the use of a weapon or violence in committing the alleged offense is included as a variable in our model. This variable is measured in binary form here, with the high value assigned to cases where a weapon or violence was used. In addition, the severity of the offence reflects basic social values, and we have incorporated this variable in the model developed. We use a ranking of the severity of the primary offence, with offences grouped into eight ordered categories.[1] Finally, the prior record of the convicted felon is incorporated in the model as a variable reflecting the offender's past threat to the fundamental values of society. This variable is measured as a simple count of the actual number of prior convictions.

The structural perspective considered in this chapter requires the inclusion of several *court-related* variables, seldom considered in research on the determinants of sentencing (but see Bernstein et al., 1977a). This set of factors is temporally subsequent to offender- and offence-related factors, but antecedent to the recommendation variables shown in figure 4.1. The offender's initial plea is included in the model on the expectation that the efficiency needs of the court organization require a penalty for those defendants who insist on the expense of a trial. This variable is measured in a binary form, with a high value assigned in those cases involving a guilty plea. The pre-trial release status (or bail status) of the offender is included in the model on the expectation that early professional judgement regarding the offender affects later organizational decisions. In this analysis release status is measured as a binary variable, with a high value assigned to cases released prior to the trial. Although a variety of legal and extra-legal factors are alleged to influence decisions about bail (Landes, 1974), the decision itself is not intended to influence the ultimate determination of sentence. A number of discussions (e.g., Matza, 1964) suggest, however, that expressions of professional judgement, wherever they occur in the process, are organizationally useful in the sentencing decision.

Our previous discussion emphasized the importance of the probation officer as the professional agent of individualization and the prosecutor as the more powerful agent of the state. In terms of our conceptual model the *recommendations* of these agents are hypothesized to be significant in the eventual disposition of sentence (see figure 4.1). The absolute and relative magnitudes of these influences, as well as the basis for the exercise of influence, indicate structural properties of the criminal court system. We have argued that the system of criminal justice involves a loosely coupled set of subsystems – which separately include the judge, the prosecutor and the probation officer – and we have maintained that, as a historical response to the needs of the individual offender, the role of the probation officer is largely ceremonial, preserving the myth of individualization in the court process in the face of a more powerful prosecutorial role. The probation officer is organizationally the most active participant in the sentencing process, engaged in extensive pre-sentence investigations and the preparation of elaborate pre-sentence reports; but we expect that this input is frequently muted. From a structural viewpoint this involves a *decoupling* of one subsystem, the probation department, from the ultimate decision, either by ignoring the officer's evaluation/recommendation, by weighing the recommendation lightly, or by not requesting a recommendation.

Previous research into the role of the probation officer (Carter and Wilkins, 1967; Hagan, 1975b) has considered probation officer influences in sentencing only in samples where pre-sentence reports have been requested. The present data, therefore, allow a broader assessment of the importance of the probation officer. Also, to the best of our knowledge, no previous research has measured the prosecutor's recommendation for sentence and assessed its relative impact. The net result of this omission is to underestimate the relative power of the prosecutor and thereby to help perpetuate the myth of individualization. Our anlysis seeks to take into account the extent to which the actions of these two agents – the prosecutor and the probation officer – are related.

The final source of variation depicted in the model in figure 4.1, the *judge*, allows another means of pursuing the issue of coupling. It may be recalled that one definition of loose coupling requires some evidence of independence or separateness among subsystems (Weick, 1976). Our model pursues this issue in two ways. First, we consider judge differences (this is the variable labeled 'Judge' in figure 4.1). It frequently is argued (cf., Carter and Wilkins) that probation officers make their recommendations to judges in a sycophantic manner, anticipating the predispositions of judges and recommending sentences accordingly. In order to examine this aspect of what is essentially the hypothesis of tight coupling, we developed a measure of the differential predisposition of each judge to award a particular sentence. We will briefly describe the methods we used. We first coded each of twenty judges in our sample as separate binary or 'dummy' variables.[2] Next, we regressed our sentence outcomes (described below) individually on this set of judge dummies and the offender-, offence- and court-related characteristics (but not the recommendation variables). The result of these regressions provided an effect for each judge which is interpretable as the likelihood of assigning a particular sentence, *independent of offender, offence- and court-related factors associated with a particular offender.* This effect was then assigned to the judge as a measure of predisposition to sentence in a particular way, independent of the characteristics of the case (offender, offence, and court). This variable is included in our model as a potential influence on the recommendations of the prosecutor and the probation officer, and we may thereby test the hypothesized influence of the judge on these recommendations.[3]

The second manner by which we pursue the issue of system coupling, insofar as the judge is concerned, involves the interpretation of the residual in our analysis. By definition, the residual (labeled "V" in figure 4.1) is independent of all measured variables which have been included in the model– offender-, offence-, and court-related factors, judge differences, and the probation and prosecution recommendations – and as such it may be interpreted as the individual power of the judge to affect the disposition of sentence. We term this the 'residual power of judge'. In a tightly coupled criminal justice system, the judge acts in concert with other subsystems (the probation and prosecution subsystems), and one would expect there to be relatively minor effects of the judge, i.e., little residual power. By contrast, in a less cohesive system – a loosely coupled system – the size of the residual may be large. A relatively large residual (i.e., a low coefficient of determination (R^2)), then, provides evidence of a loosely coupled system.

Finally, we use the severity of sentencing as the dependent variable in our model. Five categories of sentence were possible in the court system we study: (1) deferred sentence; (2) suspended sentence; (3) probation (no jail time); (4) probation with jail time; (5) incarceration. The deferred sentence, used in slightly over half of the cases, is clearly the least severe of the five categories. Persons given this sentence must satisfy a brief probationary period, but after these conditions are met the judge can erase all record of conviction. All other categories represent more severe forms of treatment. Given the even distribution of cases over this category vs. all others (0.54 vs. 0.46), we decided to use a binary variable representing this distiction, where cases receiving a deferred sentence were assigned a high value. At the opposite pole of the severity continuum is the incarceration sentence. This sentence differs from probation with jail time in both the length of confinement (incarceration sentences are for one or more years; jail time is less than one year) and the nature of the institutional confinement (incarceration involves confinement in the state prison or reformatory; jail time is served in the county jail). As an adjunct to the 'deferred' category we performed similar analyses using a binary variable based on the incarceration vs. all others distinction, where persons given an incarceration sentence were assigned a high value.

Our use of the extreme categories of sentencing in parallel analyses allows us to approximate a concept of sentence severity. If there is a single dimension of severity, we should expect to find similar effects of opposite signs for all our determinants of sentencing.[4] The use of binary dependent variables allows us to interpret regression coefficients for predictor variables as expected increments or decrements in the probability of receiving a particular sentence (for example, a deferred sentence).[5]

Our analysis makes use of structural equation models estimated by ordinary least squares. We estimate several sets of reduced-form equations for the sentence outcomes, beginning with the offender-related characteristics and adding groups of variables in sequence following the causal ordering portrayed in figure 4.1. For example, we first estimate a regression equation for 'deferred' sentence including the sex, race, work history and family integration variables, then we estimate an equation including these variables plus the offence characteristics, then one including offender, offence and court-related characteristics, and so on until all determinants of sentencing are included. This approach allows us to decompose the effects of all variables in the analysis into their direct and indirect effects (see Alwin and Hauser, 1975). This method permits us to trace the means by which a given variable exercises its effect, as well as an assessment of its relative importance compared to other variables. In addition, we examine in more detail the relative influences of the offender-, offence-, and court-related variables and judge differences on the recommendation variables. Although these may be inferred from the preceding analysis, this separate analysis will speak more directly to an important aspect of the loose coupling hypothesis, namely that subsystems which are loosely coupled respond to different influences (Glassman, 1973). To the extent, then, that prosecutors' and probation officers' recommendations depend on similar aspects of the case, the system may be viewed as tightly coupled; but, to the extent that they depend on different factors, the system can be viewed as loosely coupled.

FINDINGS

The descriptive univariate statistics for the variables in our analysis are given in table 4.1. Tables 4.2 and 4.3 present the reduced-form and structural coefficients (in both metric and standard form) for the two codings of the dependent variable. The first column of each table presents the regression of sentence on the offender characteristics viewed as important by instrumental conflict theorists – sex, race, work history, and family integration. The second column then adds the offence-related characteristics emphasized by the consensus perspective – the severity of the offence, the use of weapon or violence in the commission of the offence, and the offender's prior record. The third, fourth and fifth columns then add the variables we have associated with the structural view – first, the offender's plea and bail status; then (in the fourth column) the judge differences variable; and finally (in the fifth column) we add the prosecutor's and probation officer's recommendations. The coefficient associated with a variable in the first equation in which it appears is the variable's total effect. The differences in the coefficients in any two adjacent columns thereafter represent the indirect effects of variables in the prior column by way of variables added in the subsequent column. Finally, coefficients in column 5 are the direct effects of the variables (see Alwin and Hauser, 1975).

Our findings indicate that being female, white, having a stable work history and family ties increase the likelihood of a deferred sentence and reduce the likelihood of an incarceration sentence. All of these effects are judged to be statistically significant ($p < 0.05$). These effects are uniformly reduced when the variables suggested by the consensus perspective – offence severity, prior record and use of a weapon and violence – are introduced into the equation (column 2). For example, the effects of race are reduced by 63 and 51 per cent in tables 4.2 and 4.3 respectively, below statistical significance. This indicates that the white vs. non-white distinction affects the sentence a person receives because non-whites are more likely to be charged with more severe offences, more likely to have used violence in the offence, and more likely to have had a prior record of convictions; and these factors all influence the eventual sentence (especially prior record). In other words, the race effect is largely indirect. A similar observation may be made regarding the effects of being in the surplus population and to a lesser extent sex and family integration. The effects of sex on the deferred and incarceration sentences are reduced by 40 and 80 per cent respectively by removing their indirect effects through the offence-related variables. In the case of the deferred sentence, a statistically significant effect remains, and it is possible for us to state that, independent of the offence characteristics, being female increases one's likelihood of receiving a deferred sentence by 15 per cent. It is also worth noting that being in a stable family increases the likelihood of a deferred sentence by 12 per cent, net of offence factors, and decreases the likelihood of incarceration by 10 per cent. Since there is considerable uncertainty about the legal versus extra-legal meaning of variables like prior record (see Farrell and Swigert, 1978b), it is not possible to say whether the effects of such variables as being in the surplus population are here legal or extra-legal.

The offence-related variables all affect the sentencing outcome in some way, controlling for offender characteristics. The most sizeable effect is that associated with prior record: the likelihood of receiving an incarceration is

TABLE 4.1 Descriptive statistic for variables in analysis-convicted felony cases, King County, Washington, 1973 (N = 504)

Variable	X	S
Sex	0.794	0.405
Race	0.675	0.469
Work	0.287	0.453
Family	0.724	0.447
Severity of offence	3.355	2.333
Weapon or violence	0.153	0.360
Prior record	0.352	0.478
Plea	0.879	0.326
Bail	0.762	0.426
Judge-deferred sentence	0.369	0.075
Judge-incarceration sentence	0.466	0.053
Probation recommendation-deferred sentence	0.425	0.495
Probation recommendation-incarceration sentence	0.095	0.294
Prosecutor recommendation-deferred sentence	0.377	0.485
Prosecutor recommendation-incarcertaion sentence	0.214	0.411
Sentence-deferred	0.538	0.499
Sentence-incarceration	0.149	0.356

14 per cent greater for persons with one prior conviction, and the likelihood of a deferred sentence for such persons is 43 per cent less than persons with no prior record. The use of a weapon or violence increases the likelihood of an incarceration sentence by 19 per cent and decreases the likelihood of a deferred sentence by 13 per cent. The severity of the primary offence charged is much less important than the prior offence variable for the deferred sentence, but about equal in its effect on incarceration. Offenders whose offences differ by as much as one standard deviation on our offence severity scale (2.3) differ by only 4.5 and 6.5 in their resulting likelihoods of receiving deferred and incarceration sentences respectively.

Our findings up to this point provide some evidence for both the instrumental Marxist emphasis on offender characteristics and the Durkheimian consensus emphasis on offence-related factors. But more significantly, our results illustrate the interdependence of both sets of factors in affecting sentencing. Specifically, we note that the offender characteristics measured here depend on the offence-related factors to transmit their effects, or stated in another way, variation in the offence-related factors depends to some extent on the offender characteristics. We must also note, however, that while both perspectives suggest important variables, the combination of the

TABLE 4.2 *Reduced form and structural equations for deferred sentences-convicted felony cases, King County, Washington, 1973 (N = 504)*

	(1)	(2)	(3)	(4)	(5)
A *Metric*					
Sex	− 0.258[a]	− 0.153[a]	− 0.134[a]	− 0.135[a]	− 0.082[a]
Race	0.103[a]	0.038	0.023	0.025	0.047
Work	0.166[a]	0.064	0.019	0.027	0.001
Family	0.189[a]	0.124[a]	0.082[a]	0.071	0.054
Offence		− 0.019	− 0.012	− 0.012	− 0.013
Weapon		− 0.134[a]	− 0.045	− 0.050	0.044
Record		− 0.426[a]	− 0.360[a]	− 0.354[a]	− 0.172[a]
Plea			0.151[a]	0.164[a]	0.073
Bail			0.303[a]	0.298[a]	0.184[a]
Judge				0.998[a]	0.956[a]
Probation recommendation					0.153[a]
Prosecutor recommendation					0.416[a]
Intercept	0.489	0.758	0.372	0.759	− 0.150
B *Standard form*					
Sex	− 0.209[a]	− 0.124[a]	− 0.108[a]	− 0.109[a]	− 0.067[a]
Race	0.097[a]	0.036	0.022	0.023	0.045
Work	0.151[a]	0.058	0.018	0.025	0.001
Family	0.170[a]	0.111[a]	0.074[a]	0.064	0.049
Offence		− 0.087	− 0.056	− 0.055	− 0.061
Weapon		− 0.097[a]	− 0.032	− 0.036	0.032
Record		− 0.408[a]	− 0.345[a]	− 0.338[a]	− 0.166[a]
Plea			0.099[a]	0.107[a]	0.048
Bail			0.259[a]	0.254[a]	0.158[a]
Judge				0.150[a]	0.145[a]
Probation recommendation					0.152[a]
Prosecutor recommendation					0.404[a]
R^2	0.125	0.304	0.365	0.387	0.537

[a] Significant at 0.05 level.

two sets of variables does not account for a majority of the variation in sentence severity: the R^2s are 0.304 and 0.226.

Columns 3, 4 and 5 of tables 4.2 and 4.3 bring us to a consideration of the variables we have associated with a structural view of sentencing. Taking first the court-related factors (see column 3), it is clear that plea and bail have notable effects on sentence severity. Holding the offender and offence characteristics constant, a guilty plea increases the likelihood of a deferred sentence by 15 per cent and decreases the likelihood of an incarceration

TABLE 4.3 *Reduced-form and structural equations for incarceration sentences-convicted felony cases, King County, Washington, 1973 (N = 504))*

	(1)	(2)	(3)	(4)	(5)
A *Metric*					
Sex	0.091[a]	0.018	0.001	− 0.006	− 0.025
Race	− 0.094[a]	− 0.046	− 0.029	− 0.034	− 0.006
Work	− 0.115[a]	− 0.064[a]	− 0.026	− 0.032	− 0.034
Family	− 0.126[a]	− 0.095[a]	− 0.063[a]	− 0.075[a]	− 0.062[a]
Offence		0.028[a]	0.022[a]	0.022[a]	0.021[a]
Weapon		0.190[a]	0.109[a]	0.107[a]	− 0.008
Record		0.138[a]	0.078[a]	0.076[a]	0.019
Plea			− 0.189[a]	− 0.169[a]	− 0.069[a]
Bail			− 0.253[a]	− 0.253[a]	− 0.114[a]
Judge				1.002[a]	0.803[a]
Probation recommendation					0.259[a]
Prosecutor recommendation					0.377[a]
Intercept	0.265	0.082	0.462	− 0.001	− 0.180
B *Standard form*					
Sex	0.103[a]	0.020	0.001	− 0.007	− 0.029
Race	− 0.124[a]	− 0.061	− 0.039	− 0.045	− 0.008
Work	− 0.146[a]	− 0.081[a]	− 0.033	− 0.041	− 0.043
Family	− 0.158[a]	− 0.119[a]	− 0.079[a]	− 0.094[a]	− 0.078[a]
Offence		0.182[a]	0.143[a]	0.144[a]	0.139[a]
Weapon		0.192[a]	0.110[a]	0.108[a]	− 0.009
Record		0.185[a]	0.105[a]	0.101[a]	0.025
Plea			− 0.173[a]	− 0.155[a]	− 0.063[a]
Bail			− 0.304[a]	− 0.303[a]	− 0.137[a]
Judge				0.149[a]	0.119[a]
Probation recommendation					0.213[a]
Prosecutor recommendation					0.435[a]
R^2	0.089	0.226	0.327	0.348	0.549

[a] Significant at 0.05 level.

sentence by 19 per cent. Similarly, a released status increases the likelihood of a deferred sentence by 30 per cent and reduces the chances of incarceration by 25 per cent. The court-related factors mediate some of the influence of the prior variables. Of particular note is the fact that about two-thirds of the effect of the use of a weapon or violence on deferred sentence is mediated by plea and bail, while slightly less than half of the effect on incarceration sentence is so mediated. About 16 per cent of the effect of prior record on deferred sentence and about 45 per cent of its effect on incarceration is mediated by plea and bail. While this does not provide a complete interpretation of the effects mediated by these court-related factors, we have summarized the important indirect effects. We should reiterate that ideally plea and bail status should have no impact on sentencing. The fact that they have moderately strong effects not only assists us in the interpretation of the effects of prior variables, but underscores the importance of structural factors for sentencing as well.

In column 4 of tables 4.2 and 4.3 we have introduced the variable which measures the judge's predisposition to sentence in a particular way. The metric coefficients for this variable in these tables are not interpretable, because of the way we have constructed the variable. The standardized coefficients are interpretable as the square roots of the proportions of variance in the sentence outcome which lie between judges after the offender, offence and court characteristics have been controlled. Squaring the standardized coefficients gives the proportions of variance attributable to judge differences, about 2 per cent in either case. More importantly, however, we wish to examine the extent to which the recommendations of prosecutors and probation officers depend on the known predispositions of judges to sentence in particular ways. By comparing the judge effects which are recorded in columns 4 and 5 of the tables we are provided with the first evidence of loose coupling among the court subsystems. The very small reductions in the coefficients associated with the judge variable with the introduction of the two recommendation variables indicates that judge differences can account for very little of the variation in the recommendations they receive from either the probation officer or the prosecutor. This finding is in sharp contrast to the frequent suggestion that such recommendations are simply a formality. This suggestion is also contradicted by the effects of the probation officer and the prosecutor recommendations recorded in column 5 of the tables. With all other variables held constant, a positive recommendation of a deferred sentence by the prosecutor increases the likelihood of such a sentence by 42 per cent, while a prosecutor's recommendation of an incarceration sentence increases the likelihood of incarceration by nearly 38 per cent. The comparable figures for probation officers' recommendations are 15 and 26 per cent. It is clear from this that the prosecution's recommendation is more powerful than the probation department's recommendation. Thus, in spite of the attention given by the courts to the philosophy of individualization at the institutional level, and despite the introduction of this philosophy into the court through the profession of probation, it remains that the principal agent of the state's interest in mass processing, the prosecutor, exercises the dominant influence on sentencing. We interpret the relative importance of these two factors in terms of the myth and ceremony surrounding the notion of individualization and the participation of probation workers in the pre-sentencing process.

By incorporating the variables suggested by the structural perspective into the equations for sentencing we have substantially improved the explained variance: R^2s of 0.537 and 0.549 for deferred and incarceration sentences respectively. The relative improvements may be gauged by comparing these R^2s with those obtained before introducing the structural variables – the unique contributions of the entire set of structural variables are 0.233 and 0.323 for deferred and incarceration sentences respectively. Even though we can explain slightly over one-half of the variance in the sentencing outcomes with the array of variables measured in the present research, unmeasured factors unique to each case, termed here the residual discretionary power of the judge, also have a strong effect on the sentence outcome. The residual path coefficients for column 5 of the tables are 0.680 and 0.671 for the deferred and incarceration sentences. Given the specification of our model as a relatively complete accounting of the known determinants of sentencing, we have few alternatives but to interpret this residual in terms of the judge's influence. However, this also provides evidence for the hypothesis of a loosely coupled system of criminal justice. Although the probation officer and especially the prosecutor are significant influences on the judge's decision, the major influences on the judge's decision are unrelated to these recommendations. Compare, for example, the standardized (path) coefficients for the probation officer, the prosecutor, judge differences, and 'within' judge factors. In the case of the deferred sentence they are 0.152, 0.404, 0.145 and 0.680; and in the case of the incarceration sentence they are: 0.213, 0.435, 0.119 and 0.671. There is little doubt that, measured in terms of factors which affect the sentencing decisions of judges, the criminal court system is a loosely coupled structure.

Our final task is to assess the different bases of influence on the recommendations of the prosecutor and the probation officer. The recommendations of these two subsystems are potentially responsive to different sets of factors, and to the extent this occurs, these subsystems may be described as loosely coupled. Table 4.4 presents the regressions of deferred and incarceration sentences on all the prior variables – offender, offence, court-related characteristics, and judge differences. Generally, comparing the metric coefficients for both dependent variables reveals that the prosecutors give somewhat more attention to both offence and court factors than do probation officers, but neither appears to be overly sensitive to the attributes of the offender (although the prosecutor is more likely to recommend a deferred sentence for females, other things being equal). These findings suggest some correspondence in factors which influence the recommendations of these agents of the system, but with one distinctively important theoretical difference. The offender's plea has a statistically significant impact on the prosecutor's recommendation, increasing the

TABLE 4.4 *Structural equations for probation officers' and prosecutors' recommendations, deferred and incarceration sentences-convicted felony cases, King County, Washington, 1973 (N = 504)*

	Probation officers' recommendations		Prosecutors' recommendations	
	Metric	Standard	Metric	Standard
A Deferred sentences				
Sex	− 0.077	− 0.062	− 0.097	0.081[a]
Work	0.054	0.049	0.043	0.040
Race	− 0.015	− 0.014	− 0.049	− 0.047
Family	0.057	0.051	− 0.021	0.018
Offence	− 0.001	− 0.001	− 0.003	0.015
Record	− 0.280[a]	− 0.270[a]	− 0.333[a]	− 0.326[a]
Weapon	− 0.168[a]	− 0.123[a]	− 0.163[a]	− 0.121[a]
Plea	0.107	0.071	0.177[a]	0.119[a]
Bail	0.197[a]	0.169[a]	0.199[a]	0.175[a]
Judge	0.485	0.074	− 0.801	− 0.012
	Intercept = 0.140 R^2 = 0.230		Intercept = 0.312 R^2 = 0.270	
B Incarceration sentences				
Sex	0.006	0.008	0.046	0.045
Work	− 0.011	− 0.016	0.011	0.012
Race	− 0.053	− 0.084	− 0.039	− 0.044
Family	0.014	0.022	− 0.044	− 0.048
Offence	0.003	0.021	0.001	0.002
Record	0.038	0.062	0.125	0.145[a]
Weapon	0.135	0.166[a]	0.213	0.187[a]
Plea	− 0.037	− 0.040	− 0.241	− 0.191[a]
Bail	− 0.142	− 0.206[a]	− 0.270	− 0.281[a]
Judge	− 0.087	− 0.016	0.587	0.076
	Intercept = 0.257 R^2 = 0.140		Intercept = 0.300 R^2 = 0.301	

[a] Significant at 0.05 level.

likelihood of a deferred sentence by 18 per cent and decreasing the chance of incarceration by 24 per cent. The plea variable, however, has no significant effect on the probation officer's recommendation. This difference is very likely due to the prosecutor's sensitivity to the structural need to encourage the efficient resolution of cases, a sensitivity which leads the prosecutor to reward those who assist in meeting efficiency demands by pleading guilty. It is this pressure toward efficiency and the mass production of cases that undercuts the court's commitment to individualization and makes it more likely that the probation officer's recommendation for sentence is a ceremony in service of a myth.

DISCUSSION AND CONCLUSIONS

Contemporary theories of crime and punishment often assume a tight fit between structure and function in the criminal courts. Instrumental Marxian theory often asserts that the criminal courts serve the interests of the rich by directly oppressing the poor, while the Durkheimian consensus perspective assumes that a more even-handed enforcement of law functions to preserve values that members of society share in common. The present analysis, like most of its predecessors, fails to provide strong support for these viewpoints. We have argued that the assumption of a tight fit between structure and function is a key source of error in these earlier models, offering in their place a view of criminal justice decision-making as the product of a loosely coupled system.

One of the sources of loose coupling in the criminal justice system is the historical shift from a classical to a positivist philosophy of crime and punishment. Positivism focused new attention on the social needs of individual offenders as represented in the call for a new, individualized justice. The emergence of the probation profession and the involvement of probation offficers in the pre-sentencing process are the structural products of this philosophical change, providing a new source of legitimation for the activities of the court. However, the goals of court efficiency and individualization are contradictory. One means of resolving this contradiction involves the decoupling of probation work from much of the courts' decision-making, substituting the influence of the prosecutor for that of the probation officer in the pre-sentencing process. The prosecutor's distinctive impact on the sentencing process reflects the court system's need to reward and punish offender compliance in efficiently resolving cases. Meanwhile, the maintenance of the formal involvement of probation officers in the pre-sentencing process allows perpetuation of the myth of individualization, if only in a ceremonial form.

We have discussed at length the implications of loose coupling, and we offer some final comments on the possible consequences of tight coupling. Criminal justice systems are formally hierarchical in their organization, and under conditions of tight coupling, then, such systems are likely to find their direction from the top. Marxist theory correctly warns of the potential implications of such a situation, emphasizing the point that law can become an instrument of coercion used by a ruling class, and/or a source of protection for that class. In view of our findings, the greatest threat of such an outcome may lie in the prosecutor's influence increasing in undesired or undesirable ways, through a unique and tighter coupling to the judiciary. We have seen some evidence of this kind of tighter coupling in the preceding chapters: in the highly politicized sentencing of black big dealers in drug cases and in the prosecution and sentencing of lower level managers rather than their employers in cases of securities violations. It is therefore important to emphasize that the alternative to the system of ceremonial justice we have described, involving a more proactive and tightly coupled system, is not *necessarily* a type of justice that many of us would ideally prefer. A better match between preference and performance in the field of crime and punishment must await a clearer understanding of the articulation of the organizational units we optimistically designate 'the criminal justice system'.

NOTES

1 Thirty different offences were recorded in the sample. These were initially categorized into eight categories according to the nature and severity of the offence as follows: (a) crimes against the person I (manslaughter, rape, and personal assault); (b) crimes against the person II (robbery and attempted robbery); (c) property crimes I (burglary and attempted burglary); (d) property crimes II (auto theft, arson, and the destruction of property); (e) property crimes III (forgergy, credit theft, and credit card forgery); (f) property crimes IV (grand larceny and attempted grand larceny); (g) violation of the Uniform Controlled Substances Act (drug violations); and (h) all other offences (carnal knowledge, soliciting a minor, violations of firearms laws, professional gambling, sodomy, bestiality, and criminal trespass). These categories were constructed to parallel as closely as possible those developed by Rossi et al. (1974). However, because differences in the primary data make this comparison uncertain, we undertook an additional empirical assessment of our categorization. The offence categories were ordered by ranking them first in terms of their likelihood of receiving a particular sentence disposition (see text). The average rank over the four sentence outcomes was used to order the categories (we combined sentence categories ii and iii for these purposes). The resulting ranking appears to confirm our theoretical inferences in that the ordering deduced from Rossi et al. persists. This ranking is as follows (beginning with the least severe):

1 Drug violations (1.5)
2 Property crimes IV (3.0)
3 Property crimes III (3.5)
4 Other offences (4.5)
5 Property crimes II (4.7)
6 Property crimes I (5.25)
7 Crimes against the person II (6.25)
8 Crimes against the person I (7.25).

It is worth noting that in terms of explaining variation in the dependent variables used in the present analysis, this variable performs as well as the use of a set of dummy variables representing the eight categories of offence.

2 There were actually more than thirty judges in the sample, but only twenty judges had ten or more cases in our sample. Those judges having fewer than ten cases were assigned to a common category which served as the 'omitted category' in our regression analyses described here (see text).

3 We have essentially used an analysis of covariance model (see Fennessey, 1968) to adjust the judge means for differences in offender, offence, and court variables. Then, the resulting 'adjusted means' are assigned to individual cases to represent the differences in judges' propensities for using a particular sentence. Our method is analogous to methods used to assess school context effects (see Alwin, 1976).

4 We should qualify this statement to take into account the fact that our recommendation variables in an equation for a given dependent variable correspond to the sentence represented by the dependent variable. For example, where 'deferred sentence' is the dependent variable the two recommendation variables index the prosecutor's and probation officer's recommendations of a deferred sentence ('1' if yes, '0' if no). So, the signs of the coefficients for the recommendation variables will be positive regardless of the dependent variable of concern.

5 Other analytic solutions may be found in limited-dependent variable approaches, in polytomous dependent variable approaches, or in multiple discriminant analysis.

5

Race, Class and the Perception of Criminal Injustice

INTRODUCTION

The meaning of criminal justice, like the meaning of crime, is symbolic and variable. Criminal justice is *symbolic* in that the criminal law and its enforcement are expected to embody fundamental principles in our society. Criminal justice is *variable* in that these symbols and principles are varied, both in their legal conception and in their public perception. Philosophers, from Plato and Aristotle to Rawls (1971), have fought these facts by searching for those elusive principles that could give the idea of justice absolute meaning. They have failed because conceptions and perceptions of justice are determined in large part by the times, places, and positions in the social structure from which they are derived (Nettler, 1979: 28–31). This does not mean that there are no standards by which criminal justice can be measured or that criminal justice itself is standardless. However, it does suggest that our standards of criminal justice, such as 'equality before the law', will be ambiguously and impermanently conceived, as well as variably perceived.

For example, Nettler (1979: 30) is able to identify three common meanings of equality (numerical, proportional and subjective equality), all of which are regarded as important in some form of legal behaviour. Nettler goes on to draw an important connection between social change and criminal justice by noting that the specific meaning of equality as applied in the pursuit of justice often varies with consideration of the vantage point. Thus in an earlier era when laws involving the crimes of women and children developed in this country, an *assumption* of subjective equality (or equity) dictated that unequal treatment be mandated by legislation for what were then regarded as unequal members of society. Although these laws often encouraged differential leniency, and although they were justified as 'protective', they perpetuated symbolically an unequal status for women and children. Today as women, and sometimes children, are recognized as equals, equal treatment (numerical equality) is also demanded, and the older laws in turn are now more likely to be regarded as 'discriminatory'.

Sociologists interested in studying criminal justice have responded typically to the situation above by trying to make the existing law explicit and by then attempting to expose disparities between legal statutes and legal behaviour. An example of this approach includes the large and expanding literature that looks for systematic links between the status characteristics of criminal offenders and the sentences they receive. Much of this work has included an effort to test a conflict theory of crime. The results are inconsistent; while there are a variety of studies that find little (e.g., Bernstein et al., 1977a) or no (e.g., Chiricos and Waldo, 1975) relationship between status characteristics and sentencing, there are also a few that find these relationships to be significant (e.g., Swigert and Farrell, 1977; Lizotte, 1978) and others that find these relationships to be contingent on particular circumstances (e.g., Hagan, Nagel and Albonetti, 1980). In response to such studies, conflict theorists increasingly concede the point that relationships between status characteristics and court outcomes are neither as large nor as consistent as is frequently assumed. Indeed they have sometimes argued that such findings are actually quite consistent with the theory, suggesting that 'discrimination is not only in principle unnecessary but also likely to be counterproductive in contributing to the demystification of the structure of legal control' (Turk, 1976: 292) and that 'ruling classes have a general interest in promulgating and reproducing the stability of the social order as a *whole*, and . . . an important way of achieving this is by somehow ensuring that the severity of sanctions *ought* not significantly to be correlated with social class' (Beirne, 1979: 378, emphasis in original).

One might be tempted to infer from the research above that the symbols of criminal justice are reasonably intact in American society. This kind of inference is further encouraged by a different kind of research designed to measure crime seriousness. The pioneering work in this area is Sellin and Wolfgang's (1964) scaling of 141 criminal offences in terms of public rankings of their seriousness. Part of the initial motivation for this work was probably Sellin's (1938) early appreciation of the potential role of conflict in the definition of crime. More recently, researchers (Rossi, Waite and Berk, 1974; Thomas, 1976; Newman, 1976) interested in testing conflict hypotheses about crime have used similar measurement strategies to determine if significant class, race, and other divisions exist in public rankings of crime seriousness. The implicit assumption has been that if group-linked variations in public rankings were found that diverged from the penalties imposed by criminal statutes, this would signal a way in which the criminal law is used unjustly by some groups to impose their interests and values on others. However, research in this tradition has failed to find substantial group-linked differences in public rankings of crime seriousness. Indeed, from Sellin and Wolfgang to Newman, the data suggest rather remarkable levels of societal agreement, and it has been demonstrated more recently that these seriousness rankings correlate well with the severity of sentences received by convicted offenders (Blumstein and Cohen, 1980). Conflict theorists have responded by arguing that these findings actually are consistent with the theory. Thus Turk (1976: 289) suggests that 'a high degree of consensus on the relative seriousness of crimes can be interpreted as evidence of the successful control and mobilization of ideological resources so as to minimize the divergence of beliefs otherwise expected to result from social inequalities.' Similarly, Michalowski and Bohlander (1976) speak of a 'false consensus' (97) and argue that 'sub-groups tend to agree upon what is serious, not because this definition serves their own or society's interests but because it is difficult to understand a social creation such as crime outside the social context in which it is presented' (105).

The arguments above make conflict theory difficult to test (see also Hagan and Leon, 1977). More important, however, this form of argument may be interpreted as conceding more than it should. Uniformity in criminal justice decision-making cannot be demonstrated to exist apart from an unambiguous knowledge of what the legal standards of these decisions should be. Knowledge of these legal standards requires a clear division between legal and extra-legal variables in these decisions. Bernstein et al. (1977b: 367) identify three obstacles to this division:

First, there is considerable variation from one jurisdiction to another in the procedural law that stipulates what factors are legal versus those that are extra-legal in criminal justice decisions. Second, what is specified in a statute as legal for one stage of criminal justice processing may not be legal for another stage, e.g., community ties (flight risk) is generally a legal consideration for pre-trial release status decisions, but not for plea bargaining or sentencing decisions. Third, some variables ordinarily placed in the 'legal' category (e.g., prior record of convictions) may themselves have resulted from some combination of consideration of legal and extra-legal variables in some prior processing.

Similarly, no widespread 'false consensus' can be known to exist apart from a demonstration that various publics in some more general way actually perceive the operations of our criminal justice system to be just. A correspondence between public estimations of crime seriousness and legal sanctions is only a part of this requirement (Turk, 1976). It is not clear that critics of conflict theory have claimed more than this.

Meanwhile, the irony is that no one has analysed public *perceptions* of criminal injustice and assessed the capacity of conflict theory to explain them. Claims of criminal injustice represent a significant form of conflict because they raise fundamental doubts about the operational meaning of principles (like equality before the law) on which democratic societies are based. This chapter seeks to determine how race and class positions, among other variables, may organize the expression of this conflict. In doing this, we will make the further point that criminologists have not appropriately operationalized the concept of class or developed a clear understanding of the relationship between class and race in the determination of crime-related conflicts. An analysis of race, class, and the perception of criminal injustice is an appropriate place to begin this work.

THE DATA

The data for this study come from a national survey designed to measure perceptions of, and experience with, local, state, and federal courts, as well as more general attitudes toward the administration of justice and legal actors. The study was conducted by Yankelovich, Skelly and White Inc. (1977), under the direction of the National Center for State Courts, for the Law Enforcement Assistance Administration of the US Department of Justice. The study is based on interviews conducted between October and December 1977 with a single-stage, stratified, replicated random sample of Americans 18 years of age and older (for a more detailed discussion of the sampling procedures, see Inter-University Consortium for Political and Social Research (IUCPSR) (1979: ii–v). Analyses reported in this paper involve 1,049 persons for whom a head of household was known to be employed and on whom occupational information was available, and fifty-nine persons for whom a head of household was known to be unemployed and *not* retired or a student or a housewife. These constraints were imposed so that all persons considered in this study could be classified in terms of class position. We have introduced these data here because they are central to the following discussion of the concepts and indicators that organize our research.

A RELATIONAL MEASURE OF CLASS

Although the concept of class is central to conflict theories of crime and criminal justice (Chambliss and Seidman, 1971; Quinney, 1975; Taylor, Walton and Young, 1973; Turk, 1969b), little attention has been given by conflict criminologists to the actual operationalization of this concept. As we have noted in earlier chapters, however, Marxist scholars have begun to operationalize the concept of class for more general purposes. No single prevailing Marxian measure of class has emerged from this work, and there are several reasons to doubt that one will. First, Wright (1980: 323) points out that 'while class is perhaps the pivotal concept within Marxist theory, Marx himself never provides a systematic definition of class.' Second, there appears to be widespread agreement among Marxists that class categories cannot be made exact. Sweezy (1953: 24) makes this point when he suggests that 'it would be a mistake to think of a class as perfectly homogeneous internally and sharply marked off from other classes. Actually there is variety within the classes; and one class sometimes shades off very gradually and almost imperceptibly into another.' Third, there seems to be no urgency among Marxists to come to a resolution of this issue. Braverman (1974: 409) suggests that such an issue 'cannot always be solved neatly and definitively, nor, it should be added, does science require that it must be solved'.

The approach we take to measurement of class is informed by Marxian ideas. For example, it begins with a premise noted repeatedly in this book and that probably all Marxists accept: that classes are to be defined in relational rather than in gradational terms (Wright 1980: 325). The point is that the classes we consider are not simply conceived as 'above' or 'below' one another; instead, these classes are defined in terms of their social relation to one another, with each class representing a common structural position within the social organization of work relations.

We use three conceptual criteria to distinguish four class positions. The three conceptual criteria considered are ownership of the means of production, relationship to the means of production, and relationship to labour power. The four class positions are employers, the professional-managerial class, the working class, and unemployed workers, whom, as elsewhere in this book, we call the surplus population. The relationships between the conceptual criteria and class positions are presented in Table 5.1. A discussion of each class in terms of these criteria follows.

Employers are first of all *owners* of the means of production, as indicated by an answer of yes to a survey item, 'Do you now own a business?' Second, their relationship to the means of production is classified as *accumulative* on the basis of our knowledge that they are owners of a business and that the occupation of the head of household falls within one of these survey categories: official, proprietor, manager, or professional. Use of this occupational information eliminates from our employer category persons who own their own businesses but are engaged in clerical, sales, service, or other kinds of skilled and unskilled labouring activities, such as crafts; these respondents are categorized as members of the petty bourgeoisie who have very little opportunity to accumulate capital. (We do not consider the latter class in our analysis because Marxists typically argue that 'the petty bourgeoisie represents a remnant from an earlier era of capitalist development and, as a class, . . . is progressively becoming less important' (Wright and

TABLE 5.1 *Criteria for class categories*

	Ownership of means of production	Relation to means of production	Relation to labour power	Distribution
Employers	Owner	Accumulative	Buys labour	7.7% (85)
Professional-managerial class (PMC)	Non-owner	Reproductive	Sells labour	27.8% (308)
Working class	Non-owner	Productive and unproductive	Sells labour	59.2% (656)
Surplus population	Non-owner	Unproductive	Unable to sell labour	5.3% (59)

Perrone, 1977: 43).) Third, employers are identified as *buyers of labour power*, an inference drawn from the fact that it is virtually impossible to be an official, proprietor, manager, or professional and to own your own business without employing labour power beyond your own. Defined this way, employers constitute 7.7 per cent (N = 85) of our sample. This figure is within a few decimal percentage points of a class category of the same name measured in a somewhat different way by Wright (1978; also Wright and Perrone, 1977). We refer to the occupants of this class position as 'employers' rather than 'capitalists' because most of the persons in this type of category employ fewer than ten workers (Wright, 1978: 1370).

Our second class category, the professional-managerial class (PMC), is drawn from the work of the Ehrenreichs (1978; see also Walker, 1978), who define this class 'as consisting of salaried mental workers who do not own the means of production and whose major function in the social division of labour may be described broadly as the reproduction of capitalist class relations' (12). This definition is readily translated into our criteria. First, members of the PMC are identified as *non-owners* on the basis of their answers to the question about business ownership. Second, they are identified occupationally as officials, proprietors, managers, or professionals and (as non-owners) assumed to be in a *reproductive* relationship to the means of production; that is, they are assumed to be much more involved in the co-ordination and control of the social relationships necessary for capitalist production than in the creation of these relationships or in the actual production of commodities. Finally, members of the PMC are classified as *sellers of labour* on the basis of an item indicating that they are employed and our previous knowledge that they are not owners of businesses. Defined in this way, the PMC constitutes 27.8 per cent (N =

308) of our sample. The Ehrenreichs' own estimate is that this class makes up 20–25 per cent of the population.

Our third class category is the working class. Members of this class obviously are also *non-owners* of the means of production, as indicated by the business ownership item. The relationship of this class to the means of production is classified as *productive or unproductive* on the basis of its members' identification occupationally as being involved in skilled and unskilled labouring activities, including being craftsmen and foremen, or in clerical, sales, and service work. While the former occupations are productive in the sense of creating use value, the latter are not. Finally, workers are identified as *sellers of labour* in the same manner as the PMC, the difference being that the workers' occupations are not reproductive in character. Defined in this way, the working class constituted 59.2 per cent (N = 656) of our sample. The Ehrenreichs' (1978: 14) own estimate is that 65–70 per cent of the American population is working class. However, when Wright (1980: 368) operationalizes the Ehrenreichs' definition, he arrives at an estimate of the working class as 63.1 per cent of the population, while Wright's own operational definition of working-class membership yields an estimate of 41.6 per cent. He then points out deficiencies in his own definition and concludes that a more meaningful estimate might be 55 per cent (368n.). Our figure is close to this.

Surprisingly, recent Marxist operationalizations of class structure (e.g., Wright, 1978; Wright and Perrone, 1977; Robinson and Kelly, 1979) have not included consideration of unemployed workers. This is ironic because Marx (1912: pt. 7) attached great importance to this 'surplus population' in developing his General Law of Capitalist Accumulation, and because Marxists more generally (see Zeitlin, 1967: chapter 4) have regarded this grouping as crucial to the changing character of class relations. Marxian criminologists have recently noted the significance of this category in terms of the problems of regulation presented by this class and the consequences of these regulatory problems in terms of crime and criminal-justice-related conflicts. Carter and Clelland (1979: 98–9; see also Spitzer, 1975; Balkan, Berger and Schmidt, 1980: chapter 3) make these points in arguing that 'the very system which creates this "surplus population" . . . generates massive discontent. . . . Because such shifts are basic threats to the political economy of capitalism, the capitalist state is faced with the problem of the regulation of surplus labour. This problem is accommodated by the increasing intervention of formal systems of social control, criminal and juvenile courts, into the private socio-cultural life of the marginal fractions of the working class.'

Implicit in this statement is a use of the concept of class that is closer to the purposes of Marx than are the recent quantitative studies of income inequality. For Marx, the concept of class was first and foremost an analytic tool for explaining structural change in the capitalist system. Crucial to the prospect of structural change in the Marxian scheme is the emergence of class consciousness. A common response of the surplus population to their presumed position *vis-à-vis* the criminal justice system could be taken as one important indication of class consciousness. Quinney (1980: ix) argues that 'the future of criminal justice will be determined by changes in the objective conditions of the last stages of capitalism and by a rising consciousness, especially among that expanding portion of the working class now relegated to the status of surplus population.' We will be particularly attentive in this chapter to the possibility of the surplus population showing signs of being such a 'class for itself'.

Thus the last category in our classification consists of unemployed workers, whom as elsewhere in this volume we call the surplus population. The surplus population consists of *non-owners* of the means of production, as indicated by our business ownership question; they are *unproductive*, as indicated by the fact that they are not actively involved in any occupational category; and they are *unable to sell their labour*, as indicated by their designation as unemployed. Defined in this way, the surplus population constitutes 5.3 per cent (N = 59) of our sample.

RACE AND OTHER CONFLICT VARIABLES

Conflict theorists have not focused on class alone (e.g., Collins, 1975; Turk, 1977). For this reason we will consider other status positions of our respondents in terms of their race, education, income, region, age, sex and area of residence as well. Among the latter variables, race is expected to be salient. The history of conflict between black and white Americans is manifest, as is the connection of that conflict to crime issues (e.g., Wolfgang and Cohen, 1970) and criminal justice (e.g., Wolfgang and Reidel, 1973). Our sample is limited to black and white Americans, and race is coded as a dummy variable, with blacks coded 1. The assumption is that blacks are much more likely than whites to perceive criminal injustice.

Collins (1971; 1975; 1979) makes the case for conflict among educational status groups. He argues that education transmits status culture by providing instruction in styles of speech, dress, taste, manners, and so forth that are later translated into occupational placement: 'The mechanism proposed is that employers use education to select persons who have been socialized into the dominant status culture: for entrants to their own managerial ranks, into elite culture; for lower employees, into an attitude of respect for the dominant culture and the elite which carries it' (1971: 1011). From this perspective, education should diminish perceptions of criminal injustice. We have operationalized education as a quasi-credential scale in which 1 = postgraduate college, 2 = graduated college, 3 = some college, 4 = graduated high school, 5 = some high school, and 6 = grade school or less.

Income is an obvious conflict variable, often accorded a dependent position in conflict analyses. In this study, income is treated as an independent variable, and it is measured as total family income. Families with incomes of less than $5,000 are coded 8, those with incomes to $7,499 are coded 7, those with incomes to $9,999 are coded 6, and so on in $5,000 intervals up to an income of $35,000 or more, which is coded 1. To the extent that income influences the perception of criminal injustice, lower incomes might be expected to increase this perception.

The South is a unique region in American society, with its own particular history of conflict, aggravated by its rapid development under agrarian capitalism, its Civil War defeat and subsequent underdevelopment, and its 'rotten borough' role in the national Democratic party (Hamilton, 1972). From the time of early lynchings to the reinstatement of capital punishment, this conflict has been widely thought to be expressed in forms of criminal injustice. Region is coded as a dummy variable, with southerners coded 1, to see if persons from this part of the country perceive more criminal injustice than other Americans.[1]

What makes age status a unique conflict variable (Friedenberg, 1965; Flacks, 1971) is that for each respondent it constantly changes. The earlier periods of this change are more likely to produce conflict than later periods, as reflected by the fact that younger adults are more likely than older adults to have experience with the criminal law (e.g., Richards, 1979). Respondents 18–20 years old are coded 11, those 21–4 years old are coded 10, and so on in four-year intervals to those 65 years of age and older, who are coded 1.

It is difficult to know how the conflict of the sexes might influence the perception of criminal injustice. In contrast to the perception of their experiences with other institutions, women are widely thought to receive lenient treatment from agencies of crime control (Simon, 1975; Adler, 1975; Hagan, Simpson and Gillis, 1979). It may be men, then, who are most likely to perceive criminal injustice, and in this dummy coding, men are therefore coded 1.

The last of our conflict variables considers whether the respondents in our survey reside in the central cities of America or in more peripheral areas of the country. This distinction draws importance from Frank's (1967) neo-Marxian work on developed and underdeveloped areas. Although Frank (1978; 1979) has focused most of his attention on the world stage, he also notes that 'this contradictory metropolitan center-peripheral satellite relationship, like the process of surplus expropriation/appropriation, runs through the entire world capitalist system in chain-like fashion from its uppermost metropolitan world center, through each of the various national, regional, local, and enterprise centers' (1967: 10). Following the premise that one consequence of this metropolitan-periphery relationship of domination and dependency is a colonization of attitudes, we will assume that conflicts about issues like criminal injustice are more likely to be explicit in the center than in the periphery of American society. That is, we expect that residents of central cities will be more likely than persons in the periphery to perceive criminal injustice. For this reason, central city residents are coded 1, and residents of the periphery zero, in our analysis.[2] We can turn now to the measurement of our dependent variable.

THE PERCEPTION OF CRIMINAL INJUSTICE

The perception of criminal injustice has a variety of components, a number of which are considered in our data. We begin with ten problems of criminal injustice indicated in table 5.2: two of them involve law enforcement officials/police, four involve the courts, two involve juries, and one each involves lawyers and judges. All of the problems relate directly or indirectly to the justness of decisions reached in the criminal justice system, with special attention given to the experiences of economic and ethnic minorities with problems of equality before the law. Each of the problems was referenced in the interviewing to the respondent's state, and the problems were presented in random order. Respondents first ranked the seriousness (no problem, small, moderate, serious, very serious) of each problem and then the frequency of its occurrence (never, once in a while, some of the time, most of the time, all the time). We have combined the seriousness and frequency rankings of each item into a single variable ranging from 1 to 10, and we have combined the ten problem variables into a 100-point scale. In this chapter we will consider these variables separately and as a scale. A preliminary issue, however, is whether this combination of variables can be said to constitute a scale.

Table 5.2 presents correlations between each of the ten variables and the 10-variable scale, with and without correction for inclusion of the specific variable considered. The lowest of these correlations is 0.60. A factor analysis of these variables resulted in one factor (with loadings presented in table 5.2) that explained 100 per cent of the common variance of the variables; this indicates that the scale is unidimensional. Measures of the reliability of the scale are very encouraging: Cronbach's (1951) alpha is 0.91 and Heise and Bohrnstedt's (1970) omega is just over 0.91. Measures of

TABLE 5.2 *Perceived criminal injustice scale*

Item[a]	r[b]	Corrected r[c]	Factor loadings[d]
Law enforcement officials/police who do not treat poor suspects the same as well-to-do-suspects (PCI-1)	0.76	0.69	0.73
Law enforcement officials/police who do not represent a cross-section of the community in which they work (PCI-2)	0.68	0.60	0.65
Courts that disregard a defendant's constitutional rights (PCI-3)	0.74	0.67	0.72
Juries that do not represent a cross-section of the people in the community (PCI-4)	0.71	0.63	0.67
Juries that are biased and unfair when it comes to deciding cases (PCI-5)	0.75	0.69	0.73
Lawyers who do not treat their poor clients the same as their well-to-do clients (PCI-6)	0.72	0.65	0.69
Judges who are biased and unfair (PCI-7)	0.76	0.70	0.73
Courts that do not treat poor people as well as well-to-do people (PCI-8)	0.80	0.74	0.78
Courts that do not treat blacks and other minorities the same as whites (PCI-9)	0.76	0.68	0.74
Courts that are influenced by political considerations (PCI-10)	0.68	0.60	0.63

[a] Each item is ranked separately on a Likert Scale by respondents in terms of seriousness as a problem and frequency of occurrence (see text).
[b] Correlations between the item scores and the total scale score.
[c] Correlations between item scores and total scale score corrected for inclusion of the item considered (see Scott, 1968: 219).
[d] Factor loading based on a principal factor analysis with iterations.

internal or trait validity are also highly supportive: Heise and Bohrnstedt's validity measure is over 0.95. Their measure of invalidity is effectively zero (0.003), indicating that there is very little variation among the index items due to causes or factors other than the one underlying dimension being measured. These variables, then, clearly do form a scale of the perception of criminal injustice. Means and standard deviations for this scale and all other variables considered in this study are presented for the full sample and within class categories in table 5.3.

TABLE 5.3 *Means and standard deviations of variables used in regression equations*

	Full sample	Employers	Professional-managerial class	Workers	Surplus population
Race	0.10 (0.30)	0.02 (0.15)	0.07 (0.25)	0.11 (0.31)	0.22 (0.42)
Education	3.46 (1.24)	3.04 (1.28)	2.69 (1.18)	3.82 (1.05)	3.95 (1.34)
Income	4.23 (1.77)	3.17 (1.54)	3.33 (1.55)	4.59 (1.56)	6.59 (1.85)
Region–South	0.35 (0.48)	0.34 (0.48)	0.32 (0.47)	0.37 (0.48)	0.36 (0.48)
Age	7.12 (2.55)	5.82 (2.40)	7.05 (2.43)	7.24 (2.59)	8.07 (2.33)
Sex	0.49 (0.50)	0.45 (0.50)	0.52 (0.50)	0.49 (0.50)	0.41 (0.50)
Residence–Central City	0.38 (0.49)	0.29 (0.46)	0.36 (0.48)	0.40 (0.49)	0.44 (0.50)
PCI-1	6.47 (1.96)	6.52 (1.93)	6.21 (1.89)	6.52 (1.99)	7.20 (1.79)
PCI-2	5.34 (1.82)	5.27 (1.58)	5.39 (1.85)	5.26 (1.81)	6.08 (2.11)
PCI-3	4.89 (2.01)	4.75 (2.10)	4.69 (1.88)	4.90 (2.00)	6.10 (2.34)
PCI-4	5.30 (1.95)	5.12 (1.83)	5.34 (1.99)	5.27 (1.93)	5.64 (2.06)
PCI-5	5.22 (1.88)	4.79 (1.67)	5.05 (1.84)	5.26 (1.87)	6.20 (2.10)
PCI-6	6.60 (1.91)	6.54 (1.82)	6.29 (1.86)	6.67 (1.90)	7.44 (2.08)
PCI-7	5.57 (1.89)	5.54 (1.94)	5.43 (1.74)	5.56 (1.91)	6.47 (2.04)
PCI-8	6.27 (2.13)	6.18 (1.94)	6.09 (2.15)	6.29 (2.14)	7.16 (1.90)
PCI-9	5.78 (2.21)	5.21 (1.92)	5.71 (2.17)	5.77 (2.24)	7.03 (2.08)
PCI-10	6.50 (1.96)	6.53 (1.80)	6.37 (1.93)	6.49 (1.98)	7.22 (1.87)
PCI-scale	57.93 (14.56)	56.46 (12.26)	56.57 (14.92)	57.99 (14.35)	66.58 (15.04)

Note: Standard deviations are in parentheses.

EQUATIONS

In the first part of our analysis we estimate the following regression equations:

$$\text{Perceived Criminal Injustice} = a + b_1 \text{ Race} \qquad (5.1)$$
$$\text{Perceived Criminal Injustice} = a + b_1 \text{ Workers} \qquad (5.2)$$

and

$$\text{Perceived Criminal Injustice} = a + b_1 \text{ Race} + b_2 \text{ Workers}$$
$$+ b_3 \text{ Employers} + b_4 \text{ Education}$$
$$+ b_5 \text{ Income} + b_6 \text{ South} + b_7 \qquad (5.3)$$
$$\text{Age} + b_8 \text{ Sex} + b_9 \text{ Central City}$$

This set of equations is estimated for each of the ten perceptions of criminal injustice variables, and then for the scale, using the sample of 1,049 persons with an employed head of household. This preliminary part of our analysis parallels quantitative Marxian studies of income determination (Wright and Perrone, 1977; Wright, 1978) in its use of a three-class model. We are particularly concerned in equations (5.1) and (5.2) with determining separately how being black and being a worker may influence the perception of criminal injustice; in other words, in how being positioned in these separate locations in the social structure may influence perceptions of criminal injustice. However, as noted above, many conflict theorists characterize positions within a social structure along dimensions other than those of race and class. Equation (5.3) takes into account the race and class distributions of these other positions within the social structure as well as the distribution of race and class within one another. Thus, for example, if blacks are found in equation (5.1) to perceive significantly more criminal injustice than whites, and if this in fact is due to the greater concentration of blacks in the working class and/or the greater education of whites that puts them into a dominant status culture that assumes equality before the law, then, when class position and education are included in equation (5.3), the difference in perceived injustice between the races should be reduced substantially or eliminated. Equation (5.3) actually holds constant the full range of status positions identified above that have a plausible claim to being important determinants of relationships among race, class, and perceived criminal injustice. To the extent that race and class coefficients found in equations (5.1) and (5.2) persist in equation (5.3), with all these structural positions taken into account, we can argue with increased confidence that these coefficients are direct, unmediated consequences of the race-class positions themselves.

Following consideration of the three-class sample, we turn to an analysis of the four-class model that now includes the surplus population of unemployed workers. The analysis outlined above is repeated in this larger sample, with the exception that equations (5.2a) and (5.3a) (see table 5.5 below) include within them the surplus population instead of workers as the b_1 and b_2 coefficients, respectively.

Up to this point, we have considered only an additive, linear model of the perception of criminal injustice. However, this may tell us only part of the story. The last part of our analysis examines the interaction of class with the other status positions by estimating two regression equations within each of the four class categories. This part of the analysis is built around equation (5.1) and a new equation (within class categories):

$$\text{Perceived Criminal Injustice} = a + b_1 \text{ Race} + b_2 \text{ Education} + b_3 \text{ Income} + b_4 \text{ South} + b_5 \text{ Age} + b_6 \text{ Sex} + b_7 \text{ Central City} \quad (5.4)$$

The latter equation allows examination of the class-race interactions, with other status positions held constant. We are particularly interested here in how the influence of race may be conditioned by class position. For example, there is some reason to expect that the influence of race may be larger in some class categories than others (Wright, 1978). The final part of our analysis explores this possibility.

RESULTS

Table 5.4 presents the results of estimating our regression equations in the three-class sample with the ten measures of the perception of criminal injustice and the combined scale. The salient finding in this table is clearly the persistent and often striking influence of race on the perception of criminal injustice. In equation (5.1), with the other status positions of the respondents uncontrolled, the relationship of race to the perception of criminal injustice varies from a low β of 0.16 to a high of 0.28, all significant at the 0.001 level. These perceptions of injustice are largest for those items involving law enforcement officials/police (PCI-1, PCI-2) and for the item involving courts not treating blacks and other minorities the same as whites (PCI-9). Using the 100-point scale as a summary measure and turning our attention to the unstandardized coefficients, we can note that on average, with other class and status positions held constant, blacks score nearly thirteen points higher (b = 12.98) than whites in their perceptions of criminal injustice.

In contrast, there is little evidence in table 5.4 that workers perceive more criminal injustice than members of other classes or that employers perceive less. For three of the ten dependent measures for which equation (5.1) is estimated, workers perceive significantly more injustice than others; however, all of these relationships are below 0.10 in magnitude, and only one, that involving the treatment the poor receive from lawyers (PCI-6), remains significant when the other status positions of the respondents are held constant in equation (5.3). The worker coefficients for the summary scale are both small and non-significant.

Of the remaining measures of status position, residence in a central city has the most interesting influence. For six of the ten dependent measures in equation (5.3), residing in a central city significantly increases the perception of criminal injustice, even when all other status measures, including race and class, are taken into account. In terms of the summary scale, central city residents score more than three points (b = 3.32) higher than residents of other areas. The remaining status positions show only scattered influence in table 5.4.

Table 5.5 presents the results of re-estimating a modified set of the regression equations above for the four-class sample that now includes the surplus population; this surplus population replaces workers in two of the equations ((5.2a) and (5.3a)). The most striking difference between the findings reported in tables 5.5 and 5.4 is the influence of the added class: for nine of the ten dependent measures and the summary scale, members of the surplus population are significantly more likely than others to perceive criminal injustice. The influence of this class position on the perceptual measures is not as large or as varied as the influence of race; however, it does withstand controls for all other status positions in equation (5.3a). Using unstandardized coefficients and the summary scale as our point of reference, before controlling for their other status positions, we find that members of the surplus population on average score approximately nine points higher than others in their perceptions of criminal injustice; and, after we control for status positions, members of the surplus population on average score nearly seven points ($b = 6.90$) higher. Use of a four-class model, then, is crucial to the class-based concerns of this paper. Elsewhere, the results of changing from a three- to a four-class model are slight. Central city residential status continues to have a notable influence, and race continues to have a striking influence; both withstand controls for other status positions in equation (5.3a).

Part A of table 5.6 presents the results of estimating regression equations (5.1) and (5.4) for the summary scale within each of the four classes. Most significantly, this table reveals that the importance of these class categories extends beyond what our preceding analysis suggests. Our focus in this part of the analysis is on the influence of race within each of the classes, or, in other words, on race-class interactions. As one might expect, there are few blacks in the employer class, and only two blacks of this class are in our sample. Thus race could not be expected to have a statistically significant impact on employers' perceptions of criminal injustice, and we have therefore omitted this variable from the equations estimated in this class category. However, what interests us most is the influence of race in each of the other three classes: this influence decreases with each step down the class structure. Looking first at equation (5.1) in the professional-managerial class, we see that blacks on average score twenty points higher ($b = 20.09$, $\beta = 0.34$) than whites in their perceptions of criminal injustice. In equation (5.4), with other status positions held constant, this difference slips only slightly to 18.45 points. On the other hand, black workers score an average of about twelve points ($b = 12.12$, $\beta = 0.26$) higher than white workers on this scale in equation (5.1), and this difference again drops only slightly to 11.30 in equation (5.4). Finally, black members of the surplus population on average score only about five points higher ($b = 5.18$, $\beta = 0.10$) in equation (5.4).

TABLE 5.4 *Regressions of criminal justice items on independent variables in three equations for three class sample (N = 1049)*

	PCI-1	PCI-2	PCI-3	PCI-4	PCI-5	PCI-6	PCI-7	PCI-8	PCI-9	PCI-10	PCI scale
Equation (5.1):											
Race: b	1.75[c]	1.64[c]	1.50[c]	1.16[c]	1.36[c]	1.07[c]	1.12[c]	1.40[c]	2.14[c]	0.94[c]	14.08[c]
Beta (SE)	0.25 (0.21)	0.26 (0.19)	0.22 (0.21)	0.17 (0.21)	0.21 (0.20)	0.16 (0.20)	0.17 (0.20)	0.19 (0.23)	0.28 (0.23)	0.14 (0.21)	0.28 (1.49)
Constant	6.28	5.15	4.69	5.18	5.04	6.45	5.42	6.09	5.52	6.37	56.19
Equation (5.2):											
Workers: b	0.25[a]	−0.10	0.20	−0.02	0.27[a]	0.33[b]	0.11	0.18	0.17	0.08	1.45
Beta (SE)	0.06 (0.12)	−0.03 (0.11)	0.05 (0.13)	−0.01 (0.12)	0.07 (0.12)	0.08 (0.12)	0.03 (0.12)	0.04 (0.14)	0.04 (0.14)	0.02 (0.13)	0.05 (0.92)
Constant	6.28	5.36	4.69	5.29	4.99	6.34	5.45	6.11	5.60	6.41	56.54
Equation (5.3):											
Race: b	1.62[c]	1.57[c]	1.35[c]	1.15[c]	1.16[c]	0.91[c]	1.05[c]	1.28[c]	2.04[c]	0.86[c]	12.98[c]
Beta (SE)	0.24 (0.21)	0.25 (0.19)	0.20 (0.21)	0.17 (0.21)	0.18 (0.20)	0.14 (0.21)	0.16 (0.21)	0.16 (0.24)	0.27 (0.23)	0.13 (0.22)	0.26 (1.53)
Workers: b	0.28	−0.07	0.02	0.10	0.07	0.35[a]	0.09	0.17	0.04	0.11	1.16
Beta (SE)	0.07 (0.15)	−0.02 (0.13)	0.01 (0.15)	0.03 (0.15)	0.02 (0.14)	0.09 (0.14)	0.02 (0.14)	0.04 (0.16)	0.01 (0.16)	0.03 (0.15)	0.04 (1.07)
Employers: b	0.47[a]	0.08	0.16	0.01	−0.12	0.32	0.23	0.22	−0.23	0.23	1.35
Beta (SE)	0.07 (0.23)	0.01 (0.21)	0.02 (0.24)	0.01 (0.23)	−0.02 (0.22)	0.05 (0.22)	0.03 (0.23)	0.03 (0.26)	−0.03 (0.26)	0.03 (0.24)	0.03 (1.70)
Education: b	0.04	−0.15[b]	0.09	−0.21[c]	0.03	−0.07	−0.02	0.05	−0.05	−0.03	−0.49
Beta (SE)	−0.02 (0.06)	−0.10 (0.05)	0.06 (0.06)	−0.13 (0.06)	0.02 (0.05)	−0.05 (0.05)	−0.01 (0.05)	−0.03 (0.06)	−0.03 (0.06)	−0.02 (0.06)	−0.04 (0.40)
Income: b	−0.01	0.02	0.03	0.01	0.03	0.04	0.02	0.01	−0.02	−0.01	0.12
Beta (SE)	−0.01 (0.04)	0.02 (0.04)	0.03 (0.04)	0.01 (0.04)	0.03 (0.04)	0.04 (0.04)	0.02 (0.04)	0.01 (0.04)	−0.01 (0.04)	−0.01 (0.04)	0.01 (0.29)
South: b	0.26[a]	0.05	−0.15	−0.04	−0.05	0.25[a]	−0.20	0.33[a]	0.14	0.17	0.74
Beta (SE)	0.06 (0.12)	0.01 (0.11)	−0.04 (0.13)	−0.01 (0.12)	−0.02 (0.12)	0.06 (0.12)	−0.05 (0.12)	0.07 (0.14)	0.03 (0.14)	0.04 (0.13)	0.03 (0.96)
Age: b	0.04	0.03	0.01	0.05[a]	0.03.	−0.01	0.02	0.03	0.10[c]	0.01	0.31
Beta (SE)	0.05 (0.02)	0.05 (0.02)	0.01 (0.12)	0.07 (0.02)	0.05 (0.02)	−0.01 (0.02)	0.12 (0.02)	0.04 (0.03)	0.11 (0.03)	0.01 (0.02)	0.06 (0.17)
Sex: b	0.08	0.11	0.13	0.30[a]	0.20	−0.24[a]	0.14	0.12	0.36[b]	0.20	1.40
Beta (SE)	0.02 (0.12)	0.03 (0.11)	0.03 (0.12)	0.08 (0.12)	0.05 (0.11)	−0.06 (0.12)	0.04 (0.11)	0.03 (0.13)	0.08 (0.13)	0.05 (0.12)	0.05 (0.85)
Central city: b	0.22	0.40[c]	0.47[c]	0.33[b]	0.56[c]	0.20	0.40[c]	0.22	0.31[a]	0.19	3.32[c]
Beta (SE)	0.06 (0.12)	0.11 (0.11)	0.11 (0.12)	0.08 (0.12)	0.15 (0.12)	0.05 (0.12)	0.11 (0.12)	0.05 (0.14)	0.07 (0.14)	0.05 (0.13)	0.11 (0.89)
Constant	5.75	5.16	4.00	5.19	4.25	6.26	5.08	5.66	4.77	6.15	52.26

[a] Significant at the 0.05 level.
[b] Significant at the 0.01 level.
[c] Significant at the 0.001 level.

While the race coefficients in equations (5.1) and (5.4) are both highly significant in the PMC and among workers, this is not the case in the surplus population. However, the small number of persons in the surplus population (N = 59) limits the importance that can be attached to the latter finding. Much more meaningful are the *t*-values presented in part B of table 5.6 for the three possible comparisons of class category race coefficients[3] All six of these *t*-values are statistically significant at the 0.001 level, indicating that comparisons of race coefficients between the surplus population and workers, between the surplus population and the PMC, and between workers and the PMC all involve differences that are highly unlikely to be products of change.

An intuitive way of clarifying the findings above is to calculate predicted values using equation (5.4) for each of the race-class combinations discussed. To do this it is necessary to establish at what values of the independent variables in equation (5.4) we wish to make our comparisons. Our approach to this problem follows Duncan (1969) by substituting the most advantaged group's means into the other groups' equations. This approach tells us how the other groups would do if they had the same mean values as the most advantaged group in the independent variables considered. A second approach, used by Wright (1978), is to sum the means of the groups involved and then divide by the number of groups. This approach attempts to establish a middle ground as the point of comparison. With our data, both approaches yield very similar results. The following results come from using Duncan's approach and substituting the white employers' means into each of the six equations involved: in the surplus population, whites score an average of 64.50 on the criminal injustice scale, while blacks score an average of 68.13; in the working class, whites score an average of 55.80, while blacks score an average of 67.10; and in the PMC, whites score an average of 54.57, while blacks score an average of 73.02. These scores suggest that in the surplus population there is a consciousness of class position *vis-à-vis* the criminal justice system that largely overcomes factors of race. However, as we move up the class structure to the working class and into the PMC, blacks and whites are increasingly divided in their perceptions of criminal injustice. This occurs in the following way. On the one hand, whites tend to moderate their views as they move up the social structure: white workers perceive less criminal injustice than white members of the surplus population, and white members of the PMC are slightly less likely still to perceive criminal injustice. On the other hand, blacks in the working class are much more like blacks in the surplus population in their levels of perceived criminal injustice, and black members of the PMC are the most likely persons in the sample to perceive criminal injustice. Put back into more abstract summary terms, class position conditions the influence of race in the perception of

TABLE 5-5 *Regressions of criminal justice items on independent variables in three equations for four class sample (N = 1106)*

	PCI-1	PCI-2	PCI-3	PCI-4	PCI-5	PCI-6	PCI-7	PCI-8	PCI-9	PCI-10	PCI scale
Equation (5.1):											
Race: b	1.67[c]	1.62[c]	1.54[c]	1.15[c]	1.37[c]	1.03[c]	1.13[c]	1.31[c]	2.05[c]	0.86[c]	13.71[c]
Beta (SE)	0.25 (0.19)	0.26 (0.18)	0.23 (0.20)	0.17 (0.20)	0.22 (0.19)	0.16 (0.19)	0.18 (0.19)	0.18 (0.21)	0.27 (0.21)	0.13 (0.20)	0.28 (1.42)
Constant	6.31	5.18	4.74	5.19	5.08	6.50	5.46	6.14	5.58	6.41	56.60
Equation (5.2a)											
Surplus population: b	0.77[b]	0.79[b]	1.27[c]	0.36	1.04[c]	0.89[c]	0.96[c]	0.95[c]	1.33[c]	0.76[b]	9.14[c]
Beta (SE)	0.09 (0.26)	0.10 (0.24)	0.14 (0.27)	0.04 (0.26)	0.12 (0.25)	0.11 (0.25)	0.11 (0.25)	0.10 (0.28)	0.13 (0.29)	0.09 (0.26)	0.14 (1.93)
Constant	5.66	4.51	3.54	4.91	4.12	5.66	4.56	5.27	4.37	5.69	48.31
Equation (5.3a):											
Race: b	1.52[c]	1.53[c]	1.32[c]	1.13[c]	1.10[c]	0.84[c]	1.02[c]	1.12[c]	1.89[c]	0.74[c]	12.23[c]
Beta (SE)	0.23 (0.20)	0.25 (0.19)	0.19 (0.20)	0.17 (0.19)	0.17 (0.19)	0.13 (0.20)	0.16 (0.20)	0.16 (0.22)	0.25 (0.22)	0.11 (0.21)	0.25 (1.47)
Surplus Population: b	0.53[a]	0.58[a]	0.98[c]	0.20	0.70[b]	0.61[a]	0.77[b]	0.75[a]	1.05[c]	0.71[b]	6.90[c]
Beta (SE)	0.06 (0.27)	0.07 (0.25)	0.11 (0.28)	0.02 (0.27)	0.08 (0.26)	0.07 (0.27)	0.09 (0.25)	0.08 (0.29)	0.11 (0.30)	0.08 (0.27)	0.11 (1.96)
Employers: b	0.30	0.12	0.14	-0.03	-0.16	0.12	0.18	0.11	-0.27	0.15	0.65
Beta (SE)	0.04 (0.22)	0.02 (0.20)	0.02 (0.23)	-0.01 (0.22)	-0.02 (0.21)	0.02 (0.22)	0.03 (0.21)	0.01 (0.24)	-0.03 (0.24)	0.02 (0.22)	0.01 (1.60)
Education: b	0.01	-0.13[b]	0.08	-0.17[b]	0.04	-0.01	0.01	-0.02	-0.04	-0.02	-0.27
Beta (SE)	0.01 (0.05)	-0.09 (0.05)	0.15 (0.05)	-0.11 (0.05)	0.03 (0.05)	-0.01 (0.05)	0.01 (0.05)	-0.03 (0.06)	-0.03 (0.06)	-0.02 (0.05)	-0.02 (0.37)
Income: b	0.01	0.01	0.03	0.02	0.05	-0.06	0.01	0.01	-0.02	-0.02	0.18
Beta (SE)	0.01 (0.04)	0.01 (0.03)	0.03 (0.04)	0.02 (0.04)	0.05 (0.04)	0.05 (0.04)	0.01 (0.04)	0.01 (0.04)	-0.02 (0.04)	0.02 (0.05)	0.02 (0.27)
South: b	0.26[a]	0.07	-0.15	-0.04	-0.07	0.21	-0.20	0.33[a]	0.15	0.19	0.75
Beta (SE)	0.06 (0.12)	0.02 (0.11)	-0.03 (0.12)	-0.01 (0.12)	-0.02 (0.12)	0.05 (0.12)	-0.05 (0.12)	0.07 (0.13)	0.03 (0.13)	0.05 (0.12)	0.03 (0.88)
Age: b	0.04	0.04	0.01	0.05[a]	0.03	0.01	0.02	0.04	0.10[c]	0.01	0.33
Beta (SE)	0.05 (0.02)	0.05 (0.02)	0.01 (0.02)	0.07 (0.02)	0.04 (0.02)	0.01 (0.02)	0.03 (0.02)	0.04 (0.03)	0.11 (0.03)	0.01 (0.02)	0.06 (0.17)
Sex: b	0.08	0.11	0.14	0.27[a]	0.20	-0.27[a]	0.11	0.09	0.35[b]	0.18	1.27
Beta (SE)	0.02 (0.11)	0.03 (0.11)	0.03 (0.12)	0.07 (0.12)	0.05 (0.11)	-0.07 (0.11)	0.03 (0.11)	0.02 (0.13)	0.08 (0.13)	0.05 (0.12)	0.04 (0.83)
Central city: b	0.21	0.34[c]	0.41[c]	0.31[a]	0.54[c]	0.13	0.35[b]	0.19	0.25	0.16	2.87[c]
Beta (SE)	0.05 (0.12)	0.09 (0.11)	0.10 (0.12)	0.08 (0.12)	0.14 (0.11)	0.03 (0.12)	0.09 (0.12)	0.04 (0.13)	0.05 (0.13)	0.03 (0.12)	0.10 (0.87)
Constant	5.21	4.50	3.10	4.85	3.57	5.60	4.31	4.89	3.75	5.53	45.32

[a] Significant at the 0.05 level.
[b] Significant at the 0.01 level.
[c] Significant at the 0.001 level.

criminal injustice. We will note a significant analogue to this finding in the conclusion of this chapter.

Two other findings in table 5.6 are worthy of note, although we will not dwell on them here. The first is that there are signs that central city residential status is conditioned by class position in a manner similar to race. In particular, members of the PMC show signs of perceiving more criminal injustice when they reside in central cities (b = 5.89, $p < 0.001$). This finding does not contradict the work of Frank, and it is fully consistent with the Ehrenreichs' (1978) focus on radical movements within the PMC. The second finding is that among employers in table 5.6, it is highly educated men who are least likely, and less educated women who are most likely, to perceive criminal injustice. We will only note here that, following Collins, it is tempting to interpret the more highly educated male view as an expression of successful indoctrination into elite culture.

CONCLUSIONS

Two prominent research literatures, one dealing with criminal sentencing and the other with public rankings of the seriousness of crimes, have failed to find evidence supportive of a conflict theory of criminal justice. We have addressed issues raised by this theory in a different and more direct way: we have examined divisions, particularly those of race and class, in public perceptions of criminal injustice. In this chapter we have presented a scale of perceived criminal injustice that shows every sign of being highly reliable and valid. Our analysis of a national survey including this scale and its components parts produced three major findings: (1) that black Americans are considerably more likely than white Americans to perceive criminal injustice; (2) that regardless of race, members of the surplus population are significantly more likely than members of other classes to perceive criminal injustice; and (3) that class position conditions the relationship of race to the perception of criminal injustice, with the division between the races in these perceptions being most acute in the professional managerial class. In contrast to the prior research literatures considered in this chapter, then, we have found substantial evidence that race and class conflict exist with regard to issues of criminal injustice in America. In addition, we found evidence that the perception of criminal injustice is more pronounced in the metropolitan centres than in peripheral parts of America.

The third finding above, involving the race-class interaction and the observation that the races are most divided in the PMC, deserves separate comment. This finding parallels in an interesting way the finding of Wright (1978) that blacks also receive the smallest returns in income for their

TABLE 5.6 *Comparisons within class categories*

A Regressions of criminal justice scale on independent variables in two equations within class categories

	Employers[d]	Professional-managerial class	Workers	Surplus population
Equation (5.1):				
Race: *b*	—	20.09^c	12.12^c	5.18
Beta (SE)	—	0.34 (3.18)	0.26 (1.74)	0.14 (4.71)
Constant	—	55.20	56.67	65.43
Equation (5.4):				
Race: *b*	—	18.45^c	11.30^c	3.54
Beta (SE)	—	0.31 (3.19)	0.25 (1.81)	0.10 (5.74)
Education: *b*	2.50^a	− 0.65	− 0.63	1.48
Beta (SE)	0.27 (1.15)	− 0.05 (0.70)	− 0.05 (0.55)	0.13 (1.82)
Income: *b*	− 0.53	− 0.41	0.47	0.16
Beta (SE)	− 0.07 (0.93)	− 0.04 (0.53)	0.05 (0.37)	0.02 (1.29)
South: *b*	2.47	− 0.04	0.63	0.33
Beta (SE)	0.10 (2.80)	− 0.01 (1.71)	0.02 (1.14)	0.01 (4.44)
Age: *b*	1.09	0.05	0.30	0.01
Beta (SE)	0.21 (0.57)	0.01 (0.33)	0.05 (0.22)	0.01 (0.93)
Sex: *b*	− 5.53^a	2.30	1.50	0.46
Beta (SE)	− 0.23 (2.74)	0.08 (1.61)	0.05 (1.08)	0.02 (4.30)
Central Cities: *b*	− 1.53	5.89^c	2.50^a	− 5.42
Beta (SE)	− 0.06 (2.95)	0.19 (1.68)	0.09 (1.12)	− 0.18 (4.13)
Constant	45.99	54.74	52.88	60.87

B Comparisons of class category race coefficients

	Surplus population compared to workers		Surplus population compared to PMC		Workers compared to PMC	
	Equation (5.1)	Equation (5.4)	Equation (5.1)	Equation (5.4)	Equation (5.1)	Equation (5.4)
Difference in race coefficients	6.94	7.76	14.91	14.91	7.97	7.15
t-value of difference	4.92^c	5.35^c	7.72^c	7.89^c	5.39^c	4.77^c
Surplus population %	0.43	0.31	0.26	0.19	—	—

^{a} Significant at 0.05 level.
^{b} Significant at 0.01 level.
^{c} Significant at 0.001 level.
^{d} Race is omitted from equation (5.4) in this class category; see text for explanation.

education in the managerial class: that is, that income discrimination by race may be the largest in this class. The latter finding increases our confidence in the former and encourages several alternative explanations of it. One possibility is that black members of the PMC who perceive income discrimination may be sensitive to the perception of injustice elsewhere as well. Another possibility is that a consciousness of race among blacks in the PMC, and their more recent movement into this class, is associated with a consciousness of prior class position that continues to influence significantly their perceptions of the surrounding world. Finally, it may be that whites who manage to stay out of the surplus population also are able to avoid criminal injustice, while working class blacks and black members of the PMC may continue, directly or indirectly, to experience criminal injustice, perhaps partly as a consequence of the apparent contradiction in their race and class positions. Our data do not allow us to do more than suggest these possibilities and their suitability as subjects for further research.

The findings we have reported are important for Marxists and non-Marxists alike. For Marxists they are a vindication of the point that class position is indeed significant to the understanding of crime and criminal-justice-related conflicts. In particular, Marxian criminologists who have emphasized that consideration of the surplus population is especially important in understanding such conflicts receive support from these data and, beyond this, encouragement with regard to this class being and/or becoming a 'class for itself' in terms of common consciousness of its position in relation to the criminal justice system. Non-Marxists, some of whom may be reluctant to concede that class injustice actually exists in America, will nonetheless likely agree that *perceptions* of this injustice do exist, and they can now join in the important task of explaining these perceptions. In doing so they will undoubtedly note that the influence of class is apparently smaller than that of race in explaining the perception of criminal injustice; and they could reasonably argue from this that while Marxian *theory* finds some support in these kinds of data, nonetheless, the base of class consciousness for bringing about the revolutionary events that Marx predicted, and some Marxian criminologists foresee, is small. There is much room here for research and debate. Our point is simply that Marxists and non-Marxists alike will benefit from operationalizing the concept of class, and issues of criminal injustice, in ways that parallel those suggested in this chapter. Indeed, our data indicate that any model of the perception of criminal injustice that does not include measures of race and class similar to these is likely to be incompletely specified.

NOTES

Data utilized in this chapter were made available by the Inter-University Consortium for Political and Social Research. The data for *Public Image of the Courts, 1977: General Publics Data* were originally collected by the Law Enforcement Assistance Administration. Neither the collector of the original data nor the consortium bears any responsibility for the analyses or interpretations presented here.

1 Assuming that region might also interact with race, we estimated equation (5.3a) of an interaction effect, and therefore the possibility of this interaction is not discussed further in this chapter.

2 In these data a central city consists of 50,000 inhabitants or more in the 1960 or 1970 census, or of two cities 'having contiguous boundaries and constituting, for general social and economic purposes, a single community with a combined population of at least 50,000, with the smaller city having a population of at least 15,000' (US Department of Commerce, 1977).

3 Our paired comparisons of the race slopes for the different groups are based on the following t-test:

$$t = (b_{11} - b_{12})/\sqrt{(v_1 S^2 b_{11} + v_2 S^2 b_{12})/(v_1 + v_2)}$$

where b_{11} is the race coefficient for group 1; b_{12} is the race coefficient for group 2; $S^2 b_{11}$ and $S^2 b_{12}$ are the standard errors of the coefficients for groups 1 and 2, respectively; and v_1 and v_2 are the degrees of freedom for groups 1 and 2, respectively.

PART II

Social Structure, the Family and Delinquency

6

A Power-Control Theory of Gender and Delinquency

INTRODUCTION

In the second part of this book we develop and explore a structural framework for the study of gender and delinquency that we call power-control theory. Although class and gender are widely studied correlates of juvenile delinquency, little attention is given to their combined role in the explanation of delinquent behaviour. In its most general form, power-control theory asserts that the class structure of the family plays a significant role in explaining the social distribution of delinquent behaviour through the social reproduction of gender relations. 'Family class structure' and 'the social reproduction of gender relations' are not commonly used concepts in sociological criminology, and so we begin with some definitions.

Family class structure consists of the configurations of power between spouses that derive from the positions these spouses occupy in their work inside and outside the home. Spouses often gain power in the family through their work outside the home. So the occupational advances of women in recent decades are of particular interest to our understanding of family class structure.

The social reproduction of gender relations refers to the activities, institutions, and relationships that are involved in the maintenance and renewal of gender roles, in the family and elsewhere. These activities include the parenting involved in caring for, protecting and socializing children for the roles they will occupy as adults. According to power-control theory, family class structure shapes the social reproduction of gender relations, and in turn the social distribution of delinquency.

Of course, other institutions, such as schools, churches and governments are also involved in the social reproduction of gender relations. The activities of all these institutions are socially and historically contingent: they vary across time and place. In the second part of this volume we are concerned with social and historical variation in the reproduction of gender relations. More specifically, we are concerned with the impact of this variation on the connection between gender and delinquency.

We believe the above considerations have important implications for theory construction. The failure to consider family class structure and the social reproduction of gender relations has impeded the development of a sociological theory of crime and delinquency; this kind of ommission may also help to account for a recent dormancy of sociological interest in the etiological study of crime and delinquency. One of our purposes is to reawaken this interest.

OLD AND NEW ETIOLOGIES

We begin by considering briefly the historical background of contemporary theories of crime and delinquency. Textbooks typically trace such theories to the work of the Italian criminologist, Cesare Lombroso (see Wolfgang, 1960). Of course, Lombroso is best known for his view that criminals are atavistic throwbacks to primitive beings, and for his hypothesis that 'true criminals' can be identified by observing their physiological characteristics. This thesis is testable, and Lombroso is today better remembered for embarking on such tests, than for the rigour of his research or for the capacity of his thesis to survive such tests, when properly conducted.

Yet if Lombroso left a legacy, it was not only a growing interest in the empirical study of criminality, but also a skepticism about the possibilities of determining causes of criminal behaviour. It is not difficult to see how this two-edged legacy developed. America at the turn of the century had a better developed physiological than sociological margination (some might say this is still the case today: see Wilson and Hernstein, 1985). As a result, the suggestion that criminal behaviour had physiological roots was eagerly entertained at the turn of the century in Europe and the United States. However, as the evidence mounted that Lombroso's thesis was unsubstantiated (e.g., Goring, 1913), questions also were raised, especially by sociologists, as to the usefulness of studying the etiology of criminal behaviour at all. Although sociologists understandably were quicker to accumulate evidence on the absence or weakness of physiological (Lindesmith and Levin, 1937) and psychological (Schuessler and Cressey, 1950) causes of criminal behaviour, the issue ultimately was confronted in terms of social causes as well. Perhaps predictably, it was an historian with sociological interests, Franklin Tannenbaum (1938), who first asked if we might better shift our focus to the study of reactions to such behaviour, especially delinquency. In a famous phrase, 'the dramatization of evil', Tannenbaum focused new attention on the 'reactors' to crime and delinquency and anticipated a shift in theoretical attention that was to characterize much, if not most, sociological study of crime and delinquency for nearly a half century to follow.

Some of this early work retained an etiological component, attempting to explain 'secondary deviance', the behaviour that followed the responses of the police and other guardians of official morality to what usually were regarded as random or non-problematic behaviours (Lemert, 1967). However, secondary deviance itself often became secondary to a growing interest in the official control agents themselves. Nonetheless, this research tradition established that both actors and reactors, actions and reactions, are important in the study of crime and delinquency. A result is that there are now new opportunities to achieve a better balance in crime and delinquency research.

A renewed interest in the role of gender in the study of crime and delinquency is part of such an opportunity. The correlation of gender with criminal and delinquent behaviour is one of the few findings from the beginnings of criminological research that although questioned, never was doubted seriously. From the pioneering explorations of official crime statistics by Quetelet (1842), to the more modern tabulations by Radzinowitz (1937), Pollak (1951), Adler (1975), Simon (1975), and Smart (1977), such statistics have consistently shown that men are more criminal than women. The addition of victim (Hindelang, 1979) and self-report (Smith and Vischer, 1980) data sources to the traditional official tabulations (Steffensmeier, 1978; 1980) added to the assurance of a gender-based behavioural reality. Perhaps only age is better known for the consistency of its correlation with criminality, however measured (Hirschi and Gottfredson, 1983). The question therefore endures (Simon, 1975; Adler, 1975; Harris, 1977): can gender differences in criminal and delinquency behaviour be explained?

Feminist scholars have done the sociological study of crime and delinquency a service by refocusing attention on this important question. The effect is to suggest alternative paths that the development of the causal explanation of criminal and delinquency behaviour might usefully have taken much earlier. The paths originally chosen by Lombroso and those who followed his lead again were fundamentally wrong, but nonetheless instructive in unintended ways.

Confronted with the observed fact that women were less criminal than men, Lombroso might have been expected to argue that this was so because they were less atavistic than men. Instead, Lombroso (1895: 107) insisted woman was 'atavistically nearer to her origin than the male', and that her lesser criminality was explained by 'piety, maternity, want of passion, sexual coldness, weakness and an undeveloped intelligence' (151). It may well be that Lombroso's theory of female criminality gained currency because it both asserted women's biological inferiority and warned of the dangers of arousing her passions or developing her intelligence. In any case, Lombroso's arguments are today more easily seen as justifications for paternalistic social policies than as causal explanations of gender differences in criminality. And again, if these were the kinds of pathways to be travelled in the development of the causal explanation of gender differences in criminality, it is easy to see why few sociologists were interested in travelling them.

However, alternative possibilities were available, even at the turn of the century when American scholars chose to embrace the works of Lombroso. Most notable, perhaps, were some of the early thoughts of Willem Bonger. Bonger (1916) recognized the importance of the connection between gender and criminality and gathered cross-national data to test explanations of this correlation. Sociology, not physiology, was at the core of Bonger's thinking. He argued that 'the smaller criminality of woman is not to be sought in innate qualities, but rather in the social environment' (477). Bonger reasoned that if the gender-crime connection was social as well as or more than physical, then the strengths of this connection should vary across social conditions. Specifically, he argued that the correlation between gender and criminality should weaken as the social circumstances that confronted women as well as men declined. That is, the strength of the correlation between gender and crime should vary directly with social class.

Bonger's cross-national data admittedly allowed only a weak test of his thesis, but the results were nonetheless encouraging, and this is reason for further dismay that Lombroso's work attracted the greater attention during the formative years of American criminology. Indeed, Bonger received almost no attention at all (see Turk, 1969a). Note, furthermore, that in this early work Bonger was bringing together the concepts of class and gender. We will argue below that a missing component in Bonger's preliminary efforts was a consideration of the reproductive role of patriarchal family structure. Still, the point is easily made that most sociologists would have found Bonger's framework a more congenial start than was Lombroso's for the etiological study of gender differences in criminal behaviour. That Lombroso was the early focal point perhaps does much, then, to explain a long hiatus in the etiological study of gender and crime, and of etiological theory more generally. A new etiology that assigns primacy to gender relations points the way to a new beginning in the development of a sociological explanation of criminal and delinquent behaviour.

This new beginning receives encouragement from feminist scholars, such as Catherine MacKinnon (1982), who argue that an exclusive attention to official control agents and the state misses a rather fundamental aspect of the situation that confronts women, particularly those who are victims of crimes by men. As MacKinnon notes, whether some sexual crimes of men against women are called assault or rape, or whether they are dealt with in a court system whose functionaries are men or women, the behaviours themselves remain much the same and largely unexplained. This point does not, of course, diminish the importance of arguments about language and the elimination of sexual discrimination in the hiring of police and court officials. Rather, the point is to reassert that there is an underlying behavioural reality involving male criminality, often directed against women, that requires further explanation. MacKinnon makes this point provocatively:

Initiatives are . . . directed toward making the police more sensitive, prosecutors more responsive, judges more receptive, and the law, in words, less sexist. This may be progressive in the liberal or left senses, but how is it empowering in the feminist sense? Even if it were effective in jailing men who do little different from what nondeviant men do regularly, how would such an approach alter women's rapability? Unconfronted are why women are raped and the role of the state in that. Similarly, applying laws against battery to husbands, although it can mean life itself, has largely failed to address, as part of the strategy for state intervention, the conditions that produce men who systematically express themselves violently toward women, women whose resistance is disabled, and the role of the state in this dynamic. Criminal enforcement in these areas, while suggesting that rape and battery are deviant, punishes men for expressing the images of masculinity that mean their identity, for which they are trained, elevated, venerated, and paid. These men must be stopped. But how does that change them or reduce the chances that there will be more like them? Liberal strategies entrust women to the state.

MacKinnon's arguments return us to fundamental behavioural questions, and to the source of these behaviours in the social organization of gender relations.

But feminist scholars not only bring us back to fundamental questions about the causal explanation of criminal and delinquency behaviour, they also redirect our attention to the role of the state, and especially to family structure, in the explanation of these behaviours. Wilkinson (1974) notes that the family has not sustained the interest of sociologists, including those who have remained concerned with the explanation of criminality. The decline in interest in the family preceded the rise of the reaction theories of crime that could have been expected to replace a focus on the family with attention to official control agents. The decline seems more closely linked to a time early in this century when functions of the family were increasingly assumed by other institutions, most notably the schools, and when Americans were becoming more tolerant of divorce. While earlier interest had focused on the role of family breakdown in the causation of delinquent behaviour, concern now increasingly was directed to peers, schools, and to the quality of family life (McCord, 1982), which often improved with the separation and divorce of parents. The reform of family court procedures and divorce law became primary concerns. Studies which focused on variations in family structure often seemed in this context to attract attention to problems associated with family dissolution, and therefore this research frequently was seen as counterproductive. Perhaps as a result, Michael Hannon (1982: 65) writes that, 'In recent years the study of marriage and the family has become an intellectual backwater in sociology' (see also Nye and Berardo, 1981: 6; Berk and Berk, 1983).

However, feminist scholarship assigns renewed importance to the family and to variations in its structure. In particular, it brings attention to the role of patriarchal family relations in developing, perpetuating, and thereby reproducing gender differences in behaviour. Much of this discussion focuses on issues of power and control, concepts that are also, of course, central to the classical theories of delinquency. These concepts of power and control are central to the way we tie together our interest in class and gender. They are the conceptual cornerstones of our theory of class, gender and delinquency.

POWER, PATRIARCHY AND DELINQUENCY

The concepts of power and control typically are treated as being, respectively, macro and microstructural in content. The macro-micro distinction may or may not be one of simple aggregation, as for example, when classes are thought of as all persons found in common social relations of production, or as in addition sharing views of these conditions that result in group-based actions organized and carried out in ways that go beyond any simple summation of individual preferences (see Coleman, 1986). In either event, conceptual and empirical considerations of power typically occur at higher levels of aggregation and abstraction than do discussions of control, and they therefore are characteristically kept separate.

Considerations of power and control nonetheless have important features in common: for example, they are both relational in content. Power theories often focus on relations of domination in the workplace, while control theories frequently focus on relations of domination in the family. We do both here. Essential to the conceptualization and measurement in both areas of theory construction is the effort to capture a relational component of social structure. In power theories of the workplace, the relational structure may be that between owner and worker, or between supervisor and supervisee. In control theories of the family, the relational structure may be that between parent and child, or between parents themselves. In both cases, however, it is a sociological concern with relational and hierarchical structure that drives the conceptualization and measurement.

Power-control theory brings together these relational concerns in a multi-level framework. In doing so, this theory highlights another concern that the power and control traditions share. This common concern is with the conditions under which actors are free to deviate from social norms. Both the presence of power and the absence of control contribute to these conditions. A particular concern of power-control theory, for example, is to identify intersections of class and family relations that provide the greatest freedom for adolescent deviation. Power-control theory assumes that the concept of patriarchy is of fundamental importance in identifying such intersections.

Curtis (1986: 171) persuasively argues that patriarchy should not be seen as a theoretical concept with a standard definition, but as a generalization about social relations that calls for sociological investigation and explication. This generalization involves the propensity of males to create hierarchical structures through which they dominate others. It is important to emphasize here that these others may be male as well as female. So the study of patriarchy includes within it the analysis of structures through which men exercise hierarchical domination over both males and females, for example, including children of both genders in the family. Curtis goes on to point out that patriarchy is extremely widespread, including structures of the state (such as police, courts, and correctional agencies) as well as the workplace and the family. But the source of patriarchy nonetheless is assumed to be the family. Millett (1970: 33) calls the family patriarchy's 'chief institution', suggesting that the family is the fundamental instrument and the foundation unit of patriarchal society, and that the family and its roles are prototypical.

We are now in a position to begin sketching the outlines of a power-control theory of delinquency. We begin with the three levels of the theory, as illustrated in figure 6.1. These include, in order of level of abstraction, *social-psychological processes* involving the adolescents whose behaviours we wish to explain, *social positions* consisting of the gender and delinquency roles in which these adolescents are located, and the class *structures* by which families are socially organized. Five kinds of links, described further below, bring together the social positions and social-psychological processes that are the core of power-control theory.

We begin with the connections between the social positions and social-psychological processes identified in figure 6.1. Link 1 is the correlation between gender and state-defined delinquency that criminologists long have observed. We need only note here that gender and delinquency both constitute ascribed positions that are socially designated and legally identified. Our interest is in establishing the family class structures and social psychological processes that account for these social positions being joined in the correlations so consistently recorded by criminologists. Note

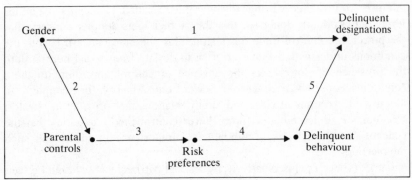

Family Class Relation

Figure 6.1   A power-control theory of gender and delinquency

that the interest of power-control theory is in individuals only insofar as they are located as occupants of these positions, and not, therefore, in these individuals *per se*. By virtue of the premises noted above, the question power-control theory inevitably asks is: how and why are individuals located in male adolescent positions freer to deviate in ways defined by the state as delinquent than are individuals located in female adolescent positions?

The reference to state definition above indicates that the connection between officially defined delinquency and delinquent behaviour is not assumed. Nor is a consensus assumed about what is to be called delinquent behaviour. Indeed, it is assumed that police and court practices sometimes operate to inflate the gender-delinquency correlation. As we will discuss further below, the effect of this inflation is to reinforce a sexual stratification of family and work activities, with females ascripted disproportionately for the former, and males appropriated disproportionately for the latter. Nonetheless, a sufficient consistency is hypothesized between police processing and delinquent behaviour to make the above kind of question relevant in behavioural terms.

Note also that while the above question makes no value judgements as to the 'goodness' or 'badness' of delinquency, it does nonetheless imply that there is a pleasurable or enjoyable aspect of delinquency. Indeed, power-control theory assumes that delinquency can be fun, if not liberating, as well as rewarding in other ways. Bordua (1961) notes that theories of delinquency too often, at least implicitly, assume that delinquency is a grim and somewhat desperate pursuit. In contrast, our assumption is that delinquency frequently is fun – and even more importantly, a kind of fun infrequently allowed to females. Said differently, delinquency may involve a spirit of liberation, the opportunity to take risks, and a chance to pursue publicly some of the pleasures that are symbolic of adult male status outside the family. One reason why delinquency is fun, then, is because it anticipates a range of activities, some criminal and some more conventional, that are more open to men than women. The interests of power-control theory are in how a sense of this sexually stratified world of licit and illicit adult pleasures, and restrictions of access to them, are communicated and reproduced across generations through gender relations.

Link 2 takes the first step in addressing such issues by explicating a connection between gender positions and the parental control of children. This link first calls attention to the proposition that parental controls are imposed selectively: that is, daughters are controlled more extensively than sons. Conceptually we represent this by noting that parents are characteristically the instruments of familial controls, while children are the objects; but most significantly, *daughters* are disproportionately the objects of this socially structured domination. So the instrument-object relationship established between parents and children is applied more selectively and extensively to daughters than sons. Beyond this, within patriarchal family structures mothers are particularly likely to be placed in the primary position of implementing this instrument-object relationship: that is, mothers more than fathers are assigned responsibility for perpetuating this instrument-object relationship.

Of course, control can be established through ties of affiliation as well as through subordination. Indeed, it might well be argued that a lot of affiliation and a little subordination is the most effective basis of social domination. Again, however, power-control theory predicts that ties of affiliation selectively and more extensively will be applied to daughters than sons. We will refer to these affiliative ties as relational controls, as contrasted with more instrumental kinds of controls involving supervision and surveillance. However, it is again the sexual asymmetry that is of greatest importance here, with power-control theory predicting that the larger burden of these controls is imposed on daughters rather than sons. Furthermore, it is mothers more than fathers that the patriarchal family holds responsible for the everyday imposition of these controls, again, on daughters more than sons.

Links 3, 4 and 5 in our theoretical framework lead us to a consideration of the consequences of this sexual stratification of social control. In link 3 the focus is on the risk preferences of adolescents. Risk-taking can be regarded as an expression of freedom, an expression that power-control theory predicts will be allowed selectively and more extensively to males than females. Delinquency can be regarded as an adolescent form of risk-taking (hence links 4 and 5) that we have argued can carry with it an element of pleasure, excitement, and therefore fun. The interest of power-control theory is in how a taste for such risk-taking is channelled along sexually stratified lines.

Link 3 in our theoretical framework predicts that gender differences in risk preferences will be observed and that they are mediated by the structures of parental control introduced above. That is, parents control their daughters more than their sons, and in so doing they diminish the preferences of daughters to take risks. The logical links in this theory therefore predict that daughters will be more risk-averse than sons, and that therefore daughters will be less delinquent in their behaviour than sons. In an important sense, then, what a power-control theory of delinquency is saying is that the higher likelihood of delinquency among boys than girls, and ultimately the higher likelihood of crime among men than women, is an expression of gender differences in risk preferences, which in turn are a product of the different patterns of parental control imposed on daughters compared to sons. In a still more ultimate sense, however, power-control theory goes beyond this to locate the source of such gender differences in a patriarchal connection between the family and the world of work outside it. We turn next to an explication of this connection between work and family.

CLASS, STATE AND HOUSEHOLD

We have made recurring references to the role of the patriarchal family in reproducing the five links presented in figure 6.1 as the core of power-control theory. In this section we will argue that the patriarchal family is one distinct type of family class structure. Power-control theory predicts that the links identified in figure 6.1 are strongest within this family class relation, and therefore that this type of family structure plays a central role in accounting for a strong connection between gender and crime. Because patriarchal family structures historically have played such a prominent role in the development of industrial capitalist societies, the effects of this family structure may be seen throughout our society, even within families that seek to reduce or eliminate patriarchy. We live, in short, in a patriarchal society. Nonetheless, if power-control theory is correct, it should be possible to identify variations in the effects of patriarchy across family class structures. The second part of this volume includes several tests of our theory. First, however, we consider the historical roots of the patriarchal family structure to which we attach so much importance, and the place of this family structure in the theory we propose.

Power-control theory focuses on the social organization of gender relations. It is concerned with the ways in which gender relations are established, maintained, perpetuated, or in other words, reproduced. The social reproduction of gender relations occurs across generations, and so adolescence provides a crucial context in which to address such issues. Meanwhile, societies vary in the social organization and reproduction of their gender relations, and so it is highly significant that our development of power-control theory occurs within an industrial capitalist society. Indeed, the question we must initially confront is: what is it about the macrolevel development of industrial capitalist societies that accounts for the way in which they reproduce gender relations?

Weber (1947) answers this question by noting that an important juncture in the development of modern capitalism involved the separation of the workplace from the home. Two distinct spheres, which Weber regarded as crucial to the rationalization of an industrial capitalist economy, resulted from this separation: the first was populated by women and focused on domestic labour and consumption, and the second was populated by men and centred around labour power and direct production. Weber refered to these respectively as the consumption and production spheres.

The differentiation of the production and consumption spheres is significant for the social reproduction of gender relations. The reproduction of gender relations occurs in both spheres. The state (through police, courts, and correctional agencies) assumes responsibility for reproductive functions in the production sphere, while the family assumes responsibility for such functions in the consumption sphere. These reproductive functions are inversely related and sexually stratified.

The inverse relationship derives from the fact that as the reproductive activities of the family and kinship groups decline, the reproductive activities of state agencies increase. So, for example, we have elsewhere (Hagan et al., 1979) tested the thesis that as informal social controls of family and kinship groups decrease, contact with state agencies such as the police increases. This inverse relationship between state and family based systems of social control is discussed by Donald Black (1976) and Andrew Scull (1977), among recent sociologists interested in issues of social control. The important point here is that this differentiation of state and family reproductive functions, and the inverse relationship between them, also has its source in the separation of the workplace from the home that accompanied the emergence of Western capitalist societies. So the separation of the workplace from the home brought a change in production relations that in turn resulted in changes in reproductive relations, both of which had profound implications for gender relations. Among the most significant of the new gender relations was an intensification of the sexual stratification of reproductive functions.

The sexual stratification of reproductive functions in the production and consumption spheres inheres in the fact that while females disproportionately are the instruments and objects of the informal social control activities of the family, males disproportionately are the instruments and objects of formal social control agencies of the state, such as the police. The overall effect of the sexual stratification of these functions is to perpetuate a gender division in the production and consumption spheres, with females restricted to the home-based consumption sphere, and males appropriated to the production sphere; where, among other things, males are more liable to police contact.

The reproductive structures of both the production and consumption spheres are patriarchal in form. However, the family is the primary source of patriarchal relations, and as a result in following chapters we give greater attention to the reproductive activities of the family than the state. Our attention turns now to the role of the patriarchal family in reproducing the separation of the production and consumption spheres, and to recent evidence of change in these arrangements.

The new family that emerged from the separation of work and home assumed responsibility for reproducing the gender division of the production and consumption spheres (Vogel, 1983). This family was patriarchal in form and created a 'cult of domesticity' around women (Welter, 1966). Today, however, Coser (1985) notes that there is a declining division of the consumption and production spheres which is reflected in the increased participation of women in the labour force. Coser goes on to note that as women have joined the labour force, they have gained new power in the family, particularly in the upper classes. The result is considerable variation in family class structure that we model in chapter 7. For the moment, we consider a highly abridged version of this model of family class structure, noting that these structures vary between two extreme family class relations that form real-life counterparts to two ideal-type families.

The first of these ideal types is largely a residue from an earlier period in which the consumption and production spheres were more strictly divided by gender. To reflect this legacy, we will call this the patriarchal family. Of the family class relations we identify in the next chapter, the one that should most closely correspond to the ideal-type patriarchal family consists of a husband who is employed outside the home in a position with authority over others, and a wife who is not employed outside the home. Power-control theory predicts that patriarchal families will tend to reproduce daughters who focus their futures around domestic labour and consumption, as contrasted with sons who are prepared for participation in direct production. We say more about how this happens below. Here we simply repeat that Weber regarded this process of social reproduction, and implicitly the social reproduction of gender relations, as crucial to the rationalization of industrial capitalism.

At the other extreme is an ideal type we call the egalitarian family, in which the consumption and production spheres are undivided by gender. Of the family class relations we identify in the following chapter, the one that should most closely correspond to the ideal type egalitarian family includes a mother and father who both are employed in positions with authority over others outside the home. Power-control theory predicts that egalitarian families tend to socially reproduce daughters who are prepared along with sons to join the production sphere. Such families are therefore a part of an overlapping of the consumption and production spheres, which a post-industrial society no longer so clearly keeps apart; such families are a part as well as a product of changing economic relations.

So the patriarchal family perpetuates a gender division in the consumption and production spheres, whereas the egalitarian family facilitates an overlapping of these spheres. The question is how this occurs. How does this happen and what are its consequences? Power-control theory answers these questions by joining a class analysis of the family with an analysis of the division of parental social control labour discussed above. The link is that parents socially reproduce their own power relationships through the control of their children. The key process involves the instrument-object relationship described under link 2 of figure 6.1 above, which is assumed to be at its extreme in the patriarchal family. Here fathers and especially mothers (i.e., as instruments of social control) are expected to control their daughters more than their sons (i.e., as objects of social control). In regard to mothers, we should emphasize that our point is not that they are, in any ultimate causal sense, more important than fathers in the control of daughters, but rather that mothers in patriarchal families are assigned a key instrumental role that involves them more in the day-to-day control of their children, especially their daughters. This imbalanced instrument-object relationship is a product of a division in domestic social control labour and it is a distinguishing feature of the control of daughters in patriarchal families. This instrument-object relationship is a key part of the way in which patriarchal families socially reproduce a gender division in the spheres of consumption and production.

Alternatively, a reduction of this relationship enables egalitarian families to reproduce an overlap of the production and consumption spheres. This does not mean that in these families fathers are as involved as mothers in the parental control of children; indeed, evidence mounts that this is not the case (e.g., Huber, 1976). What it does mean is that parents in egalitarian families will redistribute their control efforts so that daughters are subjected to controls more like those imposed on sons. In other words, in egalitarian families, as mothers gain power relative to husbands, daughters gain freedom relative to sons. In terms of the social reproduction of gender relations, the presence of the imbalanced instrument-object relationship helps perpetuate patriarchy, and its absence facilitates equality.

Our final task at this stage is to link this discussion of ideal-type families and the instrument-object relationship with predicted gender differences in common delinquent behaviour. This final intervening connection involves the attitudes toward risk-taking involved in the discussion of links 3 and 4 in figure 6.1. At one extreme, the patriarchal family and its acute instrument-object relationship between parents and daughters engenders a lower preference for risk-taking among daughters. Risk-taking is the antithesis of the passivity that distinguishes the 'cult of domesticity'. So, in patriarchal families, daughters are taught by their parents to be risk-averse. Alternatively, in egalitarian families, daughters and sons alike are encouraged to be more open to risk-taking. In part, this accommodation of risk is an anticipation of its role in the entrepreneurial and other activities associated with the production sphere, for which daughters and sons are similarly prepared in egalitarian families.

Control theories often regard delinquency as a form of risk-taking (Thrasher, 1927; Hirschi, 1969), sometimes as an unanticipated consequence of a rewarded willingness to take risks. The result is a correspondence in delinquent and entrepreneurial orientations that is reflected in Veblen's frequently quoted observation that, 'the ideal pecuniary man is like the ideal delinquent in his unscrupulous conversion of goods and persons to his own ends, and in a callous disregard of (i.e., freedom from) the feelings and wishes of others or the remoter effects of his actions' (1967: 237). Power-control theory does not regard this parallel as simple irony, but as an unintended consequence of a patriarchal social structure that is valued for its capacity to foster entrepreneurial, risk-taking orientations. With this in mind, power-control theory predicts that patriarchal families will be characterized by large gender differences in common delinquent behaviour, while egalitarian families will be characterized by smaller gender differences in delinquency. In egalitarian families, daughters become more like sons in their involvement in such forms of risk-taking as delinquency.

We will go no further here in developing the model of family class relations that we will use in further exploring and testing power-control theory. It is sufficient to note that a range of households beyond the forms we have yet considered will be analysed. The extreme forms of patriarchal and egalitarian family structures discussed so far anticipate a set of scope conditions for expanding the application of power-control theory. We have set the groundwork for the development and testing of this theory. However, before such tests can be initiated, it is important to be explicit about what exactly we are trying to explain.

COMMON DELINQUENCY AND BEYOND

To this point we have operated as if what was to be explained by power-control theory was a given. However, as criminologists have long appreciated, delinquency is a concept of rather uncertain meaning. This was particularly the case at the time our research was undertaken in Canada. In Canada delinquency is defined by federal legislation, which until recently designated within the concept of delinquency 'sexual immorality or any similar form of vice' (see Hagan and Leon, 1977). Something more specific than this is required if we are to have a more explicit sense of what we are seeking to explain.

In this and following chapters we focus on what we call 'common forms of delinquent behaviour', or simply 'common delinquency'. Before becoming more specific about these behaviours to be explained, it may be useful to indicate why we have selected among the forms of delinquency we could have considered. We decided at the outset not to focus on sexual offences. We decided this in part because we collected no data on sexual activity, but also because such offences often are so open-ended in definition that it becomes difficult to know what they mean, or how they would be treated if they were discovered by authorities. There is a cost in not considering sexual offences, in that they are often central to discussions of female delinquency. However, since our interest is comparative, this cost is less relevant than it might otherwise seem. Burnett (1986: 203) notes that a recent emphasis on sex specific offences has resulted in 'the separation of the study of women from the study of men', and that 'social policies which separate (or segregate) women from men are only half as valuable as policies or theories which recognize and take account of both groups.' Our point, of course, is not that sexual offences should go unstudied, but that they are simply not a part of this analysis.

Alternatively, there is another range of delinquent behaviour that is distinguished both by its frequency in Western capitalist societies and, most importantly, by its relevance to the power-control theory we wish to develop and test. The theory we wish to consider assumes that the presence of power and the absence of control both exercise their influence through cognitive processes in which actors evaluate courses of action. In particular, a key intervening process in power-control theory involves choices made by actors among behaviours based on their risk preferences and assessments. For actors to be influenced by such processes of risk assessment, the behaviours involved must be products of calculation. Our premise is that this is likely to be truer of minor forms of theft, vandalism and physical aggression (measurement of these behaviours is described in greater detail in the following chapter) than it will be of more serious forms of criminal and delinquent behaviour, particularly the crimes of violence emphasized in indices of 'serious' crime and delinquency. In short, ours is a theory of common delinquent behaviour. In chapter 9 we turn our attention briefly to other kinds of deviant behaviour, and to the broader possibilities for the application of power-control theory. We turn now to a brief description of the data we analyse in the following chapters.

DATA AND ORGANIZATION

Hirschi and Selvin (1967: 11–12) tell the intriguing tale of an experiment on the analysis of data conducted with three experienced investigators (Charles Glock, William Nicholls, and Martin Trow) who were given the same data set to analyse under similar 'hothouse' conditions. At the end of a long day of independent inquiry involving full access to computing resources and the support of autonomous teams of research assistants, the three analysts independently drafted reports of their findings and specified further lines of likely inquiry. The results revealed a great diversity in plans of analysis that Hirschi and Selvin undoubtedly are correct in observing would have been even more diverse had each investigator begun independently at the design stage, rather than being given identical data sets to analyse.

We take from this tale the moral that researchers might well be more forthcoming in indicating decisions made along the way in the development of their theories and their resultant data anlyses. It would undoubtedly be wasteful and tedious to preserve all such detail. However, the alternative tendency to reconstruct the research experience as a series of logically connected decisions, each flowing in pre-arranged sequence, may distort as much as it orders the record of events. In the following chapters we have chosen to preserve some of the sequence of the events that led to the theory proposed and tested. This means that both the theory and methods of analysis found in the following chapters undergo significant changes. In some cases this is because the theory began in a primitive form and developed in unexpected, or at least unplanned, directions. In other instances the changes reflect the state of our knowledge of the techniques available to undertake our analyses, so that, for example, while we began with ordinary least squares regression and little attention to scale construction, we ended with covariance structure models and an explicit consideration of measurement issues. All of this could be reorganized in a form other than it originally took. However, we have chosen to present the results of our work much as they emerged. The intention is to convey the ways in which theoretical and empirical choices actually were made, thereby making the alternatives explicit. The theory could, and doubtless should, be developed in ways other than it has been. We stake ourselves to the asumption that all good theories are provisional, subject to change. Certainly power-control theory is, and intentionally so. Hopefully this record of our work might encourage such changes.

The survey analysed in the following chapters was conducted in the greater Toronto metropolitan area during the first four months of 1979. The sample was drawn from seven schools and stratified so as to ensure sufficient numbers of subjects living in all types of housing and neighbourhoods – particularly higher density, poorer areas. School board lists of addresses with apartment and unit numbers were used to create the sampling frame, and sampling fractions were established for each school such that inhabitants of single and multiple dwelling units were selected in equal numbers. Subjects were offered a five dollar inducement to complete the questionnaire after school. By paying the students and assuring them of the confidentiality of their responses, we attempted to communicate to them the seriousness of the study. We believe this increased the quality as well as the quantity of participation. The questionnaire was administered orally to groups of the subjects to avoid reading problems encountered in earlier surveys of this kind (see Hirschi, 1969). One of the investigators read the questionnaire aloud, with the respondents following along and filling out their own questionnaires. The response rate to the survey was 72 per cent. Parents of students included in our survey were followed up by telephone, and we collected from them the information needed to construct our measure of family class position, as discussed in the following chapter. Analyses reported in following chapters are based on 463 adolescents. For all of these respondents a head of household was known to be either employed or unemployed, and additional occupational information was available on the former.

In chapter 7 we provide an operationalization of family class structure. This operationalization is then used in testing the assertion of power-control theory that the parental control of children varies in predictable ways across family class structures. In turn, this analysis considers the theory's predictions about the roles of gender and parental control in the sexual stratification of risk preferences. The chapter concludes by examining the role of these intervening variables in explaining delinquent behaviour.

In chapter 8 we provide a more refined analysis of the influence of parental controls. This analysis examines a distinction introduced earlier in this chapter between relational and instrumental controls, and explores the consequences of adding this new dimension of parental control across class categories, as well as the possibility that parental controls exercise their influence differently by gender. The latter undertaking allows us to speak to an important debate in the feminist literature between genetic and structural theories of gender. Covariance structure models also are introduced for the first time in this chapter.

Chapter 9 is the last empirical essay of the book. It brings a shift in focus by changing the behaviours to be explained. In this chapter we consider what insights power-control theory might provide in understanding thoughts about running away from home and suicide, which we conceptualize as a search for deviant role exits. In the process, this chapter offers empirical speculation about the role of parental control in responding to gender-connected problems of what often in the literature on medical sociology is called emotional distress. First, however, we turn to more familiar issues involving juvenile delinquency.

7

The Class Dynamics of the Family and Delinquency

INTRODUCTION

It is widely recognized that family life in Western capitalist societies changed dramatically following the end of World War II. The changes took several forms (Cherlin, 1983). The late 1940s and the 1950s brought a sustained baby boom, a lower average age at marriage, and a stable divorce rate. In the 1960s, these trends were overtaken by a sharp decline in fertility, a similarly sharp rise in divorce, an increase in non-marital cohabiting relationships, and, most importantly for our purposes, a large increase in the labour force participation of married women. All of these changes meant that the family was now a more variable social structure than previously had been the case. In this chapter we will explore some of the microstructural consequences of these macrostructural changes in work and the family, focusing particularly on issues of gender, risk-taking and delinquency. However, it is important first to place the above relatively recent changes in the family within a broader historical context.

SOCIAL CHANGE AND FAMILY STRUCTURE

We noted in the preceding chapter that a primary consequence of industrialization was the movement of production out of the household. Pre-industrial production characteristically was organized around the home in the form of what Tilly and Scott (1978) call the 'family economy'. Early industrialization brought a shift to a 'family wage economy', in which husbands, their children, and sometimes older sons and daughters worked outside the home, but nonetheless contributed to a common family budget. However, women, especially mothers, remained tied to the home and its domestic labour.

Over time, and with an increase in real wages, the place of women in the home became still more definite. A 'cult of domesticity', the 'woman's sphere', became a dominant part of family ideology. Cott (1977) has documented in historical detail the process by which this ideology took root, during the commercialization and then early industrialization that transformed late eighteenth-century New England. Within the 'woman's sphere', the traditional domestic values of 'intimacy, piety and virtue' became prominent; and the family became, in Christopher Lasch's (1977) apt phrase, a 'haven in a heartless world'. However, perhaps the most crucial aspect of the emergence of this distinctive 'woman's sphere' was its physical as well as ideological separation from the world of work. It is this separation that is the basis of Weber's distinction between the production and consumption spheres, with men assigned to the former, and women to the latter.

Against this backdrop, the imagery of the housewife of the 1950s (Friedan, 1963) can be understood as a creation of industrial capitalism. However, Cherlin (1983: 58–60) also argues that the family patterns that reached their peak in the 1950s were historically transient, and that this family structure, at its very pinnacle, was on the threshold of major change. Cherlin's point is that the baby boom of the 1950s, and the focus on domesticity that it brought, could only temporarily overshadow other important forces that would subsequently, and relatively quickly, bring important changes in family patterns. Among these forces for change were increasing wages and demands for semi-skilled, moderately-to-well-educated workers in the service sector, which included many sex-typed jobs: such as teachers, nurses, secretaries and clerks. Cherlin (1983: 59) writes that,

Because of the smaller cohort size and the trend toward earlier marriage, single women, who traditionally had filled these sex-typed jobs, were in short supply (Oppenheimer, 1970). In addition, the earlier age at first birth and closer child-spacing of the 1950s (Ryder, 1980) meant that many women were ending the stage of raising preschool children at a relatively young age.

The results of these forces are well known: women began joining the work force in increasing numbers, and 'the normative 1950s family', with its high fertility and withdrawal of wives from paid labour, became less common. Cherlin (63) concludes that, 'it is more enlightening to view the middle-class, single-earner family of the 1950s as a consequence of the disruptions of the Depression and World War II, the existence of a postwar economic boom, and the persistence of an ideology of domesticity, than merely as a timeless form that fits the needs of advanced capitalist societies.'

One way in which these changing family forms have been conceptualized is in terms of linkages between the occupational and family systems. Constantina Safilios-Rothschild (1976) has noted that in Parsonian functionalism, 'dual linkages' (involving husbands as well as wives) between the occupational and family systems were regarded as detrimental to family relationships. Parsons reasoned that dual linkages were likely to produce competition between spouses in terms of relative prestige, income and power. Families linked to the occupational sphere only through the husband's work were regarded as more functional, with the husband conferring his positional advantages on the wife and children. However, Safilios-Rothschild observes that while a husband's linkage to the occupational sphere may sometimes increase a spouse's prestige, it rarely increases her power. Increases in power, she reasons, are much more likely when wives are freed from the status linkages of their husbands, and when dual linkages are formed to the occupational sphere. Similarly, Pleck (1977) discusses linkages between 'the work-family role systems' and highlights the asymmetrically permeable boundaries between work and family roles for each sex. Both Pleck and Safilios-Rothschild attract attention to issues of gender and power as they are related to connections established between work and the family.

Our interest is in how power relations in the workplace and the household relate to gender differences in risk-taking and delinquency. Power-control theory begins with the premise that Western capitalist societies are characterized by a form of patriarchal family and a microstructure of parental controls that account for much gender variation in delinquency. However, while power-control theory assumes a predominance of patriarchy in Western industrial families, it also acknowledges variation in family structure. In chapter 6 we noted the importance of linking a microstructural account of family relations with a macrostructural understanding of connections between the work and family spheres. Indeed, we began with the premise that class structures the distribution of delinquency through the social reproduction of gender relations in the family. Below we further develop this premise with a model of class relations in the family. These class relations take the form of power relations, and they vary with gender-based linkages between work and family role systems. It is important, therefore, that we consider the changes in power relationships in the household that have resulted from the decline of 'the normative 1950s family', and the increasing participation of women in the labour force.

It is increasingly evident that power relationships within the family derive in significant part from the linkages formed by both husbands and wives between family and work systems (Coser and Coser, 1974). Summarizing a large research literature, Coser (1985: 1) writes that,

. . . power depends on resources, and women who do not have occupational resources are in a poor position to share it equally with their husbands (Coser and Coser,

1974). Conversely, the fact that the distribution of power in the family changes in favor of the wife wherever she contributes financial means to the household has been amply demonstrated. Blood and Wolfe (1960: 40–1) and others have shown this to be true for the United States, and Hyman Rodman (1967) examined this for all countries for which data are available – Belgium, Denmark, Finland, France, Germany, Ghana, Greece, Japan, the United States, and Yugoslavia – and found this to be true throughout.

Coser cautions that these power gains for women may be more evident in higher than in lower classes, but the more general point persists: power in the family derives from the positions in the workplace of wives as well as husbands.

The question for power-control theory therefore is this: what differences do the relative positions of husbands and wives in the workplace make for gender variations in the parental control, risk preferences and delinquent behaviour of adolescents? We anticipated this question in the preceding chapter when we discussed the variable ways patriarchal and egalitarian family structures are involved in the social reproduction of gender relations. The essence of our argument is that patriarchal families socially reproduce a gender division in the production and consumption spheres through a division along gender lines in the parental control of their children. Alternatively, we argued that egalitarian families are more likely to reduce gender differences in parental control and to thereby socially reproduce daughters as well as sons who are prepared to enter the production sphere. In a later section of this chapter we present a more complete model of family class relations that allows us to test such predictions and their implications for the relationship between gender, risk-taking and delinquency. As we note next, the development of such a model can make explicit a feature of power-control theory that might otherwise remain unnoticed: namely, that power-control theory subsumes two earlier deprivation and liberation theories of gender and delinquency.

The ability of power-control theory to subsume earlier formulations is important because, as Homans (1967: 27) points out, a good test of a theory is its ability to deduce a variety of empirical findings from a limited number of general propositions, 'with the help of a variety of given conditions'. Below we demonstrate that circumstances of deprivation and liberation constitute scope conditions within which power-control theory makes important, and perhaps surprisingly similar, predictions. However, specification of these scope conditions requires an analysis of the class dynamics of the family. The beginnings of this class analysis can be seen in the deprivation and liberation theories of gender and delinquency.

FROM DEPRIVATION TO LIBERATION

While it is well known that men markedly exceed women in criminality, until recently it was believed that only economic deprivation might appreciably alter this relationship. For example, early in this century Bonger (1916: 477) articulated the important effect that deprivation may have on gender and crime, observing that 'the criminality of men differs more from that of women in the well-to-do classes than in classes less privileged.' Bonger reasoned that differences in the 'manner of life' for the sexes decrease as we descend the social scale, and that therefore only in the underclasses should the criminality of women be expected to approach that of men.

A moden version of this deprivation theory of gender and crime is offered by Giordano, Kerbel and Dudley (1981: 81), who argue that contemporary increases in the criminality of women 'reflect the fact that certain categories of women (e.g., young, single, minority) are now in an even more unfavourable position in the labour market at the same time that they are increasingly expected to function independently'. The Giordano et al. formulation focuses particular attention on female-headed households, which are of recurring concern in contemporary studies of delinquency and poverty (see McLanahan, 1985). These households are of special interest for our extension of power-control theory and our analysis of the class dynamics of the family. Because men are not an integral part of these households, these families constitute a unique comparison group that is useful in assessing the impact on children of power relations between husbands and wives in households with two active parents.

The 'expectations of independence' noted by Giordano et al. bring us to the liberation theory of gender and crime. This theory is most provocatively formulated by Freda Adler (1975), who asserts that female criminal behaviour has become widespread in recent years largely as a result of the women's movement. Adler (1979: 93–4) argues that we are observing 'a gradual but accelerating social revolution in which women are closing many of the gaps, social and criminal, that have separated them from men'. This is clearly a different kind of formulation than the writings about deprivation and gender discussed previously. However, there is a parallel in that both deprivation and liberation are assumed to decrease differences between men and women. 'The closer they get,' writes Adler (1979: 94), 'the more alike they look and act . . . Differences do exist . . . but it seems clear that these differences are not of prime importance in understanding female criminality.

Perhaps the most interesting fact about the deprivation and liberation theories is that, although they both specify conditions under which men and women seem to become more alike, both socially and in terms of criminality, they do so by pointing to opposite ends of the class structure. While deprivation theory points to the lower end, and, increasingly, to female-headed households, liberation theory points to the upper end, where the liberation of women may be most likely to occur. Empirical tests of deprivation and liberation theories of gender and crime have produced equivocal results (for a recent review of this literature, see Box and Hale, 1984). We believe this is because the structural relationships that can result in gender equality and that are found at high and low positions in the class hierarchy have not been adequately conceptualized or operationalized.

CLASS RELATIONS IN THE FAMILY

Class location can be defined as a position in a structure of power relations within which production and reproduction occurs (cf., Cohen, 1978: 73). The particular model of class relations we propose for the purpose of developing and testing power-control theory links together the work and family role systems by considering the dual positions of spouses in the household and the labour force. This model of family class relations is a departure from older and more recent conventions in the stratification literature. These conventions tend to be individualistic. For example, the status attainment tradition focuses predominantly on male heads of households (Acker, 1973), neglecting the kinds of dual linkages between the work and family systems that Parsons saw as dysfunctional. By using males as proxies for families, and thereby implicitly assuming that families with heads of similar status had similar power structures, this tradition neglected an important source of variation in family relations that may be crucial to understanding many kinds of family transmitted gender differences, including gender differences in risk-taking and delinquency. Huber (1973) and others have correctly identified this androcentric bias in stratification theory and have proposed that an explicit focus on individuals replace the older convention of using males as proxies for families. However, as Curtis (1986) notes, the effect of such proposals is to replace one kind of individualistic bias with another. It is the household unit, and the variable structure of this unit based on the relation of household members, that may be the most useful focus of attention. In any case, it is clear from our earlier discussion that households organized as families are the essential units for the development and testing of power-control theory.

We briefly introduced our model of family class relations in the preceding chapter. The model is bounded by two polar ideal types of power relations that we designated as patriarchal and egalitarian. Although the patriarchal family may be most commonly associated with 'the normative family of the

1950s', it has its origin in the industrial revolution, and in the separation of the production and consumption spheres discussed by Weber. The egalitarian family is most often associated with the feminist movement, but also has an origin in the increasing movement of married women into the labour force since World War II. This family class relation is a part of a declining gender division in the production and consumption spheres.

In terms of the actual empirical model of family class relations developed below, the patriarchal family is one in which the husband is employed in an authority position in the workplace and the wife is not employed outside the home. The egalitarian family is one in which the husband and wife are both employed in authority positions outside the home. Power-control theory focuses on the mechanisms by which such families socially reproduce themselves.

Essential to this conception of the reproductive process is the assumption that as mothers gain power relative to fathers through their separate linkages into the occupational sphere, daughters as well gain freedom relative to sons. In turn, it is assumed that this will be reflected in the form of variation in the instrument-object relationship between parents and children discussed in earlier chapters.

For example, the patriarchal family socially reproduces a gender division between the production and consumption spheres through the sexual stratification of the instrument-object relationship between parents and children, in which mothers especially are held responsible for controlling their daughters more than their sons. Alternatively, the egalitarian family encourages an overlapping of the production and consumption spheres by diminishing the instrument-object relationship between mothers and daughters, thereby making the control of daughters more like that of sons. Included among the important consequences of such differences in the gender stratification of the parental control of children are differences in the desire to take risks. Power-control theory predicts that because in patriarchal families daughters are controlled more than sons, they will be less inclined to take risks. Alternatively, the greater relative freedom extended to daughters in egalitarian families encourages an attitude toward risk-taking that is more like that of sons. Daughters gain freedom, and in other words power, in egalitarian families, which makes them more like sons in their risk preferences, as well as ultimately in their risk-taking behaviour, including delinquency. It is on this basis that power-control theory predicts bigger gender differences in delinquent behaviour in patriarchal than in egalitarian families.

Note that we have not yet said anything about either the female-headed households emphasized in deprivation theory or the various other kinds of households that we will be considering. We have formulated the theory in terms of households with both parents present and in terms of the polar ideal types of power relations (patriarchal and egalitarian) that can result. However, the theory does have important implications for female-headed households, as well as for other kinds of families. For example, because fathers are not an integral part of female-headed households, there should be no manifest power imbalance between parents, and therefore, here too daughters should gain freedom relative to sons. These female-headed households provide a unique kind of comparison group; a special kind of egalitarian family that allows us to test our theory further. The expectation is that female-headed households should parallel other kinds of egalitarian households in many of the characteristics and consequences so far discussed. It is the common focus on freedom from male domination in these different kinds of households that allows our extension of power-control theory to subsume both deprivation and liberation theories of gender and delinquency.

This discussion of patriarchal, egalitarian, and female-headed households provides a set of scope conditions to be used in testing our extension of power-control theory. Each condition carries with it a predicted set of consequences in terms of gender variations in parental control, risk-taking and common forms of delinquent behaviour. These conditions take into account a range of circumstances that previously generated separate deprivation and liberation theories of gender and delinquency. However, many other kinds of households also exist. We turn now to a more inclusive model of family class relations that can be used in a more extensive test of our theory.

A MODEL OF FAMILY CLASS RELATIONS

The extension of power-control theory tested here asserts that the gender-based relationships we have discussed are conditioned by the combined class positions of fathers and mothers (i.e., the class composition of the household). The survey described in the preceding chapter provides the data base for the development of our model of family class relations. Parents of 463 students from this survey conducted in 1979 in the Toronto metropolitan area were followed up by telephone to collect the information we now use to construct a model of family class relations.

Our model of family class relations is based on Dahrendorfian conceptions of power and authority and their use in the control of collective units. Following Dahrendorf (1959: 198), these collective units include all 'imperatively co-ordinated associations': that is, they include the family as well as the workplace. Because they occupy so central a place in most people's lives, authority relations in industrial production often overshadow and determine authority relations in other collective units, including the family (cf., Litwak, 1968). In fact, this is our fundamental point – that to understand the effects of class position in the workplace on crime and delinquency it is necessary to trace the way that work relations structure family relations, including, for example, the instrument-object relationships between parents and daughters we have discussed previously. The crucial consideration that we now add to our test of power-control theory is the variable role of women in the workplace and its impact on the social organization of domestic social control.[1]

Dahrendorfian classes (see Dahrendorf, 1959: 166–74) are distinguished on the basis of their relations to authority. We follow Lopreato (1968) and Robinson and Kelly (1979) in using the terms 'command class' and 'obey class' to distinguish Dahrendorfian class positions. Members of the *command class* exercise authority, regardless of whether they are subject to it themselves. In contrast, persons in the *obey class* are subject to the authority of others and exercise none themselves. Finally, a small *classless* group neither exercises authority nor is subject to it; its members work on their own. Robinson and Kelly (1979: 44) demonstrate that separating the latter classless group from the obey class adds nothing to the explained variance in their analysis of income and attitudes, and therefore these classes are collapsed in our analysis.

We use the above ideas in the following ways: we begin with households in which both parents are present and the father is employed (female-headed households are brought into our analysis below). In these households, fathers are categorized as exercising authority on the basis of affirmative responses to questions asking whether there are people who work for them or are supervised by them. Where these conditions are not met, fathers are categorized as not exercising authority. Mothers are divided into three categories being considered: (1) as unemployed if they indicate, in response to a question asking about full- or part-time work, that they were 'not employed during the past year'; or, (2) if they are or were employed part- or full-time during this period, as exercising or not exercising authority on the basis of responses to items like those for fathers. The dichotomized measure of father's workplace authority is then cross-classified with our trichotomized measure of mother's workplace authority to generate the six family class relations indicated in table 7.1.

In three of the class categories indicated in table 7.1 both parents are located in the same class, and the class relation therefore has an unambiguous meaning in Dahrendorf's scheme. For example, when both the father and mother have authority in the workplace, the family is located in what we call the joint command class (12.45 per cent of our sample). This

Social Structure, the Family and Delinquency

TABLE 7.1 *Dahrendorfian model of familial class relations*

Wife's authority in workplace	Husband's authority in workplace	
	Has authority	Has no authority
Has authority	Joint command class: husband and wife in command class 12.45% (57)	Husband obey class/wife command class 6.77% (31)
Has no authority	Husband command class/ wife obey class 20.96% (96)	Upper obey class: husband and wife in obey class 18.12% (83)
Not employed	Husband command class/ wife not employed 16.38% (75)	Lower obey class: husband obey class/wife not employed 10.48% (48)

Balanced class relations

Unbalanced class relations

Female-headed household 14.85% (68)

is the class relation that we have described previously as most closely corresponding to the ideal-type egalitarian family. When neither the father nor mother has workplace authority, the family is located in the obey class. Two obey classes are distinguished in table 7.1 by whether the mother is employed. In the upper obey class, the mother is employed (18.12 per cent); in the lower obey class, the mother is not employed (10.48 per cent). Upper and, to a lesser extent, lower obey class families could also be thought of as egalitarian, in the sense that both spouses occupy obey class positions. However, given the lesser likelihood noted by Coser (1985) of women's work being translated into power in lower class families, we probably should qualify our egalitarian expectations for upper obey class families, and the expectations for lower obey class families are certainly no higher. In any case, the egalitarian family is an ideal type and we can look to the data to see how closely these families approximate the relationships that power-control theory would otherwise predict for families approaching this form. In the first part of the analysis reported below we take advantage of the common class locations of husbands and wives in these families to form an aggregate that is designated in table 7.1 as 'balanced class relations'. This grouping is subsequently disaggregated into the more refined class categories described above.

The three remaining family class relations in table 7.1 are each characterized by an unbalanced authority-subject relationship, in that one member of the household has authority in the workplace while the other does not. In two of these conditions, the father occupies a position of authority while the mother is either unemployed outside the home (16.38 per cent) or employed in a position without authority (20.96 per cent). These are the family class relations that come closest to matching the conditions of the ideal type patriarchal family described above, with the first relation providing the clearest empirical match. The final and most unusual family class relation (6.77 per cent) shows the father employed in a position without authority and the mother employed in one with authority. Because this kind of family is so atypical, in size as well as meaning, we do not consider it in subsequent analyses.[2] The power differentials in the above families are indicated in table 7.1 by their aggregate designation as 'unbalanced class relations'. Aggregated and disaggregated analyses of these class relations are presented below.

It may be of interest to consider how our new model of family class relations corresponds to the more traditional analysis of socio-economic status, as measured through father's occupation. In our survey we asked the adolescent respondents to provide a one or two sentence description of their father's occupation. These descriptions were then used to assign scores on Duncan's (1960) socio-economic index of occupations. The results are presented in table 7.2. As might be expected, fathers in the obey classes have lower index scores (37.159 and 35.195) than fathers in the command classes (49.194, 57.397, and 56.222). Of particular interest, however, is the fact that the last two scores, belonging to fathers whose wives are not employed outside the home and to fathers whose wives are also in the command class, are so close. These are respectively the patriarchal and egalitarian families in which power-control theory predicts the most extreme differences in parental control, risk preferences and delinquent behaviour. The fact that fathers' statuses in these families are so similar underlines the significance of bringing the positions of mothers into power-control theory. The theory encourages distinctions that otherwise would not be apparent. It remains to be demonstrated below, of course, that this distinction makes a difference.

Table 7.1 is not intended as an exhaustive categorization of family class relations. For example, we have not considered families where both parents are present and the father is unemployed. Because there are few such

TABLE 7.2 *Mean socio-economic status of father's occupation within family class categories*

Family class	Mean SES
Lower obey class	37.159
Upper obey class	35.195
Husband commands/wife obeys	49.194
Husband commands/wife not employed	57.397
Joint command class	56.222

families in our sample, we can only discuss them briefly below (see note 4). However, there are a substantial number of female-headed households (14.85 per cent; N = 68) and, for reasons indicated above, we include this category as a comparison group[3] that is predicted to produce many of the same consequences we expect in more conventional egalitarian families.[4]

Finally, a Marxian dimension can be added to the above model by including consideration of business ownership as a means of distinguishing, within the Dahrendorfian upper command class, between spouses in the 'capitalist' or 'employer class' and spouses in the 'managerial class'. This further distinction allows us to isolate a class that comes even closer to the social relations that should form the basis of the ideal type egalitarian family (i.e., families in which the spouses are both managers) and a class that reintroduces the potential for patriarchy (i.e., a family class structure in which the husband is an employer while the wife is only a manager). However, this modification of our model involves the creation of very small class categories, and we will therefore defer their consideration until later in this chapter.

Again, our basic premise is that authority in the workplace is translated into power in the household, with consequent effects on the relationship between gender and delinquency. More specifically, our refined power-control theory predicts that the relationship between gender and delinquency should be reduced in those family class relations in which the potential for existence of more balanced, egalitarian family relations is greatest, that is, in the lower levels of the class structure (e.g., in the upper obey class and in female-headed households) and also in the higher levels of the class structure (e.g., in the upper command class).

Alternatively, the relationship between gender and delinquency should be most intense in the unbalanced family class relations that most closely approximate an ideal-type patriarchal family, that is, in those situations in which the father has authority in the workplace and the mother is either unemployed or employed in an obey class position.

The intervening theoretical link in these predictions is that, in the class relations that characterize life in female-headed, upper obey class and joint command class families, mothers and fathers are less likely to reproduce, through the control of their daughters, the aversion to risk-taking that produces large gender differences in delinquency. In these more balanced, egalitarian families, daughters and sons alike are prepared for life in the production sphere. Alternatively, it is precisely this instrument-object relationship that our theory predicts will characterize the unbalanced class relations identified above, especially, for example, the family class relation that forms the most likely base for the ideal-type patriarchal family in our data, that is, that family class relation in which the husband occupies a command class position and the spouse is either not employed or is employed in a position without authority. It is here that we expect the instrument-object relationship between parents and daughters and the gender differences in risk preferences to be particularly apparent – and the gender-delinquency relationship consequently to be quite strong. These relationships, power-control theory argues, are part and parcel of patriarchy. They are the basis of the 'cult of domesticity' and an accompanying gender division between the consumption and production spheres. Before we test these predictions, however, some additional issues of measurement must be addressed.

MEASUREMENT OF INTERVENING AND DEPENDENT VARIABLES

Parental controls are the key intervening variables in our proposed power-control theory. Alpha coefficients are reported below for operationalizations of each of these variables. Our additively scaled measures of maternal (α = 0.66) and paternal (0.78) control ask, 'Does your (father/mother) know (where you are/who you are with) when you are away from home?' We use these items to explore the instrument-object relationship emphasized between parents and daughters.

'Taste for risk' is a socially acquired attitude expected to mediate further the link between gender and delinquency. Taste for risk (0.67) is measured by adding Likert-scaled responses to two statements: 'I like to take risks' and 'the things I like to do best are dangerous'. Power-control theory predicts that taste for risk is sexually stratified and that this attitude in turn stratifies perceived risks of getting caught in delinquent behaviour, our last intervening link. Three 'risk of getting caught' items from the work of Jensen, Erickson, and Gibbs (1978) form an additive scale (0.76). They involve the following estimations: 'Could you (break into a spot/steal from a store/write graffiti) and not get caught?'

As we have noted, we are certainly not the first to consider the importance of risk-taking in the explanation of delinquency. An important context in which the role of risk-taking previously has been considered involves studies of perceived sanction risk and delinquency. Jensen, Erickson and Gibbs (1978) report important survey research that reveals a strong inverse relationship between perceived risk of legal sanctions and self-reported delinquency. This work is important for our own because it places an emphasis on risk and includes the scale items noted above. However, there is also a way in which this and related work, wrongly understood, could easily be misleading for the purposes of the gender-based theory we are proposing.

The potential confusion occurs when Jensen et al. control for gender in a test of the influence of other variables on the strong relationship they find between perceived sanction risk and self-report measures of delinquency. They report that 'the relation between perceived risk and delinquency is neither specific to males nor spuriously attributable to common links with gender'. Similarly, Anderson, Chiricos and Waldo (1977), in a rare and important attempt to simultaneously examine formal and informal sanctioning, find an inverse relationship between both types of perceived sanction risk and self-reported delinquency. They too report that these relationships are undiminished by a control for gender of respondent. However, in spite of the central causal role we assign to gender in power-control theory, analyses like those undertaken in these studies actually should not be expected to produce any diminishing effect when gender is controlled.

The above studies treat gender as a potential source of spuriousness in the relationship between sanction risk and delinquency variables. However, power-control theory asserts a rather different causal relationship, namely, with regard to the Jensen et al. configuration of variables, that gender causes differences in risk assessment, which in turn cause differences in delinquent behaviour; and with regard to the Anderson et al. configuration, that gender causes differences in informal social controls, which, in turn, cause differences in formal social control. Hirschi and Selvin (1967: 83) point out that if 'A causes B and B causes C, the relation between B and C will not disappear when A is held constant'; or in the Lazarsfeldian terms that many readers may recall from their graduate training, 'if B interprets the relation between A and C, then A cannot explain the relation between B and C' (89n). So, from the perspective of power-control theory, the results of the above studies should come as no surprise. On the one hand, they suggest concepts and measures involving risk and sanctioning that are of considerable importance for the analyses we wish to undertake, while on the other hand their results are consistent with the causal structure proposed by power-control theory.

We use an adapted version of Hirschi's (1969) self-report delinquency scale as our dependent variable. The six-item additive scale asked how often in the last year the respondents had taken little things (worth less than $2/ between $2 and $50/and more than $50) that did not belong to them; taken a car for a ride without the owner's permission; purposely banged up something that did not belong to them; and, not counting fights with a brother or sister, purposely beaten up anyone or hurt anyone (0.78).

THE ANALYSIS

Our extension of power-control theory explicitly predicts that the relationship between gender and delinquency is conditioned by family class composition. Our analysis therefore proceeds within the aggregated and disaggregated family class relations and female-headed households identified in table 7.1. This analysis includes a series of within-class correlations presented in table 7.4, a set of bar graphs to illustrate within-class gender differences in figures 7.1–7.5, and the results of estimating a series of reduced form and structural regression equations in tables 7.5–7.10. Between-class comparisons of gender regression coefficients are presented in table 7.11, and a refinement of our class analysis, anticipated in table 7.4 and above, is presented in table 7.12. Descriptive statistics for our variables are presented in table 7.3.

Our first interest is in determining whether the instrument-object relationship postulated by our theory varies as predicted with family class relations. Correlations relevant to this issue are presented in table 7.4. Discussion of the 'refined' findings reported toward the bottom of this table is reserved until later when these categories are described. The first column in this table presents correlations between gender and the maternal control scale within the aggregated and disaggregated family class categories. This column of results confirms that mothers control their daughters more than their sons. Note further that the correlations between gender and maternal controls are generally stronger than the correlations between gender and paternal controls, shown in the second column. In table 7.3 we can also see that mean levels of maternal control are uniformly higher than paternal levels of control. Across classes, then, mothers are more involved than fathers as instruments of parental controls, and the objects of these controls are more often daughters than sons. Overall, then, these results provide evidence of the instrument-object relationship that is emphasized in power-control theory.

TABLE 7.3 *Means and standard deviations[a] of variables used in regression equations*

Variables	Unbalanced class relations	Husband commands/ wife not employed	Husband commands/ wife obeys	Balanced class relations	Lower obey class	Upper obey class	Joint command class	Female-headed households
Gender	0.550 (0.499)	0.547 (0.501)	0.552 (0.500)	0.527 (0.501)	0.542 (0.504)	0.556 (0.499)	0.456 (0.503)	0.324 (0.471)
Maternal control	5.702 (1.451)	5.667 (1.446)	5.729 (1.462)	5.622 (1.422)	5.688 (1.518)	5.639 (1.393)	5.544 (1.402)	5.765 (1.467)
Paternal control	4.947 (1.610)	4.733 (1.536)	5.115 (1.654)	4.963 (1.489)	5.000 (1.624)	5.000 (1.465)	4.877 (1.428)	3.971 (1.079)
Taste for risk	6.322 (1.975)	6.547 (2.107)	6.146 (1.858)	6.218 (1.094)	6.167 (1.837)	6.205 (1.962)	6.281 (1.906)	6.662 (1.707)
Perceived risk	8.926 (2.513)	8.533 (2.554)	8.677 (2.626)	8.926 (2.513)	9.042 (2.657)	9.000 (2.249)	8.719 (2.541)	8.838 (2.629)
Self reported delinquency	9.140 (3.544)	9.280 (3.570)	9.031 (3.538)	9.021 (3.458)	8.896 (3.502)	8.759 (3.165)	9.509 (3.823)	9.779 (4.370)

[a] Standard deviations are in parentheses.

However, a further premise of our theory is that such instrument-object relationships have an origin in family class relations between husbands and wives. If this premise is accurate, the correlations reported in table 7.4 should vary across family class relations in predictable ways. Using this premise, we predicted that the more egalitarian (i.e., balanced) class relations that characterize the obey and upper command classes – and, by default, female-headed households – will moderate the instrument-object relationship between parents and daughters. Alternatively, our extension of power-control theory leads us to predict that these instrument-object relationships will be more characteristic of unbalanced class relations, including, for example, the most unbalanced family class relation which most resembles the ideal-type patriarchal family, that is, the family with a command class husband and an unemployed wife. In this class relation, we should find fathers, and especially mothers, to be particularly controlling of their daughters.

Table 7.4 generally confirms the above predictions. It is in the female-headed households and the upper command class that the maternal instrument-object relationships are weakest (0.025 and − 0.156), and it is when the head commands and the spouse is not employed that this instrument-object relationship is most acute (− 0.398). However, this relationship remains rather strong in the lower (− 0.275) and upper obey (− 0.369) classes, as well as in the class in which the husband commands and the wife obeys (− 0.297). The latter finding is consistent with Coser's suggestion that women in the lower classes are least likely to benefit from

TABLE 7.4 *Correlations within aggregated and disaggregated class categories of gender with maternal and paternal controls, risk preferences, perceived risks and delinquent behaviour*

Class categories	Maternal control	Paternal control	Risk preferences	Perceived risks	Delinquent behaviour
Unbalanced class relations	-0.341^d	-0.257^d	0.267^d	-0.272^d	0.422^d
Husband commands/ wife not employed	-0.398^d	-0.264^c	0.263^c	-0.294^c	0.480^d
Husband commands/ wife obeys	-0.297^c	-0.256^c	0.275^c	-0.256^c	0.377^c
Balanced class relations	-0.275^d	-0.081	0.120^b	0.194^c	0.265^d
Lower obey class	-0.275^b	-0.156	0.084	-0.049	0.310^b
Upper obey class	-0.369^d	-0.167^a	0.229^b	-0.242^b	0.319^c
Joint command class	-0.156	0.104	-0.006	-0.276^b	0.202
Refinement: husband employer/ wife manager	-0.446^b	-0.498^b	0.164	-0.470^b	0.489^a
Husband and wife managers	-0.024	0.347^c	-0.060	-0.185	0.047
Female-headed households	0.025	0.078	0.119	-0.114	0.180

[a] Significant at 0.10 level.
[b] Significant at 0.05 level.
[c] Significant at 0.01 level.
[d] Significant at 0.001 level.

changes in family power relations, even when they join the work force. Overall, the maternal instrument-object relationship is stronger in unbalanced than in balanced class relations and weakest in female-headed households.

A more concrete sense of the relationships that we have emphasized here and in chapter 6 is provided in figure 7.1, which graphs the maternal control scores of sons and daughters in the most patriarchal (i.e., where the husband commands and the wife is not employed outside the home) and egalitarian (i.e., the joint command class) family class relations, as well as in female-headed households. In this figure note that the highest (6.294) and lowest (5.146) maternal control scores are found in the most patriarchal households, for daughters and sons respectively. The respective scores for daughters and sons in the egalitarian households are 5.742 and 5.308, and in the female-headed households these scores are 5.739 and 5.818. These scores provide further support for the proposition that the acute instrument-object relationship between mothers and daughters is a product of patriarchal family class relations.

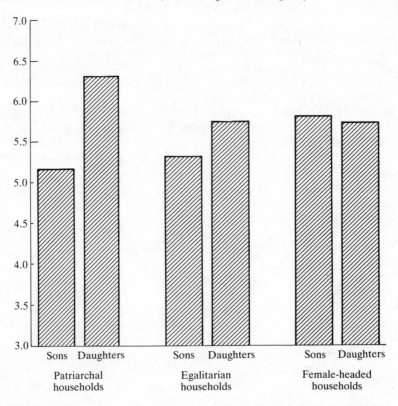

Figure 7.1   Levels of maternal controls for sons and daughters in patriarchal, egalitarian and female-headed households

The within-class gender-paternal control correlations in table 7.4 parallel those reported above, but as expected, at lower levels. Thus the correlation between gender and paternal control is stronger in unbalanced class relations ($r = -0.257$) and most acute in those families that are most patriarchal ($r = -0.264$). The corresponding correlations are weaker in the more balanced class relations ($r = -0.081$), including the more egalitarian joint command class ($r = 0.104$) and female-headed households ($r = 0.078$). The remaining family class relations produce results that, as expected, are somewhere between these extremes. The paternal control scores that underwrite some of the above correlations are again presented graphically in figure 7.2. Note that in this figure the disparity in the paternal control of daughters (5.176) and sons (4.366) is again greatest in the most patriarchal households. In the egalitarian households, fathers on average actually control daughters (4.742) slightly less than sons (5.038). As expected, fathers in female-headed families are least evident in their control of both daughters and sons, and the levels of control that are reported are almost identical (3.913 and 4.091).

The fact that mean levels of maternal control are essentially constant across the family class categories in table 7.3 shows that the instrument-object relationships do not vary across these class categories simply as a result of the time that mothers spend in or away from home; overall levels of maternal control remain approximately the same, regardless of whether mothers work. Variations in the instrument-object relationships must therefore occur as a result of the redistribution of maternal controls *vis-à-vis* sons and daughters in these homes.

The final sets of correlations in table 7.4 concern risk preferences and perceived risks. In all class categories in which the correlation of risk preference with gender is significant, the relationship is in the

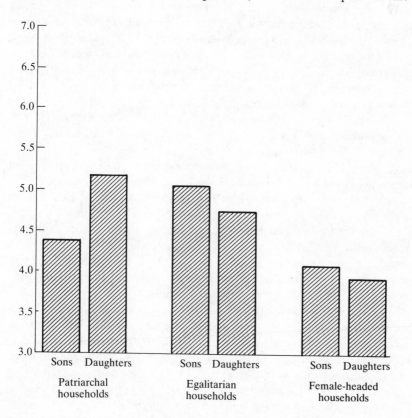

Figure 7.2   Levels of paternal controls for sons and daughters in patriarchal, egalitarian and female-headed households

expected direction of sons more than daughters preferring risk-taking. The correlations of gender with perceived risks are consistently negative, indicating that daughters perceive greater risks in delinquency than do sons. However, of greater interest is the finding that the correlations between gender and the risk variables are stronger in the unbalanced than in the balanced class relations; although this is more clearly the case for risk preferences than for perceived risks. For example, the correlation between gender and risk preference is strongest in those patriarchal classes in which the husband commands and the wife is either not employed (0.263) or employed in a position without authority (0.275), and is weakest in the more egalitarian settings of the joint command class (− 0.006), the lower obey class (0.084), and in female-headed households (0.119). The correlation of gender with risk preference in the upper obey class is perhaps somewhat stronger than expected (0.229), as are the correlations between gender and perceived risks in the upper obey class (− 0.242) and the joint command class (− 0.276); but otherwise these findings are quite consistent with the intervening role assigned to risk-taking in a power-control theory of gender and delinquency. Furthermore, the unexpectedly strong correlation just noted between perceived risk and gender in the joint command class is accounted for in a later refinement of this class category. Patriarchal families do seem to discourage risk-taking among daughters as compared with sons, while egalitarian families seem more likely to encourage a preference for risk among daughters as well as among sons. Overall, the implications are similar for the measure of perceived risk.

The gender differences in risk preferences across family settings are well illustrated in figure 7.3. In patriarchal families, the average risk preference score for sons is 7.049, while it is only 5.976 for daughters. However, in egalitarian families, the scores for sons are reduced (6.269) and the scores for daughters are increased (6.290), eliminating almost any indication of gender difference. Risk preferences in female-headed households are higher than in egalitarian families, for both sons (6.995) and daughters (6.522), but these scores are still quite similar to one another, and both are lower than the male scores in patriarchal families.

We noted above that the correlations between gender and perceived risks did not vary as predictably across class categories as did those between gender and risk preferences. The point is illustrated again in figure 7.4. Daughters (9.353 and 9.355) are more likely than sons (7.854 and 7.962) to perceive delinquency as involving risks in both the most patriarchal and egalitarian families. These estimations (8.409 and 9.043) converge somewhat in female-headed households, and there is further evidence of convergence in the refined class analysis that we report below. Nonetheless, it seems likely on the basis of findings reported so far that risk preferences would be

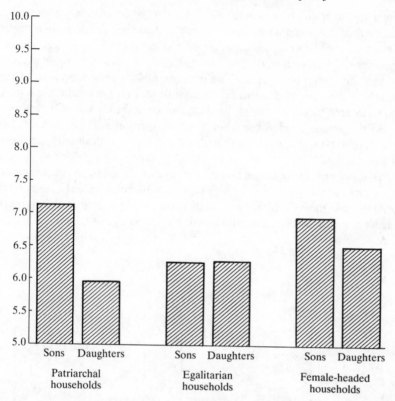

Figure 7.3   Levels of risk preference for sons and daughters in patriarchal, egalitarian and female-headed households

of greater importance than perceived risks in explaining gender differences in delinquent behaviour. We examine this possibility in the multi-variate analysis below.

The final correlations reported in table 7.4 are between gender and delinquent behaviour. These correlations are consistent with the predictions of power-control theory and the pattern we have thus far observed for the intervening variables. In the aggregated unbalanced class relations the correlation between gender and delinquency is 0.422, while in the more balanced class relations this correlation is 0.265. Furthermore, the strongest disaggregated relationship between gender and delinquency ($r = 0.480$) is in the most patriarchal class relation, where the husband commands and the wife is not employed; while the weakest gender-delinquency correlations are in the joint command class ($r = 0.202$) and in female-headed households (0.180). The correlations between gender and delinquency are somewhat larger in the lower (r = 0.310) and upper (r = 0.319) obey classes, but still smaller than in either of the more unbalanced class relations. In terms of the actual scale scores graphed in figure 7.5, the disparity across genders is again largest in the most patriarchal families, with sons scoring on average 10.829 and daughters 7.412. The average male scores (10.346) decline slightly in the more egalitarian families, while to a greater extent the female scores (8.806) increase in these families. However, the highest of both scores are in the female-headed households, where sons on average score 10.909 and daughters 9.239. Again, patriarchy is associated with disparity, at least at the bivariate level.

We move now to the estimation of a series of reduced form and structural equations in tables 7.5–7.10. The purpose of these equations is to further explore the theory's refined specification of the gender-delinquency relationship across class categories and, more specifically, the operation of

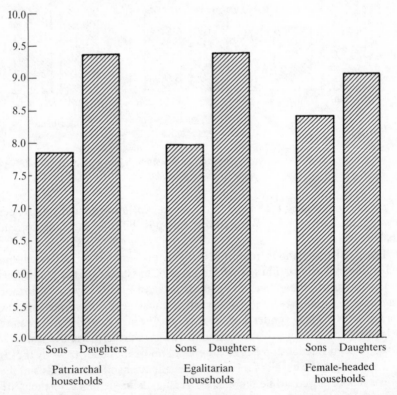

Figure 7.4   Levels of perceived risk for sons and daughters in patriarchal, egalitarian and female-headed households

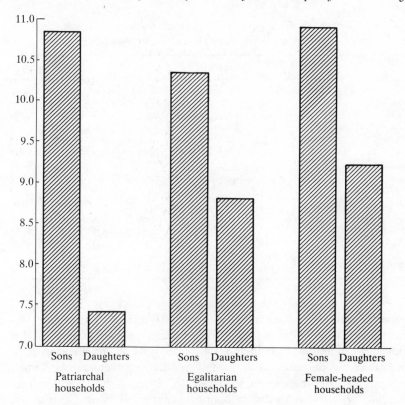

Figure 7.5 Levels of self-reported delinquency for sons and daughters in patriarchal, egalitarian and female-headed households

its postulated intervening links between gender and delinquency within these class categories.

We begin with the reduced form equations estimating risk preferences within the aggregated balanced and unbalanced family class categories analysed in table 7.4. These equations are central to understanding the role of family classes and parental controls in producing the gender-based variations in risk preferences reported above. The results in table 7.5 of estimating equation (1), which includes only gender, reveal that on average in unbalanced families sons score about one point higher (b = 1.058, p = 0.001) than daughters on our additive scale of risk preferences. In balanced families, the difference is less than half this (b = 0.475, p = 0.101). Equations (2)–(4) respectively introduce maternal and paternal controls, separately and then jointly. Power-control theory asserts that in more patriarchal families mothers are assigned an instrumental role in

TABLE 7.5 *Regressions within aggregated balanced and unbalanced class categories of risk preferences on independent variables in four equations*

Independent variables	Equation (1)		Equation (2)		Equation (3)		Equation (4)	
	Unbalanced	Balanced	Unbalanced	Balanced	Unbalanced	Balanced	Unbalanced	Balanced
Gender: *b*	1.058	0.457	0.634	0.046	0.780	0.378	0.618	0.055
Beta	0.267	0.120	0.160	0.012	0.197	0.099	0.156	0.014
Standard error	0.293	0.277	0.298	0.267	0.091	0.269	0.298	0.270
Sig.	0.001	0.101	0.035	0.863	0.009	0.162	0.039	0.840
Maternal control: *b*			− 0.428	− 0.526			− 0.310	− 0.506
Beta			− 0.314	− 0.393			− 0.228	− 0.378
Standard error			0.103	0.094			0.134	0.123
Sig.			0.000	0.000			0.022	0.000
Paternal control: *b*					− 0.335	− 0.326	− 0.160	− 0.028
Beta					− 0.273	− 0.255	− 0.130	− 0.022
Standard error					0.091	0.091	0.118	0.113
Sig.					0.000	0.000	0.177	0.805
Constant	5.740	5.978	8.412	9.150	7.553	7.637	8.537	9.175

imposing controls on daughters which diminish their preferences for risk-taking, especially compared to sons. We emphasize that our point is not that fathers are uninvolved in this process. The focus of this proposition on patriarchal families makes clear that fathers have a very central role. Rather, the point is that mothers in particular are assigned the greater role in carrying out the day-to-day monitoring activities. If these assertions of power-control theory are correct, then adding maternal controls in equation (2) should substantially reduce the relationship between gender and risk preferences observed in equation (1). This is indeed the case: the gender-risk preference relationship is reduced by about 40 per cent between these equations, from 1.058 to 0.634. Alternatively, introducing paternal controls alone in equation (3) reduces the gender-risk preference relationship by about 20 per cent, to 0.780; while the combination of maternal and paternal controls in equation (4) reduces the effect of gender on delinquency to 0.618. A similar pattern of relationships is observed in the more balanced families, but at reduced levels. The clearest implication of these findings is that the instrument-object relationship established between mothers and daughters plays a prominent role in explaining the greater attraction that risk-taking holds for boys compared to girls, especially in more unbalanced patriarchal family class relations.

The results from table 7.5 can now be disaggregated into the family class categories from table 7.1. Doing so in table 7.6 again indicates the strength of the relationship between gender and risk preference in the two most patriarchal family class relations, in which the husband commands and the wife is not employed ($b = 1.108$) or is employed in an obey class position ($b = 1.022$). The relationship between gender and risk preference is not half as strong in any of the other family classes. Maternal controls also play a greater role in explaining the relationship between gender and risk preferences in both of these family structures, although this is more clearly the case in the more patriarchal of these class relations: where the wife is not employed outside the home, adding maternal controls alone to the equation reduces the gender-risk preference relationship below statistical significance, from 1.108 to 0.705 ($p = 0.169$). When the husband is in the command class and the wife is employed in the obey class, it is necessary to add both maternal and paternal controls to the equation to reduce this relationship below statistical significance (from 1.022 to 0.582, $p = 0.105$). Note, however, that the addition of paternal controls to this equation produces only a marginal futher reduction in this relationship (from $b = 0.608$ to 0.582). So it would still seem the case that mothers play the primary role in reducing the risk preferences of daughters compared to sons, by imposing greater control on daughters in patriarchal families. Maternal controls are negatively and significantly correlated with risk preferences across all of the family classes in table 7.6, but it is only in the more patriarchal class relations that these controls play a major role in explaining the relationship between gender and risk preferences. The implication is that it is a patriarchal family structure that produces the instrument-object relationship between mothers and daughters, thereby reducing the interest of daughters in these families in risk-taking. These findings, of course, speak to the core of power-control theory.

In table 7.7 we return to the aggregated balanced and unbalanced class categories and the estimation of equations for perceived risks. As indicated earlier in table 7.4, the relationship between gender and perceived risks of delinquent behaviour is greater in the unbalanced ($b = -1.411$) than balanced family classes (-0.974). Equally interesting in this table, however, is the finding that risk preferences ($\beta = -0.175$) have a greater net impact than any of the other variables on perceived risks, although paternal controls come very close ($\beta = 0.173$). The implication of the former finding is that as risk preferences rise, perceived risks decline: that is, those who like risk more, perceive less of it. Risk preferences also play an important role in reducing the relationship between gender and perceived risks in the unbalanced family classes: from -0.932 ($p = 0.019$) to -0.790 ($p = 0.046$), between equations (4) and (5) in table 7.7. This means that the effect we already have seen exercised directly on risk preferences by maternal controls is now exercised indirectly on perceived risks through risk preferences. These findings are disaggregated into the full set of family

TABLE 7.6 *Within-class category regressions of risk preferences on independent variables in four equations*

Independent variables	Female-headed households	Lower obey class	Upper obey class	Husband commands/ wife not employed	Husband commands/ wife obeys	Joint command class
Equation (1)						
Gender: *b*	0.433	0.307	0.091	1.108	1.022	− 0.021
Beta	0.120	0.084	0.229	0.263	0.275	0.006
SE	0.432	0.536	0.426	0.478	0.369	0.512
Sig.	0.331	0.569	0.037	0.022	0.007	0.967
Constant	6.522	6.00	5.694	5.942	5.581	6.290
Equation (2)						
Gender: *b*	0.463	− 0.160	0.482	0.705	0.608	− 0.287
Beta	0.128	− 0.044	0.123	0.168	0.164	− 0.076
SE	0.421	0.504	0.443	0.507	0.360	0.468
Sig.	0.276	0.753	0.280	0.169	0.001	0.542
Maternal control: *b*	− 0.381	− 0.564	− 0.407	− 0.351	− 0.476	− 0.613
Beta	− 0.328	− 0.466	− 0.289	− 0.241	− 0.375	− 0.451
SE	0.135	0.167	0.159	0.176	0.123	0.168
Sig.	0.006	0.002	0.012	0.050	0.001	0.001
Constant	8.709	9.460	8.225	8.151	8.538	9.807
Equation (3)						
Gender: *b*	0.370	0.120	0.827	0.990	0.646	0.128
Beta	0.102	0.033	0.210	0.236	0.174	0.034
SE	0.436	0.519	0.431	0.493	0.352	0.481
Sig.	0.399	0.818	0.059	0.048	0.069	0.790
Paternal control: *b*	0.351	− 0.373	− 0.152	− 0.144	− 0.445	− 0.504
Beta	0.222	− 0.330	− 0.113	− 0.105	− 0.396	− 0.378
SE	0.191	0.161	0.147	0.161	0.106	0.169
Sig.	0.072	0.025	0.304	0.374	0.001	0.004
Constant	5.149	7.968	6.496	6.686	8.066	8.682
Equation (4)	Maternal and paternal controls in equation					
Gender: *b*	0.381	− 0.168	0.469	0.707	0.582	− 0.160
Beta	0.105	− 0.046	0.119	0.168	0.157	− 0.042
SE	0.403	0.511	0.446	0.512	0.356	0.481
Sig.	0.347	0.743	0.296	0.172	0.105	0.741
Constant	7.246	9.455	8.117	8.129	8.587	10.074

classes in table 7.8. However, rather than now discuss these findings further, we turn instead to the estimation of equations for self-reported delinquency. Results from these equations reveal, among other things, that risk preferences have a substantially larger effect on delinquency than perceived risks. This is why we do not labour the importance of the perceived risk results in this analysis. We turn instead to the delinquency equations.

We begin again with the aggregated balanced and unbalanced family class categories. Recall that Bonger's (1916) deprivation theory predicted that the relationship between gender and delinquency would increase with upward movement through the class structure, and decrease with movement down. However, power-control theory subsumes both deprivation and liberation theories of gender and delinquency by taking into account the combined class positions of spouses; the modified prediction is that when both parents occupy positions of authority (i.e., circumstances of liberation) or when neither have such positions (i.e., circumstances of deprivation), a rough balance will be established and a more egalitarian pattern should be expected – and, therefore, the relationship between gender and delinquency should decline. The weaker correlations we observed for such families in table 7.4 between gender and maternal as well as paternal controls, between gender and the risk variables, and between gender and delinquency were consistent with the predictions of power-control theory. The unstandardized gender coefficients resulting from the estimation of equation (1) in the first two columns of table 7.9 further confirm this prediction: the zero order gender coefficient in the unbalanced class relation ($b = 2.996$) is much larger than the gender coefficient in the balanced class ($b = 1.833$). These results are disaggregated in table 7.10 and compared with those in female-headed households. Here we find that the largest gender coefficients are, as expected, in the most unbalanced and patriarchal of families – that is, in those in which the father commands and the mother is not employed ($b = 3.420$) or is employed in a position without authority ($b = 2.668$). Meanwhile, the smallest gender coefficient in this table ($b = 1.540$) is in the balanced joint command class, and the coefficient for gender in female-headed households is only slightly larger ($b = 1.670$).

Gender coefficients from these equations are compared further across classes in size and statistical significance in table 7.11. Our first interest is in determining if the gender coefficient in the aggregated unbalanced class relation is significantly larger than the gender coefficient in the aggregated balanced class relation. It is ($t = 2.369$). In turning next to the disaggregated results, our interest is in whether the gender coefficient in the most unbalanced and patriarchal family we have considered, that in which the father commands and the mother is not employed, is significantly larger than the gender coefficient in the more egalitarian families we have considered –

TABLE 7.7 Regressions within aggregated balanced and unbalanced class categories of perceived risks on independent variables in five equations

Independent variables	Equation (1) Unbalanced	Equation (1) Balanced	Equation (2) Unbalanced	Equation (2) Balanced	Equation (3) Unbalanced	Equation (3) Balanced	Equation (4) Unbalanced	Equation (4) Balanced	Equation (5) Unbalanced	Equation (5) Balanced
Gender: b	− 1.411	− 0.974	− 0.962	− 0.392	− 1.047	− 0.848	− 0.932	− 0.433	− 0.790	− 0.406
Beta	− 0.272	− 0.194	− 0.186	− 0.078	− 0.202	− 0.169	− 0.180	− 0.086	− 0.152	− 0.081
Standard error	0.384	0.361	0.397	0.343	0.383	0.345	0.393	0.346	0.394	0.320
Sig.	0.003	0.008	0.016	0.254	0.007	0.015	0.019	0.212	0.046	0.206
Maternal control: b			0.453	0.744			0.220	0.650	0.149	0.400
Beta			0.254	0.421			0.123	0.368	0.083	0.152
Standard error			0.137	0.121			0.178	0.157	0.178	0.227
Sig.			0.001	0.000			0.218	0.000	0.405	0.009
Paternal control: b					0.440	0.518	0.315	0.136	0.279	0.122
Beta					0.274	0.307	0.196	0.080	0.173	0.072
Standard error					0.119	0.116	0.156	0.145	0.155	0.134
Sig.					0.000	0.000	0.044	0.350	0.073	0.364
Risk preference: b									− 0.229	− 0.493
Beta									− 0.175	− 0.373
Standard error									0.101	0.807
Sig.									0.025	0.000
Constant	9.390	9.438	6.562	4.950	7.012	6.801	6.314	4.827	8.268	9.346

that is, those in which both parents command (the joint command class), obey (the upper obey class), or where the household is female-headed. The *t*-values reported in column 3 of this table reveal that as power-control theory predicts, all three of these comparisons are statistically significant. That is, the gender-delinquency relationship is significantly stronger in the patriarchal class relation than in any of the more egalitarian class relations (t = 2.186, 2.010, 2.103).

Now we must demonstrate that the intervening links proposed in our theory and considered previously in-and-of-themselves help to explain these gender-delinquency relationships. We turn first to the intervening role of the instrument-object relationship between mothers and daughters. We have already seen in table 7.3 that mothers are more involved than fathers in the control of their children; and in table 7.4 we have seen that mothers, more than fathers, control their daughters more than their sons, particularly in unbalanced, patriarchal families. Equations (2), (3) and (4) in table 7.9 further explore the roles of maternal and paternal controls in explaining the gender-delinquency relationship by separately and then jointly adding these scales to equation (1). Both procedures yield similar conclusions; we therefore will only summarize the latter. The results of entering the parental control variables jointly in table 7.9 indicate that maternal controls ($b = -0.526$) have a slightly larger direct effect than paternal controls ($b = -0.461$) on delinquency in the aggregated unbalanced class relation and a much larger direct effect ($b = -0.864$ and 0.028 respectively) in the aggregated balanced class relation. The implication in causal terms is that, in unbalanced, patriarchal families, with gender held constant, mothers and fathers play important roles in controlling the delinquency of their children. However, we already have noted that in relative terms mothers are more involved as the instruments of this control, especially with daughters as their objects, and the compound path that estimates the indirect effect of gender on delinquency in these families through maternal control ($-0.992 \times -0.526 = 0.522$) is again greater than the comparable path that estimates the effect of gender through paternal control ($-0.887 \times -0.461 = 0.409$). Of course, power-control theory emphasizes that fathers play a key role in that it is they who assign an instrumental role to mothers in domestic social control in patriarchal families. So it would be inappropriate to infer from this analysis that mothers are in any ultimate causal sense more important than fathers. Our data simply demonstrate the instrumental influence of maternal controls in patriarchal families. Meanwhile in the balanced families, the strong direct effect of maternal controls and the diminished direct effect of paternal controls is of further interest. The latter finding implies that it is the decrease in paternal power more than the increase in maternal power that may account for the more egalitarian

Social Structure, the Family and Delinquency

TABLE 7.8 *Within-class category regressions of perceived risks on independent variables in five equations*

Independent variables	Female-headed households	Lower obey class	Upper obey class	Husband commands/ wife not employed	Husband commands/ wife obeys	Joint command class
Equation (1)						
Gender: b	− 0.634	− 0.259	− 1.177	− 1.499	− 1.343	− 1.393
Beta	− 0.114	− 0.049	− 0.242	− 0.294	− 0.256	− 0.276
SE	0.682	0.777	0.525	0.570	0.524	0.655
Sig.	0.356	0.741	0.023	0.010	0.012	0.038
Constant	9.043	9.182	9.067	9.353	9.419	9.355
Equation (2)						
Gender: b	− 0.693	0.412	− 0.696	− 0.667	− 1.118	− 0.936
Beta	− 0.124	0.078	− 0.143	− 0.131	− 0.213	− 0.185
SE	0.625	0.732	0.550	0.575	0.546	0.537
Sig.	0.272	0.576	0.209	0.250	0.043	0.087
Maternal control: b	0.743	0.810	0.467	0.725	0.259	1.053
Beta	0.415	0.463	0.268	0.410	0.144	0.581
SE	0.201	0.732	0.197	0.199	0.187	0.192
Sig.	0.001	0.002	0.020	0.001	0.169	0.000
Constant	4.777	4.214	6.759	4.791	7.812	3.310
Equation (3)						
Gender: b	− 0.631	0.139	− 1.068	− 1.180	− 0.944	− 1.608
Beta	− 0.113	0.026	− 0.219	− 0.231	− 0.180	− 0.318
SE	0.690	0.699	0.531	0.578	0.520	0.603
Sig.	0.364	0.844	0.048	0.045	0.073	0.010
Paternal control: b	− 0.021	0.789	0.223	0.394	0.472	0.725
Beta	− 0.009	0.482	0.135	0.237	0.297	0.408
SE	0.301	0.217	0.181	0.189	0.157	0.212
Sig.	0.944	0.001	0.220	0.040	0.003	0.001
Constant	9.127	5.022	8.487	7.311	6.784	5.916
Equation (4)						
Gender: b	− 0.649	0.308	− 0.692	− 0.649	− 1.056	− 1.029
Beta	− 0.116	0.058	− 0.142	− 0.127	− 0.201	− 0.204
SE	0.627	0.722	0.554	0.579	0.525	0.556
Sig.	0.305	0.672	0.215	0.257	0.047	0.070
Constant	5.569	4.147	6.785	4.614	7.697	3.116

TABLE 7.8 cont.

Equation (5)						
Gender: b	− 0.383	0.244	− 0.362	− 0.566	− 0.860	− 1.061
Beta	− 0.069	0.046	− 0.074	− 0.111	− 0.164	− 0.210
SE	0.569	0.704	0.463	0.588	0.521	0.553
Sig.	0.503	0.731	0.437	0.340	0.102	0.061
Maternal control: b	0.465	0.125	0.158	0.627	− 0.436	0.856
Beta	0.259	0.071	0.091	0.355	− 0.243	0.473
SE	0.203	0.381	0.206	0.235	0.273	0.253
Sig.	0.026	0.745	0.445	0.010	0.114	0.001
Paternal control: b	0.078	0.560	0.036	0.103	0.612	0.119
Beta	0.032	0.342	0.022	0.062	0.386	0.067
SE	0.268	0.327	0.179	0.206	0.241	0.238
Sig.	0.773	0.094	0.839	0.618	0.013	0.620
Risk preference: b	− 0.698	− 0.381	− 0.704	− 0.118	− 0.337	− 0.200
Beta	− 0.453	− 0.264	− 0.569	− 0.097	− 0.238	− 0.150
SE	0.176	0.207	0.116	0.135	0.151	0.158
Sig.	0.002	0.073	0.000	0.386	0.028	0.210
Constant	10.623	7.751	12.503	5.569	10.591	5.135

outcomes in these families. This possibility deserves further consideration, some of which is provided in later chapters.

When maternal and paternal controls are entered separately in equations (2) and (3) for the disaggregated class relations in table 7.9, the effects of maternal controls are again larger than those of paternal controls. The joint effects of these controls can be seen in the reduced gender effects between the estimations of equations (1) and (4) in tables 7.9 and 7.10.[5] For example, in families in which the husband commands and the wife is not employed, the reduction is from 3.420 to 2.615; and in families in which the husband commands and the wife obeys, the reduction is from 2.668 to 1.738. Maternal and paternal controls of daughters relative to sons are important in explaining the gender-delinquency relationship in these patriarchal families.

All the intervening variables in our theoretical discussion are finally entered into equation (5) and the results of estimating this equation are presented in tables 7.9 and 7.10. In addition to maternal and paternal controls, this equation includes our scales of taste for risk and perceived risk of capture. Both these scales exercise significant effects on delinquency; the effects of taste for risk are particularly pronounced. A central premise of a power-control theory of gender and delinquency is that the instrument-object relationship established with daughters particularly discourages risk-

TABLE 7.9 Regressions within aggregated balanced and unbalanced class categories of self-reported delinquency scale on independent variables in five equations

Independent variables	Equation (1)		Equation (2)		Equation (3)		Equation (4)		Equation (5)	
	Unbalanced	Balanced	Unbalanced	Balanced	Unbalanced	Balanced	Unbalanced	Balanced	Unbalanced	Balanced
Gender: b	2.996	1.833	2.136	1.173	2.367	1.717	2.092	1.164	1.576	1.043
Beta	0.422	0.265	0.301	0.170	0.333	0.249	0.295	0.164	0.222	0.151
Standard error	0.495	0.488	0.491	0.478	0.478	0.480	0.485	0.483	0.464	0.418
Sig.	0.000	0.000	0.000	0.015	0.000	0.000	0.000	0.017	0.001	0.004
Maternal control: b			−0.867	−0.845			−0.526	−0.864	−0.333	−0.339
Beta			−0.355	−0.348			−0.215	−0.355	−0.193	−0.139
Standard error			0.169	0.168			0.219	0.219	0.208	0.201
Sig.			0.000	0.000			0.017	0.000	0.111	0.094
Paternal control: b					−0.760	−0.481	−0.461	0.028	−0.308	0.075
Beta					−0.345	−0.207	−0.210	0.012	−0.140	0.032
Standard error					0.148	0.161	0.192	0.202	0.181	0.174
Sig.					0.000	0.003	0.107	0.890	0.092	0.669
Taste for risk: b									0.437	0.810
Beta									0.243	0.446
Standard error									0.120	0.123
Sig.									0.000	0.000
Perceived risk: b									−0.264	−0.178
Beta									−0.193	−0.130
Standard error									0.090	0.096
Sig.									0.004	0.065
Constant	7.494	8.056	12.909	13.155	11.599	10.504	13.273	13.129	11.218	6.564

taking among the latter. From this perspective, it should be expected that the gender-delinquency relationship in equation (5) should be substantially reduced from those in equation (1) and they are. The overall role that gender-linked thoughts about risk-taking play in mediating the effect of gender on delinquency can be measured by comparing the gender coefficients in equation (5) with those in equation (4), in which both the maternal and paternal control scales are included, but the risk-taking variables are not; for example, when the risk variables are introduced in those patriarchal families in which the husband commands and the wife is not employed outside the home, the gender coefficient declines from 2.615 to 2.051. Differences in attitudes about risk-taking therefore play the expected role in mediating the effects of gender on delinquency within this and other family class categories.

Further evidence of the intervening role of the risk variables can be observed in the reductions of the effects of the maternal and paternal control variables in the estimations of equations (4) and (5) in table 7.9. Finally, turning to the last two columns of table 7.11, we see that controlling for our intervening variables has the theoretically predicted result of removing all significant differences between the gender-delinquency relationships in the unbalanced and more patriarchal families, as compared with the more balanced and egalitarian families. In other words, delinquency is more strongly related to gender in the unbalanced and patriarchal class relations because of the instrument-object relationship and differences in risk taking emphasized in power-control theory.

Looking back over the analysis, it is clear that the joint command class is, as predicted, the class that varies most from Bonger's original expectation that the relationship between gender and delinquency should increase with upward movement through the class structure. We will now make two final points about how this relationship declines in the joint command class, and about how its reappearance can also be predicted on the basis of our theory. When equation (1) is estimated in the joint command class in table 7.10, the constant (8.806) attains a value that is exceeded only by that for female-headed households (9.239). Because gender is the only variable in equation (1) and is treated as a dummy variable with females coded zero, the row of constants for this equation in table 7.10 reflects the mean score of females within each class on the self-reported delinquency scale. The average male scores can be calculated by adding the unstandardized gender coefficient to the constant within each class. Doing so shows that the relationship between gender and delinquency decreases in the joint command class not because the average male score declines, but because the female score increases. The same can be said of female-based households. Our data indicate that girls

TABLE 7.10 *Within-class category regressions of self-reported delinquency scale on independent variables in five equations*

Independent variables	Female-headed households	Lower obey class	Upper obey class	Husband commands/ wife not employed	Husband commands/ wife obeys	Joint command class
Equation (1)						
Gender: b	1.670	2.157	2.027	3.420	2.668	1.540
Beta	0.180	0.310	0.319	0.480	0.377	0.202
SE	1.123	0.975	0.668	0.732	0.676	1.004
Sig.	NS	0.032	0.003	0.000	0.002	0.131
Constant	9.239	7.727	7.611	7.412	7.558	8.806
Equation (2)						
Gender: b	1.728	1.452	1.700	2.699	1.803	0.904
Beta	0.186	0.209	0.268	0.372	0.255	0.119
SE	1.095	0.951	0.717	0.770	0.645	0.862
Sig.	NS	NS	0.020	0.001	0.006	NS
Maternal control: b	− 0.739	− 0.852	− 0.318	− 0.669	− 0.995	− 1.462
Beta	− 0.248	− 0.369	− 0.140	− 0.271	− 0.411	− 0.537
SE	0.352	0.316	0.256	0.267	0.221	0.309
Sig.	0.040	0.010	NS	0.015	0.000	0.000
Constant	13.479	12.952	9.586	11.623	13.737	17.211
Equation (3)						
Gender: b	1.640	1.882	2.016	3.064	1.840	1.852
Beta	0.177	0.271	0.318	0.430	0.260	0.244
SE	1.134	0.963	0.682	0.747	0.618	0.934
Sig.	NS	0.050	0.004	0.001	0.004	0.053
Paternal control: b	0.170	− 0.546	− 0.022	− 0.436	− 0.980	− 1.053
Beta	0.042	− 0.253	− 0.010	− 0.189	− 0.458	− 0.393
SE	0.495	0.299	0.232	0.244	0.187	0.329
Sig.	NS	0.074	NS	0.078	0.000	0.002
Constant	8.576	10.606	7.726	9.672	13.025	13.800
Equation (4)	Maternal and paternal controls in equation					
Gender: b	1.659	1.431	1.668	2.615	1.738	1.073
Beta	0.179	0.206	0.263	0.367	0.246	0.141
SE	− 0.272	0.965	0.720	0.775	0.626	0.892
Sig.	NS	0.023	0.001	0.007	NS	NS
Constant	12.231	12.939	1.720	2.615	13.858	17.564

TABLE 7.10 cont.

Equation (5)						
Gender: b	1.041	1.528	1.107	2.051	1.290	0.908
Beta	0.112	0.175	0.220	0.288	0.182	0.119
SE	0.972	0.810	0.588	0.724	0.619	0.843
Sig.	NS	0.066	0.064	0.006	0.041	NS
Maternal control: b	− 0.058	− 0.374	0.010	− 0.160	− 0.334	− 0.685
Beta	− 0.019	− 0.162	0.009	− 0.065	− 0.138	− 0.251
SE	0.360	0.438	0.262	0.302	0.324	0.411
Sig.	NS	NS	NS	NS	NS	NS
Paternal control: b	− 0.218	− 0.102	0.149	− 0.159	− 0.487	− 0.094
Beta	− 0.054	− 0.047	0.069	− 0.068	− 0.228	− 0.035
SE	0.457	0.389	0.226	0.252	0.292	0.352
Sig.	NS	NS	NS	NS	0.099	NS
Taste for risk: b	1.410	1.121	0.592	0.472	0.379	0.711
Beta	0.445	0.588	0.367	0.279	0.199	0.355
SE	0.334	0.248	0.178	0.165	0.181	0.236
Sig.	0.001	0.000	0.001	0.006	0.039	0.004
Perceived risk: b	− 0.282	0.298	− 0.408	− 0.354	− 0.216	− 0.271
Beta	− 0.170	0.226	− 0.313	− 0.253	− 0.160	− 0.180
SE	0.214	0.175	0.143	0.146	0.123	0.204
Sig.	NS	0.097	0.006	0.018	0.082	NS
Constant	5.541	1.101	7.272	9.746	12.268	11.242

TABLE 7.11 *Comparison of class category gender coefficients*

	Equation (1) difference in gender b's	t-value of difference	Equation (5) difference in gender b's	t-value of difference
Comparison of balanced class relation with:				
Unbalanced class relation	1.163	2.369[a]	0.533	0.661
Comparison of command class father/mother not employed with:				
Joint command class	1.880	2.186[a]	1.143	1.473
Upper obey class	1.393	2.010[a]	0.944	1.439
Female-headed households	1.750	2.103[a]	1.010	1.158

[a] Significant at the 0.05 level.

are most delinquent in the joint command class and in female-headed households.

Power-control theory explains these increases in female delinquency by focusing on conditions of gender equality that characterize both kinds of households. We will consider several features of the joint command class before making further comment on the female-headed households. Prior research indicates that in the joint command class husbands and wives tend to translate their parallel positions of authority in the workplace into parity positions of power in the household. In the joint command class this results in a diminished instrument-object relationship between parents, especially mothers, and their daughters; or, in other words, in an increase in the freedom of daughters relative to that of sons. Yet we should not too easily assume that because husbands and wives from this class both have authority positions in the workplace they are entirely equal in power.

Marxian conceptions of power would superimpose on the Dahrendorfian scheme that we have used a consideration of business ownership that goes beyond simple authority in the workplace. We have resisted including this Marxian dimension because it results in small class categories and because the Dahrendorfian link between authority relations in the workplace and the home is so clear. However, in table 7.12 we extend our analysis in this direction by drawing a distinction between joint-command-class husbands who are in the employer rather than the managerial class (see Wright and Perrone, 1977; Robinson and Kelly, 1979).

Employer-class husbands own businesses and have one or more employees, while managerial-class husbands do not own businesses but do have subordinates. When the joint command class, with its command-class spouses, is subdivided in this way, the class becomes polarized, with one set of class relations moving in the direction of greater balance (i.e., becoming more egalitarian in form) and the other set moving toward greater imbalance (i.e., toward patriarchy). Power-control theory therefore predicts that when the husband is in the employer class and the wife is in the managerial class, the instrument-object relationship between mothers and daughters should reappear, along with the gender-delinquency relationship, and that when both spouses are in the managerial class, both of these relationships should further decline.

The refined results presented in tables 7.4 and 7.12 confirm the above predictions. Recall first that the overall joint-command-class relationship in table 7.4 between gender and maternal controls was -0.156 (with mothers controlling their daughters more than they did their sons). However, when an imbalance is reintroduced in this class by separating out situations in which the father is an employer and the wife a manager, the above relationship jumps to -0.446. Alternatively, when both spouses are managers, the relationship is reduced to -0.024. The predicted changes in the gender-delinquency relationship resulting from our refinement of these class categories and the expected changes in the gender-maternal control relationship are shown in table 7.12. Although there are only fourteen cases in the former (unbalanced class) relation, the unstandardized gender coefficient is significant and increases to 6.833 (p < 0.05). Meanwhile, in the latter (balanced class) relation, this coefficient declines to 0.198 (p > 0.10). This coefficient is not only statistically insignificant; it is almost nonexistent. Furthermore, the difference between these two gender coefficients is, as predicted, significant at the 0.001 level.

TABLE 7.12 *Marxian refinement of joint command class*

	Husband employer/ wife manager (N = 14)	Both spouses managers (N = 43)
Equation (1)		
Gender: b	6.833[a]	0.198
Beta	0.489	0.047
SE	3.129	0.651
Constant	9.250	8.652
	Difference in gender bs = 6.635	
	t-value of difference = 4.160[a]	

[a] Significant at the 0.001 level.

Finally, it is of interest to note points of similarity that exist between the new joint-managerial-class relationships we have identified and the female-headed households we discussed earlier. In both kinds of households the instrument-object relationships between mothers and daughters, and the relationships between gender and risk preference, as well as between gender and delinquency are weak, while the average levels of female participation in delinquency are relatively high. The implication is that daughters are most free to be delinquent in families where mothers either share power equally with fathers, or do not share power with fathers at all.

DISCUSSION AND CONCLUSIONS

Power-control theory revives two traditions in delinquency research. The first of these traditions involves studies of class position and delinquent behaviour; the second tradition consists of research on family relationships and delinquency. Both traditions are stalled, the first by uncertain results

(Tittle, Villemez and Smith, 1978) and the second by a decline in interest (Wilkinson, 1974). Our point is that, when reconceived and combined through power-control theory, these two traditions can contribute to a new understanding of the relationship between class and delinquency. However, a key to this new understanding is a full appreciation of the role of gender in the class dynamics of the family and in delinquency.

The social organization of work and family relations influences the social distribution of delinquency through the gender stratification of domestic social control. To recognize this point fully it is necessary to incorporate both husbands and wives into models of family class structure. Traditional theories of crime and delinquency do not fully incorporate the role of both spouses into their class analyses. The extension of power-control theory presented here does so by making the relative positions of husbands and wives a basis for a new model of family class relations.

Central to our development of power-control theory is a reconceptualization of class and family that focuses on power relations in the workplace and the home. A key premise of our theory is that positions of power in the workplace are translated into power relations in the household and that the latter, in turn, influence the gender-determined control of adolescents, their preferences for risk-taking, and the patterning of gender and delinquency.

We have argued that a predominantly male pattern of delinquency results from the class structure of modern patriarchal families. This patriarchal family structure is historically rooted in a separation of family from work that Weber saw as crucial to the rationalization of modern industrial capitalism. In these families an instrument-object relationship takes the form of fathers, and especially mothers, controlling their daughters more than their sons. This relationship plays a key role in the social reproduction of a gender division between family and work, that is, between a sphere focused on domestic labour and consumption, and a sphere concerned with labour power and direct production. Our argument is that the instrument-object relationship that characterizes the parent-daughter relationship in patriarchal families tends to prepare daughters for a 'cult of domesticity' that makes their involvement in delinquency comparatively unlikely.

First, using a Dahrendorfian model of family class relations, our power-control theory predicts that the instrument-object relationship between parents and daughters will be most acute – and disparities in risk preferences and delinquency by gender most apparent – in unbalanced, patriarchal families: for example, those in which husbands are employed in positions of authority and their spouses are either not employed or employed in positions without authority. Alternatively, our theory predicts that this instrument-object relationship will be least acute – and disparities in risk preferences and delinquency by gender therefore least apparent – in more balanced, egalitarian kinds of families in which husbands and wives occupy more balanced class positions: for example, families in which neither or both are in positions of authority in the workplace, or in which fathers are mostly absent, i.e., in female-headed households. In these egalitarian kinds of families, daughters gain a kind of freedom that is reflected in a reduced control by fathers and mothers and an increased openness to risk-taking that includes (among adolescents) some common forms of delinquent behaviour.

Our data are generally consistent with this extension of power-control theory. For example, in our most patriarchal families (fathers have authority in the workplace and mothers are not employed outside the home) the instrument-object relationship is most acute, daughters are discouraged from taking risks, and sons are more delinquent than daughters. In more egalitarian kinds of families, for example, those in which mothers and fathers both have authority in the workplace, the instrument-object relationship between parents and daughters is reduced, risk preferences of daughters are more like those of sons, and gender differences in delinquency decline, with average levels of delinquency among daughters increasing. Interestingly, these latter patterns also prevail in families in which fathers are largely absent (i.e., in female-headed households). So, circumstances of both liberation and deprivation can apparently produce the results we have described. Power-control theory notes that what both these kinds of circumstances have in common is a freedom from male domination. That is, our analyses demonstrate that gender differences result from unbalanced and patriarchal as compared with more balanced and egalitarian kinds of family class structures and, in turn, confirm that these differences can be removed when variables associated with unbalanced, patriarchal class relations are taken into account. When daughters are freed from patriarchal family relations, they too become delinquent.

A Marxian consideration of business ownership provides an interesting kind of additional evidence for our theory. This refinement of our class analysis further specified power relations that increased and decreased gender-control and gender-delinquency relationships. More specifically, within the joint command class we are able to show that extremely large gender differentials in maternal control and delinquency occur when the father is in the employer class and the mother is in the manager class, and that these differentials are almost entirely absent when both spouses occupy managerial positions. The latter is the most egalitarian kind of family structure we are able to establish in our data, with the possible exception of female-headed households from which fathers are largely absent. These are the two kinds of families in our data in which daughters are most free to be delinquent.

We should again emphasize that by giving particular attention here to the instrument-object relationship between mothers and daughters we have not meant to imply that mothers are in any ultimate causal sense more responsible than fathers for the control of daughters. Our point is that, in patriarchal settings, mothers in particular are assigned an instrumental role in imposing this selective control. Our theory actually implies that fathers and/or a patriarchal social structure are the sources of this role assignment. Exactly how, why, and with what consequences this role assignment occurs are important issues for further research. One purpose of power-control theory is to call attention to such issues.

By fully incorporating power relations between spouses into our class analysis, using a common set of concepts, and focusing on power relations at low and high ends of the class structure, we can use power-control theory to account for declines in gender-delinquency relationships that previously went unexplained or required for their explanation separate theories of deprivation and liberation. We have reduced those two theories to one power-control theory.

Power-control theory encourages a new approach to the study of class and delinquency. What is most significant is that it encourages class analysis of delinquency to become attentive to family power relations. Our approach focuses first on the relational positions of spouses in the workplace, and second on how these determine spouses' relations to one another in the home. The theory then focuses on gender-specific authority relations between parents and adolescents and on how these influence the attitudes and behaviours of adolescents. The combination of these interlocking relationships suggests a gender-based link between class and delinquency. The implication is that in explaining the relationship between social structure and common delinquent behaviour, it may no longer be sufficient to consider only the fathers' years of education, dollars of income, units of ocupational prestige, or even relational positions in the workplace. Our theory and data indicate that important relationships between class, gender, and delinquency are only discovered by taking account of the relative positions of husbands *and* wives in the workplace. These relative positions are changing as more egalitarian family class structures replace more patriarchal forms of family life. In this sense, the changing class dynamics of gender and delinquency are part of a larger process of social change that involves the declining gender division between consumption and production spheres in post-industrial society.

NOTES

1 Others, notably Kohn (1977) and Miller and Swanson (1958), also analyse relationships between features of the workplace and the structure of the family.

Our perspective differs from these important efforts. Kohn is concerned primarily with the influence of work technologies on the formation of attitudes that influence socialization processes. Miller and Swanson are concerned mainly with the influence of relations between persons in the workplace on socialization attitudes. Neither Kohn nor Miller and Swanson emphasize, as we do, the central importance of the presence or absence of dominance relations on gender-linked control processes, or the importance of considering the class positions of wives relative to those of husbands. In recent papers, Kohn et al. (1986) consider the separate influence of mothers' and fathers' social positions on childrens' values, and Mirowsky (1985) examines the effects of marital power on depression. By bringing women into their analyses, both these papers come closer to our concerns – although not, of course, in the context of gender-linked control processes and delinquency.

2 It is not that we regard this class category as unimportant but rather that we have too little data and too few cases to undertake a proper analysis here. We are disproportionately sampling this class relation in a study currently under way. Meanwhile, our decision to exclude this class from the current analysis is similar to the decision made by Wright and Perrone (1977: 43) and others to exclude the petty bourgeoisie from class analyses of survey data.

3 Our operational definition of a female-headed household is one in which the mother is not married and has affirmatively answered a question asking whether she is the sole or major source of family income. This operationalization excludes 11 cases in which the spouses are no longer married but the spouse is still the major source of income. These cases illustrate a more general point – that when fathers leave, they nonetheless often maintain some kind of presence in the family. That is why we include a paternal control variable in our analysis of female-headed families. Female-headed households may be heterogeneous in terms of the class positions of the women that head them. However, only twenty-five of the women heading the households in our sample are in the command class and removing them does not substantially alter our results. Finally, it should be noted that there are more girls than boys (see table 7.3) in the female-headed households in our sample. This may result from a selection out of the more delinquent (older) boys through non-response, selection out of school (and therefore from the sampling frame), and/or different living arrangements (possibly with fathers or on their own). Each of these possibilities should be reflected in a mean age difference between sons and daughters in female-headed households. However, these means are nearly identical (being 15.032 and 15.157, respectively). Nonetheless, the selection issue is interesting and deserves further research.

4 It is of interest to consider whether the effect of gender in the female-headed households is similar to that in households where the husband is present but unemployed. Although it must be noted that there are only fourteen such families in our sample, the gender effect in these families is comparable ($b = 1.711$, $p = 0.10$).

5 Because maternal and paternal controls are strongly correlated (r between 0.5 and 0.6) and because the number of cases in each of the disaggregated family classes is

reduced, the estimates of the maternal and paternal coefficients in equation (4) of table 7.10 become slightly less stable. However, if a 0.10 rather than a 0.05 level of significance is applied, the substantive pattern of results is essentially the same. We have conserved space by not presenting the maternal and paternal coefficients from equation (4) in table 7.10. They are available on request.

8

Feminist Scholarship and Power-Control Theory

INTRODUCTION

This chapter extends the development of power-control theory in two ways, one conceptual and the other methodological. Conceptually, we introduce a distinction between what we referred to earlier as relational and instrumental sources of social control. This is a distinction that derives most immediately from the feminist scholarship of Nancy Chodorow (1978) and Carol Gilligan (1982). Our interest is in developing this distinction, both conceptually and methodologically, as it relates to a power-control theory of gender and delinquency.

In doing this we will treat relational and instrumental controls as latent, or unobserved, concepts, that are measured using covariance structure models estimated with the statistical program LISREL (Joreskog, 1973; Joreskog and Sorbom, 1985). This analytic framework brings together the estimation of factor analytic and structural equation models. An attractive feature of covariance structure models is that they explicitly give theory priority over method. That is, conceptualization and theory construction must precede measurement. This chapter therefore begins with a reconsideration of feminist scholarship as it can further inform a power-control theory of gender and delinquency.

RELATIONAL THEMES IN FEMINIST SCHOLARSHIP

One of the most widely read books in contemporary feminism is Carol Gilligan's *In a Different Voice* (1982). Gilligan is a social-psychologist interested in the topic of moral development. As we will see, the topic of moral development has important implications for our understanding of gender differences in social control. First, however, we will explore the relational theme as it has developed in feminist writings.

Gilligan began her work with Lawrence Kohlberg (see Kohlberg and Gilligan, 1971), who produced a theory of moral development (see Kohlberg, 1958; 1981) based on empirical observations of eighty-four boys followed for a period of over twenty years. Gilligan observes that this research originally simply ignored women. However, even more significant is that when women finally were brought into research designs intended to explore Kohlberg's theory (Edwards, 1975; Holstein, 1976; Simpson, 1974), it was reported that women exemplified the third stage of Kohlberg's six-stage sequence, a stage in which morality is conceived in interpersonal terms and goodness is equated with helping and pleasing others. Alternatively, men were found at higher stages where relationships were subordinated to rules (stage four) and rules to universal principles (stages five and six). Kohlberg (see Kohlberg and Kramer, 1969) implied that this reflected a moral deficiency in women that is nonetheless functional, insofar as women disproportionately focus their lives around the home and its problems.

Put most simply, Gilligan's point is that women are indeed different, but certainly not deficient. She suggests that the problem lies in misleading divisions and stereotypes.

The stereotypes suggest a splitting of love and work that relegates expressive capacities to women while placing instrumental abilities in the masculine domain. Yet looked at from a different perspective, these stereotypes reflect a conception of adulthood that is itself out of balance, favoring the separateness of the individual self over connection to others, and leaning more toward an autonomous life of work than toward the interdependence of love and care. (1982: 17)

It is interesting to note that this critique can be read as a rejection of the separation of work and home life and the production and consumption spheres that so concerned Weber in his discussion of the emergence of industrial capitalism.

Gilligan develops her position by considering the different ways in which the genders resolve moral dilemmas, including dilemmas used experimentally in Kohlberg's original research. Perhaps the best known of these dilemmas is explored through Gilligan's discussion of Amy and Jake, two eleven-year-old children asked to consider whether a man named Heinz should steal a drug he cannot afford so as to save the life of his dying wife. Amy and Jack resolve the dilemma in quite different ways, with Amy using a more relational, and Jake a more instrumental, kind of logic. Gilligan's analysis of this case focuses attention on fundamental differences in gender-linked patterns of thought. These are the 'different voices' of the genders.

Gilligan is careful to note that the gender differences she highlights have been observed and explored by others, perhaps most notably by Nancy Chodorow. And Chodorow in turn notes that the feminine tendency to submerge the self in responsibility and connection to others has been explored by many women writers, including Simone de Beauvoir, Kate Chopin, Doris Lessing, Tillie Olsen, Christina Stead and Virginia Woolf. So Gilligan's contribution may be more that of delineating these differences, as well as their consequences and their neglect in a prototypical theoretical and research paradigm, than in explaining the differences observed. Indeed, Gilligan (2) is rather explicitly agnostic on the issue of causation, noting that, 'No claims are made about the origins of the differences described or their distribution in a wider population, across cultures or through time.' Meanwhile, Chodorow charts a somewhat different course.

Chodorow's purpose is to account for 'the reproduction within each generation of certain general and nearly universal differences that characterize masculine and feminine personality and roles' (1974: 43). These differences are seen as deriving in significant part from the fact that women are largely responsible for early child care and later female socialization. This makes the mother-daughter relationship the focal point, as it is also in power-control theory, in explaining gender differences: 'A woman identifies with her own mother and, through identification with her child, she (re)experiences herself as a cared-for child'(47). Chodorow sees this 'double identification' as producing differences in which the 'feminine personality comes to define itself in relation and connection to other people more than masculine personality does' (44).

The factor emphasized most by Chodorow in this process is that while sons are encouraged to separate and individuate their experiences from the mother, daughters are encouraged to maintain the maternal link.

It seems likely that from their children's earliest childhood, mothers and women tend to identify more with daughters and to help them to differentiate less, and that processes of separation and individuation are made more difficult for girls. On the other hand, a mother tends to identify less with her son, and to push him toward differentiation and the taking on of a male role unsuitable to his age, and undesirable at any age in his relationship to her.

A result is that sons and daughters learn their gender roles in rather different ways, that Chodorow labels respectively 'positional' and 'personal' identification. The key to this distinction is the father's immediate absence, because he is so often away at work, and the mother's immediate presence, because she is so often tied to the home, in gender role identification processes. A consequence is that the son must identify positionally with an absent male role model, while the daughter can identify personally with an omnipresent female role model. So,

... a boy's male gender identification often becomes a 'positional' identification, with aspects of his father's clearly or not-so-clearly defined male role, rather than a more generalized 'personal' identification . . . that could grow out of a real relationship to his father.

Our interest in these differing processes, of course, is that they are suggestive of different control strategies by mothers of sons and daughters. The implication is that daughters will be connected to mothers in strong relationships of direct identification that are inherently controlling, while sons are much less likely to be subjected to these kinds of relational controls. Previous to this chapter, we have focused on a much more instrumental kind of social control (i.e., the kind of constraint emphasized in Joyce Carol Oates' suggestive short story titled *Where Have You Been, Where Are You Going?*) that we have demonstrated is imposed on daughters more than on sons. It might well be argued that this focus gives a male, or instrumental, kind of bias to power-control theory. So we now incorporate into the theory a distinct and more relational kind of control – based on the themes of affiliation, connection and caring exemplified in feminist writings above – that we again propose is more likely to involve daughters than sons. We additionally will posit that these relational kinds of social control form a base for the more instrumental controls that we have considered in previous chapters. However, before we move to an operationalization and test of this new component of a power-control theory, it is useful to consider further the issues of how relational processes vary by gender, as well as what might further account for this variation.

CAUSAL RELATIONS?

First, it is unclear whether the relational characteristics attributed by some feminist scholars to women's thoughts and actions are considered to be only quantitatively, or as well qualitatively, different from those attributed to men. Carrie Menkel-Meadow (1985: 62) puts the question well: 'Are these different voices gender-based or just two thematically different ways of looking at the world?' The importance of this question lies in the implications of its answers. As we will see below, the first possibility implies biological differences, while the second is more consistent with cultural and/or structural interpretations.

Although Gilligan often seems to imply a qualitative difference between men and women in her description of their thought processes, she also disclaims such a position in the introduction to her book. She asserts that

The different voice I describe is characterized not by gender but theme. Its association with women is an empirical observation, and it is primarily through women's voices that I trace its development. But this association is not absolute, and the contrasts between male and female voices are presented here to highlight a distinction between two modes of thought and to focus a problem of interpretation rather than to represent a generalization about either sex.

The implication is that the association between relational processes and gender is variable and subject to change. If this is the case, the question becomes one of how, where and why such variation might occur. However, as suggested above and as we will see again below, Gilligan provides few answers to these kinds of questions. Perhaps they are outside the social psychologist's domain.

Chodorow comes closer to providing answers when she reviews Mitscherlich's (1969) discussion of male gender role identification in Western advanced capitalist societies. Chodorow (1978) notes the division between work and home in such societies and the resulting need for indirect male gender role identification. Chodorow gives further attention to the role of social structure in producing gender divisions in her important work on *The Reproduction of Mothering*.

However, a recent conference exchange (*Buffalo Law Review*, 1985) involving Gilligan, MacKinnon and others, makes the issue of causation even more explicit. MacKinnon (73–4) responds to the different voice that Gilligan describes in the following way:

I don't think the attributes she advanced are biological but I do think that accurate social regularities were found – and for me gender is a social regularity. On the other hand, what is infuriating about it (which is a very heavy thing to say about a book that is so cool and graceful and gentle in its emotional touch), and this is a political infuriation, is that it neglects the explanatory level. *Why* do women become these people, more than men, who represent these values? This is really very important. For me, the answer is clear: the answer is the subordination of women. (emphasis in the original).

Gilligan (76) responds:

Basically, I am in disagreement with Kitty MacKinnon. Trying to make gender fit the inequality model is the most traditional way to deal with gender, and it will not work. Gender is not exactly like social class. It is not simply a matter of dominance and subordination. There is no way to envision gender disappearing as one envisions, in utopian visions of society, class disappearing or race becoming a difference that makes no difference. The fact that gender is a difference that one cannot envision disappearing is why it makes so many people so angry.

An interesting feature of Gilligan's position is that it does not fully discount the dominance-subordination argument, but it also offers no guidance about the extent to which it may be true. Gilligan has only said that dominance-subordination will not explain all of the gender difference. Does it explain some of the difference, most of it, or almost none? If not dominance-subordination, then what? And, to return to a prior question, is there evidence that relational processes influence women's thoughts and actions differently than men's thoughts and actions? Or, is the difference simply one of degree? Few answers are given to such questions in Gilligan's work. The issue of causation usually is rendered moot by randomizing relevant differences among respondents in her quasi-experiments, while the implication is often left that the relational qualities observed are, disclaimers notwithstanding, gender rather than thematically based. Beyond Gilligan, there is relatively little empirical research with which to consider such questions. Our purpose is to fill a part of this void, in the context of gender differences in the relational control of adolescents, and in terms of the implications of such for delinquent behaviour.

FROM RELATIONAL TO INSTRUMENTAL CONTROL

Carchedi (1977: 6) writes that '. . . supervision has a double character under capitalism – the work of "co-ordination and unity" required of any co-operative labour process and the work of "control and surveillance" that arises from the antagonistic character of the capitalist labour process.' What Carchedi says of the macrostructure of work supervision in capitalist economies may be no less true of the microstructure of child supervision in the family units of the surrounding societies. Children and adolescents must be 'co-ordinated and unified' within the family unit, and they are also, sometimes alternately and sometimes simultaneously, subjected to 'supervision and surveillance'. These are the dual aspects of parental relational and instrumental control that we wish to emphasize in our elaboration of the microstructure of power-control theory, noting particularly that these microstructural control processes are stratified by gender.

As we have noted in earlier chapters, delinquency research has often focused on the role of parental controls in studying adolescents. Hirschi (1969) regards parental controls, which he calls attachments, as a key element in the social bond that makes conformity and delinquency respectively more and less likely. Numerous studies (e.g., Jensen, 1972; Matsueda, 1982; Wiatrowski et al., 1981; Menard and Morse, 1984; Liska and Reed, 1985) have since pursued the nature of this linkage between parental control and delinquent behaviour. Each of these studies confirms the importance of such controls as causal factors in delinquent behaviour.

However, none of the above studies draws distinctions among measures of these controls, some of which are clearly relational and others of which are more clearly instrumental. Nor do any of these studies call attention to the variable correlation of these measures with gender, or to their roles in explaining the relationship between gender and delinquent behaviour. Instead, the tendency is to regard measures of parental control as functional substitutes and to use one or the other kind of measure, but rarely both, in explaining delinquency, without regard to gender. This point can be made more concretely below by briefly considering four recent studies (Wiatrowski et al., 1981; Liska and Reed, 1985; Matsueda, 1982; and Menard and Morse, 1984).

In table 8.1 we present the many measures of parental control that are used in the four recent studies of delinquency cited above. The range of these items is impressive, as is the variety of names given to the concepts measured: attachment to mother/father, parental supervision, home alienation, parental communication, and parental affectivity. However, most of the conceptual content of these items can be characterized more parsimoniously as involving relational or instrumental control. For example, the items in the attachment (Wiatrowski et al., 1981), alienation (Menard and Morse, 1984) and communication (Liska and Reed, 1985) scales largely involve indicators of closeness, identification, talking, listening, mutual influence and understanding, all of which are relational themes noted in the work of Gilligan, Chodorow and others. Alternatively, the parental supervision items (e.g., Matsueda, 1982) that we all remember from our youth (i.e., 'Where are you going?', 'Out', 'What are you doing?', 'Nothing') are more clearly instrumental variations on the theme of surveillance. Only Liska and Reed's (1985) parental affectivity scale defies easy categorization as relational or instrumental; it would appear to be both. All of these studies have appeared within the last five years in two of our most important journals, the *American Journal of Sociology* and the *American Sociological Review*. What is intriguing for our purpose is that all of these studies either include relational (Wiatrowski et al. and Menard and Morse) or instrumental (Matsueda) items, or mix them together (Liska and Reed), but the two kinds of items are never clearly distinguished, or considered in relation to gender. There is an oversight here that echoes the Gilligan experience with the moral development paradigm.

Our solution to this problem is to treat relational and instrumental controls as theoretically and empirically distinct concepts to be included within a structural model of a power-control theory of gender and delinquency. This brings us to a discussion of LISREL.

TABLE 8.1 Concepts and indicators in recent studies of parental control and delinquency

Study	Concept name	Indicators	Concept content
Wiatrowski et al. (1981)	Attachment to mother/father	How close do you feel to your mother/ father? How much do you want to be like the kind of person your mother/father is?	Relational
Matsueda (1982)	Parental supervision	Do your parents (mother/father) know who you are with when you are away from home? Do your parents (mother/father) know where you are when you are away home?	Instrumental
Menard and Morse (1984)	Home alienation	Family members were always close Parents never understood me Agree with mother/father on right and wrong	Relational
Liska and Reed (1985)	Parental communication	How often do your parents listen to your side of the argument? How often do your parents talk over important decisions with you? How often do your parents act fair and reasonable in what they ask of you? How much influence do you feel you have in family decisions that affect you?	Relational

	Parental affectivity	How often do your parents:
		  act as if they don't care about you anymore?
		  disagree with each other when it comes to raising you?
		  actually slap you?
		  take away your privileges?
		  blame you or criticize you when you don't deserve it?
		  threaten to slap you?
		  yell, shout or scream at you?
		  disagree about punishing you?
		  nag at you?
			Relational to Instrumental?

MEASUREMENT AND STRUCTURAL MODELS WITH
UNOBSERVED CONCEPTS

LISREL is a statistical programme developed by Karl Joreskog and Dag Sorbom (1985) for the estimation of what are more generally called covariance structure models. Such models attempt to explain relationships among sets of manifest or observed variables in terms of a typically smaller number of latent or unobserved variables. Joreskog and Sorbom's LInear Structural RELationships programme makes the linkages between unobserved and observed variables explicit. It does this by first linking the observed variables to the unobserved variables through the estimation of measurement or factor analytic models common in psychometrics; and second by estimating the causal relationships among the latent variables through structural equation models associated with econometrics. The term covariance structure model is used to refer to the simultaneous specification of a factor analytic model and a structural equation model that is undertaken in such programmes as LISREL. Such programmes can therefore be thought of as synthesizing fundamental ideas from the fields of psychometrics and econometrics (see Goldberger, 1971; Goldberger and Duncan, 1973). Excellent introductions to LISREL in the social sciences generally (Long, 1983), and in sociology (Bielby and Hauser, 1977) and criminology (Smith and Patterson, 1985) specifically, are available elsewhere, so we offer only a brief discussion here.

Unobserved concepts are inferred within the LISREL framework from the relationships among observed variables that are measured directly, for example, with survey items. The unobserved concepts can be thought of as a synthesis of the observed indicators. One attraction of this analytic framework is that it tests the potential unreliability and invalidity of the observed variables as indicators of the unobserved concepts. LISREL does this by considering the latent or unobserved variables as constructs that have hypothesized and observable effects on corresponding manifest or observed variables.

This feature of LISREL is perhaps best communicated in the form of an example. Consider maternal relational control as a latent concept, a concept that we consider in the analysis presented below. Within the LISREL framework we hypothesize that the positions of individuals on the distribution of this unobserved construct will causally affect their responses to survey questions about the frequency with which they talk to their mothers and their preferences to be the kind of persons their mothers are. LISREL factor analyses these observed variables and estimates the extent to which the unobserved concept (i.e., maternal relational control) accounts for covariance among these survey items.

As unobserved variables or latent concepts and their indicators are added to the analysis, an important difference becomes apparent between the kind of 'confirmatory factor analysis' involved in LISREL and the more traditional or 'exploratory' versions of factor analysis. The difference is that theoretical and/or substantive premises are used in LISREL to specify constraints on relationships between the observed and unobserved variables, which are then tested (i.e., confirmed) by comparison with the observed data. For example, in the analysis below we also consider maternal instrumental control as an unobserved variable indicated by survey items asking whether the respondents' mothers know who they are with and where they are when they are away from home. In this analysis we posit that the latter survey items are affected by the latent concept of maternal instrumental control alone, and that the survey items discussed in the previous paragraph are solely affected by the latent concept maternal relational control. LISREL provides statistical tests to determine if the observed data are consistent with these imposed constraints. In this sense, theoretically generated premises are tested against sample data. This avoids the *ad hoc* character of the more traditional use of exploratory factor analysis.

Of course, measurements of observed variables will generally not be determined perfectly by the unobserved concept under consideration. There are two obvious sources of this imperfection: errors in measurement and in the linkages of observed variables to the unobserved constructs. Regardless of source, these errors can bias the estimation of parameters in causal models. By incorporating a factor analysis component into the estimation of structural equation models, LISREL reduces this potential for biased parameter estimation. The programme provides estimates of measurement error for the observed variables, of the 'true scores' that these measurement variables represent, and of the relationships between the true scores in causal models of the unobserved latent concepts. That is, a covariance structure model such as is estimated in LISREL allows for both errors in variables, as in the factor analytic model, and errors in equations, as in the structural equation model.

One final feature of LISREL is relevant to the analysis we report next. In the LISREL framework it is possible to further test whether or how well a model that is specified in theoretical terms fits data that are observed in more than one context. For example, we noted above the question as to whether relational processes are gender or thematically biased. We have already proposed in the context of our development of power-control theory that relational kinds of controls are imposed more extensively by mothers on daughters than on sons. However, use of the adverb 'more' here indicates that sons as well as daughters experience relational controls. This is a difference of quantity, not quality; of theme in association with gender, rather than of gender itself. If, on the other hand, the difference is one of gender in-and-of-itself, we might expect relational controls to operate only on daughters, or, perhaps more plausibly, for these controls to influence other variables in our theoretical model differently among daughters than sons. LISREL allows us to explore such possibilities by testing whether our theoretical model operates in the same way when our sample is divided by gender.

Similarly, power-control theory explicitly predicts that the linkages proposed between gender and delinquency are more characteristic of patriarchal than non-patriarchal families. In other words, power-control theory proposes, with MacKinnon and others, that dominance-subordination relationships between the genders are a source of the differences in relational and other kinds of control that we have considered as intervening variables in the gender-delinquency relationship. LISREL again allows us to assess such theoretical predictions by testing whether our theoretical model operates in the same way in patriarchal and non-patriarchal families. We move now to the use of LISREL in testing a version of a power-control theory of gender and delinquency that is elaborated in terms of this chapter's discussion of relational control.

MEASURES AND MODELS

Several models are estimated in this chapter. We begin with a simplified power-control model of gender and delinquency presented in figure 8.1. A more complex model presented in figure 8.2 is estimated later in this chapter. Both of these models include relational as well as instrumental control constructs. The difference is that the simplified model presented in figure 8.1 omits paternal control and perceived risk constructs. The paternal control constructs are omitted because they result in problems of model identification that are more usefully considered later in the chapter, and because the feminist work we have considered in this chapter does not give much attention to these constructs. Rather, it is the mother-daughter relationship that is emphasized. The perceived risk construct is only considered later largely because it was found to have a limited causal influence in the preceding chapter. Figure 8.1 represents a parsimonious statement of power-control theory in terms of its most powerful variables, in which we now propose on the basis of the above discussion of feminist work to include maternal relational control.

One exogenous and four endogenous latent constructs are included in

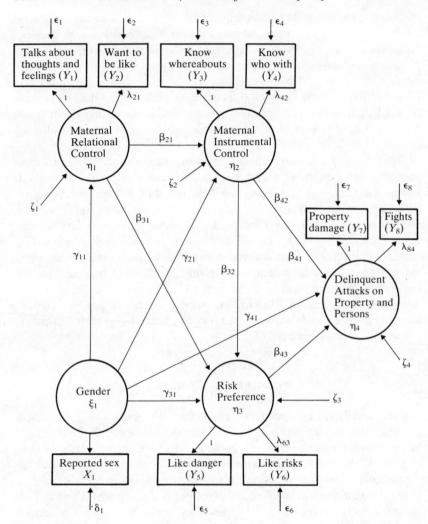

Degree of freedom = 18

$x^2 = 35.33$

Probability value = 0.009

Goodness of fit index = 0.982

Average goodness of fit index = 0.955

Figure 8.1 Simplified power-control model of gender and delinquency

figure 8.1. The exogenous latent construct is gender (ξ_1), indicated by reported sex (X_1) in a fixed-x model. The causally ordered endogenous variables are maternal relational control (η_1), maternal instrumental control (η_2), risk preference (η_3), and delinquent attacks on property and persons (η_4). The observed variables based on survey items used to measure the latent constructs in figure 8.1 are presented in table 8.2. This table also presents the means and standard deviations for each of these observed variables in the full sample and in the sub-samples that we consider later in this chapter. Note that the last of the latent constructs is a less global designation than delinquency. This reflects the fact that to reduce identification problems we have limited our indicators of delinquency to two measures of property damage (Y_7) and fighting (Y_8). These are, of course, two standard indicators of delinquency found in scales that attempt to measure more as well as less serious forms of this behaviour.

Two indicators each are also included for the latent constructs of risk preference (η_3) and maternal instrumental control (η_2). These are survey

TABLE 8.2 *Variables, means and standard deviations for total sample, sons and daughters, patriarchal and non-patriarchal families*

Variable		Total sample $\bar{x}$	SD	Sons $\bar{x}$	SD	Daughters $\bar{x}$	SD	Patriarchal $\bar{x}$	SD	Non-patriarchal $\bar{x}$	SD
ξ_1	*Gender*										
X_1	Reported Sex (female = 0; male = 1)	0.504	0.501	—	—	—	—	0.550	0.499	0.384	0.488
η_1	*Maternal relational control*										
Y_1	'Do you talk with your mother about your thoughts and feelings?'[a]	2.225	0.894	1.995	0.794	2.458	0.930	2.205	0.867	2.448	0.963
Y_2	'Would you like to be the kind of person your mother is?'[b]	2.684	1.057	2.502	1.058	2.868	1.026	2.696	1.041	2.712	1.054
η_2	*Maternal instrumental control*										
Y_3	'Does your mother know your whereabouts when you are away from home?'[a]	2.923	0.826	2.767	0.804	3.080	0.819	2.947	0.828	2.888	0.844
Y_4	'Does your mother know who you are with when you are away from home?'[a]	2.754	0.830	2.544	0.795	2.967	0.811	2.754	0.853	2.776	0.771
η_3	*Risk preference*										
Y_5	'I like to take chances.'[c]	3.576	1.033	3.674	1.066	3.476	0.990	3.556	1.063	3.672	0.974
Y_6	'The things I like to do best are dangerous.'[c]	2.754	1.148	2.972	1.148	2.533	1.107	2.766	1.165	2.816	1.132
η_4	*Attacks on property and persons*										
Y_7	'How often in the last year have you intentionally banged up something that did not belong to you?'[d]	1.623	0.925	1.833	1.018	1.410	0.764	1.655	0.960	1.616	0.914
Y_8	'Excluding fights with a brother or sister, how often in the last year have you intentionally beaten up or hurt anyone?'[d]	1.714	1.006	2.056	1.101	1.368	0.758	1.766	1.086	1.752	0.989

[a] Coded: (1) never; (2) sometimes; (3) usually; (4) always.
[b] Coded: (1) not at all; (2) in a few ways; (3) in some ways; (4) in most ways; (5) in every way.
[c] Coded: (1) strongly disagree; (2) disagree; (3) undecided; (4) agree; (5) strongly agree.
[d] Coded: (1) never; (2) once; (3) two or three times; (4) often; (5) many times.

items used in earlier chapters, in the former case measuring mother's knowledge of where (Y_3) and who (Y_4) their children are with, and in the latter case measuring the respondent's liking for danger (Y_5) and taking chances (Y_6).

Maternal relational control (η_1) is the entirely new latent construct considered in this chapter. The two indicators of this construct are survey items asking: 'Do you talk to your mother about your thoughts and feelings?' (Y_1) and 'Would you like to be the kind of person your mother is?' (Y_2). We believe this emphasis on communication and identification is central to Gilligan's notion of a 'different voice' and Chodorow's discussion of 'double identification'. The measurement model component of the LISREL analysis that follows is intended to test this expectation, among the others outlined above.

Before we turn to the results, a final word should be said about causal order. The endogenous variables are ordered as indicated above. Maternal relational control is given precedence over the other endogenous variables because, as the feminist literature emphasizes, the relational connection between mothers and daughters is nurtured from birth. Maternal instrumental controls are presumed to follow later as the child begins to move away from the home into more extended networks of contact. Risk preferences are presumed to follow from the imposition of both relational and instrumental controls, and to mediate much of the impact of these constructs on delinquent attacks on other persons and their property.

RESULTS

We consider first the results of the measurement model included within figure 8.1. These results are presented in Panel B of table 8.3. To identify the latent endogenous constructs in this model, the scale of each is set to the metric of its first indicator (i.e., the unstandardized λ is set equal to 1.0). Each construct represents the common or shared variance of its indicators, and the results in Panel B reveal that each construct has a statistically significant (p < 0.01) and substantial loading (λ coefficient) on its observed measures. This suggests that each latent construct is a common factor with respect to its observed measures.

The structural parameters for the model portrayed in figure 8.1 are presented in Panel A of table 8.3, with the unstandardized (maximum likelihood estimates) regression coefficients above the diagonal, standardized coefficients below, and standard errors in parentheses. Each parameter reported in this table represents the effect of one latent construct on another. The effects of the exogenous construct, gender, on the endogenous

TABLE 8.3 Regression and measurement coefficients for simplified power-control model of gender and delinquency (N = 427)

A Regression coefficients[a] gender (ξ_1)	Maternal relational control (η_1)	Maternal instrumental control (η_2)	Risk preference (η_3)	Attacks on property on persons (η_4)
Gender (ξ_1)	—	-0.330^f (0.069)	-0.098 (0.077)	0.080 (0.076)	0.299^f (0.069)
Maternal relational control (η_1)	-0.311	—	0.838^f (0.119)	0.015 (0.171)	-0.265^e (0.149)
Maternal instrumental control (η_2)	-0.078	0.703	—	-0.546^f (0.154)	0.049 (0.133)
Risk preference (η_3)	0.060	0.012	-0.523	—	0.482^f (0.085)
Attacks on property or persons (η_4)	0.251	-0.236	0.052	0.533	—

B Measurement coefficients (MLS)[b,c]

$$\lambda_{21} = 1.411; \quad \lambda_{42} = 0.874; \quad \lambda_{63} = 1.429; \quad \lambda_{84} = 1.250$$

[a] Unstandardized regression coefficients above the diagonal; standardized regression coefficients below the diagonal; standard errors in parentheses.
[b] $p \leq 0.01$ for all coefficients.
[c] $\lambda_{11}, \lambda_{32}, \lambda_{53}, \lambda_{74}$, fixed at 1.00.
[d] $p < 0.10$, one-tailed.
[e] $p < 0.05$, one-tailed.
[f] $p < 0.01$, one-tailed.

constructs are represented in figure 8.1 as gamma coefficients (γ), and the effects of the endogenous constructs on one another are represented as beta coefficients (β).

The results reported in table 8.3 reveal that gender has strong direct and indirect effects on attacks against property and persons. The standardized direct effect is in the expected direction ($\gamma_{41} = 0.251$, p < 0.01), with sons more likely to engage in such attacks. Indirect effects of gender operate through all of the mediating variables predicted by power-control theory. Most notably, in terms of the interests of this chapter, maternal relational control is imposed much more strongly on daughters than sons ($\gamma_{11} = -0.311$, p < 0.01), and this control also has a strong direct effect ($\beta_{41} = -0.236$, p < 0.05) that reduces the likelihood of personal and property attacks. Beyond this, maternal relational control leads to maternal instrumental control ($\beta_{21} = 0.703$, p < 0.001), which in turn decreases preferences for risk-taking ($\beta_{32} = -0.523$, p < 0.01). Finally, preferences for risk-taking greatly increase the likelihood of delinquent attacks on property and persons ($\beta_{43} = 0.533$, p < 0.01).

Overall, the above simplified power-control model of gender and delinquency fits the observed data reasonably well. The model has a X^2 of

35.33 (df = 18, p < 0.009). Given the sensitivity of X^2 to sample size (N = 427), this is a relatively good fit. With large sample sizes significant X^2s are likely to result, not because the theoretical model fits the observed data less well, but because in large samples smaller differences are detectable as being more than mere sampling fluctuations (Hayduk, 1987). To adjust for this problem, Joreskog (1969) suggests dividing X^2 by the degrees of freedom. Wheaton et al. (1977) propose that a X^2 five times the degrees of freedom is acceptable, while Carmines and McIver (1981) suggest that two to three times is more acceptable. The ratio in this case is 1.96.

The arbitrariness involved in selecting an acceptable level for the above ratio encourages alternative means of assessing model fit. Another approach to this issue involves using the X^2 to judge the comparative fit of alternative models. To this end, we estimated a model consisting of only the main effects of each of the exogenous and endogenous variables on delinquent attacks on property and persons. Prior research suggests that each of these constructs should have a main effect on such delinquency, but says little about the relationships between them. So there is a substantive basis for estimating this alternative model. The result is a X^2 of 251.55 with twenty-four degrees of freedom. The simplified power-control model provides a significant improvement over this alternative model.

A further approach to the assessment of fit involves inspecting the matrix of normalized residuals that is provided by LISREL. This matrix indicates the number of standard deviations the observed residuals are away from the 'zero residuals', or a perfectly fitting model. None of the normalized residuals in our estimated model exceed 2.0, which suggests that only random errors remain in these residuals (Joreskog and Sorbom, 1981).

Overall, then, there is considerable reason to accept this specification of our model. Much of the effect of gender on delinquent attacks against persons and property is accounted for by the greater tendency of daughters compared to sons to experience relational and instrumental controls imposed on them by mothers, which in turn reduce daughters' preferences for risk-taking and delinquent behaviour. The model estimated indicates that the relational controls introduced in this chapter play a particularly important role in mediating the effect of gender on delinquency, and therefore the addition of this latent construct represents an important modification of power-control theory that would not have been apparent without consideration of the feminist writings above.

A DIFFERENCE OF THEME OR GENDER?

We turn now to the question of whether these relational controls are simply more pronounced in their imposition by mothers on daughters than on sons, or whether these controls are gender-based in the sense of operating in significantly different ways in the mediation of the behaviours of daughters than sons. For example, one might expect on the basis of Gilligan's analyses to find relational controls more influential among daughters in reducing delinquency, while instrumental controls might be more influential among sons. This is the kind of issue raised by Menkel-Meadow in her response to Gilligan's work noted above, when she asks whether relational processes are gender or thematically based. Gilligan often seems to imply, disclaimers notwithstanding, that the genders actually think in qualitatively different ways, not just in ways that differ by degree. In the language of multivariate analysis, the thematic model is an additive or main effects model, while the gender-based model is a non-additive or interaction effects model. Recall that a common response to the gender-based position, as noted above by MacKinnon, is to see it as implying an inherent difference of biology between the genders.

Our attempt to address these issues in the context of power-control theory makes use of a feature of LISREL which allows one to set equality constraints on parameters between groups. When an equality constraint for a parameter is imposed, the groups are analysed simultaneously holding that parameter constant across the groups (e.g., see Gottfredson, 1981). We use this feature now to estimate the simplified power-control model within sub-samples divided by gender.

If the relational processes we have examined involving mothers and their children operate in the same way within groupings of sons and daughters, setting equality constraints on the parameters estimated across the sub-samples of daughters and sons should result in a model that fits the simultaneously analysed data approximately as well as when these parameters are set free. In other words, the measurement and structural parameters of causal models for daughters and sons should not be significantly different. Such an outcome does not discount what we have already seen, namely that daughters experience more relational and instrumental control than do sons, and as a result are more risk-averse and conforming than sons in their behaviours. Rather, such an outcome would instead indicate that there is no evidence of further difference between the genders, for example, in the way relational and instrumental controls operate when they are present. For example, such an outcome would suggest that there is no differential sensitivity between the genders in their responses to relational and instrumental controls, regardless of the levels at which they experience them. Or to put the matter still differently, such an outcome implies that if fewer relational and instrumental controls were imposed on daughters, they, like sons, would also be more open to risk-taking and delinquency. The difference is one of amount, not kind. Differences in amount are presumably more amenable to change than are differences of kind.

Equality constraints across son and daughter sub-groups were manipulated for segments of a model (measurement and structural) like that shown in figure 8.1, except, of course, that now gender is removed from the model, and maternal relational control becomes the exogenous construct, with the other constructs remaining endogenous. The relative goodness of fit of the different models was assessed. The results are presented for Models A to D in table 8.4.

TABLE 8.4 *Chi-squares and degrees of freedom for constrained and unconstrained models with respondents grouped by gender*

Model name and description[a]	X^2	Degree of freedom (df)	Probability value (p)	Goodness of fit index (GFI)
A No equality constraints across groups	23.27	28	0.719	0.987
B Structural coefficients constrained to be equal across groups	27.09	34	0.794	0.985
C Measurement coefficients constrained to be equal across groups	23.91	32	0.848	0.987
D Structural and measurement coefficients constrained to be equal across groups	27.53	38	0.895	0.985

[a] See text for a full description of models estimated.

In Model A no equality constraints were imposed across the groups, in Model B the structural coefficients were constrained to be equal across groups, in Model C the measurement coefficients were constrained to be equal, and in Model D both types of coefficients were constrained to be equal across groups. The crucial comparison in this case is between Models A and D. This is because the difference in fit between these models ($X^2D - A = 4.26$, df = 10) is non-significant, indicating that freeing both the structural and the measurement coefficients fails to significantly improve the correspondence between the modelled and observed data. Another way to see this is to examine table 8.5, where the coefficients estimated under each of these models are presented. Note that in Model A, where no equality constraints are imposed, the coefficients estimated for sons and daughters are quite similar. For example, the unstandardized regression coefficients for the effects of maternal relational control on maternal instrumental control are large and significant for both sons (1.073) and daughters (0.963), and they are also almost identical in size. This is only slightly less the case for the direct effects of maternal relational controls on risk-taking and delinquency.[1] So, despite the fact that daughters experience more maternal relational control than do sons, the causal effect of this control on other variables in our model is comparable for sons and daughters. Put differently, the reason maternal relational control results in less delinquency among daughters than sons is not because daughters are more sensitive to maternal relational control, but simply because they experience more of it. Or said yet another way, daughters are not less delinquent because they are inherently different, but because they are treated differently. The question therefore endures, if not by inherent reason of gender, then why?

MATERNAL RELATIONAL CONTROL IN PATRIARCHAL AND NON-PATRIARCHAL FAMILIES

The answer offered by power-control theory lies in patriarchal family relationships. A test of this component of power-control theory is to again divide the sample, this time in terms of family class structure. Of the family class relations we considered in the previous chapter, two were considered to be most patriarchal: where the husband had authority in the workplace and the wife was either not employed outside the home, or was employed in a position without authority. Alternatively, two family structures considered in the previous chapter also were considered to be least patriarchal: where both the husband and wife had authority in the workplace and female-headed households. In the next part of our analysis we manipulate equality constraints across these two groupings of patriarchal and non-patriarchal families.

The manipulations involve both measurement and structural segments of the simplified power-control model presented in figure 8.1. The results are presented in tables 8.6 and 8.7. We begin as we did in the previous section by comparing Model A, in which the measurement and structural coefficients are set free, with Model D, in which these coefficients are constrained to be equal. However, in this case the difference is significant (23.02, df = 14, $p < 0.05$), indicating that an improvement in fit results from freeing one or more parameters in the respective models. Comparisons of Model D with Models B and C suggest that freeing the measurement

TABLE 8.5 Regression coefficients for constrained and unconstrained models with respondents grouped by gender

	Unstandardized regression coefficients[b]											
	Delinquency on:						Risk on:				MIC on:	
	MRC		MIC[d]		Risk		MRC		MIC		MRC	
Model name[a]	Sons	Daughters	Sons	Daughters	Sons	Daughters	Sons	Daughters	Sons	Daughters	Sons	Daughters
Model A	-0.188 (0.265)	-0.231 (0.180)	0.097 (0.174)	-0.135 (0.140)	0.703 (0.147)	0.445 (0.141)	-0.139 (0.268)	0.008 (0.162)	-0.373 (0.179)	-0.385 (0.133)	1.073 (0.254)	0.963 (0.175)
Model B	-0.226 (0.149)		-0.016 (0.107)		0.586 (0.103)		-0.038 (0.141)		-0.392 (0.106)		1.003 (0.144)	
Model C	-0.205 (0.264)	-0.225 (0.180)	0.097 (0.173)	-0.130 (0.140)	0.719 (0.143)	0.432 (0.133)	-0.117 (0.255)	-0.005 (0.174)	-0.363 (0.165)	-0.410 (0.131)	1.074 (0.236)	0.963 (0.167)
Model D	-0.228 (0.149)		-0.014 (0.107)		0.588 (0.103)		-0.039 (0.143)		-0.395 (0.106)		1.003 (0.144)	

[a] See previous table and text for description of models.
[b] Standard errors are in parentheses.
[c] Maternal relational controls.
[d] Maternal instrumental controls.

TABLE 8.6 *Chi-squares and degrees of freedom for constrained and unconstrained models with respondents grouped in patriarchal and non-patriarchal families*

Model name and description[a]	X^2	Degree of freedom (df)	Probability value (p)	Goodness of fit index (GFI)	X^2 goodness of fit, corrected for degrees of freedom[b]
A No equality constraints across groups	44.33	36	0.160	0.969	8.33
B Structural coefficients constrained to be equal across groups	56.05	46	0.147	0.959	10.05
C Measurement coefficients constrained to be equal across groups	53.38	40	0.077	0.961	13.38
D Structural and measurement coefficients constrained to be equal across groups	67.35	50	0.051	0.946	17.35

[a] See text for a full description of models estimated.
[b] This statistic is computed by subtracting the models' degrees of freedom from their x^2 values.

coefficients ($X^2 D - B = 11.30$, df = 4, p < 0.05) significantly improves the fit, while freeing the structural coefficients ($X^2 D - C = 13.97$, df = 10, p > 0.10) does not. We also calculated a X^2 goodness of fit measure, corrected for degrees of freedom, for the four models. Doing so reveals that allowing only the measurement of the constructs to vary across groups accounts for nearly 81 per cent of the difference between the best and worst fitting models, while allowing the structural coefficients to vary accounts for only 44 per cent of this difference. The above results suggest the usefulness of comparing structural coefficients for patriarchal and non-patriarchal families in Model A, where both the measurement and structural coefficients are set free.

Such a comparison is presented in table 8.7. Note that the differences between structural coefficients in patriarchal and non-patriarchal families increase from Model C to Model A, where measurement coefficients are set free to 'correct' for differential measurement reliability across family settings. Perhaps the most important difference beween these family settings involves the effects of gender on maternal relational control. In patriarchal families this effect is large (− 0.251), while in non-patriarchal families this effect is modest (− 0.092). A *t*-test of the difference in strength of these coefficients is highly significant ($t = 2.74$, p < 0.02). The implication of this finding is strong support for MacKinnon's argument and the premise of power-control theory, namely, that the tendency of mothers to impose relational controls on their daughters is greater in patriarchal than in non-patriarchal families. That is, patriarchal family relations are a source of the sexual stratification of maternal relational control. Note that this is evidence

TABLE 8.7 Regression coefficients for constrained and unconstrained models with respondents grouped in patriarchal and non-patriarchal families

| | Unstandardized regression coefficient[b] | | | | | | | | | |
| | Delinquency on: | | | | Risk on: | | | MIC on: | | MRC on: |
Model name[a]	Gender	MRC[c]	MIC[d]	Risk	Gender	MRC	MIC	Gender	MRC	Gender
Model A										
Patriarchal	0.162 (0.068)	0.016 (0.289)	−0.297 (0.279)	0.356 (0.135)	0.103 (0.066)	0.088 (0.285)	−0.461 (0.269)	−0.099 (0.076)	0.840 (0.190)	−0.251 (0.066)
Non-patriarchal	0.092 (0.044)	−0.428 (0.192)	0.141 (0.125)	0.444 (0.165)	0.031 (0.057)	0.022 (0.199)	−0.362 (0.160)	0.033 (0.076)	0.966 (0.229)	−0.092 (0.051)
Model B										
Patriarchal										
Non-patriarchal	0.155 (0.038)	−0.409 (0.144)	0.108 (0.113)	0.450 (0.100)	0.061 (0.043)	0.030 (0.168)	−0.401 (0.143)	−0.034 (0.053)	0.935 (0.148)	−0.162 (0.046)
Model C										
Patriarchal	0.145 (0.053)	−0.058 (0.240)	−0.178 (0.201)	0.217 (0.102)	0.100 (0.062)	0.042 (0.295)	−0.406 (0.241)	−0.105 (0.075)	0.939 (0.201)	−0.216 (0.058)
Non-patriarchal	0.126 (0.059)	−0.499 (0.219)	0.204 (0.178)	0.594 (0.181)	0.029 (0.064)	0.013 (0.214)	−0.391 (0.171)	0.048 (0.079)	0.905 (0.189)	−0.112 (0.070)
Model D										
Patriarchal	0.133 (0.042)	−0.387 (0.162)	0.086 (0.133)	0.435 (0.100)	0.064 (0.045)	0.030 (0.176)	−0.415 (0.150)	−0.034 (0.054)	0.919 (0.145)	−0.172 (0.047)
Non-patriarchal										

[a] See text for full description of models estimated.
[b] This statistic is computed by subtracting the models' degrees of freedom from their x² values.
[c] Maternal relational controls.
[d] Maternal instrumental controls.

in favour of a social rather than biological account of the relational processes emphasized by Gilligan.

In both patriarchal and non-patriarchal families, maternal relational controls exercise a strong influence on maternal instrumental controls (0.840 and 0.966), and in both kinds of families maternal instrumental controls strongly influence risk preferences ($-$ 0.461 and $-$ 0.362). These effects are statistically significant within both types of family class relations, and the differences between family types are non-significant. Maternal instrumental controls are significantly stronger (p $<$ 0.10) in their direct effects on delinquency in patriarchal compared to non-patriarchal families ($-$ 0.297 and 0.141 respectively), while maternal relational controls are significantly stronger (p $<$ 0.10) in their direct effects on delinquency in non-patriarchal compared to patriarchal families (0.428 and 0.016 respectively). The greater direct effect of gender on delinquency in the patriarchal families (0.162 compared to 0.092) is of marginal statistical significance (p $<$ 0.10, one-tailed).

Overall, the total effect of gender on delinquency in patriarchal families is 0.329, compared to 0.145 in non-patriarchal families; while the total indirect effect of gender on delinquency is 0.167 in patriarchal families, compared to 0.053 in non-patriarchal families. Both of these differences are consistent with the expectations of power-control theory. However, what is perhaps most interesting is the way in which the indirect effect of gender is exercised in patriarchal families. This indirect effect flows through all of the mediating links proposed in power-control theory, including maternal relational and instrumental controls, as well as risk preferences. Meanwhile, it is not that maternal relational controls are unimportant in non-patriarchal families. We have seen that in such families these controls have a large and significant direct effect on delinquency, which they do not in patriarchal families. However, the crucial difference is the absence of a link between gender and maternal relational controls in non-patriarchal families. Apparently, in the latter families maternal relational controls are imposed more equally on sons and daughters, and this is important in accounting for the absence of gender differences in these familes.

AN ELABORATED POWER-CONTROL MODEL

In this final section of the chapter we specify and attempt to estimate a more fully elaborated power-control model of gender and delinquency. In doing so, we will 'bring fathers back in' and also reintroduce the perceived risk variables considered in the last chapter. The result is a much more complex model with attendant identification problems in non-patriarchal families.

Nonetheless, the exercise still proves useful in providing a more comprehensive conception of power-control theory, particularly as it includes fathers and the roles that they play in patriarchal families.

The descriptive statistics for the new matrix of observed and unobserved variables included in the more elaborate power-control model are presented in table 8.8, while the model itself is presented in figure 8.2. Several features of this model should be noted. Most notably, these features involve the inclusion of the paternal control constructs and indicators. First, it did not seem sensible to us that maternal relational controls would causally influence paternal instrumental controls. Mothers may causally influence fathers in their instrumental control, but if this does occur we posit that it is more likely through a mediating causal link involving maternal and paternal relational control. That is, the communication and identification that occurs between mothers and their children may encourage a similar process of communication and identification between children and their fathers, and this in turn may cause paternal instrumental control. However, this is an indirect causal process. We have therefore omitted a direct causal link between maternal relational and paternal instrumental controls in figure 8.2. This also assists in the identification of this model.

Second, the assumptions of power-control theory make it more likely that paternal instrumental control causally influences maternal instrumental control than vice versa. Although mothers form the first relational links with their children and are assigned the greater instrumental responsibility in their socialization and control, power-control theory implicitly predicts that it is fathers who determine the form, strength and content of the control that occurs. To test this expectation we estimate causal effects flowing in both directions in figure 8.2.

Third, while separating maternal from paternal relational control and maternal from paternal instrumental control is obviously desirable in terms of power-control theory, it is also equally obvious that mothers and fathers do not operate only as individuals, but also as members of family units with various mechanisms of contact. To take an obvious example, our maternal and paternal instrumental control constructs contain as indicators items asking if the mother and father know who the child is with when that child is away from home. Such information may be communicated separately and directly to the mother and father, but it may also be communicated jointly and indirectly, for example, through written notes left for both parents or by siblings, housekeepers or other third parties. Similar kinds of possibilities are involved with each of our indicators of maternal and paternal controls. As a result, we freed the correlation between the measurement errors of each of the parallel indicators of these controls, to take these various sources of covariance into account.

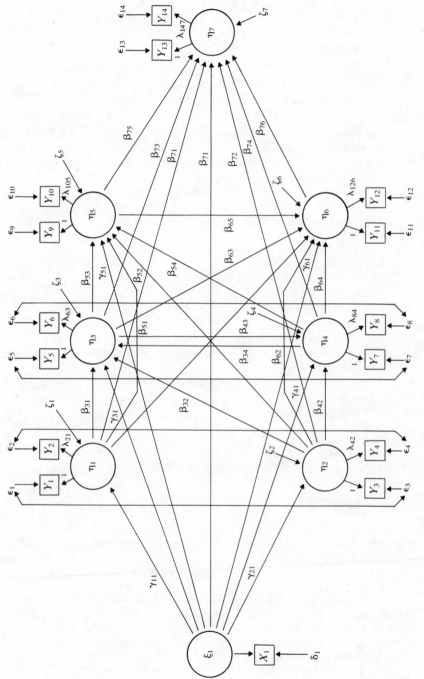

Figure 8.2   An elaborated power-control model of gender and delinquency (Model E)

TABLE 8.8 *Variables, means and standard deviations for total sample*

		Total sample	
Variable		$\bar{x}$	SD
ξ_1	*Gender*		
X_1	Reported Sex (female = 0; male = 1)	0.504	0.501
η_1	*Maternal relational control*		
Y_1	'Do you talk with your mother about your thoughts and feelings?'[a]	2.225	0.894
Y_2	'Would you like to be the kind of person your mother is?'[b]	2.684	1.057
η_2	*Paternal relational control*		
Y_3	'Do you talk with your father about your thoughts and feelings?'[a]	1.829	0.742
Y_4	'Would you like to be the kind of person your father is?'[b]	2.890	1.092
η_3	*Maternal instrumental control*		
Y_5	'Does your mother know your whereabouts when you are away from home?'[a]	2.923	0.826
Y_6	'Does your mother know who you are with when you are away from home?'[a]	2.754	0.830
η_4	*Paternal instrumental control*		
Y_7	'Does your father know your whereabouts when you are away from home?'[a]	2.450	0.836
Y_8	'Does your father know who you are with when you are away from home?'[a]	2.349	0.829
η_5	*Risk preference*		
Y_9	'I like to take chances.'[c]	3.576	1.033
Y_{10}	'The things I like to do best are dangerous.'[c]	2.754	1.148
η_6	*Perceived risk*		
Y_{11}	'Do you think you could break into a store without getting caught?'[d]	3.208	1.024
Y_{12}	'Do you think you could do graffiti without getting caught?'[d]	2.597	1.071
η_7	*Attacks on property or persons*		
Y_{13}	'How often in the last year have you intentionally banged up something that did not belong to you?'[e]	1.623	0.925
Y_{14}	'Excluding fights with a brother or sister, how often in the last year have you intentionally beaten up or hurt anyone?'[e]	1.714	1.006

[a] Coded: (1) never; (2) sometimes; (3) usually; (4) always.
[b] Coded: (1) not at all; (2) in a few ways; (3) in some ways; (4) in most ways; (5) in every way.
[c] Coded: (1) strongly disagree; (2) disagree; (3) undecided; (4) agree; (5) strongly agree.
[d] Coded: (1) definitely yes; (2) yes; (3) uncertain; (4) no; (5) definitely no.
[e] Coded: (1) never; (2) once; (3) two or three times; (4) often; (5) many times.

The above paragraphs introduce a series of model modications that can be tested for the improvement they might make in fitting the observed data. Table 8.9 provides the basis for such comparative tests. Model A fits the simplest of these formulations, a recursive model based on the single exogenous and seven endogenous variables and their indicators found in figure 8.2, with the only omitted link between maternal relational and paternal instrumental controls. The result is a X^2 of 358.08 with sixty-four degrees of freedom. Although the goodness of fit index for this model is nearly 0.91, the X^2 is more than five and a half times the degrees of freedom, with an associated probability beyond 0.001. Model B significantly improves this fit ($X^2A - B = 206.01$, df $= 2$, p < 0.001) by correlating the errors for maternal and paternal instrumental controls. Model C again significantly improves this fit ($X^2B - C = 55.3$, df $= 2$, p < 0.001) by correlating the errors for maternal and paternal relational controls. Finally, Model D introduces non-recursiveness into figure 8.2 by allowing paternal instrumental controls to causally influence maternal instrumental control. Theoretically, this may be the most interesting feature of the elaborated power-control model, because it tests the implication of power-control theory that fathers are a source of the instrumental control that mothers impose more strongly on daughters than sons. Adding this non-recursive effect to the model significantly improves its fit with the observed data ($X^2C - D = 5.19$, df $= 1$, p < 0.05).

Overall, Model D fits the data quite well. The goodness of fit index is 0.973, the ratio of the X^2 to its degrees of freedom is 1.55, and the probability value for the model is 0.004. Furthermore, the squared multiple correlations for the observed variables and latent constructs are reasonably large, and none of the normalized residuals exceed 2.0. There is, however, one potential source of uncertainty about the model. The largest eigen-value of *BB'*, the stability index, is 2.0. A value of this index of less than 1.0 is sufficient, but not necessary, to assure the stability of a model. We therefore used several procedures to test the identification of Model D (see Hayduk, 1987: chapter 5).

First, we re-estimated the model coefficients several times, starting each estimation from a different set of 'start values' for the coefficients. The maximum likelihood procedure converged repeatedly to the same set of final estimates, giving us reasonable certainty that the estimated coefficients were distinguishable from their neighbouring values and hence identified. Second, the estimated coefficient that is most likely the source of instability in the model is also the non-recursive effect that is of greatest theoretical interest in the model, the effect of paternal instrumental controls on maternal instrumental control. To test the identification of this particular coefficient we re-estimated the model with this coefficient fixed at a value

TABLE 8.9 *Goodness of fit measures for alternative power-control models of gender and delinquency in the full sample*

Model name and description[a]	Degree of freedom (df)	X^2	Probability value (p)	Goodness of fit index (GFI)
A Recursive model	64	358.08	0.000	0.908
B Recursive model with two sets of correlated errors	62	152.07	0.000	0.956
C Recursive model with four sets of correlated errors	60	96.77	0.002	0.971
D Non-recursive model with four sets of correlated errors	59	91.58	0.004	0.973

[a] See text for a full description of models estimated.
[b] This statistic is computed by subtracting the models' degrees of freedom from their X^2 values.

(0.05) thought to be minimally yet substantially different than the estimated value (0.312). The result was a significant ($p < 0.05$) decrement in fit compared to Model D ($X^2 = 95.41$), our final model, which again is evidence that this coefficient's value is uniquely determined by the combined model and data constraints.

A final indication that the elaborated power-control model presented in figure 8.2 and estimated in Model D is well identified is that the pattern of results closely parallels those found for the simplified model in figure 8.1. In general, then, coefficient estimates presented in table 8.10 contain few surprises and overall support for the theory. The important mediating roles of maternal relational and instrumental controls again are confirmed, as is the mediating role of risk preference. The pattern in this model is consistent with the fundamental premise of power-control theory that mothers relationally and instrumentally control their daughters more than their sons, and that this leads daughters to have lower levels of risk preference than do sons, making them also less likely to engage in delinquent attacks on other persons and their property. However, of greater interest in this model, because they were not contained in the simplified model, are the effects of paternal controls.

Perhaps the key finding with regard to paternal relational control, in terms of our interest in explaining gender differences in delinquency, is that sons experience more relational control than do daughters from their fathers. That is, as Chodorow predicts, sons communicate and identify more with their fathers than do daughters. With maternal relational control held constant, the effect of gender on paternal relational control is substantial

(0.328) and significant. Nonetheless, gender has the opposite effect on paternal instrumental control (− 0.271). So notwithstanding the fact that fathers have more relational control over sons, they exercise more instrumental control over daughters. Put differently, sons communicate and identify more with their fathers, while fathers monitor the associations and whereabouts of their daughters more than their sons. Daughters are the focus of instrumental control from both parents, while relational control is differentiated more by gender. Finally, it may be of interest to note that paternal relational control has a marginally significant ($p < 0.10$, one-tailed) positive effect on delinquency.

However, the most interesting finding in table 8.10 is that paternal instrumental control has a positive and significant (0.312) effect on maternal instrumental control, while the opposite path, from maternal instrumental control to paternal instrumental control is non-significant. As we noted above, this is a finding of considerable theoretical interest, since it is consistent with the power-control notion that fathers have much to do with the role mothers are assigned in instrumentally controlling their children, especially their daughters.

Our analysis turned finally to the estimation of the model we have been discussing in the sub-samples of patriarchal and non-patriarchal families. As we indicated above, we at this stage encountered problems in achieving a proper solution. The problem appears to derive from the sub-sample of non-patriarchal families, where a negative covariance in the theta epsilon matrix appears. This should perhaps not be surprising, since earlier when we fit the simplified power-control model in the patriarchal and non-patriarchal families sub-samples we found indications of notable differences. Indeed, our theory predicts that there should be notable differences. Distinct elaborated models for the patriarchal and non-patriarchal sub-samples can be successfully estimated, but the results largely mirror what we have found before with the simplified model and above in the more fully elaborated model: namely, that differences in the control and resulting risk preferences and delinquency of daughters and sons remain strong in the patriarchal families, and diminish in the non-patriarchal families. Given the similarity in outcomes, the more parsimonious model is probably preferable. We therefore bring this part of our analysis to a conclusion.

DISCUSSION AND CONCLUSIONS

This chapter has resulted in an important modification of power-control theory. This modification reflects an emphasis placed on relational processes in contemporary feminist scholarship. These processes involve an emphasis

TABLE 8.10 Structural and measurement coefficients for elaborated power-control model of gender and delinquency (N = 427)

A Regression coefficients[a]	Gender (ξ₁)	Maternal relational control (η₁)	Paternal relational control (η₂)	Maternal instrumental control (η₃)	Paternal instrumental control (η₄)	Risk preference (η₅)	Perceived risk (η₆)	Attacks on property and power (η₇)
Gender (ξ₁)	—	−0.301[i] (0.066)	0.328[i] (0.062)	−0.022 (0.100)	−0.271[h] (0.117)	0.134[f] (0.104)	−0.006 (0.125)	0.228[h] (0.096)
Maternal relational control (η₁)	−0.298	—	0.382[i] (0.084)	0.798[i] (0.126)	0.000[b]	0.052 (0.210)	0.259 (0.243)	−0.416[h] (0.199)
Paternal relational control (η₂)	0.407	0.480	—	−0.301 (0.242)	1.032[i] (0.224)	0.177 (0.240)	−0.547[g] (0.297)	0.358[f] (0.247)
Maternal instrumental control (η₃)	−0.018	0.640	0.192	—	0.215 (0.312)[ch] (0.155) (0.128)	−0.565[i] (0.180)	0.089 (0.211)	0.196
Paternal instrumental control (η₄)	−0.183	0.000[b]	0.560	0.183 (0.367)[d]	—	0.030 (0.109)	0.260[h] (0.130)	−0.244[h] (0.109)
Risk preference (η₅)	0.100	0.039	−0.105	−0.529	0.033	—	−0.579[i] (0.107)	0.531[i] (0.117)
Perceived risk (η₆)	−0.004	0.170	−0.286	0.073	0.251	−0.507	—	0.103 (0.103)
Attacks on property and power (η₇)	0.194	−0.358	0.245	0.211	−0.308	0.609	0.135	—

B Disturbance terms

$\zeta_1 = 0.234$; $\zeta_2 = 0.177$; $\zeta_3 = 0.138$; $\zeta_4 = 0.292$; $\zeta_5 = 0.321$; $\zeta_6 = 0.281$; $\zeta_7 = 0.145$. (All significant at 0.25, one-tailed.)

C Measurement coefficients (MLS)[e]

$\lambda_{2,1} = 1.526$; $\lambda_{4,2} = 1.548$; $\lambda_{6,3} = 0.879$; $\lambda_{8,4} = 0.839$; $\lambda_{10,5} = 1.367$; $\lambda_{12,6} = 0.794$; $\lambda_{14,7} = 1.286$ (All significant at 0.10, one-tailed.)

D Correlation of measurement errors

$r(\epsilon_{13}) = 0.173$; $r(\epsilon_{42}) = 0.098$; $r(\epsilon_{57}) = 0.118$; $r(\epsilon_{68}) = 0.204$.

---

[a] Unstandardized regression coefficients above the diagonal; standardized regression coefficients below the diagonal.
[b] Fixed at zero.
[c] b_{34}.
[d] β_{34}.
[e] $\lambda_{1,1}$, $\lambda_{3,2}$, $\lambda_{5,3}$, $\lambda_{7,4}$, $\lambda_{9,5}$, $\lambda_{11,6}$, $\lambda_{13,7} = 1$.
[f] $p < 0.10$, one-tailed.
[g] $p < 0.10$, two-tailed.
[h] $p < 0.05$, two-tailed.
[i] $p < 0.01$, two-tailed.

on relationships of shared intimacy, mutual understanding, caring and other kinds of interpersonal affect that are assumed to be more characteristic of women than men, and of particular relevance in understanding the mother-daughter relationship. We propose that these processes result, among other things, in relational kinds of social control that are distinguishable from more instrumental forms of social control. The data analysis presented in this chapter confirms that both kinds of social control are imposed by mothers on daughters more than on sons.

Furthermore, the initial covariance structure model presented in this chapter indicates that relational controls play a crucial mediating role in a power-control explanation of gender and delinquency. Daughters are controlled by their mothers, relationally and consequently instrumentally, more than sons, which in turn leads daughters to prefer risk taking less than do sons. Daughters therefore engage in less delinquency. The inevitable question is why?

Is the difference between sons and daughters an inherent one that involves gender specific properties, for example, are daughters more sensitive to relational or instrumental controls than are sons? Or, is the matter one of theme and degree that results instead from disparities in the extent to which the genders are controlled, so that differences between sons and daughters derive from variations in levels of both kinds of control, rather than from differences in the ways in which they respond to such control?

Our data are more consistent with the second interpretation than the first. When a simplified power-control model is examined in sub-samples of daughters and sons, no major differences are found in the way relational and instrumental controls exercise their influence. That is, even though sons experience more relational and instrumental control than daughters, sons and daughters are both influenced strongly, and to similar degrees, by the amounts of relational and instrumental control they encounter. There is some slight evidence that sons respond more to their risk preferences that do daughters, but the difference is of marginal statistical significance and therefore remains in need of further study. Meanwhile, there is not enough evidence here to conclude that any inherent difference between the genders accounts for their greatly different experiences with delinquency.

On the other hand, we have found evidence that the variations in treatment of the genders that are associated with family class structure do make a difference. When a simplified power-control model of gender and delinquency is estimated in sub-samples of patriarchal and non-patriarchal families, important differences become apparent. Most significantly, the relationship between gender and maternal relational control is stronger in patriarchal families. The mother-daughter relationship is intensified in these families, and it is diminished in non-patriarchal families. Since maternal relational control is a key mediating link between gender, risk preferences and delinquency, the implication is again that patriarchal family structure is a key factor in the explanation of gender differences in delinquency. So we now have further evidence of sexual stratification in the social control of adolescents that is connected to patriarchal family structure, and that is important in the explanation of gender differences in delinquency. The implication is that these differences are social structural in origin rather than biologically inherent.

A final finding of this chapter that is deserving of further note is that when paternal controls are brought back into an elaborated power-control model, we find evidence that the instrumental form of these controls plays a role in explaining the tendency of mothers to instrumentally control their daughters more than their sons. Again, such a finding is consistent with power-control theory and the role assigned to patriarchal power in this theory. There is much evidence in this chapter that mothers exercise control on behalf of others, namely fathers, over daughters. The relational aspects of maternal control considered in this chapter can in this sense be seen as part of larger patterns of dominance and subordination.

NOTES

1 Note that there is some sign in table 8.5 that risk preference interacts with gender on delinquency. It will be of interest to see if this interaction recurs in other data sets.

9

Gender and the Search for Deviant
Role Exits

INTRODUCTION

Gender is not related to all forms of deviance in the same way. For example, while girls consistently score lower than boys on most measures of juvenile delinquency, they score as high as do boys on many measures of drug use, and higher than boys on measures of psychosocial distress, including attempted suicide. Yet little attention is given in sociological theories of deviance to this variation. Instead we tend to specialize: on juvenile delinquency, substance abuse, suicide, depression, violent crime, and so on; little attention is given to the different ways that gender is connected to these various forms of deviance. This balkanization of areas in the study of deviance may have obscured valuable opportunities for the comparative development of our theories (Cloward and Piven, 1986). In this chapter we argue that an exploration of a propensity of mothers and their daughters to search for deviant role exits, including thoughts about leaving home and attempts at suicide, represents an important opportunity to develop the comparative possibilities of a power-control theory of adolescent deviance.

THE DEVIANCE AND CONTROL DIALECTIC

Power-control theory assumes that at all times and in all places, we are subject to social control. From the time we are born until we die, in our daily lives, as well as in our fantasies and in our dreams, social controls channel, curb, and contain us. Of course, this does not mean that social controls go unchallenged or unviolated. In fact, such controls are regularly open to challenge and violation, and these controls are therefore also subject to change. Power-control theory is concerned with the forms and rates at which these challenges and violations occur. The theory proposed in this book asserts that the presence of power and the absence of control are key forces that determine the form and rate these deviations take. But the larger assumption of the theory is that control and deviation from it are universal features of social life (see Hagan, 1977a; 1983: 122 onwards). Cloward and Piven (1986: 2) put the matter well when they observe that, '. . . the dialectic between social control and resistance to it is at the core of all social life.'

However, consider the following conundrum. If the inclination to deviate is ubiquitous, is it possible that there could actually be no manifestation of this inclination among those who have too little power, and who experience too much control, to act? Can such inclinations be so efficiently and comprehensively suppressed as to persist with no expression at all? The answer with regard to gender and crime is apparently in large part 'yes'. Relatively few crimes are committed by women. However, there is, of course, more to deviant behaviour than crime.

Furthermore, there is more to deviance than behaviour. We spoke above of the *inclination* to deviate. This inclination is more ubiquitous than the deviant acts that follow from it, and this inclination may be important in its own right. For example, it is well known that women are more likely to attempt suicide than to complete this act of self-destruction. In this chapter we will conceive of such attempts as one indicator of a search for deviant role exits. This kind of search may have particularly important implications for our understanding of gender relations and deviance.

Power-control theory is concerned with the varied forms of deviance, including the search for deviant role exits, that can result from alternative combinations of power and control. As we have noted, control theory (see Hirschi, 1969) assumes that the inclination to deviance is universal. What the power tradition adds to this assumption is the suggestion that the form this inclination will take varies not only with the imposition of social control, but also with the opportunities for the expression of such inclinations that are available. The inclination to deviate is assumed; what remains to be explained is variation in the form, as well as the amount, of this inclination.

THE SEARCH FOR DEVIANT ROLE EXITS

In large part, women may simply endure the disproportionate social control that they experience. But this is not the end of the story. We have assumed that the inclination to deviate, to challenge and violate social control, is universal. So we should expect that women as well as men will at least contemplate deviation from the social control imposed on them. However, as we noted at the outset of this chapter, the form of this inclination varies. It is more likely to be recognized among women in expressions of psychosocial distress, such as attempted suicide. So while women may often simply endure the sexual stratification of social control, they also often contemplate, and as well sometimes attempt, escape from this control. The opportunities, and therefore the power, to otherwise challenge the sexual stratification of social control are limited, especially for women who are restricted to the home. For these women especially, the only alternative to endurance may be a search for escape. It is this gender-based search for role exits that is the focus of this chapter and its elaboration of power-control theory.

The fact that women in Western society experience significantly higher rates of psychosocial distress than men is nearly as well documented (see Al-Issa, 1982) as the fact that men are more criminal than women. Walter Gove (e.g., 1978) offers a compelling sociological explanation of gender differences in distress based on the assumption that women's social roles are more stress provoking and less fulfilling than those occupied by men. Consistent with this role theory explanation, Gove (1972; see also Aneshensel et al., 1981; Gove, 1979; Radloff, 1975) has demonstrated that the relationship between gender and distress is more pronounced among respondents who are married than among those who were married previously or never married at all. Similarly, across studies done since the end of World War II, married women are found consistently to report higher levels of depression and psychological distress than married men (Gove and Tudor, 1973). The clear implication is that differences in the married family roles of men and women account for the gender-distress relationship.

In looking for the features of the family roles of married men and women that more specifically explain the gender-distress relationship, attention inevitably has focused on employment outside the home. As we have noted in earlier chapters, a gender division between the home-based sphere of consumption and a work-based sphere of production is at least in part a product of the industrial revolution. This gender division has markedly declined in this century, especially since the 1950s, as women increasingly have found work outside the home. If the restriction to the home associated with women's roles in patriarchal family structures is a source of the gender-distress relationship, then the movement of women into the workplace in recent decades should have brought with it a decline in the gender-distress relationship so frequently observed in past research. Using three national and two community surveys conducted between 1957 and 1976, Kessler and McRae (1981) demonstrate that such a decline has indeed occured in the gender-distress relationship, and that part of this decline can be traced to the increased labour force participation of women. More generally, Kessler and McRae (450) conclude that their evidence is 'consistent with the view that employment outside the home provides women with a variety of concrete and symbolic rewards unavailable to homemakers and that it allows them to escape from a variety of strains to which homemakers are exposed' (see also

Welch and Booth, 1977; Gove and Geerken, 1977; Rosenfield, 1980; Gore and Mangione, 1983; cf., Pearlin, 1975; Aneshensel et al., 1981).

Within the context of the above research, Kessler and McRae also offer the intriguing suggestion that another source of the declining gender-distress relationship might involve the increasing distress of men married to women employed outside the home (see also Burke and Weir, 1976; Rosenfield, 1980; Booth, 1976; Roberts and O'Keefe, 1981). In a subsequent paper, Kessler and McRae (1982) report evidence of such a pattern from a national survey. So the convergence found earlier in men and women's levels of distress across time may result not only from improved levels of employed women's mental health, but also from increasing distress among men.

Beyond this, it may be that the disaggregation of men and women joined in different kinds of marital relationships, both in terms of their preferences about spousal work outside the home (Ross, Mirowsky and Huber, 1983) and in terms of relative levels of power within the marriage (Mirowsky, 1985; see also Seligman, 1974; Scanzoni and Scanzoni, 1981), can account for the aggregated changes that the earlier studies have observed. Ross et al. demonstrate with a national sample that both spouses are less depressed in 'parallel marriages', where spouses perform tasks on an equitable and mutually accepted basis, while Mirowsky demonstrates with the same data that each spouse is least depressed if marital power, defined as the ability to impose one's will, is shared to some extent. Insofar as contemporary marriages are moving in both of these directions, that is, toward power sharing and the satisfaction of consensually defined preferences, this would further account for a convergence by gender in levels of experienced distress.

Meanwhile, there is also evidence of convergence with regard to the more specific linkage between gender and suicide attempts. Although men are known to commit suicide more frequently than women, we also have noted that women attempt suicide more frequently than men. A recent English study finds women attempting suicide at two and a half times the rate of men (Hawton and Catalan, 1982). But there is also evidence of convergence, with regard to attempted as well as completed suicides. Using several community studies, Weissman (1974: 740) suggests that the number of unsuccessful male suicide attempters has been on the rise in recent years and that the sex difference in these rates is declining. On the other side of the equation, Davis (1981) demonstrates that between 1950 and 1969 the increased labour force participation of women has led to an increase in the rate of completed female suicides. So again there is evidence of convergence.

We take the above findings as providing important evidence of gender differences in psychosocial distress and the search for what we have called deviant role exits. Furthermore, this evidence is consistent with the suggestion that the source of these patterns involves conditions associated with the prototypical role of married women in Western industrial families; and changes over time in these patterns are again consistent with increases in the labour force participation of women, and therefore with the changing role of women in Western families. We turn next to the meaning of these findings for a power-control theory of deviance.

POWER-CONTROL THEORY AND THE SEARCH FOR DEVIANT ROLE EXITS

Power and control can be two sides of the same coin. That is, the absence of power can be synonymous with the presence of control. Paid employment outside the home has this feature in relation to the marital roles of women. Married women with paid employment outside the home have a kind of power other married women lack, while women without paid employment outside the home are controlled in a way that externally employed women avoid. Our interest is in the impact of these circumstances on mothers and their daughters. To this point, we have used power-control theory to argue that daughters in families where mothers lack the power that employment can bring are less likely to engage in behaviours defined as criminal or delinquent. However, we also have questioned the plausibility of the assumption that the kinds of controls that derive from this form of patriarchal family structure can completely suppress what is assumed to be a ubiquitous inclination to resist social control, an inclination we assume among women as well as men.

The obvious path that a power-control theory must follow, then, is to look, in a way that is analogous to the way women confronted with the interlocking web of social control that we have described might look, for the opportunities that exist within the female role to give expression to suppressed inclinations to resist, challenge and otherwise deviate from a surrounding system of social control. As suggested above, these 'opportunities' may largely involve the contemplation of escape, for example, by death or other less drastic means of departure. There is much evidence in studies reviewed above that such contemplation occurs, that is, that these deviant role exits are considered more by women than men. Our particular interest is in the implications of such considerations for daughters, who, as we have emphasized in preceding chapters, are tied to their mothers by unique and interlocking sets of relational and instrumental controls.

Recall, for example, Chodorow's point that mothers and daughters are involved in a process of 'double identification'. This process leads mothers to establish particularly intense ties with their daughters and to relive a part of their own experience through their daughters. For example, we have established that mothers engage in more relational and instrumental control of their daughters than their sons. The question now is one of how these control processes are linked into the psychosocial distress that we also know females experience more than males. For example, if daughters like mothers experience such distress, in the form of depression and the search for deviant role exits, is this truer (as the research reviewed above would suggest) among daughters of mothers who are not employed outside the home? Do relational and instrumental controls play a role in containing resulting inclinations to deviance among daughters? Might the imposition of such controls play a part in explaining why, although daughters may search for deviant role exits, they 'succeed' less often than sons in taking these exits? These are the kinds of questions we attempt to answer in the analysis that follows.

CLASS IN THE HOUSEHOLD AND THE SEARCH FOR DEVIANT ROLE EXITS

To develop answers to the above questions we must first introduce indicators of psychosocial distress and the search for deviant role exits. Our indicators of distress include responses to two items: 'Do you ever feel "there's nothing to do?"' and 'Are you lonely?'. The first is the alternative to an item ('Life is interesting') used by Kessler and McRae (1982: 217) to measure depression, while the second is used by Ross et al. (1983: 813) also to measure depression. The search for deviant role exits is measured with two distinct sets of indicators involving thoughts about running away from home and about suicide. With regard to running away, two items ask: 'Have you ever thought about leaving home?' and 'How bad would things have to get before you would want to leave home?'. With regard to suicide, three items ask: 'How bad would things have to get before you would wish you were dead?', 'Have you thought about suicide?' and 'have you ever attempted suicide?'. An item asking about actually running away from home intentionally was omitted from this analysis, since this represents more than a search for a deviant role exit; that is, this item reflects the actual act of exiting. Again, our interest is not in actual role exits, but in the contemplation of such exits.

As in chapter 7, the above items are first combined into additive scales and correlated with gender in the family class categories considered in that chapter. The results are presented in table 9.1. These results reveal that the relationship between gender and distress is most acute in two family classes.

The first is the family structure that we have consistently identified as the most patriarchal in our typology, where the father has authority in the workplace and the wife is not employed. Daughters in these families are significantly more likely than sons (p < 0.05) to report signs of depression ($r = -0.197$), to think about running away from home (-0.227), to think about suicide (-0.191), and, when the previous two sets of items are combined, more generally to search for deviant role exits (-0.254).

TABLE 9.1 *Correlations within family class categories of gender with feelings of depression, thoughts about running away, suicide and the search for deviant role exits*

Family class categories	Feelings of depression	Thoughts about running away	Thoughts about suicide	Search for for deviant role exits
Husband commands/wife not employed	-0.197^b	-0.227^b	-0.191^b	-0.254^b
Husband commands/wife obeys	0.041	0.145^a	-0.090	0.041
Lower obey class	-0.362^c	-0.252^b	-0.227^a	-0.278^b
Upper obey class	-0.136	0.088	-0.063	0.021
Joint command class	0.023	-0.144	0.081	-0.053
Female-headed household	-0.073	-0.136	-0.054	-0.116

[a] Significant at 0.10 level.
[b] Significant at 0.05 level.
[c] Significant at 0.01 level.
[d] Significant at 0.001 level.

Interestingly, there is only one other family class category in which daughters display greater signs of distress and inclinations to deviance at the bivariate level. This is in the lower obey class, where the father is employed in a position without authority and the mother is not employed outside the home. So in contrast to our findings with regard to gender and self-reported delinquency, these findings suggest that in the context of the relationship between gender and distress, it is not the disjuncture between the authority of the father and mother outside the home that is crucial, but rather whether the mother has employment outside the home at all. Indeed, the correlations between gender and distress are greater in the lower obey class than in any other setting. Here daughters compared to sons are more likely than in any of the other class relations to report signs of depression (-0.362), to think about running away from home (-0.252), to think about suicide (-0.227), and overall to show signs of searching for deviant role exits (-0.278).

Of course, what separates the two family class settings where we have observed a bivariate gender-distress relationship from the remaining family structures is the absence of maternal employment outside the home. This pattern for adolescents mirrors the results reported above for adults and resonates with Chodorow's notion of a double identification that occurs between mothers and daughters. The implication is that mothers' feelings of depression are passed on to daughters, either through a process of identification with the experience of the mother, or through an identification with the success prospects of the mother, or both.

However, recall that in the research on adults reviewed above there was evidence of an effect of wives' employment outside the home on husbands' as well as wives' feelings of distress. It may therefore be important to further consider exactly how the paid labour force participation of mothers influences sons as well as daughters. When all families in our sample where mothers are not employed outside the home are aggregated, the average score of sons on our depression scale is 4.909, and the average score for daughters is 5.534. A t-test for this difference of means is significant at the 0.001 level ($t = 3.038$). In contrast, the aggregated score in the grouping of families where mothers work outside the home is 5.006 for sons, and 5.110 for daughters. So the decline in the gender-distress relationship that results from mothers entering the paid labour force is almost entirely the result of the decreased depression of daughters.

However, the combined scale of runaway and suicide items that measures the search for deviant role exits reveals a pattern that is more like that for adults. When mothers are not employed outside the home, sons score an average of 7.167 on this scale, while daughters score an average of 8.207. A t-test for this difference of means is significant at the 0.001 level ($t = 3.082$). In families where mothers are employed outside the home, sons score an average of 7.705, and daughters score 7.864. So in terms of the search for deviant role exits, there is evidence of a convergence like that observed in studies of adults, with the distress of daughters decreasing and the distress of sons increasing.

Up to this point we have only considered the gender-distress relationship in bivariate terms, albeit as conditioned by family class structure. However, there is reason to suspect from the work that we have done thus far that the bivariate relationship between gender and distress is suppressed. We know that overall daughters are more likely to report signs of distress than are sons, while we also know from our previous work that daughters are more likely than sons to be relationally and instrumentally controlled by their mothers. Beyond this, power-control theory predicts that maternal controls reduce expressions of distress in the same way that these controls reduce other kinds of deviant inclinations and acts. Collectively, these observations predict that the gender-distress relationship should be suppressed by the pattern of mother-daughter control that we have emphasized.

We test the above prediction using the covariance structure model presented in figure 9.1. This model is based on the indicators described in table 9.2, with gender (X_1) as the exogenous variable, and maternal relational (η_1) and maternal instrumental (η_2) controls, feelings of depression (η_3), and the search for deviant role exits (η_4) as the endogenous variables. Gender,

TABLE 9.2 *Variables, means and standard deviations for total sample and for families with mothers employed in and outside home*

Variable		Total sample $\bar{x}$	SD	Mother in home $\bar{x}$	SD	Mother outside home $\bar{x}$	SD
ξ_1	*Gender*						
X_1	Reported sex (female = o male = 1)	0.504	0.501	0.845	0.500	0.487	0.501
η_1	*Maternal relational control*						
Y_1	'Do you talk with your mother about your thoughts and feelings?'[a]	2.225	0.894	2.154	0.878	2.253	0.900
Y_2	'Would you like to be the kind of person your mother is?'[b]	2.684	1.057	2.740	0.999	2.661	1.081
η_2	*Maternal instrumental control*						
Y_3	'Does your mother know your whereabouts when you are away from home?'[a]	2.923	0.826	2.919	0.845	2.924	0.819
Y_4	'Does your mother know who you are with when you are away from home?'[a]	2.754	0.830	2.756	0.833	2.753	0.830
η_3	*Feelings of depression*						
Y_5	'Do you ever feel "there's nothing to do?"'[c]	2.838	0.802	2.886	0.822	2.819	0.794
Y_6	'Are you lonely?'[c]	2.262	0.794	2.293	0.837	2.250	0.777
η_4	*Search for deviant role exits*[e]						
Y_7	Thoughts about running away[d]	3.747	1.317	3.805	1.328	3.724	1.314
Y_8	Thoughts about suicide[d]	4.000	1.235	3.911	1.274	4.036	1.219

[a] Coded: (1) never; (2) sometimes; (3) usually; (4) always.
[b] Coded: (1) not at all; (2) in a few ways; (3) in some ways; (4) in most ways; (5) in every way.
[c] Coded: (1) never; (2) rarely; (3) sometimes; (4) often.
[d] Coded: (1) never; (2) almost never; (3) half the time; (4) almost always; (5) always.
[e] See text.

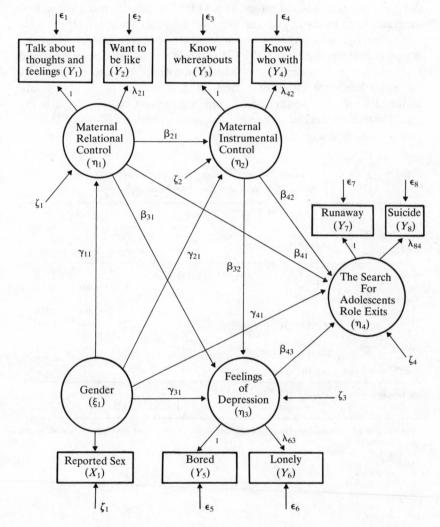

Figure 9.1   Simplified power-control model of gender and the search for adolescent role exits

maternal relational and maternal instrumental controls are measured as in the previous chapter. Feelings of depression are measured by the two indicators of boredom and loneliness described earlier. The search for deviant role exits is based on the two additive scales discussed above that measure thoughts about running away and thoughts about suicide.

The endogenous variables are ordered as presented above. As in the previous chapter, maternal relational controls are assumed to be nurtured from birth, while maternal instrumental controls are assumed to emerge as the child begins to move away from home. Feelings of depression are assumed to be a more immediate condition, but to causally precede the actual search for deviant role exits. The model is estimated with LISREL, and the results are presented in table 9.3.

TABLE 9.3 Regression and measurement coefficients for simplified power control model of gender and the search for deviant role exits

A Regression coefficients[a]	Gender (ξ_1)	Maternal relational control (η_1)	Maternal instrumental control (η_2)	Feelings of depression (η_3)	Search for adolescent role exits (η_4)
Gender (ξ_1)	—	-0.333^{f} (0.069)	-0.099^{d} (0.076)	-0.060 (0.062)	-0.295^{f} (0.090)
Maternal relational control (η_1)	-0.313	—	0.825^{f} (0.118)	-0.157 (0.134)	-0.264^{d} (0.189)
Maternal instrumental control (η_2)	-0.080	0.705	—	0.098 (0.113)	-0.344^{e} (0.159)
Feelings of depression (η_3)	-0.076	-0.214	0.156	—	0.883^{f} (0.227)
Search for deviant role exits (η_4)	-0.223	-0.212	-0.324	0.522	—

B *Measurement coefficients (MLS)[b,c]*

$$\lambda_{21} = 1.399; \quad \lambda_{42} = 0.897; \quad \lambda_{63} = 1.165; \quad \lambda_{84} = 1.578$$

[a] Unstandardized regression coefficients above the diagonal; standardized regression coefficients below the diagonal; standard errors in parentheses.
[b] ≤ 0.01 for all coefficients.
[c] $\lambda_{11}, \lambda_{32}, \lambda_{53}, \lambda_{74}$ fixed at 1.00.
[d] $p < 0.10$, one-tailed.
[e] $p < 0.05$, one-tailed.
[f] $p < 0.01$, one-tailed.

THE ANALYSIS

Overall, the model fits the data rather well. Looking first at Panel B of table 9.3, each construct has a statistically significant ($p < 0.01$) and substantial loading (λ coefficient) on its observed measures. This implies that each latent construct is a common factor with regard to its observed measures.

The results for the maternal relational and maternal instrumental constructs should not surprise us, since they carry over from the previous chapter. However, the measures of depression also appear to constitute a common factor, as do also the runaway and suicide scales as indicators of the search for deviant role exits. Again, the former results should not surprise us, since these items have been used previously in other studies to measure depression. However, the construct representing the search for deviant role exits is new, and so the latter result may be of particular importance.

As in chapter 8, the structural parameters for the model portrayed in figure 9.1 are presented in Panel A of table 9.3, with the unstandardized regression coefficients (maximum likelihood estimates) above the diagonal, standardized coefficients below, and standard errors in parentheses. Of greatest interest in table 9.3 is evidence of the predicted suppression of the gender-distress relationship. The LISREL output indicates that the total effect of gender on the search for deviant role exits is -0.118. However, the direct effect of gender on the search for adolescent role exits (γ_{41}) is -0.295 (p $<$ 0.01). As power-control theory predicts, this difference is largely a result of the fact that both maternal relational (-0.264) and maternal instrumental (-0.344) controls decrease the search for deviant role exits, and that daughters, as we have seen in earlier chapters, are subjected to greater amounts of both of these kinds of controls (-0.333 and -0.099). The result is a positive indirect effect of gender on the search for deviant role exits of 0.216 [($-0.333 \times -0.264 = 0.088$) + ($-0.099 \times -0.344 = 0.034$) + ($-0.333 \times 0.825 \times -0.344 = 0.094$)]. So the indirect effect of gender on the search for deviant role exits through maternal controls substantially suppresses the effect of gender on the search for deviant role exits. Or, said differently, were it not for the constraining influence of mothers on daughters, the inclination of daughters to look for deviant role exits would be much greater than it otherwise appears to be. This only becomes apparent when these controls are taken into account in a multivariate analysis such as above.

Overall, the above model fits the observed data reasonably well. The model has a X^2 of 49.35, with eighteen degrees of freedom, which is significant beyond the 0.001 level. However, we have noted previously the sensitivity of X^2 to sample size, and the sample size here is again rather large (N $=$ 427). The ratio of X^2 to the degrees of freedom is 2.74, which is acceptable by Carmines and McIver's (1981) standard. Furthermore, none of the standardized residuals in the estimation of this model exceeds 2.0, which suggests that the errors that remain may be random (Joreskog and Sorbom, 1981). However, we also saw above in the bivariate correlations within family class categories that family structure conditions the effect of gender on distress. So we turn next to the estimation of our model of the

TABLE 9.4 *Chi-squares and degrees of freedom for constrained and unconstrained models
with respondents grouped by mother's employment*

Model name and description[a]	X^2	Degrees of freedom (df)	Probability value (p)
A No equality constraints across groups	68.19	36	0.001
B Structural coefficients constrained to be equal across groups	85.03	46	0.000
C Measurement coefficients constrained to be equal across groups	71.19	40	0.002
D Structural and measurement coefficients constrained to be equal across groups	89.35	50	0.001

[a] See text for a full description of models estimated.

search for deviant role exits among families grouped by whether the mother is employed inside or outside the home.

We begin by comparing Model A, in which the measurement and structural coefficients are set free, with Model D, in which these coefficients are constrained to be equal. The difference in X^2s (21.16, df = 14) is significant (p < 0.10), indicating that an improvement in fit results from freeing one or more parameters in the respective models. Comparisons of Model D with Models B and C suggest that freeing the structural coefficients (X^2D − C = 18.16, df = 10, p < 0.10) significantly improves the fit, while freeing the measurement coefficients (X^2D − B = 4.3, df = 4) does not. As in the previous chapter, in the discussion that follows we will compare structural coefficients that result from the estimation of Model A, where both the measurement and structural coefficients are set free.

The effects of gender on the search for deviant role exits are quite different in families where the mother is and is not employed outside the home. To begin, the LISREL output indicates that the total effect of gender in families where the mother is not employed outside the home is − 0.179, compared to 0.003 where the mother is employed outside the home. The respective direct effects of gender on the search for role exits are − 0.132 and − 0.065. While the former is significantly larger than the latter (t = 1.2, p < 0.10), the ways in which these direct effects emerge and are combined with the indirect effects of gender are perhaps of greater importance.

Both where mothers are and are not employed outside the home, links between gender and maternal controls suppress the effects of gender on the search for deviant role exits. Where mothers are not employed outside the home, gender indirectly suppresses this search through maternal relational control ($- 0.216 \times - 0.381 = 0.082$). Where mothers are employed outside the home, gender indirectly suppresses this search through maternal relational and instrumental controls ($- 0.189 \times 0.909 \times - 0.319 = 0.055$). In both kinds of family settings, then, maternal controls reduce what would otherwise be a larger bivariate relationship between gender and the search for deviant role exits.

Meanwhile, what more clearly distinguishes the two family settings is the part that the link between gender and depression plays in explaining the gender-based search for deviant role exits in families where mothers are not employed outside the home. In these families, daughters are significantly more likely to be depressed ($t = 2.48$, p < 0.05) and the indirect effect of gender through feelings of depression on the search for deviant role exits is ($- 0.192 \times 0.619$) = 0.119. These results make clear that it is the greater tendency toward depression of daughters of mothers who are not employed outside the home that leads these daughters to search for deviant role exits.

One final point is of interest. While the analyses undertaken above in both the full sample and in the sub-samples reveal suppressed effects of gender on the search for deviant role exits, the direct effect of gender on this search is substantially greater in the full sample than in either of the sub-samples. Inspection of the correlation matrices for these analyses reveals why this is the case. First, however, note that gender is substantially more strongly correlated with maternal relational control in the full sample ($- 0.333$) than in either of the sub-samples ($- 0.216$ and $- 0.189$). Maternal relational control plays the primary role in suppressing the effect of gender on the search for deviant role exits, so it is not surprising that this suppression effect is weaker in the full sample than in the sub-samples. However, to understand why the relationships between gender and maternal relational control decline in both of the sub-samples, it is necessary to consider the correlations between gender and the observed variables that underlie this construct in each of the sub-samples.

The two observed variables involved are items that ask how extensively mothers talk with their sons and daughters about their thoughts and feelings, and how much these sons and daughters would like to be the kind of person the mother is. In the sub-sample where mothers work outside the home, daughters are substantially more likely than sons to talk to their mothers ($- 0.232$) and to want to be like their mothers ($- 0.210$). As well, these items are correlated quite strongly with one another (0.460). However, the pattern is somewhat different in the sub-sample where mothers are not employed outside the home. Here daughters are more likely still than sons ($- 0.320$) to talk to their mothers about their thoughts and feelings, but they

TABLE 9.5 *Regression coefficients for constrained and unconstrained models with respondents grouped by mothers employed in and out of home*

| | Unstandardized regression coefficients[b] | | | | | | | | | |
| | Search for role exits on: | | | | Depression on: | | | MIC on: | | MRC on: |
Model name[a]	Gender	MRC[c]	MIC[d]	Depression	Gender	MRC	MIC	Gender	MRC	Gender
Model A										
In	−0.132 (0.082)	−0.381 (0.314)	0.015 (0.189)	0.619 (0.226)	0.192 (0.093)	−0.304 (0.362)	0.251 (0.233)	−0.119 (0.104)	0.862 (0.312)	−0.216 (0.078)
Out	−0.065 (0.038)	−0.126 (0.138)	−0.319 (0.121)	0.497 (0.183)	−0.046 (0.038)	−0.067 (0.134)	0.007 (0.101)	−0.023 (0.054)	0.909 (0.140)	−0.189 (0.045)
Model B										
In	−0.097 (0.035)	−0.220 (0.129)	−0.211 (0.097)	0.620 (0.139)	−0.071 (0.035)	−0.097 (0.120)	0.045 (0.090)	−0.057 (0.045)	0.898 (0.124)	−0.191 (0.037)
Model C										
In	−0.098 (0.057)	−0.334 (0.266)	0.004 (0.155)	0.581 (0.165)	−0.173 (0.072)	−0.305 (0.345)	0.227 (0.206)	−0.134 (0.083)	1.006 (0.274)	−0.167 (0.057)
Out	−0.066 (0.038)	−0.101 (0.143)	−0.324 (0.121)	0.400 (0.143)	−0.059 (0.050)	−0.139 (0.183)	0.014 (0.142)	−0.018 (0.054)	0.899 (0.133)	−0.197 (0.046)
Model D										
In	−0.093 (0.035)	−0.223 (0.135)	−0.178 (0.099)	0.581 (0.135)	−0.098 (0.040)	−0.209 (0.158)	0.096 (0.117)	−0.057 (0.045)	0.906 (0.124)	−0.190 (0.037)

[a] See previous table and text for description of models.
[b] Standard errors are in parentheses.
[c] Maternal relational controls.
[d] Maternal instrumental controls.

are essentially no more likely than sons (− 0.078) to want to be like their mothers. A result is that these measures of maternal relational control are less strongly correlated (0.320) with one another in this sub-sample.

The implication of the above finding is intriguing. It suggests that the process of 'double identification' that Chodorow discusses breaks down in families where the mother stays at home. In these families, daughters are closely involved in relationships with their mothers. As we saw above, such a relationship would appear to go so far as to involve the daughters in the distress of the mother that derives from staying home, although the mother's relationship with the daughter also seems to reduce feelings of depression somewhat. However, these daughters are no more likely than are sons to want to be the kind of person their mother is. It is perhaps not surprising, then, that these daughters are the most likely in our analysis to search for deviant role exits. It is perhaps in this grouping that the sexual stratification of social control displays its weakest link. These daughters, to put the matter succinctly, want out. Even more to the point, they are depressed enough to consider as the means of escape running away from home and taking their own lives.

'DON'T EVEN THINK ABOUT IT': SOME CONCLUSIONS

The results reported on adolescent distress in this chapter include some fascinating parallels with research findings for adults. Perhaps the most striking of these findings is that it is the daughters of mothers who are not employed outside the home who, like their mothers, are most likely to be distressed. So while in earlier chapters we found that it is the authority of fathers relative to mothers outside the home that is most consequential in terms of the tendency of sons to be more delinquent than daughters, in this chapter we find that it is the employment of mothers outside the home that is most consequential in terms of the tendency of daughters to be more distressed than sons.

Albeit in different ways, the findings for delinquency and distress are consistent with the premise that patriarchal family relations influence the relationship between gender and deviance. When it is considered that delinquency can be fun and that distress obviously is not, an explanation for the different patterns becomes apparent. This explanation begins with the premise that authority is liberating and that unemployment is constraining. We have identified processes through which patriarchal family structures convey to sons a sense of liberation that makes their involvement in delinquency more likely, and we also have identified processes through which patriarchal family structures convey to daughters a sense of constraint that makes their distress more likely. These processes are most clearly reflected in the most patriarchal family structure that we have considered, where the husband has authority in the workplace and the wife is not employed outside the home. The role experiences of parents in this family class relation are by implication simultaneously liberating for sons and constraining for daughters.

Meanwhile, one of the most interesting aspects of the broader research literature on gender and distress is the finding that while women are more likely than men to express signs of distress, in the form of the symptoms of depression, thoughts about leaving home, and attempts at suicide, they are less likely than men to activate these feelings, for example, by actually leaving home or commiting suicide. Analysts of gender and distress have not been greatly concerned with this point, choosing instead to focus on the issue of distress itself. This is understandable, since this distress presents itself as the more manifest problem among women. Nonetheless, we believe there is an important theoretical basis for re-ordering the research problem.

Power-control theory begins with a kind of question that leads to such a re-ordering. This question asks why more wives and daughters, given their expressions of distress, don't actually leave home or commit suicide. Why do they search for, but not take, the kinds of deviant role exits they in disproportionate numbers consider? As one might expect from power-control theory, the answer we propose has to do with the relative powerlessness and control of wives and daughters. The answer is suggested by the common warning, 'Don't even think about it', that no doubt is passed on more frequently to daughters than sons. Daughters do apparently think about 'it', but they do not actually 'do it', at least not any more so than do sons.

Re-ordering the research problem in this way re-focuses the attention given in work on gender and distress around issues of power and control. This research has sometimes very effectively captured the importance of a perceived powerlessness and a felt absence of control among women in producing distress (see Mirowsky, 1985). And we have seen in this chapter that relational and instrumental controls imposed by mothers on daughters act to suppress the inclinations of daughters to search for deviant role exits. However, the tendency in the broader research literature on gender and distress is often to focus more on the social psychology of women than on the social structures in which they are located. Within this context, there may also be a tendency to see distress as an expression of social psychological weakness or deficiency. Such a tendency is a common theme in the study of deviance, especially where the form of deviance is associated with a cause that fails. However, it is also possible to see distress as a precursor of resistance and as an agent for change. Such a view gains plausibility as distress is associated with a search for deviant role exits, that is, as these role exits are seen as part of a larger search for change. We have seen evidence in this chapter that distress is associated with a search for such role exits.

So the distress and consequent search for role exits that we have seen in our sample of adolescent girls can be understood as a form of rebellion, albeit often unsuccessful. It is interesting to note that in the criminological research literature delinquency more often has been seen this way with regard to adolescent boys than adolescent girls. The inclination to rebel may be more widely dispersed than previously assumed.

Epilogue

The Future of Structural Criminology

INTRODUCTION

Our interest in this book is in the linkage of theory and data in criminological research. The premise of the book is that criminologists have ignored the methodological implications of the structural foundations of dominant theories of crime, delinquency and criminal justice. In contrast, we have emphasized a structural theme found in labelling, conflict and control theories. Although this structural theme involves social relations organized along horizontal as well as vertical dimensions, we have noted that structural relations organized along vertical, hierarchical lines of power are of greatest interest to criminologists. Structural criminology is distinguished by efforts to measure, analyse and otherwise bring these power relationships directly into the development of criminological theory.

We have offered no all-encompassing structural theory of crime, delinquency and criminal justice. Instead, this book consists of empirical essays that illustrate the methods of structural criminology. Like the field of criminology, the essays are divided roughly into two groups, the first group dealing largely with reactions to crime by criminal justice agencies, and the second group concerned primarily with an etiological theory of delinquency. Each grouping contains departures from the conventions that define it. For example, chapter 1 deals with the causes of white-collar crime as well as punishment, chapter 5 considers public perceptions of criminal justice practices, chapter 6 explores briefly the implications of a power-control theory for reactions by gender to delinquency, and chapter 9 expands power-control theory beyond the explanation of delinquency to consider what we call 'the search for deviant role exits'. Nonetheless, we offer no theory that can bring all of this together. Instead we pursue a structural methodology that is useful in unifying the study of such diverse topics in a thematic way. This epilogue consists of final thoughts about problems and prospects of a structural criminology. This discussion leads to a suggestion that we might solve some problems we confront in criminology more generally through a reconceptualization that focuses on 'crimes as social events in the life course'. First, however, we summarize problems that confront sociological criminology generally, and the work of a structural criminology more specifically.

SOCIOLOGICAL DISCONTENTS

If sociology is the scientific study of social relations, then the approach outlined in this volume is not only a structural criminology, but a sociological criminology as well. The sociological tradition has long been ascendant in criminology (see Gibbons, 1979), but today is under attack. The attack comes on one hand from those who see criminology as its own 'fully autonomous discipline' (e.g., Thomas, 1984), and on the other hand from those in other disciplines (e.g., Wilson, 1975) who believe their own or some grander combination of disciplines provides a better approach to the study of crime and delinquency. The structural approach outlined in this volume is inherently opposed to the separation of criminology from sociology, arguing instead that the structural foundations of sociology make its explanatory role necessary for an understanding of crime and delinquency.

In this regard, it is interesting to recall how sociology came to the study of crime. In its formative period, sociology was unique in its willingness to consider social problems that other established social sciences deemed unimportant or uninteresting. The study of criminal and delinquent behaviour is one example. However, the importance of sociology to the study of criminality was better understood as it was recognized that most criminal and delinquent behaviour occurred in social groupings that other social groupings attempted to control. The relations within and between these groupings were a natural focus for an emergent structural sociology, as represented, for example, in early efforts to develop American sociology at the University of Chicago (see Hinkle and Hinkle, 1954).

However, satisfying as these early explanatory efforts were to sociologists, they failed to satisfy those who more single-mindedly sought ways to effectively treat and prevent crime. Ironically, in retrospect there is reason to believe that some of the prevention strategies developed out of early work in the Chicago tradition may actually have been underestimated in terms of their ameliorative results (Schlossman, 1983). Nonetheless, modern critics, including most prominently the political scientist James Q. Wilson (1975; but see also Scheingold, 1984; Jacob, 1984), have reasoned that the sociological focus on 'ultimate' structural causes of criminal and delinquent behaviour has impeded the formation of effective crime policies. Wilson (1975: 3) writes that 'ultimate causes cannot be the object of policy efforts precisely because, being ultimate, they cannot be changed.' Regardless of whether one accepts this judgement about the malleability of the causal factors sociologists emphasize, it seems clear that Wilson and representatives of rival disciplines wish to develop criminology as a form of policy analysis. Interestingly, one of the effects of the new policy analysis of crime is to shift attention away from criminal and delinquent behaviour and onto the strategies used by control agencies in response to these behaviours. Sociologists too, particularly labelling and conflict theorists, have been much interested in the actions of control agencies. However, a fundamental premise of a structural criminology is that a one-sided attention to only these reactions of control agencies misses much of what we initially set out to study, and beyond this makes impossible a full understanding of the phenomena (i.e., both criminal behaviour and reactions to it) we wish to explain. The policy analysis of crime leaves off where the sociological study of crime and delinquency began. Sociologists, it seems, may still be uniquely suited to pursue the causes of these behaviours regarded by others as disreputable.

It bears reiteration, then, that a fundamental assumption of structural criminology is that the understanding of criminality will be built on an analysis within and between groupings of individuals, regardless of on which side of the law they reside. We have argued with examples: that to understand the class-crime connection it is necessary to take into account the relational position of individuals in the class structure, as well as the ways in which their behaviours are defined by law; that to understand variations in sentencing decisions and by implication other kinds of criminal justice outcomes it is necessary to take into account relationships between offenders, complainants and victims, as well as power relationships between persons involved in the decision-making process; and that to understand fundamental interconnections between gender, class, delinquency and crime it is necessary to take into account the work-related positions of heads and spouses in households, as well as the impact of these work-based relations on the sexual stratification of the social control of children.

STUDYING ACTIONS AND REACTIONS

In the above examples there is a necessary focus on action and reaction in the production and reproduction of crime and its control. The implication is that the power relations that are the explanatory foundations of structural criminology cannot be developed, explored or tested with one-sided methodologies. The essays that make up this volume also have emphasized that power relationships have symbolic as well as instrumental dimensions, both of which must be considered in attempts to explain criminal actions and reactions. Futhermore, we have noted that these instrumental and symbolic relationships can change over time. The implications of this are that our data collection and analyses must be both dynamic and relational, including a consideration of temporal change and the interaction of actors and reactors in the production and reproduction of crime and delinquency. In our efforts to satisfy these requirements in the preceding chapters we have presented analyses of data that derive from a division of criminological labour that characterizes our own as well as others' recent work. That is, we have worked with the kind of data that are found in criminal justice agencies and that are the basis of most empirical studies of reactions to crime, and we have collected and analysed our own survey data that are the basis of most work on the causes of delinquent and sometimes criminal behaviour. Each kind of data has characteristic advantages and disadvantages for issues that concern us.

One advantage of the data found in criminal justice agencies is that they often extend backward in time, allowing analyses of changes in processing practices across temporal periods. A major disadvantage of these data is that they usually are restricted to one or only a few sectors and/or stages of the criminal justice system, and therefore they involve highly selected samplings of offenders subjected to punishment. We, like others, have attempted to reduce these problems by various strategies. For example, in our study of white-collar crime and punishment in the securities industry we interviewed investigators in several agencies to broaden our sampling frame, and in this and the chapter dealing with the sanctioning of drug offenders we used statistical techniques to correct within the limits of our data for sample selection processes that occur across stages of the criminal justice system. However, these are presented as only partial remedies to the limitations of criminal justice data sets.

The survey data often used in the study of the causes of delinquent and criminal behaviour involve more representative samples of relevant populations. However, these data sets usually involve cross-sectional designs or limited term panels that allow little consideration of change over time. Again, like others, we have attempted to reduce these problems in various ways. For example, our development of a power-control theory of gender and delinquency began with the assumption that the mother-daughter relationships emphasized in this theory would vary in their intensity across kinds of families, and that these families are changing in predominance over time. We used our cross-sectional survey data to identify different kinds of families that ranged from patriarchal to egalitarian in form. It is usually assumed that there has been a shift over time from more patriarchal to more egalitarian families in Western industrial societies, and we in effect treated these family structures as cross-sectional proxies for slices of history. However, we also know that the meaning of different kinds of family structures can vary across time and place (see Elder, 1985: 27). The implication is that new kinds of longitudinal, historically based data are needed to set scope conditions and/or to more meaningfully test predictions of power-control theory as well as other theories of crime and delinquency.

From the beginning of this book we have made the point that the theoretical separation of the study of criminal reactions and actions is unnecessary, and inconsistent with the goals of structural criminology. It is now also apparent that data used to study issues on both sides of this divide are, for different reasons, inadequate. With these points in mind, we now propose a reconception of 'crimes as social events in the life course' that represents a new avenue along which a structural criminology might take some useful steps in synthesizing the study of criminal actions and reactions.

CRIMES AS SOCIAL EVENTS IN THE LIFE COURSE

This approach begins by placing criminal events within the broader context of life course research (Elder, 1985). A key feature of the life course conceptualization is that it leads us away from intended or unintended concentrations on restricted phases of the life cycle or on restricted groupings of persons. For example, it leads away from either a limited focus on the causes of delinquency in late adolescence, or from a restricted consideration of police or court reactions to crime in adulthood. In part, it does so by explicitly substituting the conceptualization of 'social events' for that of 'criminal careers'. The focus of this conceptualization is on the causes and consequences of events called crimes or delinquencies in the life course. The point of a life course perspective is to emphasize that social events which are called delinquent or criminal are linked into life trajectories of broader significance, whether these trajectories are criminal or non-criminal in form. A key feature of this terminology is that it does not require that the events involved are designated as criminal or delinquent: criminal events, or crimes, are social events that result from individual and collective designations. In etiological research it may often be heuristically useful to assume that certain operationalizations constitute crime and delinquency, while in police and court processing studies it may often be more appropriate to leave this designation open to exploration or test (e.g., see Hagan and Zatz, 1985). The language of 'social events' allows either possibility to apply.

Again, the point of life-course research is to emphasize that such events and transitions may be linked into life trajectories of broader significance. As Elder (1985) notes, 'transitions are always embedded in trajectories that give them distinctive form and meaning' (31), and 'the same event or transition folowed by different adaptations can lead to very different trajectories' (35). To capture the full range of these trajectories, Elder urges that we include intergenerational and historical dimensions in our research designs. Two ways of doing so are with prospective and retrospective panel designs for the collection of survey data over time. There are increasing indications that these are the research designs that will dominate criminological research in the near future. These data sets have important implications for the development of a structural criminology.

AN APPLICATION WITH POWER-CONTROL THEORY

Power-control theory asserts that adolescent experiences with delinquency are an important part of the life course, both for the boys who are involved in them, and for the girls who are not. For each, the presence or absence of these events can be a part of the intergenerational reproduction of gender roles and sex role ideology. To understand whether or not these events will occur, we need to explore the causes and consequences of them in the life course, within and between the generations involved. Doing so will include consideration of issues that would in the past have been thought of as part of societal reactions research. For example, we noted in chapter 6 that power-control theory predicts that boys more often than girls, apart from their behaviour, will be designated as delinquents through police contacts. This is a kind of prediction that is often associated with labelling theory. However, power-control theory includes such a prediction as part of its conception of the social reproduction of gender relations and the role of the state in this reproductive process. A value of life course conceptualization, and of power-control theory, is that it encourages us to take this larger view of the place of delinquency in the life cycle and society.

Retrospectively and prospectively developed panel data open up possibilities for exploring these and other issues. For example, it becomes possible to consider links between childhood experiences with families of origin, adolescent involvements in delinquency, contacts with the criminal justice system, and a wide range of adult life outcomes, including experiences with drugs, alcohol, psycho-social distress, and social mobility, to name only a few. The point is that this type of conceptualization and methodology avoids the common division between studying the antecedents and consequences of crime and delinquency that has characterized criminological research in recent years. The concern of power-control theory and a structural criminology with changes in relationships of domination and subordination, and the interest in linking actions and reactions to events defined as delinquent and criminal, fits well with the dynamic form of life course conceptualization.

Retrospectively and prospectively collected survey measures are not new to the social sciences, but there is increasing recognition of the attractions of their use, along with the techniques of event history analysis, to study the effects of social change (see Tuma and Hannan, 1984; Palloni and Sorenson, in press). There is much debate about the relative benefits of retrospective and prospective longitudinal designs (e.g., Gottfredson and Hirschi, 1986; Blumstein, Cohen and Farrington, 1988; Hagan and Palloni, 1988). However, as Blumstein, Cohen and Farrington observe (29) in comparing cross-sectional with longitudinal designs, 'The two methods are not mutually exclusive or necessarily in competition.' This is truer still of the comparison of retrospective and prospective longitudinal designs. Of course, an attraction of survey measures in general for a structural criminology is the opportunity they provide for the application and analysis of relational measures of class and other forms of positional power.

What is clear is that it is no longer useful to ignore that power relationships are a central part of criminal action and reaction; that these relationships are subject to change both in their symbolic and instrumental forms; and that it is necessary to study not only suspects and offenders who become involved in the criminal justice system, but also samples of the more general population of persons who over the life course may or may not become involved in social events that are designated individually or collectively as delinquent or criminal. A structural criminology pursued within the life course framework may open important possibilities of answering perennial questions about the causes and consequences of the social behaviours we call criminal and delinquent.

Bibliography

Acker, Joan 1973: Women and Social Stratification: A Case of Intellectual Sexism. *American Journal of Sociology* 78: 936–45.

Adler, Freda 1975: *Sisters in Crime: The Rise of the New Female Criminal*. New York: McGraw Hill.

1979: Changing Patterns. In Freda Adler and Rita Simon (eds), *The Criminology of Deviant Women*, Boston: Houghton Mifflin, 91–4.

Albonetti, C., Hauser, R., Hagan, J. and Nagel, I. 1988: Criminal Justice Decision-Making as a Stratification Process. *Journal of Quantitative Criminology*. Forthcoming.

Al-Issa, Ihsan 1982: Gender and Adult Psychopathology. In Ihsan Al-Issa (ed.), *Gender and Psychopathology*, New York: Academic, 84–103.

Alwin, D.F. 1976: Assessing School Effects: Some Identities. *Sociology of Education* 49: 294–303.

Alwin, D.F., and Hauser, R.M. 1975: The Decomposition of Effects in Path Analysis. *American Sociological Review* 40: 37–47.

Anderson, L.S., Chiricos, T.G. and Waldo, G.P. 1977: Formal and Informal Sanctions: A Comparison of Deterrent Effects. *Social Problems* 25: 103–14.

Aneshensel, Carol, Frerichs, Ralph and Clark, Viriginia 1981: Family Roles and Sex Differences in Depression. *Journal of Health and Social Behavior* 22: 379–93.

Arnold, T. 1967: The Criminal Trial. In H. Jacob (ed.), *Law, Politics and the Federal Courts*. Boston: Little, Brown.

Arnold, W. 1971: Race and Ethnicity Relative to Other Factors in Juvenile Court Decisions. *American Journal of Sociology* 77: 211–27.

Atkinson, David and Newman, Dale 1970: Judicial Attitudes and Defendant Attributes: Some Consequences for Municipal Court Decision-Making. *Journal of Public Law* 19: 68–87.

Baab, George W. and Ferguson, William R. 1968: Texas Sentencing Practices: A Statistical Study. *Texas Law Review* 45: 471–503.

Baker, Wayne 1984: The Social Structure of a National Securities Market. *American Journal of Sociology* 89: 775–811.

Balbus, Issac 1973: *The Dialectics of Legal Repression*. New York: Russell Sage Foundation.

1977: Commodity Form and Legal Form: An Essay on the 'Relative Autonomy' of the Law. *Law and Society Review* 11: 571–88.

Balkan, Sheila, Berger, Ronald J. and Schmidt, Janet 1980. *Crime and Deviance in America: A Critical Approach.* Belmont, Calif.: Wadsworth.

Baumhart, Raymond C. 1961. How Ethical are Businessmen? *Harvard Business Review* 39: 51–76.

Bayley, C.T. 1973: Annual Report of the Prosecuting Attorney of King County for the Year ending 31 December 1973. Seattle, Washington.

Beattie, John 1975: The Criminality of Women in Eighteenth Century England. *Journal of Social History* 8: 80–117.

Beauvoir, S. de 1953: *The Second Sex.* Harmondsworth: Penguin.

Beccaria, Cesare 1963: *On Crimes and Punishments.* Translated by Henry Paolucci. Indianapolis: Bobbs-Merrill.

Becker, Howard 1963: *Outsiders: Studies in the Sociology of Deviance.* New York: Free Press.

Bedeau, Hugo A. 1964: Death Sentences in New Jersey. *Rutgers Law Review* 19: 1–55.
1965: Capital Punishment in Oregon, 1903–64. *Oregon Law Review* 45: 1–39.

Beirne, Piers 1979: Empiricism and the Critique of Marxism on Crime and Law. *Social Problems* 26 (4): 373–85.

Bensing, Robert C. and Schroeder, Oliver Jr. 1960: *Homicide in an Urban Community.* Springfield, Illinois: Charles C. Thomas Co.

Bentham, Jeremy 1970: *An Introduction to the Principles of Morals and Legislation.* Edited by J.H. Burns and H.L.A. Hart. University of London: Athlone Press.

Berk, Richard 1983: An Introduction to Sample Selection Bias in Sociological Data. *American Sociological Review* 48: 386–97.

Berk, Richard and Berk, Sarah Fenstermaker 1983: Supply-Side Sociology of the Family: The Challenge of the New Home Economics. *Annual Review of Sociology* 9: 375–95.

Berk, Richard A., Brackman, Harold and Lesser, Selma 1977: *A Measure of Justice: An Empirical Study of Changes in the California Penal Code, 1955–1971.* New York: Academic Press.

Berk, Richard A., Bernstein, Paul and Nagel, Ilene 1980: Evaluating Criminal Justice Legislation. In Malcolm W. Klein and Katherine S. Teilmann (eds), *Handbook of Criminal Justice Evaluation.* Beverly Hills, California: Sage Publications, 611–628.

Bernstein, Ilene, Kelly, William and Doyle, Patricia 1977a: Societal Reactions to Deviants: The Case of Criminal Defendants. *American Sociological Review* 42: 743–55.

Bernstein, Ilene, Nagel, Ilene, Kick, Edward, Leung, Jan T. and Schulz, Barbara 1977b: Charge Reduction: an Intermediary Stage in the Process of Labelling Criminal Defendants. *Social Forces* 56 (2): 362–84.

Biderman, A.D. et al. 1967: *Report of a Pilot Study in the District of Columbia on Victimization and Attitudes toward Law Enforcement.* Washington, DC: US Government Printing Office.

Bielby, Denise and Bielby, William 1984: Work Commitment, Sex-Role Attitudes and Women's Employment. *American Sociological Review* 49: 234–47.

Bielby, William and Hauser, Robert 1977: Structural Equation Models. *Annual Review of Sociology* 3: 137–61.

Black, Donald 1976: *The Behavior of Law*. New York: Academic Press.

1985: *Toward a General Theory of Social Control*. New York: Academic Press.

Black, Donald and Reiss, Albert 1970: Police Control of Juveniles. *American Sociological Review* 35: 63–77.

Blau, Zena 1981: *Aging in a Changing Society*. New York: Franklin Watts. Second Edition.

Block, Alan 1977: Aw – Your Mother's in the Mafia: Women Criminals in Progressive New York. *Contemporary Crises* 1: 5–22.

Blood, Robert and Wolfe, Donald 1960: *Husbands and Wives: The Dynamics of Married Living*. New York: Free Press.

Blumberg, Abraham S. 1973: The Politics of Deviance: The Case of Drugs. *Journal of Drug Issues* 3: 104–14.

Blumstein, Alfred and Cohen, Jacqueline 1980: Sentencing of Convicted Offenders: An Analysis of the Public's View. *Law and Society Review* 14 (2): 223–62.

Blumstein, Alfred, Cohen, Jacqueline and Farrington, David, 1988. Criminal Career Research: Its Value for Criminology. *Criminology* 26: 1–36.

Blumstein, Alfred, Cohen, Jacqueline, Martin, Susan E. and Tonry, Michael H. 1983: *Research on Sentencing: the Search for Reform*. Volume 1. Washington, DC: National Academy Press.

Bohannan, P. 1965: The Differing Realms of Law. *American Anthropologist* 67: 33–42.

Bonger, William 1916: *Criminality and Economic Conditions*. Boston: Little, Brown.

Bonnie, Richard J. and Whitebread, Charles H. 1974: The *Marihuana Conviction*. Charlottesville, Virginia: University of Virginia Press.

Booth, Alan 1976: Wife's Employment and Husband's Stress: A Partial Replication and Refutation. *Journal of Marriage and the Family* 39: 645–50.

Bordua, David 1961: Delinquent Subcultures: Sociological Interpretations of Gang Delinquency. *Annals of the American Academy of Political and Social Science* 338: 119–38.

1967: Recent Trends: Deviant Behavior and Social Control. *Annals of the American Academy of Political and Social Science* 369: 149–63.

Bowers, William and Pierce, Glenn L. 1980: Arbitrariness and Discrimination Under Post-Furman Capital Statutes. *Crime and Delinquency* 26: 563–635.

Bowker, Lee 1981: Women as Victims: An Examination of the Results of L.E.A.A.'s National Crime Survey Program. In L. Bowker (ed.), *Women and Crime in America*. New York: Macmillan.

Box, Steven and Hale, Chris 1984: Liberation/Emancipation, Economic Marginalization or Less Chivalry: The Relevance of Three Theoretical Arguments to Female Crime Patterns in England and Wales. 1951–80. *Criminology* 22: 473–97.

Braverman, Harry 1974: *Labor and Monopoly Capital*. New York: Monthly Review Press.

Brenner, Steven N. and Molander, Earl A. 1977: Is the Ethics of Business Changing? *Harvard Business Review* 55: 57–71.

Brown, Carol 1981: Mothers, Fathers and Children: From Private to Public

Patriarchy. In Lydia Sargent (ed.), *Women and Revolution*. Boston: South End Press.

Buffalo Law Review 1985: Feminist Discourse, Moral Values, and the Law – A Conversation. *Buffalo Law Review* 34: 11–87.

Bullock, Henry 1961: Significance of the Racial Factor in the Length of Prison Sentences. *Journal of Criminal Law, Criminology and Police Science* 52: 411–17.

Burke, Ronald and Weir, Tamara 1976: Relationship of Wife's Employment Status to Husband, Wife, and Pair Satisfaction and Performance. *Journal of Marriage and the Family* 38: 279–87.

Burke, Peter and Turk, Austin 1975: Factors Affecting Post Arrest Dispositions: A Model for Analysis. *Social Problems* 22: 313–32.

Burnett, Cathleen 1986: Review Essay. *Criminology* 24: 203–11.

Byrnes, Thomas 1886: *Professional Criminals of America*. New York: Cassell.

Cameron, Mary Owen 1964: *The Booster and the Snitch*. Glencoe, Illinois: Free Press.

Carchedi, G. 1977: *The Economic Identification of Social Classes*. London: Routledge and Kegan Paul.

Cargan, Leonard and Coates, Mary A. 1974: Indeterminate Sentences and Judicial Bias. *Crime and Delinquency* 20: 144–56.

Carmines, E.G. and McIver, J.P. 1981: Analyzing Models with Unobserved Variables: Analysis of Covariance Structures. In Groge Bohrnstedt and Edgar Borgatta (eds), *Social Measurement: Current Issues*. Beverly Hills, California: Sage Publications, 65–115.

Carter, R.M., and Wilkins, L.T. 1967: Some Factors in Sentencing Policy. *Journal of Criminal Law, Criminology and Police Science* 58: 503–14.

Carter, Timothy J. and Clelland, Donald 1979: A Neo-Marxian Critique, Formulation and Test of Juvenile Dispositions as a Function of Social Class. *Social Problems* 27 (1): 96–108.

Chambliss, William 1973: Functional and Conflict Theories of Crime. *MSS Modular Publications* 17: 1–23.

   1984: White Collar Crime and Criminology. *Contemporary Sociology* 13: 160–2.

Chambliss, William and Seidman, Robert 1971. *Law, Order and Power*. Reading, Massachusetts: Addison-Wesley.

Chein, Isidor D., Gerard, Donald L., Lee, Robert S. and Rosenfeld, Eva 1964: *The Road to H: Narcotics, Delinquency and Social Policy*. New York: Basic Books.

Cherlin, Andrew 1983: Changing Family and Household: Contemporary Lessons from Historical Research. *Annual Review of Sociology* 9: 51–66.

Chiricos, T. and Waldo, G. 1975: Socioeconomic Status and Criminal Sentencing: An Empirical Assessment of a Conflict Proposition. *American Sociological Review* 40: 753–72.

Chodorow, Nancy 1971: Being and Doing: A Cross-Cultural Examination of the Socialization of Males and Females. In Gornick and Moran (eds), *Women in Sexist Society*. New York: Basic Books 173–97.

   1974: Family Structure and Feminine Personality. In M.Z. Rosaldo and L. Lamphere (eds), *Woman, Culture and Society*. Stanford: Stanford University Press.

   1978. *The Reproduction of Mothering*. Berkeley: University of California Press.

Chute, Charles 1956: *Crime, Courts and Probation*. New York: Macmillan.

Clark, John and Haurek, Edward 1966: Age and Sex Roles of Adolescents and Their Involvement in Misconduct: A Reappraisal. *Sociology and Social Research* 50: 495–506.

Clarke, Steven H. and Koch, Gary G. 1976: The Influence of Income and Other Factors on Whether Criminal Defendants Go to Prison. *Law and Society Review* 11: 57–92.

Clement, Wallace 1977: *Continental Corporate Power*. Toronto: McClelland & Stewart.

Clinard, Marshall and Yeager, Peter 1980: *Corporate Crime*. New York: Free Press.

Cloward, Richard and Ohlin, Lloyd 1960: *Delinquency and Opportunity*. Glencoe: Free Press.

Cloward, Richard A. and Piven, Frances Fox 1986: Challenge and Control as Sociology's Core. Paper presented at the American Sociological Association Meetings, August, New York.

Cloyd, Jerald W. 1979: Prosecution's Power, Procedural Rights, and Pleading Guilty; the Problem of Coercion in Plea Bargaining Drug Cases. *Social Problems* 26: 452–66.

Cohen, G.A. 1978: *Karl Marx's Theory of History: A Defense*. Princeton: Princeton University Press.

Coleman, James 1974: *Power and the Structure of Society*. New York: Norton & Co.

1986: Social Theory, Social Research and a Theory of Action. *American Journal of Sociology* 91: 1309–35.

Collins, R. Randall 1971: Functional and Conflict Theories of Educational Stratification. *American Sociological Review* 36 (December): 1002–19.

1975: *Conflict Sociology: Toward an Explanatory Science*. New York: Academic Press.

1979: *The Credential Society: A Historical Sociology of Education and Stratification*. New York: Academic Press.

Colvin, M. and Pauly, J. 1983: A Critique of Criminology: Toward an Integrated Structural-Marxist Theory of Delinquency Production. *American Journal of Sociology* 89(3): 513–51.

Conklin, John E. 1972: *Robbery and the Criminal Justice System*. Philadelphia, Pennsylvania: Lippincott.

Cook, Shirley 1969: Canadian Narcotics Legislation, 1908–23: A Conflict Model Interpretation. *Canadian Review of Sociology and Anthropology* 6: 36–46.

1970: *Variations in Response to Illegal Drug Use*. Toronto: Alcoholism and Drug Addiction Research Foundation.

Cooley, W.W. and Lohnes, P.R. 1971: *Multivariate Data Analysis*. New York: Wiley.

Coser, Rose 1985: Power Lost and Status Gained: The American Middle Class Husband. Paper presented at the American Sociological Association Meetings. Washington, DC.

Coser, Rose and Coser, Louis 1974: The Housewife and Her Greedy Family. In Louis Coser (ed.), *Greedy Institutions*, New York: Free Press, 89–100.

Cott, N.F. 1977: *The Bonds of Womanhood: 'Woman's Sphere' in New England, 1780–1835*. New Haven: Yale University Press.

Cronbach, L.J. 1951: Coefficient Alpha and the Internal Structure of Tests. *Psycholometrika* 16: 297–334.

Cullen, Francis T., Link, Bruce G. and Polanzi, Craig W. 1982: The Seriousness of Crime Revisited: Have Attitudes Toward White-Collar Crime Changed? *Criminology* 20: 83–102.

Cummings, L.D. 1977: Value Stretch in Definitions of Career among College Women: Horatia Alger as Feminist Model. *Social Problems* 25: 65–74.

Curtis, Richard 1986: Household and Family in Theory on Equality. *American Sociological Review* 51: 168–83.

Dahrendorf, Ralf 1959: *Class and Class Conflict in Industrial Society.* Stanford University: Stanford University Press.

Davis, F. James 1952: Crime News in Colorado Newspapers. *American Journal of Sociology* 57: 325–30.

Davis, Robert 1981: Female Labor Force Participation, Status Integration, and Suicide, 1950–1969. *Suicide and Life-Threatening Behavior* 11: 11–23.

Diamond, Shan Seidman and Zeisel, Hans 1975: Sentencing Councils: A Study of Sentence Disparity and its Reduction. *University of Chicago Law Review* 43: 109–49.

Duncan, Otis Dudley 1960: A Socio-Economic Index for all Occupations. In Albert Reiss (ed.), *Occupations and Social Status.* New York: Free Press.

  1969: Inheritance of Poverty or Inheritance of Race? In Daniel P. Moynihan (ed.), *On Understanding Poverty: Perspectives from the Social Sciences,* New York: Basic Books, 85–110.

  1975: *Introduction to Structural Equation Models.* New York: Academic Press.

Durkheim, Emile 1933: *The Division of Labor in Society.* New York: Macmillan.

  1950: *The Rules of the Sociological Method.* New York: Free Press.

Duster, Troy 1970: *The Legislation of Morality: Law, Drugs and Moral Judgement.* New York: The Free Press.

Edwards, Carolyn 1975: Societal Complexity and Moral Development: A Kenyan Study. *Ethos* 3: 505–27.

Ehrenreich, Barbara and Ehrenreich, John 1978: The Professional Managerial Class. In Walker (ed.), *Between Labor and Capital.* Montreal: Black Rose, 5–48.

Eisenstein, James and Jacob, Herbert 1977: *Felony Justice: An Organizational Analysis of Criminal Courts.* Boston: Little, Brown.

Elder, Glen 1985: *Life Course Dynamics.* Ithaca, New York: Cornell University Press.

Ennis, Philip 1967: *Criminal Victimization in the United States: A Report of a National Survey.* Washington, DC: US Government Printing Office.

Ermann, M. David and Lundman, Richard J. 1978: *Corporate and Governmental Deviance: Problems of Organizational Behaviour in Contemporary Society.* New York: Oxford University Press.

  1980: *Corporate Deviance: Toward a Sociology of Deviance, Social Problems and Crime.* New York: Holt, Rinehardt and Winston.

Farberman, Harvey 1975: A Criminogenic Market Structure: The Automobile Industry. *Sociological Quarterly* 16: 438–57.

Farrell, Ronald and Swigert, Victoria Lynn 1978a: Legal Disposition of Inter-Group and Intra-Group Homicides. *Sociological Quarterly* 19: 565–76.

1978b: Prior Offense as a Self-Fulfilling Prophecy. *Law and Society Review* 12: 437–53.

Fennessey, J. 1968: The General Linear Model: A New Perspective on Some Familiar Topics. *American Journal of Sociology* 74: 1–27.

Feyerherm, William 1981: Gender Differences in Delinquency: Quantity and Quality. In Lee Bowker (ed.), *Women and Crime in America*. New York: Macmillan.

Finestone, Harold 1957: Cats, Kicks and Color. *Social Problems* 5: 3–13.

Flacks, Richard 1971: *Youth and Social Change*. Chicago: Markham.

Fligstein, Neil and Wolf, Wendy 1978: Sex Similarities in Occupational Status Attainment: Are the Results Due to the Restriction of the Sample to Employed Women? *Social Science Research* 7: 197–212.

Forslund, M. 1969: Age, Occupation and Conviction Rates of White and Negro Males: A Case Study. *Rocky Mountain Social Science Journal* 6: 141–6.

Fox, John and Hartnagel, Timothy 1979: Changing Social Roles and Female Crime in Canada: A Time Series Analysis. *Canadian Review of Sociology and Anthropology* 16: 96–104.

Frank, Andre Gunder 1967: *Capitalism and Underdevelopment in Latin America*. New York: Monthly Review Press.

1978: *World Accumulation, 1492–1789*. New York: Monthly Review Press.

1979: *Dependent Accumulation and Underdevelopment*. New York: Monthly Review Press.

Frankel, Marvin 1972: *Criminal Sentences: Law Without Order*. New York: Hill, Wang.

Franklin, Alice 1979: Criminality in the Work Place: A Comparison of Male and Female Offenders. In Freda Adler and Rita Simon (eds), *The Criminology of Deviant Women*. Boston: Houghton Mifflin.

Friedan, Betty 1963: *The Feminine Mystique*. New York: Norton.

Friedenberg, Edgar Z. 1965: *Coming of Age in America: Growth and Acquiescence*. New York: Random House.

Fuller, Lon 1964: *The Morality of Law*. New Haven: Yale University Press.

Galanter, Marc 1974: Why the Have's Come Out Ahead. *Law & Society Review*.

Galliher, John F. and Basilick, Linda 1979: Utah's Liberal Drug Laws: Structural Foundations and Triggering Events. *Social Problems* 26: 284–97.

Gallup, George H. 1972: *The Gallup Poll: Public Opinion 1935–1971*. (Volume 3, 1959–71.) New York: Random House.

1978a: *The Gallup Poll: Public Opinion 1972–1977*. (Volume 1, 1972–75.) Wilmington, Delaware: Scholarly Resources, Inc.

1978b: *The Gallup Poll: Public Opinion 1972–1977*. (Volume 2, 1976–77.) Wilmington, Delaware: Scholarly Resources, Inc.

1979: *The Gallup Poll: Public Opinion 1978*. Wilmington, Delaware: Scholarly Resources, Inc.

Garfinkel, Harold 1949: Research Note on Inter- and Intra-Racial Homicides. *Social Forces* 27: 369–81.

Geis, Gilbert 1984: White-Collar and Corporate Crime. In Robert F. Meier (ed.), *Major Forms of Crime*. Beverly Hills, California: Sage Publications, 137–66.

Geis, Gilbert and Meier, Robert 1977: *White-Collar Crime*. New York: Free Press.

Gerard, Jules and Terry, T.R., 1970: Discrimination Against Negroes in the Administration of Criminal Law in Missouri. *Washington University Law Quarterly* 415–37.

Gibbons, Don C. 1979: *The Criminological Enterprise*. Englewood Cliffs, NJ: Prentice-Hall.

Gibson, James L. 1978: Race as a Determinant of Criminal Sentences: A Methodological Critique and a Case Study. *Law and Society Review* 12: 455–78.

Giffen, P.J. 1976: Official Rates of Crime and Delinquency. In W.T. McGrath (ed.), *Crime and Its Treatment in Canada*, Toronto: Macmillan of Canada.

Gilligan, Carol 1982: *In a Different Voice: Psychological Theory and Women's Development*. Cambridge, Massachusetts: Harvard University Press.

Giordano, Peggy 1978: Guys, Girls and Gangs: the Changing Social Context of Female Delinquency. *Journal of Criminal Law and Criminology* 69: 126–32.

Giordano, Peggy, Kerbel, Sandra and Dudley, Sandra 1981: The Economics of Female Criminality: An Analysis of Police Blotters, 1890–1976. In Lee Bowker (ed.), *Women and Crime in America*. New York: Macmillan.

Glasbeek, H. and Rowland, S. 1979: Are Injuring and Killing at Work Crimes? *Osgoode Hall Law Journal* 17: 506–94.

Glaser, Daniel 1974: Interlocking Dualities in Drug Use, Drug Control, and Crime. In James Inciardi and Carl Chambers (eds), *Drugs and the Criminal Justice System*. Beverly Hills, California: Sage Publications, 39–56.

Glaser, Daniel and Rice, Kent 1959: Crime, Age and Employment. *American Sociological Review* 24: 679–86.

Glassman, R.B. 1973: Persistence and Loose Coupling in Living Systems. *Behavioral Science* 83–98.

Globe and Mail 1983a: Crown Rejects Charges Against Norcen, Black. *Globe and Mail*, 10 June: 5.

1983b: Financiers Knew Loans Breached Act, Report Says. *Globe and Mail*, 15 June: 11.

1985: An Interview with Outgoing Chairman of OSC. *Globe and Mail*, 26 February: B1.

Goff, Colin H. and Reasons, Charles E. 1978: *Corporate Crime in Canada*. Scarborough, Ontario: Prentice-Hall of Canada.

Gold, David 1960: Spuriousness, Developmental Sequences, and Independent Causation in Non-Experimental Research. Paper presented at the American Sociological Association Meetings, New York, 1960.

Gold, Martin 1970: *Delinquent Behavior in an American City*. Belmont, California: Brooks/Cole.

Goldberger, Arthur 1964: *Econometric Theory*. New York: Wiley.

1971: Econometrics and Psychometrics: A Survey of Communalities. *Psychometrika* 36: 83–107.

1981: Linear Regression After Selection. *Journal of Econometrics* 15: 357–66.

Goldberger, Arthur and Duncan, Otis. D. 1973: *Structural Equation Models in the Social Sciences*. New York: Seminar.

Goodman, L. A. 1970: The Multivariate Analysis of Qualitative Data: Interactions

Among Multiple Classifications. *Journal of the American Statistical Association* 63: 226–56.

Gore, Susan and Mangione, Thomas 1983: Social Roles, Sex Roles and Psychological Distress: Additive and Interactive Models of Sex Differences. *Journal of Health and Social Behavior* 24: 300–12.

Goring, Charles 1913: *The English Convict*. London: HMSO.

Gottfredson, Denise 1981: Black-White Differences in the Educational Attainment Process: What Have We Learned? *American Sociological Review* 46: 542–57.

Gottfredson, Michael and Hirschi, Travis 1986: The True Value of Lambda Would Appear to be Zero: An Essay on Career Criminals, Criminal Careers, Selective Incapacitation, Cohort Studies, and Related Topics. *Criminology* 24: 213–33.

Gove, Walter 1972: The Relationship Between Sex Roles, Marital Status and Mental Illness. *Social Forces* 51: 34–44.

1975: *The Labelling of Deviance*. New York: Free Press.

1978: Sex Differences in Mental Illness among Adult Men and Women. *Social Science and Medicine* 12: 187–98.

1979: Sex, Marital Status, and Psychiatric Treatment: A Research Note. *Social Forces* 58: 89–93.

1982: The Effect of Age and Gender on Deviant Behavior: A Biopsychosocial Perspective. In Alice Rossi (ed.), *Gender and the Life Course*. Chicago: Aldine, 115–44.

Gove, Walter and Geerken, Michael 1977: The Effect of Children and Employment on the Mental Health of Married Men and Women. *Social Forces* 56: 66–76.

Gove, Walter and Tudor, Jeanette 1973: Adult Sex Roles and Mental Illness. *American Journal of Sociology* 78: 812–35.

Gower, L.C.B. 1969: *The Principles of Modern Company Law*. London: Stevens & Sons.

Gibbs, Jack 1977: Social Control, Deterrence and Perspectives on Social Order. *Social Forces* 56.

Gordon, S.L. 1981: The Sociology of Sentiments and Emotions. In M. Rosenberg and R. Turner (eds), *Social Psychology: Sociological Perspectives*. New York: Basic Books.

Green, Edward 1961: *Judicial Attitudes in Sentencing: A Study of the Factors Underlying the Sentencing Practices of the Criminal Court of Philadelphia*. New York: St. Martin's Press.

1964: Inter- and Intra-Racial Crime Relative to Sentencing. *Journal of Criminal Law, Criminology and Police Science* 55: 348–58.

Gusfield, Joseph 1967: Moral Passage: The Symbolic Process in Public Designations of Deviance. *Social Problems* 15: 175–88.

1975: The (F)Utility of Knowledge?: The Relation of Social Science to Public Policy Toward Drugs. *The Annals* 417: 1–15.

1981: *The Culture of Public Problems: Drinking-Driving and the Symbolic Order*. Chicago: University of Chicago Press.

Hagan, John 1974: Extra-Legal Attributes and Criminal Sentencing: An Assessment of a Sociological Viewpoint. *Law and Society Review* 8: 357–83.

1975a: Law, Order and Sentencing: A Study of Attitude in Action. *Sociometry* 38: 374–84.

1975b: The Social and Legal Construction of Criminal Justice: A Study of the Presentencing Process. *Social Problems* 22: 620–37.

1977a: *The Disreputable Pleasures.* Toronto: McGraw-Hill Ryerson.

1977b: The Basic Concepts of Social Control. In Robert Hagedorn (ed.), *Sociology.* Dubuque, Iowa: Wm. Brown.

1983: *Victims Before the Law: The Organizational Domination of Criminal Law.* Toronto: Butterworths.

Hagan, J. and Bumiller, K. 1983: Making Sense of Sentencing: A Review and Critique of Sentencing. In A. Blumstein, J. Cohen, S. Martin, M. Tonry. Washington, DC: National Academy Press.

Hagan, John and Leon, Jeffrey 1977: Rediscovering Delinquency: Social History, Political Ideology and the Sociology of Law. *American Sociological Review* 42: 587–98.

Hagan, John and Zatz, Marjorie 1985: The Social Organization of Criminal Justice Processing: An Event History Analysis. *Social Science Research* 14: 103–25.

Hagan, John, Nagel, Ilene and Albonetti, Celesta 1980: The Differential Sentencing of White-Collar Offenders in Ten Federal District Courts. *American Sociological Review* 45: 802–20.

Hagan, John, Simpson, John and Gillis, A.R. 1979: The Sexual Stratification of Social Control: Toward a Gender-based Perspective on Crime and Delinquency. *British Journal of Sociology* 30 (1): 25–38.

Halevy, Eli 1960: *The Growth of Philosophic Radicalism.* Translated by Mary Morris. Boston: Beacon Press.

Hall, D.J. 1975: The Role of the Victim in the Prosecution and Disposition of a Criminal Case. *Vanderbilt Law Review* 28: 931–985.

Hall, Jerome 1952: *Theft, Law and Society.* Boston: Little, Brown and Co.

Hamilton, Richard F. 1972: *Class and Politics in the United States.* New York: Wiley.

Hannon, Michael 1982: Families, Markets, and Social Structure: An Essay on Becker's 'A Treatise on the Family.' *Journal of Economic Literature* 20: 65–72.

Harris, Anthony 1977: Sex and Theories of Deviant Type-Scripts. *American Sociological Review* 42: 3–16.

Harris, Anthony and Hill, Gary 1981: Changes in the Gender Patterning of Crime, 1953–77. Opportunity v. Socialization. *Social Science Quarterly.*

Hawton, Keith and Catalan, Jose 1982: *Attempted Suicide: A Practical Guide to its Nature and Management.* Oxford: Oxford University Press.

Hayduk, Leslie 1987: *Structural Equation Modeling with LISREL.* Edmonton, Alberta: University of Alberta.

Heckman, James J. 1974: Shadow Prices, Market Wages, and Labour Supply. *Econometrica* 42: 679–94.

1975: Shadow Prices, Market Wages, and Labour Supply Revisited: Some Computational and Conceptual Simplifications and Revised Estimates. Mimeographed paper, University of Chicago.

1979: Sample Selection Bias as a Specification Error. *Econometrica* 45: 153–61.

Heise, David and Bohrnstedt, George 1970: Validity, Invalidity and Reliability. In Edgar F. Borgatta and George W. Bohrnstedt (eds), *Sociological Methodology, 1970*, San Francisco: Jossey-Bass, 104–29.

Hewitt, John 1975: A Multivariate Analysis of Legal and Extralegal Factors in Judicial Sentencing Disparity. Unpublished PhD dissertation, Washington State University.

Heyl, Barbara 1979: Prostitution: An Extreme Case of Sex Stratification. In Freda Adler and Rita Simon (eds), *The Criminology of Deviant Women*. Boston: Houghton Mifflin.

Hibbert, Christopher 1963: *The Roots of Evil: A Social History of Crime and Punishment*. Boston: Little, Brown and Co.

Hindelang, Michael 1971: Age, Sex and Versatility of Delinquent Involvement. *Social Problems* 18: 522–35.

　　1974a: The Uniform Crime Reports Revisited. *Journal of Criminal Justice* 2: 1–17.

　　1974b: Decisions of Shoplifting Victims to Invoke the Criminal Justice Process. *Social Problems* 21: 580–93.

　　1979: Sex Differences in Criminal Activity. *Social Problems* 27: 143–56.

Hindelang, Michael and Gottfredson, Michael 1976: The Victim's Decision Not to Invoke the Criminal Justice Process. In W.F. McDonald (ed.), *Criminal Justice and the Victim*. Beverly Hills, California: Sage Publications.

Hindelang, Michael, Hirschi, Travis and Weis, Joseph 1981: *Measuring Delinquency*. Beverly Hills, California: Sage Publications.

Hinkle, R. and Hinkle, G. 1954: *The Development of Modern Sociology*. New York: Random House.

Hirschi, Travis 1969: *Causes of Delinquency*. Berkeley: University of California Press.

　　1973: Procedural Rules and the Study of Deviant Behaviour. *Social Problems* 21: 154–73.

Hirschi, Travis and Gottfredson, Michael 1983: Age and the Explanation of Crime. *American Journal of Sociology* 89: 552–84.

Hirschi, Travis, Hindelang, Michael and Weis, Joseph 1982: Reply to 'On the Use of Self-Report Data to Determine the Class Distribution of Criminal and Delinquent Behavior. *American Sociological Review* 47: 433–5.

Hirschi, Travis and Selvin, Hanan 1967: *Delinquency Research: An Appraisal of Analytic Methods*. New York: Free Press.

Hochschild, Arlie 1973: A Review of Sex Role Research. *American Journal of Sociology* 78: 1011–29.

　　1979: Emotion Work, Feeling Rules, and Social Structure. *American Journal of Sociology* 85: 551–75.

Hofstadter, Richard 1968: *The Age of Reform*. New York: Knopf.

Hogarth, John 1971: *Sentencing as a Human Process*. Toronto: University of Toronto Press.

Holstein, Constance 1976: Development of Moral Judgment: A Longitudinal Study of Males and Females. *Child Development* 47: 51–61.

Homans, George 1967: *The Nature of Social Science*. New York: Harcourt, Brace & World.

Huber, Joan 1973: Editor's Introduction *American Journal of Sociology* 78: 763–6.

1976: Toward a Sociotechnological Theory of the Women's Movement. *Social Problems* 23: 371–88.

Humphries, Drew 1981: Serious Crime, News Coverage, and Ideology. *Crime and Delinquency* 27: 191–205.

Humphries, Drew and Greenberg, David 1984: Social Control and Social Formation: A Marxian Analysis. In Donald Black (ed.), *Toward a General Theory of Social Control*. Volume 2. New York: Academic Press.

Ianni, Francis 1974: *The Black Mafia*. New York: Simon and Schuster.

IUCPSR 1979: *Public Image of the Courts, 1977: General Public Data*. Ann Arbor, Michigan: Inter-University Consortium for Political and Social Research.

Jackson, B. 1969: *A Thief's Primer*. New York: Free Press.

Jacob, H. 1984: *The Frustration of Policy: Responses to Crime by American Cities*. Boston: Little, Brown.

Janowitz, Morris 1975: Sociological Theory and Social Control. *American Journal of Sociology* 81: 82–108.

Jeffrey, Clarence R. 1957: The Development of Crime in Early English Society. *Journal of Criminal Law, Criminology and Police Science* 47(6): 647–66.

Jensen, Gary 1972: Parents, Peers and Delinquent Action: A Test of the Differential Association Hypothesis. *American Journal of Sociology* 78: 562–75.

Jensen, Gary, Erickson Maynard and Gibbs, Jack 1978: Perceived Risk of Punishment and Self-Reported Delinquency. *Social Forces* 57: 57–78.

Jensen, Gary and Eve, Raymond 1976: Sex Differences in Delinquency: An Examination of Popular Sociological Explanations. *Criminology* 13: 427–8.

Johnson, Elmer 1957: Selective Forces in Capital Punishment. *Social Forces* 36: 165–9.

Johnson, Richard 1986: Family Structure and Delinquency: General Patterns and Gender Differences. *Criminology* 24: 65–84.

Johnston, David 1977: *Canadian Securities Regulation*. Toronto: Butterworths.

Joreskog, Karl 1969: A General Approach to Confirmatory Factor Analysis. *Psychometrika* 34: 183–202.

1973: A General Method for Estimating a Linear Structural Equation System. In A.S. Goldberger and O.D. Duncan (eds), *Structural Equation Models in the Social Sciences*. New York: Seminar Press, 85–112.

Joreskog, Karl and Sorbom, Dag 1981: *LISREL V User's Guide*. Chicago: National Educational Resources.

1985: *LISREL VI User's Guide*. Uppsala, Sweden: University of Uppsala.

Judson, Charles, Pandell, James, Owens, Jack, McIntosh, James and Matschulatt, Dale 1969: A Study of the California Penalty Jury in First Degree Murder Cases. *Stanford Law Review* 21: 1297–1431.

Kanter, Rosabeth 1974: Intimate Repression. *Sociological Quarterly* 15: 320.

Kaplan, H.B., Robbins, C., Martin, S.S. 1983: Antecedents of Psychological Distress in Young Adults: Self-Rejection, Deprivation of Social Support and Life Events. *Journal of Health and Social Behavior* 24: 230–44.

Katz, Jack 1980: The Social Movement Against White Collar Crime. In Egon Bittner and Sheldon Messinger (eds), *Criminology Review Yearbook. Volume 2*. Beverly Hills, California: Sage Publications 161–84.

Kessler, Ron and McRae, J. 1981: Trends in the Relationship Between Sex and Psychological Distress: 1957–1976. *American Sociological Review* 46: 443–52.
    1982: The Effect of Wife's Employment on the Mental Health of Married Men and Women. *American Sociological Review* 47: 216–27.
Kleck, Gary 1981: Racial Discrimination in Criminal Sentencing: A Critical Evaluation of the Evidence on the Death Penalty. *American Sociological Review* 46: 783–804.
    1982: On the Use of Self-Report Data to Determine the Class Distribution of Criminal and Delinquent Behavior. *American Sociological Review* 47: 427–33.
Kohlberg, Lawrence 1958: *The Development of Modes of Thinking and Choices in Years 10 to 16.* PhD dissertation. Chicago: University of Chicago Press.
    1981: *The Philosophy of Moral Development.* San Francisco: Harper and Row.
Kohlberg, Lawrence and Gilligan, Carol 1971: The Adolescent as a Philosopher: The Discovery of the Self in a Post-Conventional World. *Daedalus* 100: 1051–86.
Kohlberg, Lawrence and Kramer, R. 1969: Continuities and Discontinuities in Childhood and Adult Moral Development. *Human Development* 12: 93–120.
Kohn, Melvin 1977: *Class and Conformity.* 2nd ed. Chicago: University of Chicago Press.
Kohn, Melvin, Slomczynski, Kazimierz and Schoenbach, Carri 1986: Social Stratification and the Transmission of Values in the Family: A Cross-National Assessment. *Sociological Forum* 1: 73–102.
Kratcoski, Peter and Kratcoski, J. 1975: Changing Patterns of Delinquent Activities of Boys and Girls: A Self-Reported Delinquency Analysis. *Adolescence* 10: 38–91.
Kryzanowski, Lawrence 1978: Misinformation and Security Markets. *McGill Law Journal* 24: 123–35.
LaFree, Gary 1980: The Effect of Sexual Stratification By Race on Official Reactions to Rape. *American Sociological Review* 45: 842–54.
Landes, K. 1974: Legal Theory and Reality: Some Evidence on Criminal Procedure. *Journal of Legal Studies* 3: 287–300.
LaPraire, Carol 1979: The Development of Sanctions for Stock Market Manipulations in Ontario. *Canadian Journal of Criminology* 21: 275–92.
Lasch, Christopher 1977: *Haven in a Heartless World: The Family Besieged.* New York: Basic Books.
Laslett, Barbara 1980: The Place of Theory in Quantitative Historical Research. *American Sociological Review* 45: 214–28.
Lemert, Edwin 1967: *Human Deviance, Social Problems and Social Control.* Englewood Cliffs, New Jersey: Prentice Hall.
Lemert, Edwin M. and Rosberg, Judy 1948: The Administration of Justice to Minority .Groups in Los Angeles County. *University of California Publications in Culture and Society* 11: 1–28.
Levin, Martin A. 1972: Urban Politics and Judicial Behavior. *Journal of Legal Studies* 1: 193–221.
    1977: *Urban Politics and Criminal Courts.* Chicago: University of Chicago Press.
Lidz, Charles W. and Walker, Andrew L. 1980: *Heroin, Deviance and Morality.* Beverly Hills, California: Sage Publications.

Linden, Rick and Fillmore, Kathy 1981: A Comparative Study of Delinquency Involvement. *The Canadian Review of Sociology and Anthropology* 18: 343–61.

Lindesmith, Alfred and Levin, Y. 1937: The Lombrosian Myth in Criminology. *American Journal of Sociology* 42: 653–71.

Liska, Allen and Reed, Mark 1985: Ties to Conventional Institutions and Delinquency: Estimating Reciprocal Effects. *American Sociological Review* 50: 547–60.

Litwak, Eugene 1968: Technological Innovation and Theoretical Functions of Primary Groups and Bureaucratic Structures. *American Journal of Sociology* 73: 468–81.

Lizotte, Alan 1978: Extra-Legal Factors in Chicago's Criminal Courts: Testing the Conflict Model of Criminal Justice. *Social Problems* 25: 564–80.

Lombroso, Cesare 1895: *The Female Offender*. New York: Fisher Unwin.

Long, J. Scott 1983: *Covariance Structure Models: an Introduction to LISREL*. Beverly Hills, California: Sage Publications.

Lopreato, Joseph 1968: Authority Relations and Class Conflict. *Social Forces* 47: 70–9.

Lorber, J. 1975: Beyond Equality of the Sexes: The Question of the Children. *The Family Coordinator* 24: 465–72.

Lucas, Netley 1926: *Crook Janes: Study of the Woman Criminal in the World Over*. London: Stanley Paul.

MacKinnon, Catherine 1982: Feminism, Marxism, Method and the State: Toward Feminist Jurisprudence. *Signs* 8: 185–208.

Maine, (Sir) Henry James Sumner 1960: *Ancient Law*. London: Dent.

Mannheim, Herman 1960: *Pioneers in Criminology*. London: Quadrangle.

Martin, Roscoe 1934: *The Defendant and Criminal Justice*. University of Texas Bulletin No. 3437: Bureau of Research in the Social Sciences.

Marwell, Gerald 1969. Adolescent Powerlessness and Delinquent Behavior. *Social Problems* 16: 35–47.

Marx, Karl 1912: *Capital*. Vol. 1. Chicago: Kerr.

Matsueda, Ross 1982: Testing Control Theory and Differential Association: A Causal Modeling Approach. *American Sociological Review* 47: 489–504.

Matza, David 1964: *Delinquency and Drift*. New York: Wiley.

McCarthy, William and Hagan, John 1987: Gender, Delinquency and the Great Depression: A Test of Power-Control Theory. *Canadian Review of Sociology and Anthropology* 24: 153–77.

McCord, Joan 1982: A Longitudinal View of the Relationship Between Parental Absence and Crime. In John Gunn and David P. Farrington (eds), *Abnormal Offenders, Delinquency and the Criminal Justice System*. New York: Wiley.

McDonald, Lynn 1976: *The Sociology of Law and Order*. Boulder: Westview Press.

McDonald, William F. 1976: Towards a Bicentennial Revolution in Criminal Justice: The Return of the Victim. *American Criminal Law Review* 13(4): 649–73.

McLanahan, Sara 1985: Family Structure and the Reproduction of Poverty. *American Journal of Sociology* 90: 873–901.

Menard, Scott and Morse, Barbara 1984: A Structuralist Critique of the IQ

Delinquency Hypothesis: Theory and Evidence. *American Journal of Sociology* 89: 1347–78.

Menkel-Meadow, Carrie 1985. Portia in a Different Voice: Speculations on a Women's Lawyering Process. *Berkeley Women's Law Journal: 39–63.*

Merton, Robert 1938: Social Structure and Anomie. *American Sociological Review* 3: 672–82.

Meyer, John and Rowan, Brian 1977: Institutionalized Organizations: Formal Structure as Myth and Ceremony. *American Journal of Sociology* 83(2): 340–63.

Michalowski, Raymond and Bohlander, Edward W. 1976: Repression and Criminal Justice in Capitalistic America. *Sociological Inquiry* 46 (2): 95–106.

Miller, Daniel and Swanson, Guy 1958: *The Changing American Parent.* New York: Wiley.

Miller, Walter 1973: The Molls. *Society* 11: 32–5.

Millett, Kate 1970: *Sexual Politics.* Garden City, New York: Doubleday.

Millman, M. 1975: She Did It All For Love: A Feminist View of the Sociology of Deviance. In M. Millman and R. M. Kanter (eds), *Another Voice: Feminist Perspectives on Social Life and Social Science.* Garden City, New York: Anchor Press.

Milton, Catherine 1972: *Women in Policing.* Washington DC: The Police Foundation.

Mirowsky, John 1985: Depression and Marital Power: An Equity Model. *American Journal of Sociology* 3: 557–92.

Mirowsky, John and Ross, Catherine 1983: Paranoia and the Structure of Powerlessness. *American Sociological Review* 48: 228–39.

1986: Social Patterns of Distress. *Annual Review of Sociology* 12: 23–45.

Mitscherlich, Alexander 1969: *Society Without the Father.* London: Tavistock.

Moore, Mark 1977: *Buy and Bust: The Effective Regulation of an Illicit Market in Heroin.* Lexington, Mass.: Lexington Books.

Morden, Peter 1980: *A Multivariate Analysis of Bail Decisions Involving the Police.* Unpublished manuscript, Indiana University.

Mueller, John, Schuessler, Karl and Costner, Herbert 1977: *Statistical Reasoning in Sociology.* (3rd edition). Boston: Houghton Mifflin.

Musto, David F. 1973: *The American Disease: Origins of Narcotic Control.* New Haven: Yale University Press.

Myers, Martha 1979: Offended Parties and Official Reactions: Victims and the Sentencing of Criminal Defendants. *Sociological Quarterly* 20: 529–40.

Myers, Martha and Talarico, Susette 1987: *The Social Contexts of Sentencing.* New York: Springer-Verlag.

Myrdal, G. 1944: *An American Dilemma.* New York: Harper.

Nagel, Ilene 1980: The Behaviour of Formal Law: A Study of Bail Decisions. Unpublished manuscript, Indiana University.

Nagel, Ilene and Hagan, John 1983: Gender and Crime: Offense Patterns and Criminal Court Sanctions. *Crime and Justice: An Annual Review of Research* 4: 91–144.

Nelson, William E. 1967: Emerging Notions of Modern Criminal Law in the Revolutionary Era: An Historical Perspective. *New York University Law Review,* 42: 450–81.

Nettler, Gwynn 1978: *Explaining Crime.* New York: McGraw-Hill.

1979: Criminal Justice. *Annual Review of Sociology* 5: 27–52.

New York State 1979: *New York: State Statistical Yearbook* (1979–1980 ed.). Albany: Division of the Budget.

The New York Times 1969: 'Freaking Out' on Drugs. 15 July 1969: 38.

1969: Progress on the Drug Front. 22 October 1969: 46.

1969: The 'Answer' on Drugs. 8 December 1969: 46.

1970: The Price of Pot. 24 January 1970: 30.

1970: Classifying Marijuana. 30 August 1970: IV, 12.

1970: The Good-Bad Drug Bill. 26 September 1970: 28.

1971: Parting Marijuana Mists. 25 January 1971: 42.

1972: Judicial Overkill. 22 January 1972: 28.

1972: Decriminalizing Marijuana. 20 February 1972: IV, 12.

1973: Cannabis in Canada. 9 January 1973: 38.

1973: The Politics of Drugs. 9 January 1973: 38.

1973: Wrong Way on Drugs. 10 January 1973: 40.

1973: Make Drug Laws Work. 15 January 1973: 28.

1973: The D.A.'s Prescription. 9 February 1973: 34.

1973: Now, The Death Penalty. 7 March 1973: 42.

1973: Rockefeller Masquerade. 17 April 1973: 40.

1973: Law and Order. 30 April 1973: 30.

1977: 'Mister Untouchable'. *The New York Times Magazine*, 5 June 1977: 15–17.

1978: Barnes is Sentenced to Life in Drug Case. 20 January 1978.

Newman, Graeme. 1976: *Comparative Deviance: Perception and Law in Six Cultures.* New York: Elsevier.

Newman, Peter C. 1982: *The Establishment Man.* Toronto: McClelland & Stewart.

Noblet, George and Burcart, Janie 1976: Women and Crime: 1960–70. *Social Science Quarterly* 56: 651–7.

Nye, F.I. and Berardo, F.I. 1981: *Emerging Conceptual Frameworks in Family Analysis.* New York: Praeger.

Nye, F. Ivan and Short, James 1958: Scaling Delinquent Behavior. *American Sociological Review* 22: 326–32.

Oppenheimer, V. K. 1970: *The Female Labor Force in the United States.* Berkeley: Institute for International Studies, University of California.

Page, J. and O'Brian, M. 1973: *Bitter Wages.* New York: Grossman.

Palloni, Alberto and Sorenson, Aage In Press: Methods for the Analysis of Event History Data: A Didactic Overview. In Paul Battes, David Featherman and Richard Lerner (eds), *Life-Span Development and Behavior*, Vol. 10. New Jersey: Laurence Erlbaum Assoc.

Park, R. 1915: The City: Some Suggestions for the Investigation of Human Behavior in the Urban Environment. *American Journal of Sociology* 20: 577–612.

Park, R. and Burgess, E. 1921: *Introduction to the Science of Sociology.* Chicago: University of Chicago Press.

Partington, Donald 1965: The Incidence of the Death Penalty for Rape in Virginia. *Washington and Lee Law Review* 22: 43–75.

Pearlin, Leonard 1975: Sex Roles and Depression. In N. Datan and L. Ginsberg (eds), *Life Span Developmental Psychology: Normative and Life Crises.* New York: Academic Press, 191–207.

Pearlin, Leonard and Lieberman, M.A. 1979: Social Sources of Emotional Distress. In R.G. Simmons (ed.), *Research in Community and Mental Health.* Greenwich: JAI.

Peterson, Ruth 1983: The Sanctioning of Drug Offenders: Social Change and the Social Organization of Drug Law Enforcement. Unpublished PhD dissertation, Department of Sociology, University of Wisconsin-Madison.

——1985: Discriminatory Decision-Making at the Legislative Level: An Analysis of the Comprehensive Drug Abuse, Prevention and Control Act of 1970. *Law & Human Behavior* 9: 243–70.

Platt, Anthony 1969: *The Child Savers.* Chicago: University of Chicago Press.

Pleck, Joseph 1977: The Work-Family Role System. *Social Problems* 24: 417–27.

Pollak, O. 1951: *The Criminality of Women.* Philadelphia: The University of Pennsylvania Press.

Pope, Carl 1975a: *The Judicial Processing of Assault and Burglary Offenders in Selected California Counties.* National Criminal Justice Information and Statistics Service, Washington, DC: US Department of Justice.

——1975b: *Sentencing of California Felony Offenders.* National Criminal Justice Information and Statistics Service, Washington, DC: US Department of Justice.

Pound, R. 1930: The Individualization of Justice. *Yearbook of the National Probation Association.* New York: National Probation Association.

Quetelet, Adolphe 1842: *A Treatise on Man.* Gainesville, Florida: Scholars' Facsimiles and Reprints.

——1971: *The Social Reality of Crime.* Boston: Little, Brown.

——1975: *Criminology.* Boston: Little, Brown.

——1977: *Class, State and Crime.* New York: Longman.

Quinney, Richard 1970: *The Social Reality of Crime.* Boston: Little, Brown.

——1971: *The Social Reality of Crime.* Boston: Little, Brown.

——1975: *Criminology.* Boston: Little, Brown.

——1980: *Class, State and Crime.* New York: Longman.

Radloff, Lenore 1975: Sex Differences in Depression: The Effects of Occupation and Marital Status. *Sex Roles* 1: 249–65.

Radzinowitz, Leon 1937: Variability of the Sex Ratio of Criminality. *Sociological Review* 29: 76–102.

Rawls, J. 1971: *A Theory of Justice.* Cambridge, Mass.: Harvard University Press.

Reasons, Charles 1974: The Politics of Drugs: An Inquiry in the Sociology of Social Problems. *Sociological Quarterly* 15: 381–404.

Reasons, C., Ross, L. and Paterson, C. 1981: *Assault on the Worker.* Toronto: Butterworths.

Reiss, Albert 1966: The Study of Deviant Behavior: Where the Action is. *Ohio Valley Sociologist* 32: 60–6.

——1971: *The Police and the Public.* New Haven: Yale University Press.

——1981: Forward: Towards a Revitalization of Theory and Research on Victimization by Crime. *Journal of Criminal Law and Criminology* 72: 704–13.

Reitman, B. 1937: *Sister of the Road: The Autobiography of Box-Car Bertha.* New York: Macaulay.

Richards, Pamela 1979: Middle-Class Vandalism and Age-Status Conflict. *Social Problems* 26(4): 432–97.

Roberts, Robert and O'Keefe, Stephen 1981: Sex Differences in Depression Reexamined. *Journal of Health and Social Behavior* 22: 394–400.

Robin, Gerald D. 1967: The Corporate and Judicial Disposition of Employee Thieves. *Wisconsin Law Review* (Summer): 685–702.

Robinson, Robert and Kelly, Jonathan 1979: Class as Conceived by Marx and Dahrendorf: Effects on Income Inequality, Class Consciousness, and Class Conflict in the United States and Great Britain. *American Sociological Review* 44: 38–57.

Rodman, Hyman 1967: Marital Power in France, Greece, Yugoslavia and the United States: A Cross-National Discussion. *Journal of Marriage and the Family* 29: 320–4.

Rosenfield, Sarah 1980: Sex Differences in Depression: Do Women Always Have the Higher Rates? *Journal of Health and Social Behavior* 21: 33–42.

Rosenthal, Michael P. 1977: The Legislative Response to Marijuana: When the Shoe Pinches Enough. *Journal of Drug Issues* 7: 61–77.

Rosenthal, Robert (ed.) 1980: Quantitative Assessment of Research Domains. *New Directions for Methodology of Social and Behavioral Science.* Volume 5.

Ross, Catherine, Mirowsky, John and Huber, Joan 1983: Dividing Work, Sharing Work and In-Between: Marriage Patterns and Depression. *American Sociological Review* 48: 809–23.

Ross, E.A. 1901: *Social Control: The Foundations of Social Order.* New York: Macmillan.

Rossi, R., Waite, E., Base, C. and Berk, R. 1974: The Seriousness of Crimes: Normative Structure and Individual Differences. *American Sociological Review* 39 (April): 224–37.

Ryder, N. B. 1980: Components of Temporal Variations in American Fertility. In R. W. Hiorns (ed.), *Demographic Patterns in Developed Societies.* London: Taylor and Francis.

Safilios-Rothschild, Constantina 1976: Dual Linkages Between the Occupational and Family Systems: A Macrosociological Analysis. *Signs* 1: 51–60.

Scanzoni, Letha and Scanzoni, John 1981: *Men, Women and Change.* New York: McGraw-Hill.

Schafer, Stephen 1977: *Victimology: The Victim and His Criminal.* Reston, Virginia: Reston Publishing Co.

Scheingold, S. 1984: *The Politics of Law and Order: Street Crime and Public Policy.* New York: Longman.

Schlossman, S. 1983: *The Chicago Area Project Revisited.* Santa Monica, California: Rand.

Schrager, Laura Shill and Short, James F. Jr. 1978: Toward a Sociology of Organizational Crime. *Social Problems* 25(4): 407–419.

Schrager, Laura and Short, James 1980: How Serious a Crime?: Perceptions of Organizational and Common Crimes. In G. Geis and E. Stotland (eds), *White*

Collar Crime: Theory and Research. Beverly Hills, California: Sage Publications, 14–31.

Schuessler, Karl 1973: *Edwin H. Sutherland: On Analyzing Crime*. Chicago: University of Chicago Press.

Schuessler, Karl and Cressey, Donald 1950: Personality Characteristics of Criminals. *American Journal of Sociology* 55: 476–84.

Schwendiger, Herman and Schwendiger, Julia 1974: *The Sociologists of the Chair*. New York: Basic Books.

Scott, William 1968: Attitude Measurement. In Gardner Lindzney and Elliot Aronson (eds), *The Handbook of Social Psychology*. Vol. 2. Reading, Mass: Addison-Wesley, 204–73.

Scull, Andrew 1977: Madness and Segregative Controls: The Rise of the Insane Asylum. *Social Problems* 24: 346.

Seligman, Martin 1974: Depression and Learned Helplessness. In R.J. Friedman and M. M. Katz (eds), *The Psychology of Depression: Contemporary Theory and Research*, Washington, DC: V.H. Winston 83–125.

Sellin, Thorsten 1938: *Culture Conflict and Crime*. Bulletin No. 41. New York: Social Science Research Council.

Sellin, Thorsten and Wolfgang, Marvin E. 1964: *The Measurement of Delinquency*. New York: Wiley.

Shaw, Clifford 1929: *Delinquency Areas*. Chicago: University of Chicago Press.

Shearing, Clifford and Stenning, Philip 1983: Private Security: Implications for Social Control. *Social Problems* 30: 493–506.

Simmel, Georg 1950: Quantitative Aspects of the Group. In Kurt Wolff (ed.), *The Sociology of Georg Simmel*. New York: Free Press.

Simon, Rita James 1975: *The Contemporary Woman and Crime*. Washington, DC: National Institute of Mental Health.

1976: American Women and Crime. *Annals of the American Academy of Political and Social Science* 423: 31–46.

1977: *Women and Crime*. New York: Lexington Books.

Simpson, Elizabeth 1974: Moral Development Research: A Case Study of Scientific Cultural Bias. *Human Development* 17: 81–106.

Sites, P. 1973: *Control: The Basis of Social Order*. New York: Dunellen.

Skolnick, Jerome 1966: *Justice Without Trial: Law Enforcement in Democratic Society*. New York: Wiley.

Smart, Carol 1977: Criminological Theory: Its Ideology and Implications Concerning Women. *British Journal of Sociology* 28: 89–100.

Smigel, Erwin O. and Ross, H. Laurence (eds) 1970: *Crimes Against Bureaucracy*. New York: Van Nostrand Reinhold Co.

Smith, Douglas 1982: Street Level Justice: Situational Determinants of Police Arrest Decisions. *Social Problems* 29: 167–77.

1984: The Organizational Context of Legal Control. *Criminology* 22: 19–38.

Smith, Douglas and Patterson, Britt 1985: Latent-Variable Models in Criminological Research: Applications and a Generalization of Joreskog's LISREL Model. *Journal of Quantitative Criminology* 1: 127–58.

Smith, Douglas and Vischer, Christy 1980: Sex and Involvement in Deviance/Crime:

A Quantitative Review of the Empirical Literature. *American Sociological Review* 45: 691–701.

Sparks, Richard 1979: Crime as Business and the Female Offender. In Freda Adler and Rita Simon (eds), *The Criminology of Deviant Women.* Boston: Houghton Mifflin.

Spitzer, Steven 1975: Towards a Marxian Theory of Deviance. *Social Problems* 22(5): 638–51.

Spitzer, Steven and Scull, Andrew 1977: Privatization and Capitalist Development: The Case of the Private Police. *Social Problems* 25: 18–29.

Steffensmeier, Darrell 1978: Crime and the Contemporary Woman: An Analysis of Changing Levels of Female Property Crime, 1969–75. *Social Forces* 57: 566–84.

    1980: Sex Differences in Patterns of Adult Crimes, 1965–1977: A Review and Assessment. *Social Forces* 58: 1080–1108.

    1983: Organization Properties and Sex-Segregation in the Underworld: Building a Sociological Theory of Sex Differences in Crime. *Social Forces* 61: 1010–32.

Steffensmeier, Darrell and Steffensmeier, Renee Hoffman 1980: Trends in Female Delinquency: An Examination of Arrest, Juvenile Court, Self-Report, and Field Data. *Criminology* 18: 62–85.

Stinchcombe, Arthur 1963: Institutions of Privacy in the Determination of Police Administrative Practice. *American Journal of Sociology* 49: 150–60.

Stinchcombe, Arthur L., Adams, Rebecca, Heimer, Carol A., Schepple, Kim Lane, Smith, Tom W. and Taylor, D. Garth 1980: *Crime and Punishment – Changing Attitudes in America.* San Francisco: Jossey-Bass Publishers.

Susman, Ralph M. 1975: Drug Abuse, Congress and the Fact-Finding Process. *The Annals* 417: 16–26.

Sutherland, Edwin 1945: Is 'White Collar Crime' Crime?' *American Sociological Review* 10: 132–9.

    1949: *White Collar Crime.* New York: Dryden.

    1973: Crime of Corporations. In Karl Schuessler (ed.), *Edwin H. Sutherland: On Analyzing Crime.* Chicago: University of Chicago Press, 78–96.

    1983: *White Collar Crime. The Uncut Version.* New Haven: Yale University Press.

Sweezy, Paul 1953: *The Present as History.* New York: Monthly Review Press.

Swigert, V.L. and Farrell, R.A. 1977: Normal Homicides and the Law. *American Sociological Review* 42: 16–32.

Sykes, Gresham and Matza, David 1961: Juvenile Delinquency and Subterranean Values. *American Sociological Review* 26: 712–19.

Tannenbaum, Franklin 1938: *Crime and Community.* Boston: Ginn.

Tappan, Paul 1947: Who is the Criminal? *American Sociological Review* 12: 96–102.

Taylor, Ian, Walton, Paul and Young, Jock 1973: *The New Criminology.* London: Routledge and Kegan Paul.

Terry, R. 1967: Discrimination in the Handling of Juvenile Offenders by Social Control 'Agencies'. *Journal of Research on Crime and Delinquency* 4: 218–30.

Thayer, James Bradley 1898: *A Preliminary Treatise on Evidence at the Common Law.* Boston: Little, Brown.

Thomas, C. 1984: From the Editor's Desk. *Criminology* 22(4): 467–71.

Thomas, Charles W. 1976: Public Opinion on Criminal Law and Legal Sanctions:

An Examination of Two Conceptual Models. *Journal of Criminal Law and Criminology* 67: 110–16.

Thomas, C.W. and Cage, R.J. 1977: The Effect of Social Characteristics on Juvenile Court Dispositions. *Sociological Quarterly* 18: 237–52.

Thomas, W.I., 1923: *The Unadjusted Girl*. New York: Harper.

Thomson, R. and Zingraff, M. 1981: Detecting Sentence Disparity: Some Problems and Evidence. *American Journal of Sociology* 86: 869–80.

Thornberry, T. 1973: Race, Socioeconomic Status, and Sentencing in the Juvenile Justice System. *Criminology* 64: 90–8.

Thrasher, Frederick 1927: *The Gang*. Chicago: Phoenix Books.

Tiffany, Lawrence P., Avichai, Yakov and Peters, Geoffrey W. 1975: A Statistical Analysis of Sentencing in Federal Courts: Defendants Convicted After Trial, 1967–1968. *Journal of Legal Studies* 4: 369–90.

Tigar, Michael and Levy, Madeleine 1977: *Law and the Rise of Capitalism*. New York: Monthly Review Press.

Tilly, Louise and Scott, J.W. 1978: *Women, Work and the Family*. New York: Holt, Rinehart and Winston.

Timascheff, Nicholas 1941: *One Hundred Years of Probation: 1841–1941*. New York: Fordham University Press.

Tittle, Charles, Villemez, Wayne and Smith, Douglas 1978: The Myth of Social Class and Criminality: An Empirical Assessment of the Empirical Evidence. *American Sociological Review* 43: 643–56.

Toronto Star 1975: Politicians 'on take' Dredge Trial tape says. 4 June: A24.

Traill, H.D. 1899: *Social England*. Vol. I. New York: Putnam and Sons.

Tuma, Nancy and Hannan, Michael 1984: *Social Dynamics: Models and Methods*. New York: Academic Press.

Turk, Austin 1969a: Introduction. In Willem Adrian Bonger, *Criminality and Economic Conditions*. Abridged Edition, Bloomington: Indiana University Press.

1969b: *Criminality and the Legal Order*. Chicago: Rand McNally.

1976: Law, Conflict and Order: From Theorizing toward Theories. *Canadian Review of Sociology and Anthropology* 13(3): 282–94.

1977: Class, Conflict, and Criminalization. *Sociological Focus* 10: 209–20.

Udry, J.R. 1974: *The Social Context of Marriage*. New York: Lippincott.

Uhlman, Thomas and Walker, N. Darlene 1979: A Plea is No Bargain: The Impact of Case Disposition on Sentencing. *Social Science Quarterly* 60: 218–24.

US Department of Commerce 1974: *The Costs of Crimes Against Business*. Washington, DC: US Government Printing Office.

US Department of Commerce, Bureau of the Census 1977: *County and City Data Book, 1977*. Washington, DC: US Government Printing Office.

US Department of Justice 1975: *Criminal Victimization in Thirteen American Cities*. Washington, DC: US Government Printing Office.

US Department of Labor 1972: *The President's Report on Occupational Safety and Health*. Washington, DC: US Government Printing Office.

Veblen, Thorsten 1967 (1899): *The Theory of the Leisure Class*. New York: Viking Press.

Vold, George 1958: *Theoretical Criminology*. New York: Oxford University Press.

Vogel, Lise 1983: *Marxism and the Oppression of Women: Toward a Unitary Theory*. New Brunswick, New Jersey: Rutgers University Press.

Walker, Pat (ed.), 1978: *Between Labor and Capital*. Montreal: Black Rose.

Wall Street Journal 1983a: Investigation of Norcen is Dropped by Ontario Securities Commission. *Wall Street Journal*, 14 April: 6.

1983b: Canada police probes of Norcen's Hanna bid ends without charges. *Wall Street Journal*, 13 June: 18.

1983c: Ontario Report questions Whether Saudis Purchased 11,000 Apartments in Toronto. *Wall Street Journal* 20 June: 4.

Ward, David, Jackson, Maurice and Ward, Renee 1969: *Crimes of Violence by Women*. Crimes of Violence 13, Appendix 17. Washington, DC: President's Commission on Law Enforcement Administration of Justice.

Weber, Max 1947: *The Theory of Social and Economic Organization*. Glencoe, Illinois: Free Press.

1969: *Max Weber on Law in Economy and Society*. Translation by Max Rheinstein. Cambridge, Mass.: Harvard University Press.

Weick, Karl 1976: Educational Organizations as Loosely Coupled Systems. *Administrative Science Quarterly*, 21 (March): 1–19.

Weiner, C. 1975: Sex Roles and Crime in Late Elizabethan Herefordshire. *Journal of Social History* 8: 38–60.

Weis, Joseph 1976: Liberation and Crime: The Invention of the New Female Criminal. *Crime and Social Justice* 6: 17–27.

Weissman, M. 1974: The Epidemiology of Suicide Attempts, 1960 to 1971. *Archives of General Psychiatry* 30: 727–46.

Welch, Susan and Booth, Alan 1977: Employment and Health Among Married Women with Children. *Sex Roles* 3: 385–97.

Welter, Barbara 1966: The Cult of Womanhood, 1820–1860. *American Quarterly* 18: 151–74.

Wheaton, B., Muthen, B., Alwin, D. and Summers, G. 1977: Assessing Reliability and Stability in Panel Models. In David Heise (ed.), *Sociological Methodology: 1977*. San Francisco: Jossey-Bass.

Wheeler, Stanton 1968: *Controlling Delinquents*. New York: Wiley.

1976: Trends and Problems in the Sociological Study of Crime. *Social Problems* 23: 525–33.

Wheeler, Stanton and Rothman, Mitchell Lewis 1982: The Organization as Weapon in White-Collar Crime. *American Sociological Review* 47: 641–59.

Wheeler, Stanton, Weisbord, David and Bode, Nancy 1982: Sentencing the White Collar Offender: Rhetoric and Reality. *American Sociological Relview* 47: 641–59.

Whitelock, Dorothy 1952: *The Beginnings of English Society*. Harmondsworth: Penguin.

Wiatrowski, Michael, Griswold, David and Roberts, Mary 1981: Social Control Theory and Delinquency. *American Sociological Review* 46: 525–41.

Wilkinson, Karen 1974: The Broken Family and Juvenile Delinquency: Scientific Explanation or Ideology. *Social Problems* 21: 726–39.

Wilson, J.Q. 1975: *Thinking About Crime*. New York: Basic Books.

Wilson, James Q. and Hernstein, Richard 1985: *Crime and Human Nature*. New York: Simon and Schuster.

Wise, Nancy 1967: Juvenile Delinquency among Middle-Class Girls. In *Middle Class Juvenile Delinquency*. New York: Harper and Row.

Wolf, Edwin 1964: Abstract of Analysis of Jury Sentencing in Capital Cases. *Rutgers Law Review* 19: 56–64.

Wolfgang, Marion, Figlio, Robert and Sellin, Thorsten 1972: *Delinquency in a Birth Cohort*. Chicago: University of Chicago Press.

Wolfgang, Marvin 1958: *Patterns of Criminal Homicide*. New York: Wiley.

1960: Cesare Lombroso. In H. Mannheim (ed.), *Pioneers in Criminology*. London: Stevens.

1972: *Delinquency in a Birth Cohort*. Chicago: University of Chicago Press.

Wolfgang, Marvin E. and Cohen, Bernard 1970: *Crime and Race: Conceptions and Misconceptions*. New York: Institute of Human Relations Press, American Jewish Committee.

Wolfgang, Marvin and Reidel, Marc 1973: Race, Judicial Discretion and the Death Penalty. *Annals of the American Academy of Political and Social Science* 407: 119–33.

Wolfgang, Marvin, Kelly, Arlene and Nolde, Hans 1962: Comparison of the Executed and Commuted Among Admissions to Death Row. *Journal of Criminal Law, Criminology and Police Science* 53: 301–11.

Wright, Erik Olin 1978: Race, Class and Income Inequality. *American Journal of Sociology* 83: 1368–97.

1980: Varieties of Marxist Conceptions of Class Structure. *Politics and Society* 9: 299–322.

1985: *Classes*. London: Verso.

Wright, Erik Olin, Costello, Cynthia, Hachen, David and Sprague, Joey 1982: The American Class Structure. *American Sociological Review* 47: 709–26.

Wright, Erik Olin and Perrone, Luca 1977: Marxist Class Categories and Income Inequality. *American Sociological Review* 42: 32–55.

Yankelovich, Skelly and White, Inc. 1977: The Public Image of the Courts: A National Survey of the General Public, Judges, Lawyers, and Community Leaders. Unpublished Report. Available from National Criminal Justice Reference Service, Rockville, Md.

Zastrow, W. 1971: Disclosure of the Presentence Investigation Report. *Federal Probation* 36: 20–2.

Zeitlin, Irving M. 1967: *Marxism: A Re-Examination*. Princeton, N.J.: Van Nostrand.

Ziegenhagen, Edward A. 1977: *Victims, Crime and Social Control*. New York: Praeger.

Zimring, Franklin E., Eigen, Joel and O'Malley, Sheila 1976: Punishing Homicide in Philadelphia: Perspectives on the Death Penalty. *University of Chicago Law Review* 43: 227–52.

Zinberg, Norman and Robertson, John 1972: *Drugs and Public*. New York: Simon and Schuster.

Index

Index by Fiona Barr

DATE DUE